[when you're addicted to the planet]

BASED ON THE POPULAR NOW COLUMN

ECO

YOUR GUIDE TO THE MOST ENVIRONMENTALLY FRIENDLY

ADRIA VASIL

HOLIC

PRODUCTS, INFORMATION AND SERVICES IN CANADA

VINTAGE CANADA

www.randomhouse.ca

Library and Archives Canada Cataloguing in Publication

Vasil, Adria
    Ecoholic : your guide to the most environmentally friendly products, information and services in Canada / Adria Vasil.

Includes bibliographical references and index.
ISBN 978-0-679-31484-4

    1. Green products—Canada—Guidebooks. 2. Environmentalism—Handbooks, manuals, etc. I. Title.

HF5413.V38 2007   640   C2006-904695-6

Design by Kelly Hill

Printed in Canada

Printed on 100% post-consumer recycled, ancient forest–friendly paper.

10 9 8 7 6 5 4 3 2

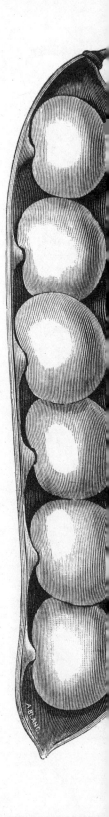

CONTENTS

INTRODUCTION

You know, it's funny: Canadians are surrounded with so much damn nature we think that automatically nominates us for outdoor MVP of the year. But when hundreds of trees fall in the boreal every minute, does anybody really care? Well, aside from a few folk singers and some placard-bearing enviro-groups, my answer just a few years ago was a reluctant no. Observers declared environmental consciousness dead. Earth Day marches had long been cancelled due to lack of attendance. Indeed, there was but a faint green pulse left in us as we dragged our recyclables out to the curb then hopped into our gas guzzlers with the a/c blasting. Memories of acid rain, dead lakes and the *Exxon Valdez* had faded to black, along with any recollection of feathered hair and shoulder pads.

Then, sometime in the last year or two, someone somewhere pulled out the defibrillators and called "clear." Was it the spike in the price of oil, forcing us to reconsider the value of spending 80 bucks a tank just to drive ourselves to the corner store? Was it the increased alarm-ringing of climate change scientists? The drowning polar bears? The breaking levies? The freak storms? The reports that DDT is still swimming in our children's bloodstreams decades after it was banned or that non-stick chemicals are sticking to bald eagles and floating in breast milk? Maybe, as my local souvlaki guy noted, it was the realization that ever-climbing hydro bills could be tackled only with conservation and sharp questions about why our government isn't more aggressively subsidizing solar panels and geothermal heat pumps. More realistically, it was all of the above: a perfect storm of factors that made us sit up and say, Holy Toledo, Dorothy, we're not in Kansas anymore.

But what's exciting about this surge, this outpouring of interest in all things green, is that everyone, from the trucker up the street to the CEO of Wal-Mart, is taking notice. And whether you're expressing your concern for the planet by reaching for organic milk, turning off the taps as you brush, driving a little less or not driving at all, it all adds up to a movement.

Sure, sticking to a five-minute shower rule may seem fruitless in the face of a melting planet and relentless emissions from the coal plant two towns down. But are we to throw our hands in the air and bury our heads in the sand as our federal government has? Every drop of water you conserve, each watt of power you save, every green pepper you purchase from a local organic grower sends a message. To paraphrase hockey dads everywhere, if you want to be on a winning team, you have to think like a winner. And sometimes, when that team is slacking, you've gotta step up and take the lead. You don't have to start a march on Parliament Hill to make a statement (though, hey, if you're itching to try out a megaphone, go ahead).

Start small. Start by leading by example. Get your workplace to turn the lights off at night and the thermostat down. Tell your grocery manager you don't need California mushrooms vacuum-packed on polysterene when he should be pushing local ones, loose. Tell your brother idling is just burning up gas (not to mention the planet) and tell your minister of Parliament you want real action on greenhouse gas emissions for once.

The tough part is that figuring out what's green and what's greenwash, what's eco-friendly and what's ozone-deadly can be downright dizzying. This is where knowledge comes in to play. The more you know, the more effective your choices, actions and movements can be. And if GI Joe was right that knowing is half the battle, just buying this book (and reading it cover to cover, of course) should turn you a finely trained eco-warrior, or at least make it easier for you to decide what cleaning products to buy. Don't worry: you don't have to give up shaving and chain yourself to a tree to be green. Just do what you can, one step at time—until you're a full-blown ecoholic.

BEAUTY SPOTS

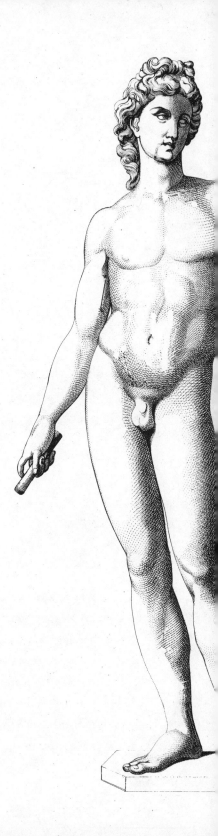

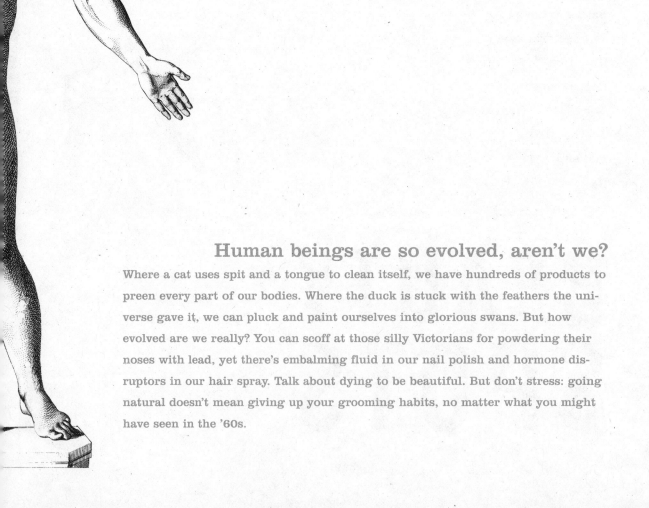

Human beings are so evolved, aren't we?

Where a cat uses spit and a tongue to clean itself, we have hundreds of products to preen every part of our bodies. Where the duck is stuck with the feathers the universe gave it, we can pluck and paint ourselves into glorious swans. But how evolved are we really? You can scoff at those silly Victorians for powdering their noses with lead, yet there's embalming fluid in our nail polish and hormone disruptors in our hair spray. Talk about dying to be beautiful. But don't stress: going natural doesn't mean giving up your grooming habits, no matter what you might have seen in the '60s.

BODY CARE

A dab of this and a spritz of that can quickly turn your morning routine into a chemical bath. The average adult uses nine personal care products a day, containing a grand total of 126 chemical ingredients, according to a report by the Environmental Working Group (EWG). The synthetic slather is even more intense for the one in four women who use more than 15 products daily. The next time you get ready in the morning, do your own count. Facial wash, shampoo, moisturizers, lip gloss—they add up quickly. And while the $5.3 billion Canadian industry likes us to believe its shampoos and creams are oh-so-natural thanks to well-advertised ingredients such as ginger and ylang-ylang, the truth is that you're

You're drenching your lips, cheeks and hair in a largely untested and lengthy list of petroleum-derived, genetically modified, animal-tested or animal-based ingredients

drenching your lips, cheeks and hair in a largely untested and lengthy list of petroleum-derived, genetically modified, animal-tested or animal-based ingredients.

There are roughly 10,500 chemical ingredients stirred into the personal care products that line shelves. It's a mind-baffling number, really, but it gets even scarier when you consider that neither Canada nor the U.S. requires much testing for these products. The result? Only about 11% have been tested for safety, according to the EWG. And those tests aren't done by Health Canada but by the cosmetics companies themselves and, in the U.S., the Cosmetic Industry Review Board.

Chemicals: Ever notice that some products make your eyes water or your skin itchy? That's because many common ingredients, such as diethanolamine (DEA) or sodium lauryl/laureth sulfate (SLS), can be just plain irritating. But beyond a little rash, over a third of the 14,000 products the EWG catalogued and cross-referenced against toxicity databases have at least one ingredient that's linked to cancer. Formaldehyde and potentially carcinogenic parabens are common preservatives. And, although you'll rarely see the word "phthalate" on a label (it's often one of the thousands of chemicals represented by the word "fragrance"), these plastic softeners are everywhere. Despite industry assurances about their safety, one type of phthalate in particular, DEHP, has been found to cause birth defects in rats, and Harvard researchers found that another, DEP, causes DNA damage in the sperm of adult men. Kind of nerve-wracking when you consider that phthalates showed up in 52 of the 72 name-brand beauty products lab-tested by a coalition of environmental and public health

5

groups (www.nottoopretty.org). They've even made their way into breast milk. Fortunately, some of the worst phthalates have been banned from plastic baby toys in Canada for a few years now. But do our regulators care that *every person* tested by the U.S. Centers for Disease Control tested positive for phthalates and that they're turning up in our waterways, soil and wildlife, with inconclusive long-term impacts? Not really, because they're still allowed in all the products we adults slather on our skin and hair every day. Some companies, such as L'Oréal and Revlon, have announced that they're voluntarily withdrawing two (but not all) types of phthalates from their products. It's a start.

Penetration enhancers help **nasty chemicals** reach your blood vessels faster

Of course, it doesn't help matters that over half of the products EWG tested had penetration enhancers—these might make your lotion seep into your skin nice and quickly, but that also means they're helping these nasty chemicals reach your blood vessels faster.

Body Care Solutions: So how do you stay away from all this junk? You're best off buying goods with a purely natural ingredient list, but don't sink your dollar into just any products labelled "natural" or "organic." Even though we have new organic food regulations, the feds aren't tackling the wild west of organic labelling in the beauty care biz. In the U.S. on the other hand, you'll find the USDA organic seal on creams and shampoos that are at least 95% certified organic. Anything less than 95% will just say "made with organic ingredients." Be aware that "hydrosol" is just a fancy name for distilled water, which is often used to pump up the organic content on a label. At the same time, keep in mind that it can be very difficult to make 100% certified organic products because many essential oils and other ingredients aren't readily available in that form.

Read ingredient lists carefully. Historically, Canada hasn't demanded that companies disclose ingredients on labels, but this changed in November 2006. You can generally spot chemical names pretty easily in so-called natural products. Not all of them are necessarily harmful; but when in doubt, look an unfamiliar term up online or ask the health store salesclerk and avoid products in which only one or two ingredients are actually organic and the rest are synthetic.

So what products get the green thumbs up *and* work wonders? High praise goes to **Dr. Hauschka**, a quality German line for body, hair and skin (including makeup). The company grows its own 100% certified organic ingredients in line with planetary rhythms and biodynamic principles.

10 BEAUTY PRODUCT INGREDIENTS TO STEER CLEAR OF

#1 Diethanolamine (DEA): A suspected carcinogen common in shampoos, body wash and makeup. Cocamide DEA, MEA and TEA may be contaminated with DEA.

#2 Formaldehyde: You might not see it on your ingredient list, but this carcinogen is found in imidazolidinyl urea, DMDM hydantoin and quaternium-15. Formaldehyde can evaporate into the air when the product is wet.

#3 Parabens: All types of parabens (methyl, ethyl, etc.) have been found to be estrogenic—meaning they mimic female hormones. Parabens have been found in breast tumour samples but haven't been conclusively linked to cancer.

#4 Petrolatum: Comes from non-renewable crude oil, kind of like tanking up at the pump. Not breathable. Mineral oil is also petroleum-based.

#5 Phenylenediamine (PPD): Also goes by the name of P-diaminobenzene. Found in brown and black hair dyes, it has been tied to increases in bladder cancer in long-term frequent users.

#6 Phthalates: You'll rarely see this controversial family of hormone disruptors listed on labels. It's often tucked away under the ingredient "fragrance."

#7 Sodium lauryl/laureth sulfate (SLS): Skin irritants; laureth is less irritating than lauryl, but can still cause dryness. Found not to cause cancer after much suspicion, but not everyone's convinced.

#8 Talc: A powder found in everything from eye shadow and blush to baby powder and deodorant. Any talc that's contaminated with asbestos fibres is a recognized carcinogen. The U.S. Department of Health's National Institutes of Health (NIH) voted to have all talc (even the non-asbestos-tainted stuff) categorized as a probable carcinogen, but it was voted down by another government body.

#9 Toluene: This powerful solvent is found in nail polishes. Long-term exposure affects the nervous system, liver and kidneys. It can also contribute to smog, making it an all-around bad guy.

#10 Triclosan: An antibacterial chemical used in everything. It's building up in our rivers and sewage sludge and can turn into carcinogenic dioxins when exposed to sunlight in water. It has been found in breast milk and has been banned by U.K. supermarkets. (See page 11 for more details.)

Druide, a much more affordable brand from Quebec, offers shower gels, soaps, shampoos and facial products, many of which are 100% certified organic. **Weleda** is well known for using a high percentage of quality organic as well as biodynamic and fair-trade ingredients and is 100% natural. A master herbalist makes all of B.C.-based **Life Root**'s products by hand in small batches of 30 or less with certified organic or wildcrafted herbs. Other solid skin and body care brands include **Terra Essentials** and **Aubrey Organics**.

For swoon-worthy perfumes, free of the hundreds of chemicals (including phthalates) found in your typical squirt-'n'-go scent, you needn't be restricted to the flower child fave patchouli. **Ecco Bella** makes some lovely eau de parfum with essential oils from fruits, herbs, flowers and spices in natural grain alcohol. And you fruity body spray lovers can easily make the switch from artificial brands to mixing your own blissfully delicious blend of essential oils such as vanilla and orange.

Even funky, swooshy, spiky hairdos can be sculpted without petroleum pastes. Health stores are full of natural aerosol-free hairsprays, mousses, gels and waxes. **Aubrey Organics**, **Jason** and **Kiss My Face** make some, and **Giovanni Natural Hair Care** is devoted exclusively to all things mop-related.

READ THE INGREDIENTS LIST

Despite what many people think, the Body Shop, which has been bought out by L'Oréal, isn't all that natural. Look at the ingredients list at www.thebodyshop.com and you'll notice that cranberry shower gel (for example) is chock full of chemicals. Its main advantage is that products aren't tested on animals and may include some fairly traded ingredients. Aveda (now owned by Estée Lauder) fares a little better. It claims to include plant-derived ingredients whenever possible (though its products still contain synthetics) and has comprehensive sustainability practices.

DANDRUFF SHAMPOO

You know those annoying commercials that use snow as a metaphor for a dandruff? Well, their solution to your scalp's weather woes is about as helpful as George Bush's response to global warming.

First of all, mainstream dandruff shampoos are loaded with super-toxic ingredients such as coal tar—the black liquid distilled from coal (found in Neutrogena Therapeutic T/Gel). The stuff has long been linked to cancer in miners, asphalt workers and chimney sweeps, but the U.S. Food and Drug Administration (FDA) says there's nothing to worry about when it's used in such small quantities. Even if you don't mind the notion of rubbing coal juice into your scalp, coal mining is highly polluting and has a history of contaminating groundwater long after a mine is in use.

Another common flake-busting ingredient is zinc pyrithione (found in Head & Shoulders). What could be wrong with zinc? you ask. Well, in this form, lots. A report by the Swedish Society for Nature Conservation states that when researchers poured 3 millilitres of dandruff shampoo with 0.8% zinc pyrithione into a 1,000-litre aquarium, waited 24 hours, then added fish, half the fish died within four days. This despite the fact that the ingredient is said to degrade quickly in water. The study also found that 1% to 2% of the added zinc could still be detected 80 days later. Considering that (depending on whom you ask) anywhere from 50% to 97% of North Americans experience dandruff at some point, a hell of a lot of the stuff washes down our drains every morning.

Another big snow-buster is selenium disulphide, which is classified as very toxic to aquatic organisms, with long-term environmental effects. It's also, according to the Environmental Protection Agency (EPA), a probable human carcinogen. Tsk, tsk.

"Second-generation" flake fighter piroctone olamine is considered about 100 times less toxic for aquatic life than zinc, but it's still a synthetic. And Procter & Gamble's own studies found that high doses of the stuff contributed to reduced body and liver weight, as well as anemia, in male rats. Sulphur and salicylic acid are other active dandruff shampoo ingredients that aren't considered toxic to water critters. No similar data could be found on ketoconazole (patented by Nizoral), but taking the potent antifungal internally has been linked to birth defects in animals. It is not recommended for use by pregnant women or nursing mothers.

Dandruff Solutions: Ironically, lots of dandruff hair washes contain a notorious skin and scalp irritant: sodium lauryl/laureth sulfate (SLS). It actually dries out your skin. Before you buy a dandruff shampoo, make sure your regular shampoo doesn't contain SLS, which might be at the root of your problem.

Make sure your regular shampoo doesn't contain SLS, which might be at the root of your problem

Most dandruff is caused by yeast or fungus. Try cutting back on sugar and refined foods, taking antifungal **oregano oil** internally and washing your hair with natural **tea tree oil** shampoos, available at health stores. You can even add a few drops of tea tree oil or essential **rosemary oil** to a palmful of regular shampoo.

Some people swear by using one part **apple cider vinegar** to three parts warm water every few days. Let it soak into your scalp before shampooing with a really mild shampoo. You can also use the pH-balancing **vinegar** straight, if you can take the pungent wake-up call.

If you see flurries only in winter, you have a dry-skin problem, not a fungal issue. Pop extra **omega fatty acids** and **vitamin B$_6$** and consider a humidifier. Rubbing pure **aloe vera** into your scalp is another soothing remedy.

BATH PRODUCTS

Who doesn't love a soak in the tub? But what's the point if you're just marinating yourself in chemicals? Ditch the dodgy synthetics and splurge on some organic, wildcrafted bath oils and bath teas, or just reach into your kitchen cupboards and drizzle 2 tablespoons (30 mL) of organic almond oil or olive oil into the water. Add a few drops of your fave essential oils to sweeten things up.

Drop the petrochemical- and fragrance-filled soap in favour of a naturally zesty bar made with freshly grated ginger or essential oils. If bath salts are your thing, make sure to buy in bulk to cut back on packaging waste. B.C.-based **Kootenay Soap Co.** makes all kinds of sweet-'n'-sassy bulk salts, like Chaispice and Merrymint. Or whip up your

own natural soaks, salts and scrubs with yummy recipes such as Cinnamon Sugar Scrub and Cucumber Coconut Skin Softener (made with fresh cucumber and coconut oil!) from www.makeyourcosmetics.com.

Even our lathering tools can froth up nature's balance. Sea sponges aren't just lying around the ocean floor, waiting to be used on your elbows, you know. They're living organisms with a life of their own. If you want to use them, make sure you're not buying from a source that may be over-harvesting them. Scrub your conscience clean with unbleached and controlled-harvest sea sponges, like the ones by **Urban Spa** (available at health stores or online at www.forever-natural.com). Or slough off dead skin with abrasive **plant-based brushes** made from jute, coconut, sisal or loofah (which comes from a relative of squash). **Pumice stones**, by the way, are made of dried, hardened lava—they're actually a type of glass. I've yet to come across any pumice protection societies, so you should be in the clear.

ANTIBACTERIAL SOAPS

They're everywhere. Lurking on every doorknob and lingering on every sponge. No, not germs—antibacterial products, silly. After news programs started scaring us with footage of microscopic particles hovering in our midst, we freaked out. No one could look at a damp dishcloth the same way again. Pretty much every company in North America took notice and started adding antibacterial ingredients (mostly triclosan) to anything and everything. Now commercials instruct you to spray the air around your children's toys with antibacterial mists, and every hand, dish and floor soap kills 99.99% of anything that comes in its path. But is this really a good idea?

By now you may have heard about how antibacterial mania is lowering our defences against germs. But there's also accumulating evidence that our obsession with these ingredients could breed drug-resistant bug strains. Research out of Tufts University found that *E. coli* that survived being treated with triclosan became resistant to 7 of 12 antibiotics. Great, like we need more super-germs in our lives.

Despite the ick factor of sharing tight spaces with coughing strangers, you should be aware that our germ-phobia is wreaking some serious havoc on the environment as well. Triclosan and triclocarbon, the active ingredients in a lot of antibacterial soaps, are scarily finding their way into rivers, streams and lakes, according to a U.S. Geological Survey. Even though the stuff is supposed to quickly break down in water, research out of Johns Hopkins University indicates that about 75% makes it down our drains and past sewage treatment plants. The thing is, researchers at the University of Minnesota found that when these chemicals are exposed to sunlight in water they create a mild dioxin (a carcinogenic hormone disruptor that accumulates in the food chain even at low levels). And when you throw chlorinated water into the mix, the result could be a much nastier form of the pollutant. If your municipality is spreading its sewage sludge on farmers' fields, as

Triclosan and triclocarbon are **essentially fertilizing the crops in your area**

many are, triclosan and triclocarbon are essentially fertilizing the crops in your area. Indeed, triclosan was found in 35 sewage samples collected from across Canada. Johns Hopkins researchers estimate that about 200 tons of the compounds are spread on farms

11

south of the border every year. And these chemicals accumulate in soil. Forget field to table, this is sink to field.

British supermarkets decided to ban the substance from their products in 2003. No word yet from Canada on this, although it is investigating the substance. Bottom line: read labels and stay away from soaps and other products containing triclosan or triclocarbon. They'll be listed. And why bother using antibacterial soaps at all when an FDA panel and the American Medical Association have said that antibacterial soaps and washes don't reduce household infections any more than washing with regular soap?

Hand Sanitizers: In our quest to be germ-free, portable hand sanitizers have become the adult equivalent of baby wipes. The good news is that those sanitizing gels don't generally have triclosan in them; ethyl alcohol (a grain alcohol used for hundreds of years as a natural antiseptic) and synthetic isopropyl alcohol (a.k.a. rubbing alcohol) are the main germ killers. Antibacterial soap critic and Columbia U prof Elaine Larson says that alcohol-based hand gels kill germs without contributing to antibiotic resistance, as triclosan might. But mainstream sanitizers also contain artificial perfumes, coal tar–derived dyes and a few petroleum-based ingredients.

Instead, reach for an all-natural hand sanitizer. **Plant Power** makes a good lavender, oregano oil and citronella spray. **EO** makes hand-sanitizing gel and wipes with organic alcohol. Do you want to use these all the time, or instead of soap? No, but for the occasional extra-sticky situation when a sink's nowhere in sight, they're not so bad.

HAIR DYE

To dye or not to dye? The answer must have been so much simpler in Shakespeare's time, before highlights, lowlights and frosted tips. A shot of colour can really liven up your locks, and it seems as if everyone and their uncle (yes, more and more men like to transform their tufts too) heads to the nearest drugstore or hair salon to do just that. But what is the eco-conscious colour-craver to do? Of course, you should love what Mother Nature gave you, but if you're looking for a little enhancement, there are several earth- and body-friendly alternatives out there.

Mainstream Dyes: If any of you are tinting your tresses with conventional dyes, it might be time to rethink that approach. Made up of a sordid stew of chemicals that definitely don't do the planet or your body much good, rivers of these dyes get washed down the drain on a regular basis by over a third of North American women and one in 10 men.

So what's in them that makes them so spooky? Besides all the well-known allergens such as ammonia and peroxide, ingredients such as PPD (p-phenylenediamine) and diaminobenzene are definitely toxic to the chemically sensitive, and even people who've been dyeing for years can suddenly develop reactions to them. Then there's the whole cancer link. Sure, many of the carcinogens have been

PPD (p-phenylenediamine) and diaminobenzene are definitely toxic to the chemically sensitive

removed from mainstream formulas since the '80s, but in 1994, the National Cancer Institute declared that deep-coloured dyes (like dark brown or black) may increase the risk of non-Hodgkin's lymphoma and multiple melanomas when used every month over a pro-longed period of time. (And you thought bleaching was bad!) Regardless of colour, a study published in the *International Journal of Cancer* found that women who dye their hair more than once a month using permanent shades were more than twice as likely to develop blad-der cancer (thanks to PPDs seeping into your skin and making their way to your bladder before you pee them out. Some of us eliminate them without a problem, others not so much). If you've been dyeing for more than 15 years, your chances jump to three times above non-dyers, and long-time hairdressers are five times more likely to develop the cancer. Semi-permanent and temporary dyes didn't share that risk. And remember, whatever doesn't penetrate your hair shaft and scalp is being washed down the sink, polluting water supplies at the end of the pipe.

Bleaching: As glaringly unnatural as stripping dark hair down to a blinding shade of blonde can look, bleach may be the least of your worries. Chemical lighteners use hydrogen peroxide (HP), which isn't all that bad. In more diluted solutions, it's even marketed as an eco-friendly cleaning product. The EPA says HP breaks down rapidly into water and air. In concentrations of 35% and above, it's extremely corrosive and irritating to the skin, eyes and mucous mem-branes, but the peroxide brushed onto your hair is usually only 6% (the kind you put on your paper cut is usually 3%). The biggest problem is that it's often mixed with ammonia, and ammonia is not only a potent skin and lung irritant, it's also toxic to fish and aquatic life.

Hair Dye Solutions: So what of the alternatives? Know that all permanent dyes, even health store brands, contain PPD—it's supposedly the only way to get the colour to stick to

13

your hair shaft. And those that say they don't? Well, either they're using one of its derivative names (benzenediamine dihydrochloride or aminoaniline dihydrochloride) or they're using toxic metals such as lead or mercury instead.

Clairol's Natural Instincts line of semi-permanents is free of ammonia and is lower in peroxide than other brands, which is great, but according to its safety data sheet, the colorant alone still contains over a dozen chemicals, and inhaling its vapours may still cause respiratory irritation.

Herbatint is a biodegradable, ammonia- and cruelty-free herbal hair colour gel that has very low concentrations of PPD and peroxide. Its semi-permanent line, as with most vegetable-based semi-permanents, is PPD-free. **Ecocolors** uses small amounts of ammonia and peroxide in a soy and flax base. **Naturcolor** is an ammonia- and cruelty-free plant-based option low in PPD that contains therapeutic herbs such as rosemary and lavender. I've tried Naturcolor to darken my hair, and it worked just as well as hair salon chems, without the nasty toxic scent wafting from your head.

GREENWASHING LABELS

Stuck on drugstore brands? Just be aware that greenwashing terms such as "natural," "herbal" and "organic" (as in "a truly organic experience") don't mean the product is without chemicals. Ditto for brands that advertise the presence of one or two herbs. Ginseng and aloe do not a chem-free dye make.

If you're looking for an entirely natural, PPD- and peroxide-free dye, you can always turn to the colourant preferred by Cleopatra. And that, of course, is **henna**. It's made from the ground-up leaves of a Lawsonia shrub. You can't lighten with it, but it's great for brown and some grey hair. (FYI, according to Health Canada, the black henna in temporary tattoos actually contains PPDs, and prolonged contact with the stuff can be very harmful and might lead to blisters, rashes and scarring.)

The old sun-baked **lemon juice** technique could help you with highlights, especially if you blow-dry the lemon into your hair and repeat the process until you're happy with the shade. It worked for me one summer in grade school. Straight-up 3% **hydrogen peroxide** from the drugstore is another fairly low-toxicity way to lighten your locks.

Now for all of you who'd rather have a pro do it. To be honest, 100% chemical-free organic salons are nearly impossible to find. **Aveda** concept salons carry the company's semi-permanent and permanent dyes, which are up to 97% plant-based. They're gentler on the earth and your body than the products used by mainstream hair stylists, which are nearly 100% synthetic and petroleum-based. If your salon doesn't offer less toxic brands, pick up a box from a health store and ask your stylist to apply it for you. If they're hesitant, tell them it'll be easier on their health as well as your head.

HAIR REMOVAL

If you believe the old stereotype, every good green boy and girl rejects our cultural obsession with being follicle-free and has the grizzly beard or hairy legs to prove it. Sure, the birth of the environmental movement kind of coincided with the explosion of hairy hippies, but this is the new millennium. Just because you shave your face or sugar your legs doesn't mean you're into waxing the planet. Of course, if you lather up with chemically laden shaving foams and reach for a new disposable blade every other day, it's time to shape up.

Shaving: According to Gillette, the largest supplier of disposable and reusable razor blades, over 1.7 billion men over the age of 15 remove hair daily. Since about 80% of them use razors, that's a hell of a lot of waste. And that doesn't factor in the women! Even if only a third of Canadians threw out a razor blade once a week, we'd be tossing over 520 million every year!

If you're hooked on razors, at least go for the reusable kind. Why throw out a handle every time you shave? And skip the mega-brands with excess packaging—most of that plastic is not commonly recycled. Even their blade refills come with a mountain of plastic (and cost more than the original razor!). Some also have a history of animal testing. Back in the '90s, Woody Harrelson grew a beard to protest Gillette's testing practices. In 1996, Gillette instituted a moratorium on animal testing, but they haven't issued a complete ban on using it in the future.

OLD-SCHOOL BARBERING

Both blade and electric razors lose in the ring against good old-fashioned straight razors. These classic barber-style blades can be sharpened and reused indefinitely. Imagine that! Yes, they're a little scary. If you're not up to living on the edge, you can order old-school metal safety razors with replaceable blades online (www.classicshaving.com).

15

For something truly hair-raising, check out **Preserve razors**, available at some health stores. The handles are 65% recycled Stonyfield Farm yogurt cups (which once housed organic yogurt), and they're recyclable in towns with #5 recycling. If your municipality doesn't take #5, you can mail your handle back to the company for recycling.

Electric razors are another great alternative. The downside is that they're filled with way more potentially toxic hardware than a simple plastic razor, but they last for years. (Mine finally died, but it was from the early '80s!) If it's the rechargeable type and the battery just isn't holding its juice, look into replacing the battery rather than buying a whole new razor. You can avoid the battery problem altogether by getting the kind that plugs straight into a socket. (See page 166 on electronics.)

Shaving Creams: Whatever type of blade you choose, you're not ecologically groomed until you stop using synthetic shaving creams and gels. They're not only filled with chemical fragrances and petroleum-derived ingredients (see waxing), they're also full of penetration enhancers, which help chemicals seep into your skin more readily. Some even contain possible carcinogens. Hardly worth all the foaming action, now is it?

> You're not **ecologically groomed** until you stop using synthetic shaving creams and gels

Luckily, there are all kinds of all-natural, chem-free shaving creams out there for both men and women, such as **Weleda**'s shaving cream, made from goat's milk and almond milk, and **Avalon Organics Moisturizing Cream Shave**. Many companies make healing aftershave balms and tonics, such as **Aubrey Organics** ginseng mint aftershave. For old-fashioned types, **Herban Cowboy** offers sweatshop-free ceramic shaving mugs (made with non-toxic glazes) and unbleached wooden shaving brushes, as well as organic grooming products.

Waxing: Most waxes are petroleum-based, so all of the eco-problems associated with digging up oil for your car are hanging off your skin. Look for natural waxes such as beeswax or tree resin–derived products (like **Parissa**). But because of the nature of the sticky resin, strips used to tear off hair are not reusable. If you prefer to get someone else to do your yanking for you, look for spas or salons in your area that use **parafin-free waxes**.

Sugaring: The ancient Egyptian art of sugaring is as earth-friendly as it gets. The sticky stuff rinses away with water, making your cloth hair removal strips reusable for years. B.C.-based **MOOM** products are made of sugar, chamomile, lemon and tea tree oil and come with reusable cotton strips. Or make your own (see recipe at www.pioneerthinking.com/bodysugaring.html). Some spa and waxing salons offer pro sugaring services, so keep your eyes peeled.

Creams: These freaky shaft dissolvers are loaded with harsh chemicals, including suspected hormone disrupters and possible carcinogens. Depilatories can even cause second-degree burns if you're not careful.

Threading: Perhaps the least product-heavy option of them all is threading. A plain cotton thread is wrapped around individual hairs in this process. It's a bit time-consuming for legs, but is perfect for eyebrows. Best to see a professional. Men are also having it done, so don't be shy to ask, boys.

Lasers/Electrolysis: Considering more permanent options? Lasers and electrolysis aren't always as lasting as you'd think, and both require electricity (and plenty of money) to power the process through several visits, but if all goes well, you shouldn't have to pick up another razor or howl through another waxing session, which ultimately cuts your product consumption.

BODY ODOUR CONTROL

Being social creatures often crammed in close quarters, we have a deep collective phobia of smelling bad. Advertisers tapped into that fear brilliantly back in the '80s. Raise your hand, they challenged us, but only if you're sure. God forbid your deodorant fails you on the treadmill, in a meeting, on a date. So we diligently douse ourselves with whatever new stick on the market promises to protect us. The question is, what the hell is stopping us from smelling so foul?

Antiperspirants: Many of us swipe our underarms with antiperspirants every morning without really thinking about why our sticks keep us from sweating. The answer? Aluminum (and/or zirconian). It closes our pores and reduces the amount of perspiring we'd normally do. Although government bodies such as Health Canada say there's nothing to worry about, the jury is still out on whether the mineral contributes to Alzheimer's, since aluminum is found in higher concentrations in the brain tissue of Alzheimer's patients. Some researchers continue to study the link, including whether applying it to shaved underarms allows a more direct path into the bloodstream. So far nothing conclusive has been found. Some say that until we know more, it's not a bad idea to avoid it. I mean, really, we line pots and cans with materials that keep our food from coming into contact with the metal, yet we smear it freely against our skin every day in the form of deodorant. Kind of contradictory, no?

> **We line pots and cans with materials that keep our food from coming into contact with the metal, yet we smear it freely against our skin**

The environmental impacts, however, aren't quite so fuzzy. As with all mining, digging up aluminum (or bauxite ore) has been tied to destructive practices around the globe, and vast amounts of energy go into processing the stuff.

Deodorants: Plain old odour-masking deodorants come with their own set of problems. Chemical fragrances are only one of a number of ingredients in deodorants that can often cause allergic skin reactions, and coal tar–based colours like the Yellow No. 6 that goes into blue-hued gel sticks pose possible liver toxicity and cancer hazards.

Formaldehyde, an air-polluting, lung-irritating volatile organic compound (VOC) and probable human carcinogen, can be found in many deodorant preservatives; according to *The Green Guide*, it might pose the greatest health (and environmental) risk in roll-on deodorants. VOCs may evaporate as the product dries and off-gas as sweat beads on your skin.

If you're a fan of spraying rather than rolling or rubbing on your deodorant, don't think you're off the hook. That label might say CFC-free, but all consumer products have had to be free of chlorofluorocarbons for a long time now. They still contain some smog inducing VOCs (though less than in the past) and you're also inhaling fossil fuels and other chems. Indeed, the main ingredients are often butane (lighter fluid), propane (barbecue fluid), and talc. Talc, found in many mainstream deodorants, can be carcinogenic if contaminated with arsenic, and it's impossible to tell if yours is. On top of that, it was discovered that talc was being illegally mined from an Indian wildlife sanctuary and tiger reserve. The U.K.'s Environmental Investigation Agency and *The Observer* reported that trees were being chopped down, holes were being blasted in the earth and water tables drained—all practices that threatened the habitat of the severely endangered creatures. And all for the sake of a little body powder. The mining company listed Uniliver, Revlon, Avon and Johnson & Johnson as its clients when the talc hit the fan in 2003.

Natural Deodorants: Don't assume that buying your scent-prevention stick from health stores means you're entirely wholesome. Many so-called natural deodorants still contain a lot of the same ingredients found in drugstore varieties. None of the alt-deos contains aluminum. Nor do they have triclosan (the antibacterial eco-contaminant found in many mainstream brands), but over half of the sticks on health store shelves still contain petrol-based propylene glycol (PG)—which, in 100% concentrations, is known as antifreeze and is extremely toxic to aquatic life. Many companies, such as Tom's of Maine, insist it's safe in small doses and point out that it's also found in fat-free ice creams (um, yuck!), while other companies have switched to PG-free formulas. Tom's says it tried to take the controversial ingredient out in 1993 but put it back in after customers complained PG-free sticks were too mushy.

Besides propylene glycol, keep an eye out for synthetics, such as the potentially carcinogenic preservative paraben. The U.S. National Institutes of Health (NIH) says it has estrogenic properties, meaning it mimics estrogen hormones. One study cited by the NIH's report on deodorant found parabens in 18 to 20 human breast tumours, but the research was inconclusive as to the source and effect of those parabens. Avalon has phased it out, though old formulations can still be found on shelves. Check the ingredients.

Some vitamin shops sell a deodorant cream called Lavalin, which is said to prevent B.O. for up to a week. Cool, but creepy. Its ingredients, such as zinc, arnica and potato starch, are largely natural, but it also contains petroleum jelly and talc.

If you're shopping for a natural deodorant, look for those with the highest organic content to avoid any controversial chemicals. Crystals made with the natural rock salt Alum can be quite effective. Also, keep in mind that body chemistries differ, so what works for some might not work so well for you. In completely unscientific observations, I've noted that natural brands may work for weeks or months then suddenly conk out. Be prepared to switch things up. It's best to reframe your expectations of just how long an application can protect you. Translation: Pack a spare stick in your purse, gym bag or briefcase for emergency reapplication.

TOOTH CARE

Brush, rinse, spit. And maybe, if you listen to your dentist, floss. It's one of those rituals we do in a haze and don't think too much about (aside from you nutbars brushing to egg timers). But what exactly are we swishing, then spitting into our water system every morning?

Toothpaste: For one, depending on where you live, you might just be adding fluoride to an already fluoridated system. Yes, scrubbing your teeth with fluoride helps prevent tooth decay, but so does general dental hygiene (regular brushing, flossing, you know the drill) and not consuming half your body weight in sugar. Swallowing fluoride in our tap water, however, has a mouthful of health and environmental implications that have even convinced the University of Toronto's head of preventative dentistry, once a vocal advocate of fluoridated water, to switch sides. Fluoride in drinking water accumulates in your bones, for one thing, and drinking it has been linked to increasing bone cancer rates in young boys and hip fractures. It's also building up in wildlife, leading, again, to fractures, lameness and poor reproduction. If your municipality has you believing they're doing your teeth a favour by putting this stuff in your water, think again. Dozens of towns have dropped it—tell your MP you think yours should too.

You're also spitting out a mouthful of eco-persistent triclosan (see page 11) every time you brush with toothpastes like Colgate Total. On top of that, with every tube you're squeezing out potentially carcinogenic saccharin, synthetic dyes and preservatives. It's enough to make you let your teeth get furry.

HOMEMADE TOOTHPASTE

If you have about two minutes to spare in the kitchen, you can skip packaging woes altogether by making your own toothpaste from scratch. Just mix 6 teaspoons (30 mL) of baking soda (your whitener), 1/3 teaspoon (1.5 mL) of salt (your mildly abrasive antiseptic), 4 teaspoons (20 mL) of vegetable glycerine (your gel) and 15 drops of an organic essential oil such as winter-green or spearmint for minty fresh flavour that comes from the earth, not the lab (recipe from Pioneer Thinking, **www.pioneerthinking.com**).

Not that every "natural" toothpaste is all that natural either. As with deodorant, many contain some of the same scorned ingredients as drugstore brands, ingredients such as propylene glycol, fluoride (Tom's of Maine provides fluoride as an option) and the sudsing irritant sodium lauryl sulfate (SLS). Read your label carefully if you'd rather avoid these. Tom's of Maine, Nature's Gate and Auromère all argue that SLS isn't a big concern. But lots of brands are SLS-free, including **Green Beaver Company**, a Canadian brand. **NewCo** is among the few that don't come in a totally unnecessary box.

Sorry to disappoint, but even if your toothpaste tube says it's recyclable, it's not in most municipalities. Yes, even the aluminum kind is lined with a plastic that makes it harder to recycle and thus too often destined for landfill. Notably, some include instructions on how to separate the plastic from the aluminum. Tom's of Maine says you can mail it back to them for recycling.

Whitener: I blame Wonder Woman for fostering our earliest obsession with impossibly bright teeth. Back when I was a tot, I used to brush two or three times in a row just to get my teeth Lynda Carter white. But besides obsessive oral hygiene and cutting out coffee, tea and wine (we all know that's asking too much), how can you lighten your smile without putting poison on your pearls? Most whitening toothpastes contain sodium hydroxide, a.k.a. lye (a caustic drain cleaner considered a poison by the Food and Drug Administration (FDA), or potassium hydroxides (found in cuticle removal products and drain cleaners) as well as dozens of other chems. Tom's of Maine makes a whitening paste that uses natural silica, but it has SLS. **Jason's PowerSmile** uses silica, calcium carbonate and renewable bamboo powder and doesn't contain SLS. You can also just add a little **baking soda** to your brush and scrub.

Mouthwash: Gargle much? You're basically swishing fake dyes and artificial ingredients in your mouth every morning. A lot of drugstore mouthwashes contain anti-parasitic thymol, which used to come from thyme way back when (corporations now use a synthetic version), so you'd assume it's safe. It's actually toxic to aquatic organisms when it ends up in rivers and lakes. **Jason's Healthy Mouth** mouthwash has organic tea tree oil and aloe vera instead. Tom's of Maine makes a peppermint baking soda mouthwash, but it contains flavour-dispersant poloxamer 335, which is derived from natural gas and oil. A maker of antibiotic, antiviral, antifungal **grapefruit seed extract** drops, **Nutribiotic**, also makes a mouthwash, but the gargle isn't all-natural—it adds a couple of synthetic ingredients. Better to just buy the extract in concentrated form and put a few drops in water. It's bitter as hell (kind of like biting into a handful of grapefruit seeds), but it works. You can also stir a few drops of anti-bacterial tea tree oil and peppermint oil into a cup of warm water and swish.

Floss: A couple brands such as Crest Glide coat their plastic with PTFE (a.k.a.Teflon) Sure, the floss won't stick between your chompers as easily, but it contains traces of PFOA, the persistent chemical used in the making of Teflon, which has been labelled a probable carcinogen. Oral Care reps at Crest say you'd have to floss 365 times a day for 75 years to be exposed to 3 milligrams of the stuff. Still, is it totally necessary? Several floss makers have actually discontinued PTFE-containing versions. **Radius Silk Floss**, on the other hand, uses biodegradable and sustainable silk threads coated with beeswax. Vegans might prefer the rice bran wax–veneered nylon in **Eco-DenT GentleFloss**. Nylon, however, is also a petroleum-based synthetic.

Toothbrushes: If we all listened to our dentists and ditched our toothbrushes four times a year, over 125 million of them would be trashed in Canada annually. Even if we changed our toothbrushes half as often, we'd still be scrapping 75 million of the petroleum sticks every year. And you can bet there's zero recycled content in the kind you pick up in your drugstore. In contrast, **Preserve** toothbrushes are made from old Stonyfield Farm yogurt cups and may be recyclable in some municipalities. You can even return them to the company, and they'll revive the handle and the nylon bristles into plastic lumber. But **Radius**, a natural floss and toothbrush maker, has stopped taking toothbrushes back because they said it wasted more energy to truck all those brushes back and recycle them than it did to make new ones.

Speaking of waste, do you need to toss the whole handle out each time, when it's only the bristles that get mashed up? Look for toothbrushes with a replaceable head like the ones made by **TerraDenT**.

For all of you hooked on the snazzy electric variety (see page 166 on electronics), the story gets more complicated. Yes, I know a certain segment of you have long sworn by your high-end (sometimes dentist-prescribed), rechargeable, plug-in types. But in recent years the market has been flooded with the cheapie battery-operated kind. As tempting as their $5 price tags can be, you should consider spending a little more on the old plug-in models. Or at the very least, use rechargeable batteries.

Whichever brush you choose, remember: old bristles are great for precision cleaning, so don't toss 'em.

MEANINGLESS TERMS

Hypoallergenic, Allergy-Tested and Dermatologist-Tested:
You'll find these labels all over beauty care products, and you generally assume they mean the product shouldn't irritate your eyes, skin or whatnot. Somehow it must be purer, more natural, even. Trouble is, these terms are fairly meaningless since they're not government-regulated. Same goes for "fragrance-free" (ever notice how drugstore products labelled fragrance-free still smell perfumy, just not as strong as the next bottle over?). In fact, the U.S. FDA says there's no such thing as a non-allergenic cosmetic, since virtually all can cause a reaction in someone somewhere.

Against Animal Testing:
This label became controversial when it was discovered that some companies just farm the testing out to outside labs, rather than test the product on bunnies and mice themselves. Same goes for the use of "cruelty-free" or "not tested on animals." Sometimes the label should really say, "not currently tested on animals, since the ingredients were already tested on them five years ago." Of course, we prefer that to "still shoving chemicals in animals' eyes and making them sick to find out the lethal dose." Still, even though the labels are totally unregulated, what they say might be true—when you see one on an organic bottle of shampoo, for instance. Your best bet is to look for "no animal testing" logos certified by the Coalition for Consumer Information on Cosmetics (CCIC) or People for the Ethical Treatment of Animals (PETA). PETA's website offers a list of animal testing policies and a cruelty-free pocket shopping guide (www.peta.org).

MAKEUP

How we've suffered for beauty (touch wrist to forehead and sigh dramatically). First there was the lead kohl eyeliner used by ancient Egyptians, then the white lead powder used to lighten the cheeks of the Greco-Romans, then more whitening lead face powder in the Renaissance. Unfortunately, we haven't yet let the lead thing die. Health Canada says

As of September 2004, our progressive friends across the pond, the E.U., banned the use of chemicals that are known to cause or are strongly suspected of causing birth defects, cancer or genetic mutations. Sounds so logical, doesn't it? Now that companies there have proven they can do without, it's just too bad the directive applies only to products sold in the E.U. The Campaign for Safe Cosmetics, however, is asking companies such as L'Oréal and Revlon to make those reformulated products available to those of us outside of Europe (over here, please!). So far, more than 150 companies have signed on, but Procter & Gamble, Estée Lauder, Revlon, L'Oréal and Unilever.

traditional dark kohl eye makeup made of the deadly neurotoxin is still available in this country. Stay away.

Of course, painting our faces hasn't involved just killing ourselves—animals have also fallen victim to our beauty trends. Okay, so plastic/aluminum/glass-based glitter may have replaced shiny fish scale bits in adding sparkle to your eyeshadow or lip gloss. And you won't find whale blubber in lipstick anymore, but you're still tinting your kisser with animal fats.

Lash-extending mascaras can even contain polluting plastics like polyurethane

Petroleum waxes, oils and chemicals, coal-tar dyes and potentially carcinogenic talc (see page 18 on talc) are included in just about everything in your makeup kit. Lash-extending mascaras can even contain polluting plastics like polyurethane. Yeesh.

Makeup Solutions: No one's asking you to put down your makeup brush and go bare. And, luckily, going green doesn't mean giving up on good eyeshadow. There are super-trendy shades of glitter made with certified organic cornstarch and natural mineral pigments—**Suncoat** makes some. They also sell lip shimmers, mascaras and blush with certified organic ingredients. For top-of-the-line foundation, lipstick, gloss and mascara plugged by celebs like Debra Messing, **Lavera** is your girl. This largely certified organic makeup is free of synthetics, mostly vegan and allergy-tested on humans. **Ecco Bella** is another high-quality company that uses organic and wild-grown herbs and oils to make its complete line of animal- and petrol-free goodies. All three brands are available at many larger health stores. For a serious selection of slickly packaged all-natural, eco-friendly, animal-free products, head online to Toronto-based **Organic Make-up Company** at www.organicmakeup.ca. In addition to the usual face paint selection, they also brew up great cleansers, masks and scrubs.

NAILS

Maybe it's the potent fumes that fill the room when you open a bottle or the harsh chemicals you need to remove it, but you can kind of guess that nail polish is one of the most toxic beauty products around. That smell comes from polluting VOCs such as the carcinogen formaldehyde and the powerful neurotoxin toluene. Breathing a lot of this stuff in can dam-

Breathing in a lot of this stuff can damage your kidneys, brain and liver

age your kidneys, brain and liver, so nail salon workers take note. Plus, most nail polish is made using the plastic softener dibutyl phthalate, which has been found in human blood and body tissues and is known to cause birth defects in animals.

As you can imagine, mainstream nail polish removers aren't much better than the polishes themselves. Liver, kidney and neural damage can also result from long-term exposure to the acetone in your nail polish remover. Companies have tried to soften the image of harsh-smelling removers by marketing the presence of natural ingredients such as vitamin E and aloe vera, but don't be fooled: there ain't nothin' natural about it. The alternatives aren't always much better. Back in 1995, Health Canada issued a warning that some non-acetone nail polish contained poisonous methanol, which is deadly to fish, birds and wildlife. Check labels to make sure your acetone-free remover doesn't contain it.

Nail Polish Solutions: **No-Miss** and **Suncoat** are two common health store nail polish brands that are free of all three of the contentious chems, although they're not entirely natural. Suncoat's 29 shades get their pigment from earthy minerals, are 70% water and are alcohol- and acetone/acetate-free. FYI, **Revlon** and **L'Oréal's Jet-Set Shine Speed Dry Nail Enamel** are also formaldehyde- and toluene-free.

For removers, **No-Miss Almost Natural Polish Remover** uses a fruit acid solvent, a lichen-derived solvent, water and natural vanilla. **Suncoat's** remover is

BEAUTY WEBSITES

www.ewg.org/reports/skindeep/
The Environmental Working Group did a hell of a job ranking over 14,000 personal care products for their safety and includes ingredient lists and breakdowns of their impact for each and every one.

www.lesstoxicguide.ca
This Canadian database lists less toxic alternatives to beauty care and baby care products and more, brought to you by Nova Scotia's Environmental Health Association.

www.nottoopretty.org
This international site offers a full assessment of which perfumes, nail polishes, deodorants and hair products tested positive for phthalates and which didn't.

100% soy- and corn-based. But if you've used a Suncoat polish, it can be removed by soaking your fingers in hot water for a few minutes, then scratching the polish off with your nail. By the way, **Organic Essentials** makes organic cotton balls, rounds and swabs. You can find them, as well as the removers, at many health stores.

WHAT NOT TO
WEAR

It's overwhelming, really.

We're inundated with endless options on how to bundle our feet, drape our bodies and adorn our earlobes. And the fact that you can now buy two pairs of pants, a few bangles and a pair of shoes for the price of a nice dinner makes us want to purchase even more of the stuff. But while falling prices might lure us into frenzied shopping sprees, sale tags only tell half the story. The full cost of each item is paid every day by the planet and workers around the world picking pesticide-laden cotton, digging for blood gems and stitching up toxic shoes.

CLOTHING

Few of us question what we wrap around our bodies, unless the fit is off or the colours clash. It's just fabric, right? How much harm can a tank top do? You'd be surprised at the ecological implications of a single singlet, as those crazy Brits like to call them. Green fashionistas take note: from our pants to our underpants, our closets are stocked with environmental woes.

Cotton: The fabric industry is one of the most polluting on the planet. Cotton soaks up 10% of the world's pesticides and 25% of its insecticides, many of which are carcinogens and extremely toxic, causing major water pollution and making workers and wildlife sick. In fact, it takes half a pound of chemicals to make one regular old T-shirt. Multiply that by what's in your closet (and drawers), and, presto, you're a major pesticide purchaser.

It takes half a pound of chemicals to make one regular old T-shirt

Genetically modified cotton is being touted as a solution, especially as high-tech crops such as Bt cotton are altered to produce naturally occurring insecticides. This might cut pesticide use at first. But some Chinese users of the crop are finding that after several years, outbreaks of other bugs get so bad farmers end up using more pesticides than ever before. Farmers are also struggling with how to prevent original cotton strains from interbreeding with genetically modified types when their seeds are blown by the wind.

Pesticide use isn't the only problem associated with the cotton industry. Human rights abuses are common, and child labour is a serious issue. According to Human Rights Watch, over one million children pick leafworm from cotton plants in Egypt alone every summer. Seasonal child labour in cotton fields is actually government sanctioned there, but only for six hours a day, not 11 hours a day, seven days a week, as is common.

MAD CLOTHING SCIENTISTS

In the category of "what are those scientists on, anyway?" genetic modification of bacteria is being tinkered with to bring us clothing complete with sweat-digesting microbes. Nasty, really. But that's not all: others have developed sports gear that secretes vitamins and jeans that release anti-cellulite cream into your thighs as you wear them. It's enough to make polyester look natural.

Synthetics: I don't know how they did it, but someone figured out that you can take oily black goop pumped out of the earth (namely petroleum) and spin it into a whole new category of fibres. It all started with pantyhose (nylon was invented by researchers at DuPont in the '30s as a substitute for silk) and snowballed from there. Now countless barrels of oil go into weaving millions of synthetic garments a year. Who knew the hunt for oil was being waged, in part, to supply your wardrobe?

Sweatshops: So you're sifting through a clothing rack and find a pretty blouse for the price of a movie ticket. Do you a) scan for defects b) think about how you have enough blouses already or c) mutter "Score!" and run to the cash register. The truth is few of us would pick option d) worry about the poor worker who had to sew the cheap thing, but come on, why else do you think you're dishing out $13 for that top?

GORE-TEX'S GORY RECORD

Whether you're trekking through the Himalayas, throwing yourself down a ski hill or just staying dry through rain, snow or sleet you're probably well acquainted with this revolutionary high-tech fabric. But Gore-Tex is basically Teflon (PTFE) with micropores in it. And Teflon is made with the extremely persistent (and likely carcinogenic) chemical PFOA, which now thoroughly contaminates our air, water, wildlife and bloodstreams.

W.L. Gore and Associates (the maker of Gore-Tex fabric) says that their PTFE is so "stable" that your coat's membrane won't off-gas or leach in landfills. In fact, it won't even decompose. (Whether you see that as a good thing is another matter.) Sealed into your coat, I'm guessing, the PTFEs are probably safer for you (and your canary) than those in a burnt non-stick pan.

So, should you toss your Gore-Tex jacket or boots as quickly as you should your non-stick pan (see page 145 on cookware)? All the suspicious health findings to date have revolved around cooking surfaces, so I'd wait on the coat front. In the meantime, at least make good use of your garment.

Take note: some of the high-performance alternatives out there might be almost as bad. Polyurethane resin, used to make comparable, though cheaper, jackets and shells, creates all kinds of hazardous by-products, including ozone-depleting CFCs during production and carcinogenic dioxins when incinerated.

Don't assume that a high price tag means you're home free. Even pricy stores have been caught using sweatshops. And workers aren't just toiling long hours with little pay in abusive conditions, they're also often working with toxic dyes to get your jeans that perfect shade of indigo—dyes that end up getting dumped in streams, rivers and waterways.

How do you know if your clothes were made under abusive conditions? Hard to say. You'll never see a dress that says "made in a sweatshop." Even buying apparel made in Canada gives you no guarantee that workers were paid the legal minimum wage. And there's no real international certification system in place, although you can look for companies that tell you they're sweatshop-free or fair trade. Or search for stuff that was union-made, like **No Sweat** (www.nosweatapparel.com). **American Apparel** doesn't run a union shop, but it used to market its clothing as sweatshop-free. For some strange reason, the company decided to stop using this as a selling point, but it does sew all of its gear and weave all of its fabrics at a relatively respected factory in L.A.

Clothing Solutions: In the quest for eco-friendly fabrics, designers have started to experiment with pretty much everything on the planet, and it seems many plants—soy and flax, for example—can be spun into beautiful material. The cool thing is, you can now get the stretch and suppleness of synthetics without relying on oil-drenched clothes.

> You can now get the stretch and suppleness of synthetics **without relying on oil-drenched clothes**

With a growing array of earth-loving fabrics at their disposal, it's no wonder higher-end designers are starting to get in on the scene. **Linda Loudermilk** is about as patchouli as a pair of Manolos, but she uses bamboo, organic cotton and soy blends in her luxury eco line (www.lindaloudermilk.com). Hollywood starlets also turn to ethereal funk machine **Deborah Lindquist** for vintage pieces and killer clothes made with recycled fabrics (www.deborahlindquist.com). Designer jeans may tax your wallet, but they don't have to tax the planet if you buy a pair of certified organic butt huggers from **Loomstate** (www.loomstate.org) or **Del Forte Denim** (available at www.thegreenloop.com). **Levi's** is also coming out with organic denim, so keep your eye out. Even rock stars are getting in on the action—Bono and his wife have launched a new ecologically sourced, fairly made line called **Edun** (nude backwards). For kick-ass selection of all the flyest eco-brands, click on to **Greenloop** (www.thegreenloop.com), **Coco's Shoppe** (www.cocosshoppe.com) and **Pangaya** (www.pangaya.com). But let's get back to basics and break down your general fabric options.

An increasingly popular fabric source is the quick-growing plant **bamboo**. Just punch in "bamboo clothing" online, and you'll get a flood of designers and stores (including www.bambooclothes.ca, which also sells bamboo fibres and yarn) offering ultra-soft T-shirts, tanks and cashmere-like sweaters that are either 100% bamboo or bamboo blends. Plus, they're said to be naturally antibacterial and very breathable, meaning a slinky bamboo tank will never stick to your body and trap unwelcome odours the way synthetics will.

Of all the alternative fabrics, **organic cotton** has taken off the most. **Mountain Equipment Co-op** offers all sorts of organic tops and pants (www.mec.ca). Active outdoor gear maker **Patagonia** has long ditched conventionally grown cotton altogether in favour of the pesticide-free type (plus they use recycled polyester and fleeces made of old plastic pop bottles). **Levi's**, **Nike** and **Gap** are all buying organic cotton and blending it into their lines so that anywhere from 1% to 3% of their jeans, tees and sports bras are made with pesticide-free fibres. It's a small percentage, but it represents a hell of a lot of organic threads. Nike buys over 2 million kilograms of the stuff a year, making it the largest retail user of organic cotton in the world. It also has a line of 100% organic gear. **American Apparel** offers racy thongs, tight tanks and tees in their line of organics, but so far they only come in, you guessed it, beige. Looking for something a little more original and a little less corporate? Vancouver's **Twice Shy** designs jaw-droppingly sexy, style-y and sustainable clothes out of organic cotton blends (www.twice-shy.com). **Under the Canopy** also stitches ultra funky outfits with the fabric (www.underthecanopy.com).

Organic wool can be more expensive than conventional types, but it's worth it when you consider that the sheep haven't been dipped in toxic pesticides to kill off lice, nor have they had a square of their flesh near the tail cut away to prevent infection, a painful and strangely common process called mulesing. (Mulesing is practised in Australia and New Zealand to prevent blowfly infestation—see www.vegsoc.org/info/sheep.html for more info and www.woolisbest.com/animal_welfare/mulesing/ for the industry's explanation, then decide for yourself.) Organic wool is fairly hard to find, but **Patagonia** uses the sustainable fabric in its sweaters and cardigans. Ontario native **Warm and Wonderful** specializes in organic wool sweaters (www.warmandwonderful.com).

An acre of hemp **absorbs five times more carbon dioxide** *than an acre of forests*

The classic hippie alternative, even non-organic **hemp** is much gentler on the earth than mainstream cotton. It naturally uses much less pesticide and herbicide, and grows faster than cotton without stripping the soil as it grows. Plus, an acre of hemp absorbs five times more carbon dioxide than an acre of forests, so it could play a role in curbing global warming. Industrial hemp contains no psychoactive THC—the trippy ingredient in weed. However, harsh chems may still be used to process it into fibres, especially if it's made in China, the world's biggest hemp fabric producer. And the stuff is still pretty rough in texture. But the National Research Council of Canada is working with Vancouver's own **Hemptown** to put out a new style of ultra-soft hemp that's processed with a sustainable enzyme technology. Rawganique.com, which has a boutique on Denman Island B.C., is a good online source for organic hemp clothing.

Super-soft **Tencel** (a.k.a. Lyocell) is made with wood pulp cellulose processed with non-toxic dissolving agents. Pure Tencel drapes like silk. **Ramie** is an ancient fabric made from a plant native to Asia.

WINTER COATS

Yes, down-filled jackets are snug and toasty in blizzards, but they come with a heavy animal welfare conundrum. Down is either purchased as a by-product of the meat industry (with which you may not want to be associated) or plucked from living birds, causing them serious distress. If you'd prefer to go synthetic in solidarity with the birdies, look for polyester-based polyfill or hypoallergenic Primaloft.

If you need a good, warm technical coat (doesn't every Canadian?), **Patagonia** has developed its own environmentally friendly polyester-based version of Gore-Tex, made with recycled fabrics. Patagonia's Inferno winter jacket is even lined with fleece made from post-consumer recycled pop bottles.

A truly dope coat option is made by **Hemp Hoodlamb**. It's a hooded all-element jacket that's half hemp, half organic cotton, with smooth vegan "lamb fur" lining and funky features such as a cellphone pocket.(**www.hood-lamb.com**).

Mens' Suits and Dress Clothes: Boys, need to dress up for work, or just like to dress to impress? Sure, a beige hemp tee is pretty easy to find these days, but will you wear it to an interview or your cousin's wedding? Probably not. Get fine organic dress shirts from **Boll Organic** (www.bollorganic.com). Need a proper suit? You can buy 100% certified organic hemp dress slacks and matching suit jackets at www.rawganique.com. Add one of their Oxford shirts in seven funky hues, wrap one of their hemp ties around your neck, and you're set! For a three-piece organic linen or tweed suit, you'll have to pay in pounds at the U.K.-based www.greenfibres.com.

You know immediately when a **lululemon** has entered your town. Soon the little om insignia that is lululemon's logo can be spotted at gyms and brunch restaurants and on campuses and street corners everywhere. The Vancouver-born company has now taken enlightenment to the next level by introducing a line called **Oqoqo** (pronounced oh cocoa). Every item of clothing is at least 75% natural, organic or sustainable in some way. And it's not all athletic gear either: we're talking slinky bamboo-blended tops you could wear clubbing, hot hemp and recycled-pop-bottle jackets, even well-cut organic jeans. And many of the getups are reversible so you can get more wear out of one item and, hopefully, buy fewer clothes. It's a concept foreign to the fashion world of buy more for less, but one that gets green fashionistas even more excited about the brand. So far, there are Oqoqo stores in Vancouver, Victoria and Toronto, and a selection of Oqoqo products is available at regular lululemon shops in Edmonton, Burnaby and Toronto. Even if you can't get Oqoqo stuff near you, pretty much every lulu location across the country carries cute tees made with a soy-based fabric so soft it's called vegetable cashmere. Plus, the stores themselves incorporate renewable building materials such as reclaimed wood flooring, and showers are installed in nearly every shop to encourage employees to run, walk or cycle to work. As if you didn't have enough reasons to love lululemon (**www.lululemon.com** and **www.oqoqo.com**).

Vintage: The most earth-friendly option of all might be every fashionista's favourite form of recycling—vintage clothing! It's amazing what you can find with a little patience and a dream. Plus, it's also the cheapest way to wear planet-friendly threads. I recommend shopping in opposite seasons. For instance, search for winter coats in the summer, when everyone's purging their closets of anything related to cold weather and the stores haven't been picked over.

If second-hand shops aren't your thing, a surge of small designers are sewing brand new dresses out of old raincoats and making funky patchwork sweaters with remnants of cardigans past (see Preloved sidebar, opposite). And the piecemeal magic doesn't stop at clothing: many designers are using old billboards, newspapers and candy wrappers to make funky bags, belts and clutches. Ask around at small boutique stores in your town, like **Not Just Pretty** in Victoria (www.notjustpretty.com), **Nokomis** in Edmonton (www.nokomisclothing.ca), **Skirt** in Toronto (www.skirtclothing.ca), **Rien à cacher** in Montreal and **Heroine** in Halifax. They tend to sell funky recycled lines by designers like **Susan Harris, On & On, Ecolo**

Chic and more. And besides reconstructed clothes, these shops are also great sources for totally original local designs.

Make Your Own: Walk into any fabric store and ask for organic textiles and you'll probably be told that all cotton is natural. Sure, it technically comes from the earth, but is it pesticide-free? Fat chance. Manufacturers also tend to use all kinds of nasty dyes and potent chemicals to process the materials, including adding a wrinkle-resistant formaldehyde finish.

For genuinely earth friendly fabrics, **Toronto Hemp Company** (www.torontohemp.com) sells hemp by the metre, including dress-worthy hemp/silk blends and hemp denim. For a broader selection, you've gotta head online. **NearSea Naturals** likely has the biggest and most inspiring collection of organic cotton prints, woven blends, wools and knits by the metre (www.nearseanaturals.com). They even sell organic thread, batting and a crazy-cool collection of buttons made of stuff like bamboo, nuts and fallen antlers. **Organic Cotton Plus**

PRELOVED

Like the idea of supporting recycled clothing, but don't have the patience to sift through second-hand bins, especially when you can never find a pair of pants with just the right fit? Well, many young designers are doing the work for you, hitting by-the-pound stores, then taking that old camel sweater up a notch by chopping it up and fusing it with an '80s tee or well-loved denim. And Toronto-raised Preloved, founded by former model Julia Grieve back in the mid-'90s, is the reigning queen of the deconstructed style. Old-man trench coats are turned into slick tube dresses suitable for work or a night out, and '70s sheets are transformed into pretty summer skirts at the hands of designer Peter Friesen. It was projected that the second-hand revivalists would use 8,000 old T-shirts, 8,000 pounds of bed sheets, 8,000 trench coats, 8,000 jeans and 35,000 discarded sweaters in 2006. No surprise, considering that Preloved's popularity has propelled it out of Toronto (although its flagship store is still on Queen Street)—the celeb-favoured boîte now has shops in Montreal and Vancouver, and the line is available in a dozen other stores across the country, from Twisted Sisters Boutik in St. John's, Newfoundland, to the Lounge Collection in Tofino, B.C. It even sells to boutiques in Norway and the U.K., as well as a few dozen shops across the States. Who knew your old Van Halen T-shirt would go so far? (**www.preloved.ca**)

We talk about cutting down our food miles (and all the greenhouse gas emissions that come with trucking a head a lettuce from California to your door) but what about clothing miles? Most of our outfits come from tens of thousands of kilometres away. Why not support all the amazing designers that live, work and stitch fabulous designs right under our noses? They tend not to sell directly online, so you'll just have to go sniffing around your hood searching out some cool Canadiana, but that's half the fun. (For some local-friendly boutiques near you, see my blurb on vintage.)

(www.organiccottonplus.com) and **Earth Friendly Goods** (www.earthfriendlygoods.com) also carry organic fabrics.

Fair Trade: Feeling guilty about that $13 shirt? Buying clothing that's fairly traded is one of the only ways to know for sure that the imported sweater you're wearing wasn't made in a sweatshop. The term applies only to goods purchased in the developing world and tells you they were sewn by worker co-ops or artisanal groups that are paid a decent income, rather than starvation wages. Fair-trade producers are also supposed to avoid using toxic dyes and unsustainable resources that would end up damaging local ecosystems and the workers that live and breathe in them. Okay, so most of the fair-trade stuff you find in local fair-trade shops such as **Ten Thousand Villages** or from online sources such as **Global Mamas** (www.globalmamas.org) is pretty earthy (think large, bright floral prints and loose clothing). But the fashionistas are moving in. The best place to find cool fair-trade clothing is actually in England (London has dozens of funky fair-trade clothing boutiques), but that doesn't mean you can't access them from here. **People Tree**'s website is full of stylish fair-trade skirts, shirts and accessories (www.peopletree.co.uk). For a list of Canadian stores that sell Bono's **Edun** line, head to www.edun.ie.

SHOES

Deciding what footwear is ecologically, socially and politically correct is enough to make any conscious consumer sweat. And with good reason. Even "all-natural" cotton canvas sneaks and sandals aren't so soft on nature when you consider that cotton is one of the heaviest users of chemical insecticides on the planet. Even your rubber soles tend to be made from petroleum.

Short of going barefoot, rest assured, there are ways to put a little heart back into your soles. Just know that I can't promise that a company is sweatshop-free—even workers' rights activists refuse to make those kinds of guarantees. So we'll just stick to what we know for sure: your shoes' ecological footprint.

Chemicals: In the shoemaking biz, sweatshops and harsh chemical use go hand in hand. In fact, the use of toxic chems in shoemaking has been decried in labour rights campaigns for the last decade. Part of what has historically made the factories so unbearable for workers is the use of adhesives containing nasty chemicals such as toluene (the smog-inducing and neurotoxic oil- and coal-refining by-product). Public pressure got major sportswear giants to switch to toluene-free, low-VOC (volatile organic compound), water-based glues or solvents. But the rest of the shoe biz is still gluing your soles with the stuff, and it's contributing to higher cancer rates among shoe workers. Contact your favourite shoe companies to ask whether they have standards around using water-based glues.

Leather: What about the shoe itself? Leather is the most popular material to wrap around our feet, but while it's nice and water-repellent and breathable, a hell of a lot of chemicals keep those hides from decomposing under your toes.

Tanneries were behind one of the worst cases of **groundwater pollution** in India's history

All sorts of nasty heavy metals go into the tanning of leather. In fact, tanneries were behind one of the worst cases of groundwater pollution in India's history, in which alarming levels of arsenic, mercury, lead and hexavalent chromium were found swimming in local water supplies. More and more leather makers are now using chrome-free processes, but that doesn't make them eco saviours.

Of course, the fact that leather producers tend to get their hides from the meat industry could be either a plus or minus for you. Some say, well, at least the animal wasn't killed for this sexy suede boot alone; the leather would just go to waste otherwise. But others point to the horrors of meat-processing plants and the ecological burden of raising animals for dinner, and say they don't want anything to do with it on their feet. Especially since the meat biz makes a pretty penny from selling its hides.

PVC: Just because your shoes are made of fake leather doesn't mean you're in the clear. Sure, vegans love this imitation material, but most faux leather footwear is made of what environmentalists consider the most noxious of plastics, PVC (vinyl). It emits dangerous carcinogenic dioxins during manufacture and incineration, as well as softening plasticizers, or phthalates, which are potential hormone disruptors and have been found to off-gas fumes of their own.

Running Shoes: When shopping for running shoes, it's impossible not to come toe to toe with the big brands on the market. You'll be happy to know that **Adidas**, **Asics**, **New Balance**, **Puma**, **Reebok** and **Nike** have all started eliminating PCVs and smoggy VOCs. Adidas and Puma gear, for instance, is nearly PVC-free. Adidas and Reebok are experimenting with using recycled rubber soles, and Nike is using what they call "an environmentally preferred rubber" that reduces toxins by 96%.

Looking to take the beef out of your bounce? **New Balance** (the celebrity-free "endorsed by no one" sneaker maker) manufactures many leather-free runners and walking shoes that are also free of PVC. Just know that the company doesn't guarantee that the glues are vegetarian.

Eco-Sneakers: If you'd rather ditch big brands altogether, why not go for the most anti-corporate street shoe in town? After years of biting attacks on mainstream shoe companies, big-biz-bashing **Adbusters** is now selling its own sneaks, called Blackspots (www.adbusters.org). The Converse-style union-made shoes are made of organic hemp, with a 70% biodegradable toe cap. Adbusters also makes a styley Blackspot Unswoosher boot with recycled tire soles. **Converse** itself has revived its hemp sneaks. And to continue with the skater theme, **Vans** has paired up with organic cotton designer **Loomstate** to make slick slip-ons (www.revolveclothing.com).

Earth-Friendly Shoes: One of the top skater shoe manufacturers, **Simple**, has exited the half-pike zone to crank out loafers, sandals and oxford types made with cool natural stuff such as jute, wool, cork, bamboo and natural latex (www.simpleshoes.com). Some hemp stores carry **Ecolution** gear, a line of organic hemp shoes, sandals, slippers, lace-up boots and even kids' stuff. If you can't find them, you can order them online at www.ecolution.com.

All you fashionistas might be moaning at the prospect of wearing hemp on your feet, but chill out, there *are* über-cool footwear options for the green at heart. Canada's own shoe designer **John Fluevog** uses veggie dyes on some shoes, plus they'll even resole your shoes if

RECYCLING SHOES

While the recycling bin might not take your old shoes, second-hand shops do. Or send unwanted sneaks (all brands accepted) to Nike's Reuse-a-Shoe program. They grind 'em up and turn them into basketball and tennis courts, as well as track and playground surfaces (**www.nikeorganics.com**).

they start to fall apart (www.fluevog.com). **Terra Plana** makes some hype toe-wear with vegetable dyes and natural rubber soles (www.terraplana.com). **La Canadienne** is a local Montreal-made brand that uses eco-friendly dyes on all their fashionable footwear (available in stores across Canada or www.lacanadienne.ca). The U.K.-based **Natural Shoe Store** has a roster of all the best and edgiest earth-friendly, socially responsible designers, like funky **Think**! and **El Naturalista** (www.thenaturalshoestore.com). El Naturalista is also carried by several Canadian stores (check out www.elnaturalista.com for store listings).

Though not quite as trendy, good old **Birkenstock** also makes some veggie sandals and clogs. And leather or not, all Birks are made with leftover cork from the wine industry, natural latex and solvent-free glues, and they're fully repairable and resoleable. No wonder hippies love them!

For top-notch comfort and a little (okay, a lot) more money, non-vegans might consider slipping into **Mephisto** walking shoes. Yes, they're leather, but they use vegetable dyes, toxin-free glues, natural rubber and no plastics. And since the name sounds kind of green, I checked out **Ecco**, another line of extra-comfy shoes and boots. Turns out they, too, use vegetable dyes and a water-based finish and are Freon-free, though their soles and insole foam are synthetic. Both Ecco and Mephisto shoes are available at www.softmoc.ca and at stores across the country (www.mephisto.com and www.eccocanada.com).

Reconstructed Footwear: And now for something completely recycled: flip-flops made with used bicycle uppers, chipped tire footbed and natural recycled hemp. The product is 100% waste-free and reused (www.splaff.com). In the kookier category, conscious footwear designers **Terra Plana** have taken it up a notch, green-wise, with their Worn Again sneaks. These babies incorporate leather salvaged from old cars, old coffee bags, unwanted jeans and surplus military jackets (www.terraplana.com).

JEWELLERY

I admit it. I have a jewellery fetish. I get weak when I see a good bangle or an oversized ring. But whether you're buying beads or browsing through Birks, picking out the right ring or bracelet is not just about personal fashion when landscapes, communities and even animal populations around the globe have been devastated to get them to you.

On average, 350 tons of ore have to be dug up and processed **to carve up a single carat**

Diamonds: Sorry ladies, but Marilyn Monroe was lying: diamonds aren't a girl's best friend, but their environmental impacts are forever. Open-pit mines involve blasting a large area, stripping it of vegetation and trees and leaving the land severely degraded. On average, 350 tons of ore have to be dug up and processed to carve up a single carat. And after all that digging, only 20% of the raw gems are considered good enough to wear! One in five diamonds are dug up from riverbeds (they're known as alluvial diamonds)—not surprisingly, vacuuming a river tends to destroy its ecosystem. Another chunk is mined from the ocean floor.

Ever heard of the term "blood diamonds"? No, it's not a reference to a new ruby-hued version of the stone, but rather a nod to the fact that part of the gem trade is run by gun-toting rebels financing vicious armed conflicts. It's the kind of scenario you can pretty much guarantee offers zero protection for the environment or for the poor people who get caught in the crossfire in places like Angola, Sierra Leone and Liberia. The industry says only a small percentage of diamonds come from such countries, but Amnesty International estimates that 10% of the world's rough diamonds are tied to groups engaged in all sorts of human rights abuses, from rape to child soldiering, as well as the forced relocation of millions.

Yes, certification schemes now say they can document the chain of custody between producers and you. In fact, the Kimberley Process, developed by industry and non-governmental organizations (NGOs) in the last few years, is supposed to ensure that all diamonds that enter or exit Canada and over 40 other countries are certified. But that only tells you that your diamond is conflict-free. The mine could still be ecologically damaging, pay its workers next to nothing and employ children (70% of diamonds by weight are polished

NORTHERN CANADIAN DIAMONDS

Northern Canadian diamonds are blood-free, and tougher environmental regulations are in place. Nonetheless, eco-groups say federal regs fail to protect water from mine toxins, the draining of lakes (20 have been sucked dry to date), according to the Canadian Arctic Resources Committee, has led to a loss of fish habitats, and the industrial boom around mines has doubled carbon monoxide emissions in the Northwest Territories. At least **Brilliant Earth** embeds Canuck diamonds in recycled gold or platinum bands (**www.brilliantearth.com**).

in India, often under appalling conditions, and at least 20,000 workers are children—although that might improve now that India's cracking down on child labour). Plus, Kimberley certificates aren't always obtained on the up and up. In fact, one group (Partnership Africa Canada) says almost a quarter of Brazil's diamond exports in 2004 were shipped out on forged papers. Activists are aiming for a fair-trade diamond certification program so you can know whether your rock came from a worker-run co-op.

Other Gems: Diamonds aren't the only friend you should mistrust. All gems have equally sordid pasts and are often traded in the same circles that run guns and drugs. Myanmar (formerly known as Burma) supplies the world with 95% of its beautiful blood-red rubies, as well as jade, sapphire and pearl, but activists say these gems have a different sort of blood on them. Many countries, including the U.S, have banned or boycotted all Burmese goods, saying that buying them only validates and funds a brutal military dictatorship. Canada restricts trade with the country, but hasn't banned it outright.

Take heart: fairly traded gems are available. **Columbia Gem House Inc.** is a fair-trade company that does its own mining, cutting and marketing. Unfortunately, no Canadian retailer sells these particular hand-mined, environmentally sensitive rocks, but check www.fairtradegems.com to find American retailers that sell online.

Metals: What about all the pretty metals that fill our jewellery boxes? Did you know it takes 20 tons of waste rock and toxic tailings to produce 1 ounce (30 grams) of gold? Or that the mercury and cyanide used to separate gold and copper from rock has a nasty habit of ending up in groundwater? Even basic silver mining communities are tarnished by groundwater pollution and toxic waste dumping, as pretty much all mines are. And the cheap silver jewellery you find on the street and in many stores could have enough lead to poison a child—no joke. Check Health Canada's website for current recalls (www.hc-sc.gc.ca). If the silver isn't cut with lead, it's probably cut with nickel, which makes the fingers of one in five people turn green. Plus, you're likely indirectly supporting nickel mining giant Inco, one of the worst polluters in Canada.

Animals: Be very cautious when buying jewellery made from animals. While ivory is outlawed here, it still gets smuggled in. And if it isn't sliced from endangered elephants, it's cut from hippos and walruses. You should also pass on trendy tortoiseshell, coral and peacock-feather trinkets.

41

LAB-GROWN DIAMONDS

All the most conscious celebs are wearing fakes to avoid the human rights and environmental implications of traditional jewels. Why not join them and get your bling from lab-grown or cultured diamonds? These man-made high-pressure, high-heat creations are started from a real diamond "seed" and end up being optically and physically the same as the gems we so aggressively extract from nature. **Gemesis** cultured diamonds come in J-Lo colours like yellow and pink, and best of all, they're completely sustainable (**www.gemesis.com** or **www. diamondscultured.com**).

There are other types of high-quality synthetic diamonds besides the cultured kind. **Moissanite** stones will even cut glass, but it's hard to get a pure white one if you're picky. **Diamond Nexus** stones, said to be excellent diamond doppelgängers, also cut glass, and they're super-cheap (**www.diamondnexuslabs.com**).

Jewellery Solutions: Don't tear your pearls out! There are plenty of ways to adorn yourself in good conscience, especially if you're willing to shop online. **GreenKarat** sells all kinds of engagement rings, wedding bands and more, made from recycled gold (sourced from watches, eyeglass frames, coins and even aerospace components). The company also ensures that the gold is refined at zero-discharge refineries. You can even design your own band and offset the carbon emissions of your puchase (www.greenkarat.com).

Eco-artware.com uses a selection of reused, recycled and natural materials to make their Scrabble earrings and pottery shard necklaces. Hemp shops tend to sell necklaces and bracelets made with fibres from the low-pesticide, high-yield crop hemp. If there's a fair-trade shop such as **Ten Thousand Villages** near you, you'll find large sections devoted to crafty necklaces, silver earrings and funky bangles, all made by worker co-ops, often using recycled material. **Snooty Jewelry** offers a ton of pearl-, leather-, shell-, bone- and silk-free toe rings, anklets and lockets (www.snootyjewelry.com). **Moonrise Jewelry**'s focus is especially cool: not only does its work/training program promote the empowerment of women of all backgrounds, but its Premier EcoJewelry Collection is made with fair-trade gems, ecologically mined materials and recycled metals (www.moonrisejewelry.com).

Finally, **antique markets** and **shops** are the ultimate jewellery recycling centres, filled with loads of one-of-a-kind rings, bracelets and brooches. Anyone wanting to score an engagement ring without contributing directly to the dirty mining biz should look here.

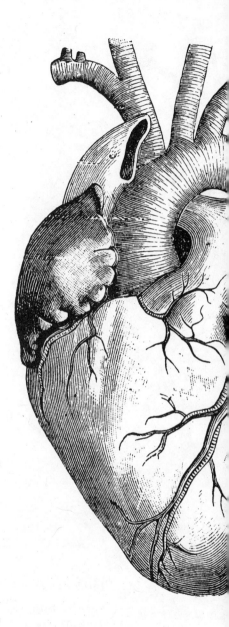

A POUND OF CURE

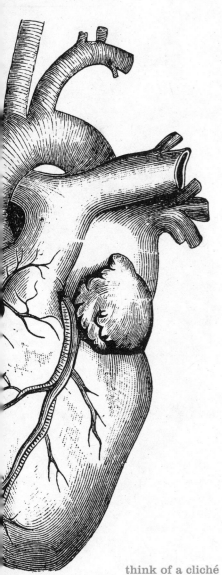

I'll give you five bucks if you can

think of a cliché that's less comforting in trying times than "at least you have your health." Still, the fear of losing that healthy status is a powerful force in North American society. Just look at our obsession with popping pills, dieting and weird ab machine infomercials. Then add up all the things you do in a day that have a potential impact, good or bad, on your body's well-being: swallowing supplements, taking a painkiller, smoking . . . Now, stop your navel-gazing and spend a moment or two learning about what all that does to the planet.

PHARMACEUTICALS

You might pop a few echinacea pills after your co-worker sneezes on your keyboard, but when full-blown infection or illness hits, most of us run to our doctors for the most hard-core prescription we can get our hands on. Canadians spent $20 billion on prescription drugs in 2005, according to University of British Columbia's *Rx Atlas*, and that doesn't even include all the pills we bought over the counter. These powerful synthetic compounds are aggressively tested on animals and, alarmingly, the world's poorest (see Sonia Shah's book *The Body Hunters: How the Drug Industry Tests Its Products on the World's Poorest Patients*). While you might be on the lookout for weird side effects, few of us are tuned in to just what happens once those meds leave our bodies. (Warning: You might need a sedative once you find out.) Not to mention all the pollution involved in making the damn things in the first place.

Production: It churns out billions of synthetic pills a year, so it's no surprise that Big Pharma also pumps out vast amounts of pollutants. The daily wastewater released by the pharmaceutical industry in 1990 was 266 million gallons, according to Environmental Protection Agency (EPA) reports (did I mention that was each and every day?). Many of the chemical solvents released are considered hazardous and can't be treated by wastewater treatment plants. Big Pharma manufacturers also emit plenty of hazardous particles into the atmosphere, including cyanide, smoggy volatile organic compounds (VOCs) and the neuro-toxin toluene. The industry has taken on waste reduction and pollution prevention practices like any other, but harmful emissions continue to be pumped out of stacks.

Sewage: Swallow a pill. Feel better. End of story, right? Wrong. Anywhere from 50 to 90% of the active ingredients found in our medications aren't broken down by our bodies, according to a report released in 2006 by the Canadian Institute for Environmental Law and Policy. To put it bluntly: we basically pee and poop them out. Luckily, sewage treatment plants degrade most drug residues, but some, like anti-seizure drugs, basically pass through the sewage treatment process unscathed. Drug residues then end up flowing into our rivers, lakes, oceans and, yup, pouring back out of our taps. Plus, plenty of raw, untreated sewage gets into waterways, thanks to storm sewage overflows (the same overflows that toss condoms and tampons up on beaches), leaks, septic tank failures and straight-piping. According to a U.S. EPA report called "Green Pharmacy," it isn't known whether sewage treatment plants could be "cost-effectively modified" to eliminate or even reduce the problem.

DO WE NEED SO MANY DRUGS?

We've finally figured out that we're taking too many antibiotics. But we still run to our doctors in increasing numbers, asking for all kinds of meds, when we should be asking ourselves if we really need them. An ounce of prevention, people! Healthy eating and regular exercise could stop you from flushing a pound of cure down the toilet.

So what *is* swimming in our water then? One test on drinking water (conducted by Enviro-Test labs for CTV) in towns across Canada turned up traces of epilepsy and cholesterol drugs, while another, conducted by the National Water Research Institute for Health and Environment Canada, found nine meds in samples taken near water treatment plants, including ibuprofen, prescription painkillers, Prozac and estrogen (at this point, the feds are testing only a few easy-to-spot acidic drugs). Overall, roughly 100 pharmaceuticals have been found in the waters of the U.S. and Europe. Okay, so they tend to be in the parts per billion or trillion range (about a drop in an Olympic-size pool). How much impact can that have? Well, so far none have been discovered in humans. But that doesn't mean they won't be. And what about the poor fishies?

Roughly 100 pharmaceuticals have been found in the waters of the U.S. and Europe

If you've read up on the ABCs of eco-friendly sex (see page 57), you'll know that faint traces of birth control pills are feminizing fish out in the wild. Much of the Western world is gearing up to research into all this, trying to figure out just what risks, if any, other drugs pose. The Canadian Water Network, established by the feds, has teamed up with the E.U. to coordinate research with a dozen university and government researchers here. The data should be out sometime in 2007.

Proper Disposal: If expired or unused drugs are collecting in your medicine cabinet, do *not* flush them. Health Canada asks that you not even toss them in the trash. Medication can leach from landfills—a bad scene, especially when you consider how many meds, including nasal sprays, eye ointments and hemorrhoid creams, contain traces of the known neurotoxin mercury. Instead, ask your pharmacy if they have a drug disposal program. This is the one time where recycling is a bad idea. Your pharmacy makes sure they're disposed of in "an environmentally sound way." Basically they're sending your old meds off to medical incinerators or chemical landfills fortified to take hazardous waste. While burning and dumping them this way seems a little dodgy, it's certainly better than burning and dumping them in regular municipal facilities not designed to handle toxic waste.

If your pharmacy can't help, call your municipality and ask if they have a drug take-back program. Many cities consider pharmaceuticals a hazardous waste and ask that you drop them off at your local hazardous waste depot.

TOXICITY TESTING

In the "Damn, shouldn't we have been doing this all along?" category, European medical guidelines recommend that any new drug undergo long-term environmental toxicity testing to see how well it biodegrades, whether it's broken down by sewage treatment plants, whether it disrupts the little micro-organisms that do all the dirty work in sewage treatment plants and just how it impacts fish, algae and water fleas. But these new guidelines won't apply to drugs already on the market. For those, testing is happening out in the real world à la mass global experiment. Don't you just love being a guinea pig? Canada's following Europe's lead, but the testing is happening more informally.

NATURAL HEALTH REMEDIES

Back in the day before pink-coated painkillers and fizzy antacids, all our meds came straight from nature. Before Big Pharma started doctoring up synthetic formulas in sterilized labs, village doctors and tribal healers prescribed hundreds of plants from the wilds to heal the worst of ailments. Of course, pharmaceutical companies know to look to nature too; otherwise, they'd never have found penicillin. Today, about 25% of all prescription drugs contain active ingredients that either originally came from plants or were designed to copy the effects of plants. Without a doubt, scientists are still picking over jungles for the next big drug. (Hey, you've seen Sean Connery in *Medicine Man*, right?)

Given all that, I guess you could say it's only natural (sorry, some puns are just unavoidable) that more of us are going back to our roots. The Canadian Health Food Association says 75% of us use natural health supplements. But just because something comes from the earth doesn't mean we extracted it in an earth-friendly way.

47

Collecting Wild Herbs: Lots of us pop ginseng to liven our step, quicken our minds and boost our immune systems. But the popular indigenous root is now scarce in North America, thanks to over-harvesting. The root's now on Canada's federal endangered species list, making it illegal to pick it on federal land. But what about the poor endangered plants that aren't on Crown turf? Well, it all depends on what province you're in. Ontario, for instance, has American ginseng on the endangered list too, but there's nothing on the books yet to protect it. The province just strongly encourages you not to rip it out of the ground. As you can imagine, policing forests for ginseng or other herb poachers can be a little difficult and is not exactly, shall we say, a high priority.

And ginseng is not alone on the missing herbs list. Wild echinacea is endangered in the U.S., and calming lady's slipper is on the list both north and south of the border. Sore throat soother licorice root has been depleted by about 60% in the wild. And goldenseal, a popular antiviral, is on the official threatened list here in Canada.

You wouldn't know any of this by walking into a health store, where the term "wildcrafted" is not only common, but revered as a sign the herb wasn't sprayed with pesticides and farmed on mega-plantations. Indeed, according to the World Wildlife Fund's (WWF) wildlife trade monitoring network, TRAFFIC, of the estimated 40,000–50,000 plants used by traditional and modern medicine around the world, the majority are snagged from the wild. Some herb companies insist that they practise ethical wildcrafting, but it's important to avoid buying any wild herb on the endangered or threatened list. For a full list of species at risk see www.sararegistry.gc.ca, or check out the Species at Risk (SAR) list in your home province. Some plants, such as yellow dock and St. John's wort, are considered so widespread that you can pick to your hearts content and still be in the clear.

Mega-farms growing medicinal herbs might take the heat off wild supplies, but in countries such as China, herbs are pushing out food crops and big corporations are moving into what was once the territory of the local medical practitioner.

Contamination: In some cases, trace pesticides are the least of your worries. In 2005, Health Canada issued a warning that about a dozen Ayurvedic tablets, powders and capsules were contaminated with high levels of heavy metals such as lead, mercury and/or arsenic. In 2006, several Chinese herbs were blacklisted by the agency because of dangerous bacterial contamination. The department says you can avoid this kind of thing by making sure you buy only authorized natural medicine, with an eight-digit Drug Identification Number (DIN), Natural Product Number (NPN) or homeopathic number (DIN-HM) as proof. It's also good idea to periodically check out Health Canada's website for a list of current advisories, warnings and recalls (www.hc-sc.gc.ca).

Endangered Wildlife: Where have all the wild things gone? The poaching of threatened and endangered animals has reached crisis proportions, in large part due to the rising popularity of traditional Chinese medicine (TCM), according to the WWF. Chinese medicine is also the number one threat to Asia's tiger, rhinoceros and bear populations, even though these are supposedly protected. Poaching is so out of control in India, for instance, that not one Siberian tiger was left at the Sariska Reserve in 2005.

TCM-motivated hunting is in no way just an Asian problem. A lot of it happens right here in Canada. Wild black bears are killed for their gallbladders and bile, used in everything from hemorrhoid creams to hair tonics. Luckily, many Canadian TCM practitioners won't prescribe the stuff anymore, and the WWF is trying to promote the use of substitutes. But that doesn't mean you can't find any. Environment Canada says several products are still being shipped in illegally. Tell your TCM doc that you want to stay far away from anything suspicious.

Fish Oil: Everyone's talking about adding healthy oils to our diets, and popping fish pills seems to be one popular way to do so. The omega-3 fatty acids they contain are good for our hearts and our brains. But make sure your supplements are made with the smallest fish on the food chain—sardines, anchovies, herring and the like—rather than cod or salmon. Why? Well, they

> Make sure your supplements are made with **the smallest fish on the food chain**

have lower levels of heavy metals, mercury and other pollutants. (FYI, ConsumerLab.com tested 41 fish oil brands and found none containing mercury or PCBs—the oils are supposedly distilled to filter out contaminants. Still, a British study found salmon and cod liver oil contaminated with flame retardants and pesticides. Make sure your brand of choice uses pharmaceutical-grade oil, rather than industrial-grade). Smaller fish are generally considered more sustainable than larger fish and show up on the green lists of sustainable seafood guides such as Monterey Bay Aquarium's Seafood Watch (www.mbayaq.org/cr/seafoodwatch.asp). American wild-caught sardines and Atlantic herring, for instance, are in the clear. Or skip the fish altogether and get your omega-3 from flaxseed oil.

7 SOUND MOVES TO PROTECT YOUR HEALTH (AND THE PLANET'S)

#1 Cut out toxic pesticides and carcinogenic and hormone-disrupting chemicals by buying organic food, shampoos, deodorants, etc.

#2 Turn to pharmaceutical drugs only when you really need them.

#3 Boost your health with sustainable natural remedies that come from the earth.

#4 Cigarettes pollute you and the ecosystem. It's time to quit.

#5 Cut your smog emissions by making your home more energy-efficient (power plants are serious air polluters). Every watt you use makes it harder for you to breathe.

#6 Clear your home of persistent chemicals, which can accumulate in your tissues. Get rid of crumbling cushions (they're full of old-generation toxic fire retardants, see page 163), toss your non-stick products (see page 145) and say no to chemical lawn pesticides (see page 228).

#7 Spend time in nature—it not only reminds us what we're fighting to protect, but it boosts serotonin levels and has been proven to speed recovery among the sick and improve attention deficit hyperactivity disorder in kids.

For more on boosting your health and that of the ecosystem, get a copy of *The Canadian Guide to Health and the Environment*, edited by the founding president of the Canadian Association of Physicians for the Environment, Dr. T. Guidotti.

Natural Health Solutions: Ask your health store clerk about smaller local manufacturers with solid reputations. Their products may cost a little more, but the cheaper drugstore or big box brands often use lower-grade ingredients, artificial dyes and hydrogenated oil fillers. **New Chapters** out of Vermont is considered a leader in eco-sustainability. Also ask about food-sourced vitamins such as **Advantage Health Matters** and **Source of Life**, which get their vitamin C, for instance, from camu berries instead of synthetic sources.

Organic Herbs: Many herbalists recommend using organic herbs, so you can be sure your meds were harvested sustainably and without toxic inputs. Buying organic is thought to be especially important for your internal health if you're using tinctures or essential oils, since the herbs are so concentrated in these forms. Health Canada's Health Product and Food Branch maintains that all manufacturers have to prove that pesticide levels aren't above a set level. Fine, so the pesticides used may not show up on your herbs, but that doesn't mean they didn't have an impact on surrounding soil, waterways and wildlife. As with food, it's a good idea to buy organic health supplements whenever possible to make sure the planet stays as fit as you do. **Natural Factors**, out of B.C., uses strictly certified organic Kelowna-grown herbs in all its herbal products, such as silica made from organic horsetail and omega oils made with organic flaxseed. Quebec's **Clef Des Champs** and Ontario's **St. Francis** also make reputable organic herb supplements.

BUG REPELLENT

Can you hear that? That buzzing? That's the sound of mosquitoes making a beeline for your neck. You might as well call it the sound of summer because, as the weather warms up, these blood-sucking creatures start looking to multiply, and the female can't lay her eggs without a little meal. That means you, and every exposed surface on your body, kiddo. But if you don't want to become a skeeter's breakfast, and West Nile phobia has got you nervous, what do you do?

Deet: As tempting as it is to douse yourself in a chemical that promises to confuse mosquitoes by biologically messing with their antennae so they can't find their target (namely you), DEET is obviously not the greenest option. Have you seen what it can do to a pair of sunglasses? It's pretty potent stuff, and the U.S. Agency for Toxic Substances and Disease Registry reports that, with daily use over several months (like, say, the length of the summer), a few people have developed shortness of breath, headaches, tremors, joint pain and even seizures. Young kids are particularly at risk, and DEET should never be used on babies under six months. For info on how much DEET kids can safely be exposed to, type in "insect repellent" at www.pmra-arla.gc.ca.) DEET, by the way, is one of the top five contaminants found in U.S. streams (likely there from washing it off our skin in the shower and sending it down the drain), which isn't great news for aquatic life.

Natural Repellents: Fear not, chemical-weary traveller, there are alternatives and, some of them do work. A much-touted study by the *New England Journal of Medicine* found that soy-based **Bite Blocker** rivalled DEET (www.biteblocker.com) in terms of effectiveness. *Consumer Reports* found **Repel's Lemon Eucalyptus Spray** performed even better than DEET. According to the *New England Journal of Medicine* study, citronella products aren't all that effective and have to be reapplied as often as every 10 to 30 minutes.

Bug Clothing: The only anti-insect clothing I'd recommend is the old-fashioned bug shirt. These lightweight pullover hoodies with mesh over the face offer a personal refuge of sorts when you're in the deep woods. Think of it as the camper's burka. The **Original Bug Company** (www.bugshirt.com) offers made-in-Canada shirts, pants, hoods and something called gaiters (which are kind of like leg warmers, but aimed more at keeping your ankles bite-free than priming them for that *Flashdance* revival). Camping stores also tend to have ecological netting products for your outdoor pleasure.

TOBACCO

Among all the images of rotting gums and black, tumour-covered lungs, never once have you seen a pack of smokes with a warning about what cigarettes do to the earth. Perhaps that's because there's just too much to say.

Chemicals: Anyone who's read the side of a cigarette pack has seen the very partial list of chemicals and heavy metals lurking in the cancer sticks. Back in 1994, American cigarette manufacturers finally released a list of 599 additives they potentially toss into the tobacco mix for flavour enhancement. Some are as harmless as chocolate, but others (like the mosquito insecticide methoprene, which has been linked to frog deformities) are far more worrying.

Some cigarette manufacturers, such as Rothman's, say their sticks are additive-free, but don't fool yourself into thinking you're off the hook, folks. You're still sending a toxic cloud of up to 4,000 chemicals into the atmosphere when you light up—things like formaldehyde, benzene and hydrogen cyanide, which are all air-polluting, smog-inducing VOCs. And in case you think your little ciggie won't make matters worse in a world saturated with chemicals, just multiply that smoke by the over 5 million Canadians who are also puffing.

Production: Meanwhile, back at the ranch, over 11.6 million kilograms (and over 450 kinds) of pesticides are used on this crop every year in the U.S. alone. But much of the production takes place in the developing world, where the protection of rivers and wildlife is about as high on the list of priorities as the risks to the workers who harvest it.

Just drying the damn leaves out has led to serious deforestation in some parts of the world. In southern Africa, about 200,000 hectares of trees a year are chopped to fuel tobacco curing, according to *World Agriculture and the Environment* by Jason Clay (put out by the WWF). In the '90s, tobacco curing and production was fingered for nearly half of South Korea's deforestation.

Litter: Finally, there are all those damn butts. With those 5 million Canadian smokers tossing their filters onto sidewalks, streets, parks and highways, we're talking a hell of a lot of litter. And they don't just disappear, people! Sure, cellulose acetate is a plastic that comes from wood pulp, so eventually it does break down, but it takes anywhere from 18 months to 12 full years to decompose. In the meantime, filters have been found in the stomachs of sick or deceased fish, birds and other unsuspecting creatures who have mistaken them for food.

Wherever they end up, be it beaches, parklands or sewers, they inevitably leach out all the thousands of nasty chemicals they absorbed from your cigarette. So stop your illicit butting, people! Oh, and by the way, dropped butts were responsible for a staggering 14,030 fires between 1995 and 1999 in Canada. Fires that killed 356 people and seared to a crisp thousands of acres of beautiful Canadian forest.

You're sending a toxic cloud of up to **4,000 chemicals** into the atmosphere when you light up

Herbal and Organic Cigarettes: What about herbal cigarettes, made of seemingly benign baking ingredients such as cloves, basil and cinnamon? What harm could they do? Turns out even these veggie sticks puff out plenty of tar and carbon monoxide (a greenhouse gas precursor that contributes to global warming). And just because they're herbal and sometimes come wrapped in pretty leaves instead of paper doesn't mean pesticides aren't used on their ingredients.

CIGARETTE PAPERS

One tree is axed and bleached for every 300 cigarettes rolled in paper. That's one tree every two weeks if you smoke a pack a day, and 26 trees for every year you've been hooked.

53

The only organic smokable I found was **American Spirit**'s line of certified organic rolling tobacco. A Vancouver store also sells dried certified organic tobacco leaves online that are said to be quite strong and should, according to the shop, be blended with other herbs like mullein (www.gaiagarden.ca). Not that organic tobacco won't kill you—oh, it will—but at least you're not partaking in the global chemical bath associated with the rest of the industry.

If you really want to stick it to the biz, grow your own. You can buy all sorts of organically produced tobacco seeds at www.eonseed.com. Of course, your greenest option is to stop smoking, but you already know that.

MENSTRUAL PRODUCTS

It's that time of the month and you're out of supplies. You run to the nearest pharmacy to stock up on whatever option has the widest wings, the driest weaving and the biggest sale. And who can blame us? Most of what we know about what's on the shelves comes from cryptic TV ads in which girls release blue water from a vial once a month. And as much as we try to keep what happens on Aunt Flow's visits behind closed doors, we're creating a massive amount of waste that can't really be discreetly flushed down the loo.

Waste: About 12 billion pads and 7 billion tampons are used once and tossed in the trash each and every year in the U.S. alone! That's a hell of a lot of landfill-clogging, ladies! Even if you're a "light days" kind of girl and don't have long, heavy periods, you're still creating plenty of waste in your lifetime.

And though companies tell us their tampon applicators are perfectly flushable, that doesn't mean sewer overflows won't wash 'em back up onto a shore or stream near you. (Horrifically, tampon applicators and other plastics were found in the stomachs of Hawaiian Laysan albatross chicks that had died in their nests.)

Production: Then, of course, there are the materials that go in to keeping you dry and happy every month. (Wouldn't want that blue water to leak.) Super-absorbent rayon (often blended with pesticide-drenched cotton) forms the basis of most pads and tampons. Menstrual product pushers are only too happy to tell you the stuff comes from trees. Yes, synthetic rayon is a wood pulp derivative, but it's not exactly natural. It's made extra-absorbent in a fairly toxic chemical process.

Companies do insist that they've ditched their old practice of bleaching the batting with chlorine gases, a process responsible for the carcinogenic and highly persistent by-product dioxin (which accumulates in fatty tissue). Instead, they say they use chlorine dioxide, oxygen and/or hydrogen peroxide in a process called "elemental chlorine–free bleaching" to "significantly minimize the potential for dioxin formation."

Tampax also says it tests its cotton fibres to ensure they don't contain detectable levels of pesticides, but while your private parts might be spared exposure, the cotton's still grown with toxic herbicides, fungicides and the like, which ain't good for the planet. And drugstore brands are chock full of plastics: synthetic latex wings, polyethylene dry-weave layers in pads and that "silky" coating on tampons. Not to mention all those damn applicators (bet you've never seen a little recyclable symbol on these) and the nasty PVC wrapper that comes with pads.

Tampons and Pads: If you're going to buy drugstore tampons, cardboard applicators are better than plastic, and applicator-free types such as **O.B.** are another step up. But you really should be using tampons from **Natracare** or **Organic Essentials**, made with 100% certified organic non-chlorine-bleached cotton. They're free of synthetics and chemical additives, come with or without cardboard applicators, and work just as well as mainstream brands. These companies also make organic chlorine-free pads and panty liners (with or without wings), as does **Seventh Generation**. Seventh Generation's pads and liners are not organic and do contain some plastic, but they also contain an absorbent gel derived from wheat. Natracare, however, uses a biodegradable plant-based bioplastic in place of petroleum plastic as a barrier layer to keep the pads from leaking.

FEMININE WIPES

Recently, big sanitary product brands have been pushing the idea of disposable wipes for gals on the rag. If you're keen on "freshening" your privates on the go, at least reach for an organic cotton wipe made with essential oils and healing calendula (Natracare makes some) instead of the chemical fragrances, petroleum-based ingredients such as propylene glycol, and even formaldehyde-releasing preservatives (namely, imidazolidinyl urea) in mainstream brands. A good old-fashioned shower will do the same job without the waste.

Cloth Pads: Still, these products are disposable, and each tampon comes individually plastic-wrapped. If you're ready to take the plunge and go even greener, your next option is reusable cloth pads (which should last you about five years). Yes, it sounds a little icky, and it isn't for everyone, but if you can get past the minor psychological hurdle, give 'em a shot. You can buy Canadian-stitched pads by companies such as **Goddess Moon** or organic unbleached styles by **Moonwit** and **Many Moons**. Many Moons also makes recycled pads using fabric ends from the clothing industry. **Lunapads** crafts both organic and non-organic versions (FYI, dark colours stain less), as well as panty liners and all-in-one padded organic "period panties," with or without a layer of nylon, in bikini, thong or brief styles (www.lunapads.com). They even offer ones with snap-on wings! To avoid all packaging problems, crafty girls can always sew their own pads (see www.bloodsisters.org/bloodsisters/pads.html).

Sponge: If you're more of a tampon type, and bulky pads and period panties sound too cumbersome, you can use the ocean's best-known absorbent: sea sponges. Sure, stuffing a dried ocean critter in your box might seem a little odd (that's right, sponges aren't just flora), but they work just as well as tampons, according to fans of the product, and you can wear them while swimming. (Note: the following might not be suitable for squeamish readers). How does it work? Well, when it gets saturated, you just rinse, squeeze and reinsert throughout the day. If you don't have a place to rinse it out, just pop a new one in (you're supposed to keep a film canister or a baggie in your purse to store used ones until you can rinse them). You can soak them in a tablespoon of apple cider vinegar or a few drops of tea tree oil and warm water overnight, but boiling them for five minutes is the only way to rid them of bacteria, and you should do this at the end of your cycle. Each sponge should last about six to eight cycles.

Keep in mind that, as with anything from the sea, you have to make sure the sponges are harvested sustainably, as **Sea Pearls** are (www.lunapads.com or www.gladrags.com). Sea Pearls are the only sea sponge legally available as a menstrual product in the U.S. They were exempt from a ban on sponges that took effect in the early '80s after the University of Iowa examined menstrual sponges and found them to contain bacteria, sand, grit and other matter. Other researchers found some to be chemically contaminated (not surprising, when you think about how we treat the oceans as toxic dumping grounds). Plus, just as with regular and organic tampons, you might get toxic shock from sea sponges if you leave them in too long. But Sea Pearls says it has never had a case of toxic shock among its users.

Reusable Cup: Since you're experimenting, you can also try a reusable cup (literally a mini cup you pop inside and empty two to four times a day). **The Keeper**, for instance, is made of natural gum rubber and lasts about a decade (www.keeper.com). If you're allergic to latex, you might want to use the silicone-based **Diva Cup** (www.divacup.com). Trust me, women that try these swear by them. Just steer clear of drugstore posers like Instead, which looks like a reusable cup but has to be thrown out after one use. What's the point?

SEX

Let's cut the foreplay and get to the nub of our dilemma: sex is dirty. Just stop emptying the wastebasket in your bedroom for a year and see how much trash your love life produces— condoms, pill packs, massage oil bottles, broken-down vibrators and, yes, those telling wads of crumpled virgin-forest tissue paper. To have an entirely eco-friendly sex life, you'd have to live alone in a hilltop monastery, but you don't have to be a monk to bring a little green to your boudoir.

Researchers found that adult trout exposed to a synthetic estrogen (estradiol) found in combination birth control **were half as fertile as fish kept in clean water**

Hormonal Birth Control: The pill has been wonderfully empower- ing for women (and a big step forward from the favoured female contra- ceptive of the '30s and '40s—Lysol disinfectant!). But it means that 1.5 million Canadian women are pissing out synthetic estrogen every day (nearly 85% of Canadian women have used oral contraceptives at some time in their lives). American researchers found that adult trout exposed to a synthetic estro- gen (estradiol) found in combination birth control were half as fertile as fish kept in clean water. Shockingly, fertility was affected even when they were exposed to super-low doses, 80 times lower than those turning up in the wild. In fact, other researchers at Trent University in Ontario found that low levels of estrogen hormones spawned hermaphrodite fish and lowered the number of males. Discharges from sewage treatment plants were fingered as the culprits.

Users of the patch, the implant, the shot and any other form of hormonal birth control are all culpable here. The patch, in particular, has been embroiled in controversy because it releases way more hormones than regular pills (60% more, in U.S. versions, and a little less in Canadian ones). And while health agencies south of the border have started issuing warnings about the impact that might have on women, flushing one down the toilet means bad news for fish downstream, especially since about 25,000 Canadians ditch a patch a week (for three out of four weeks). The manufacturer says women should instead fold them in half, then throw them in the waste bin, but even then, landfilled hormones could potentially leach into groundwater in leaky dumps. Activists want to see them returned to pharmacies for proper disposal. If you think the patch sounds bad, vaginal rings (new to the market) contain a third more estrogen when you trash them than a month's worth of discarded patches, and six times as many hormones as a month's worth of birth control pills, according to Women and Health Protection. Maybe that's why the manufacturer suggests that you reseal the ring in its triple-layered foil polyethylene and polyester pouch before you toss it.

FYI, **progestin-only pills** (which mimic the hormone progesterone and have fewer side effects but are somewhat less effective than progestin/estradiol combination pills) don't contain estrogen and have no feminizing properties.

Millions of condoms are said to slip into bodies of water every year, thanks to sewer overflow and all you boys who flush used ones down the toilet

Condoms: Latex condoms are, of course, your best bet for preventing unwanted surprises, from babies to herpes. Yes, latex comes from the sap of the rubber tree, but undisclosed additives ensure that your safes, especially lubricated models, will not decompose. (Vegans should also be aware that most condoms are made with the milk protein casein.) And, gross but true, millions of condoms are said to slip into bodies of water every year, thanks to sewer overflow and all you boys who flush used ones down the toilet. (Betcha never thought about how tying them off only helps them float to the water's surface.)

9 NAUGHTY WAYS TO GREEN YOUR SEX LIFE

#1 Crack open a bottle of certified organic wine.

#2 Choose GMO- and pesticide-free chocolate-coated strawberries.

#3 Ditch the petroleum wax candles and set the mood with beeswax or soy ones.

#4 Slip into something more comfortable, like, say, an ultra-feminine ensemble made of organic hemp/silk (**www.enamore.co.uk**) or a hot organic thong (**www.americanapparel.net**).

#5 Reach for PVC-free toys.

#6 Loosen things up with organic petroleum-free lube and massage oils.

#7 Save energy by doing it with the lights off.

#8 Cut back on hot water bills by soaping up together in the bath or shower.

#9 Make love, not war.

(Thanks to Greenpeace Netherlands for some of these tips.)

Polyurethane-based condoms (male and female) and sponges are even worse. While polyurethane might not cause reactions in people with latex allergies, it creates all kinds of nasty toxins in its manufacture and incineration, and it never breaks down.

If you're not vegetarian and aren't trying to prevent STDs, **lambskin condoms** are biodegradable. The only high-grade biodegradable vegan latex condom—**Condomi**—is only available to Canadians through www.britishcondoms.com.

IUDs: If you're with a trusted partner and your doctor thinks you're a good candidate, an **IUD** is probably the soundest eco-option. A lot of women grew nervous about IUDs after one brand, recalled in the '70s, was linked to significant increases in pelvic inflammatory disease, but technology has improved and the risks are now much lower. One small T-shaped copper thingy lasts up to 10 years! (The progestin-releasing versions last up to five.) IUDs are about 99% effective, but be warned: they hurt like hell going in and out.

Sex Toys: I hate to take the fun out of your frolicking sessions, but be aware that the majority of jelly dildos and vibrators are made with that eco mood killer vinyl (PVC) and softened using high levels of potentially endocrine-disrupting, liver-damaging phthalates. In 2000, a German study not only found that sex toys off-gas the stuff at pretty scary levels (up to 243,000 parts per million; Canada's maximum daily exposure limits allow for up to 3,000), but also discovered that 10 other chemicals off-gassed from certain sex toys. In addition, lead and cadmium have been found in jelly and vinyl toys. Also be wary of cheap metallic coatings, which might flake off in unwanted places.

Solid, high-quality **silicone** is much easier on the planet, as well as your body. And lovely **glass dildos** are the friendliest—they can even be recycled if you tire of them (pretty much all glass can be recycled). Plus, glass and silicone models last much longer than cheaper PVC types, which soon break, wear and flake. You'll be happy to know that **I Rub My Ducky**, as well as all **Big Tease Toys**, have been phthalate-free from the start, and Vibratex's popular **Rabbit Habit** vibrator was reformulated sans PVC.

Lubricants: Most of us are lookin' for lube in all the wrong places. Drugstore brands are loaded with petrochemicals, controversial preservatives and sometimes animal-based glycerine or lactic acid (not to mention spermicides, which can trigger yeast infections).

Sensua makes flavoured and unflavoured lube with aloe and grapefruit seed extract to encourage healthy body chemistry. It's also 95% certified organic and latex-compatible. **Hathor** makes a wonderful condom-friendly lube with organic ingredients such as ginseng.

Massage Oil: With all that oil and bare flesh, is a massage ever really just a massage? The next time you whip out this handy seduction technique, skip the petroleum-derived oils laced with nauseating chemical scents and reach for something alluringly all-natural. **Body Candy Lickable Massage Balm** isn't organic, but its ingredients are natural, and its yummy flavours, such as Orange Creamsicle and Cinnamon Hearts, are sweetened with herbal stevia. Health food stores often carry a variety of organic and all-natural massage oils. Even plain old almond oil would make for a nice rub-down.

FOOD
FOR THOUGHT

You know you want to eat healthy.

You know you'd rather eat food that's good for the health of the planet too. But let's face it, most of the time we reach for whatever we're in the mood for and what's on sale. The problem is, you can't tell by looking at a pear or a pepper just what it's been through to keep it looking firm and flawless even after sitting on a truck for a few days, then on shelves for another week. Was it genetically engineered, sprayed with a flurry of chemicals and zapped with gamma rays? Here's a breakdown of some of the major processes coming between you and your food, as well as solutions that will bring your appetite back.

INDUSTRIAL AGRICULTURE

Back in the day, people just called it food. Farmers had never heard of chemical fertilizers and relied on age-old techniques such as crop rotation to rebuild the soil's nutrient level. No doubt it was hard work: weeds were pulled by hand, and crops didn't always survive insect infestations. But somewhere around the Second World War, things changed. Chemicals developed for the war, such as ammonium nitrate and DDT, made their way onto farmers' fields. The explosion of advanced mechanization, large-scale irrigation and chemical inputs christened what was coined the Green Revolution. Not because it was remotely eco-friendly. No, no, the "green" part refers to the enormous jump in the sheer volume of food that could be produced on industrial-sized farms.

It was a mixed blessing. Yes, the dramatic boost in yields meant a drop in food prices (and we suddenly had more wheat than the world would ever need), but the type of farming it spawned was much more trying on the earth. And it's still with us today (it's one of the few '6os revolutions that actually stuck)—massive monoculture farms growing one lone crop, sucking up incredible amounts of water and demanding endless cycles of petroleum-based fertilizers to feed depleted soil and chemical pesticides that end up polluting local waterways and draining the soil of life. The irony, according to the David Suzuki Foundation, is that despite all the heavy spraying and new-fangled machinery being used on fields, nearly a third of crops are still lost to weeds and pests. That's a rate, says the Foundation, on par with crop losses before the era of chemical pesticides was ushered in.

Nearly a third of crops are still lost to weeds and pests. That's a rate on par with crop losses before the era of chemical pesticides was ushered in

Pesticides: Over a thousand chemicals are available for use as pesticides in Canada. Kind of scary when you consider the hormone-mimicking, neurotoxic, reproduction-impairing properties of many of the chemicals being sprayed to keep fields free of weeds, fungus and insects with relative ease and affordability. In fact, according to a parliamentary report, about 60% of pesticides currently being used (by weight) are hormone disruptors. Furthermore, the David Suzuki Foundation says 58 pesticides in use in Canada today are banned in other developed countries because of their ties to cancer, reproductive disorders and acute toxicity. And all pesticides, says the Canadian Association of Physicians for the Environment, are designed to kill one or more living things. Sure, you think, who cares about aphids? Well, it's not just pesky insects that are getting knocked off. The World Health Organization estimates that over 200,000 people die every year from pesticide poisoning. And countless animals die when they inadvertently, say, eat a grasshopper that's just been sprayed in a field. In Canada, over 30 registered pesticides are known to kill wild birds, and if they're not killing birds, they may be killing fish or important beneficial insects. Even when pesticides aren't the instant kiss of death, they might be weakening animals and creating birth defects. Canadian Wildlife Service says weakened birds may die more easily in bad weather or sing less so they're less likely to attract a mate and have little chicks of their own. You can't get much more heartbreaking than that.

Thanks to drifting winds, less than 5% of pesticides are said to reach their intended target. Those winds carry many persistent chemicals halfway across the world, to accumulate in the fatty tissues of animals far from farmers' fields, such as polar bears and whales. Even chemicals banned here 20 years ago, such as DDT, are blowing over from developing countries where they're still in use. They also keep building up in the food chain long after they're out of fashion.

Oh, but all the pesticides used in North America are tested and safe, you say. Well, many older pesticides bypassed detailed safety reviews because they were already in widespread commercial use before stricter standards came in. The good news is that Canada is currently retesting some of these. Unfortunately, we're also looking at harmonizing our pesticide regulations with the U.S. and swapping safety data for product approvals. That's kind of scary considering, in the spring of 2006, union leaders representing U.S. Environmental Protection Agency (EPA) scientists came out and said that researchers there are being pressured to gloss over testing and skip steps as they re-evaluate the safety of commonly used old-generation pesticides.

Add up the three pesticides on your apple, the one on your potatoes, the four on your salad, and you're ingesting a cocktail of chemical residues

Sure, in isolation, one pesticide might not affect us, but we eat more than one food item a day. Add up the three pesticides on your apple, the one on your potatoes, the four on your salad, and you're ingesting a cocktail of chemical residues. Yes, the vast majority fall below Health Canada safety levels, but many of those maximums were set back in the '70s, before they tested for things like the effects on children's health. And Canada hasn't historically tested pesticides in combination, though that's starting to change. One study that did so found that an average of about 4% of tadpoles died when they were exposed to 0.1 ppm (parts per million) of various pesticides, but a dramatic 35% of them died when they were exposed to the same low levels of nine different pesticides at once.

DO FRUIT SPRAYS WORK?

Who hasn't been intrigued by the promise of those fruit sprays in the produce aisle? **Fit**, for instance, says its natural product removes 98% more pesticides than washing with water alone because it lifts more of the waxes away. A microbiologist at the University of Georgia reported that Fit did as well in lab tests at removing bacteria on lettuce, tomatoes and apples as high levels of chlorine used by the industry to wash fresh cut fruit. But overall, the researcher said most fruit sprays are about as good as washing with chlorinated municipal water. As for the pesticides, it depends who you ask. Just rinsing produce thoroughly with tap water will remove many surface pesticides, say pesticide residue experts Thea Rawn and Jim Lawrence in *Carleton NOW*, a Carleton University publication. But ask the Pesticide Action Network U.K., and they'll tell you that water has little effect on pesticides such as diphenylamine (used on apples) and chlorpropham (on potatoes). The group says a product called **Veggie-Wash** got rid of 93.4% of these two chems (compared to a 6.7% and 30% reduction with water).

Ultimately, these sprays and soaks won't hurt you, but the jury's out on their value. Washing fruit with a mild natural detergent might help reduce some of the pesticide residues, but it won't get rid of all of them. Peeling also helps, but a good chunk of the nutrients are in the peel. It's a Catch-22 for fruit and veggie lovers.

While the Canadian Food Inspection Agency says it detects pesticide residues on only 20% of washed produce, World Wildlife Fund (WWF) reps say the feds are using crude analytical methods to save cash, and in any case, that's 20% too much. The bottom line, the Canadian Environmental Law Association says, is that 90% to 100% of us have pesticides in our tissues. The Canadian Association of Physicians for the Environment is pretty blunt in its assessment of the matter. Its standing position paper says that, for the health of our children, our wildlife and ourselves, synthetic pesticide use should be abandoned. Period.

The Environmental Working Group ranked pesticide levels on 46 fruits and vegetables based on over 100,000 tests by the U.S. Food and Drug Administration (FDA) and the Department of Agriculture. For a printable pocket-sized guide on which 12 produce items had the highest residues and which 12 had the lowest, go to http://foodnews.org. You should definitely think long and hard about buying organic versions of the 12 worst offenders.

If you feel like scaring yourself even more, Environmental Defence's Food Watch website (www.foodwatch.ca) lets you track your exposure to pesticides in your diet through its Toxic Tracker.

Fertilizers: Pressure to squeeze every last dollar from farmers' fields means that crops are no longer rotated to let lands lay fallow so that the soil can rebuild itself. There's no real need when you pump the soil full of potent petrochemical fertilizers. That's right, modern fertilizers don't come from pigpens (manure) or compost, but from petroleum. In fact, 31% of all the fossil fuels used by North American farms goes into fertilizers. And far too much of that ends up seeping into rivers, lakes and oceans, where too many nutrients can be a very bad thing. Overdoses of nitrogen and phosphorous from fertilizer runoff can create massive algae blooms that suffocate aquatic life, creating large dead zones.

Water: Any kindergartener knows that crops need water to grow, but bet you didn't realize that global agriculture sucks up roughly 90% of all the water we use on this planet. Yet the driest part of Canada, the Prairies, which also happens to be home to 60% of our agriculture, tends to raise some of the most water-intensive crops (grains and cattle)—not good when you factor in expert predictions that the Prairies are destined to become dust bowls.

Global agriculture sucks up roughly 90% of all the water we use on this planet

According to the Stockholm International Water Institute, within 25 years the planet's going to run short of H_2O, and there won't be enough water to grow the crops needed to feed the world's exploding population. Is anyone else feeling parched?

Transportation: Being Canadian in winter used to involve largely giving up fresh produce, other than carrots and turnips, and maybe a few oranges at Christmas. Now, of course, we snap our fingers and find blueberries and pineapples in the produce aisle of a Winnipeg grocery store, deep in the heart of blizzard season. Since we've yet to master the art of teleporting our fruit, that produce makes its way to kitchens on a circuit of planes, trains and automobiles. On average, our produce travels at least 2,500 kilometres to get to us. If you live in Halifax and you're buying a head of lettuce from California, those leaves have come about 5,000 kilometres on a spewing diesel truck. B.C. apples have to travel over 3,500 kilometres to get to consumers in Montreal, but that's spitting distance if you compare it to the 9,000 kilometres an apple has to trek to get here from New Zealand. That's a hell of a lot of greenhouse gas emissions for something we take four bites out of, then toss in the trash because it's too mealy or bruised.

Land Use: As much as we try to sprout food in test tubes and labs, you still need land to grow it on. And as the globe's population explodes by over 90 million a year, the amount of topsoil on the planet dwindles by more than 25 billion tons in the same time frame, according to the United National Environmental Program. Fertile land, it seems, is running out. It doesn't help that our farming habits have a tendency to erode soil even further. And as our cities keep bloating and spreading out into dwindling farmlands, we're losing not only valuable sources of local food, but also vital watersheds, wilderness habitats and carbon dioxide–absorbing green space. Statistics Canada says that, from 1971 to 2001, urban sprawl had crowded out 7,400 square kilometres of prime farmland, including prized fruit belts. And that number keeps on climbing.

As our cities keep bloating and spreading out into dwindling farmlands, we're losing not only valuable sources of local food, but also vital watersheds, wilderness habitats and carbon dioxide–absorbing green space.

Irradiation: Zapping our chicken or potatoes with gamma rays, X-rays or electron beams to get rid of germs sounds like a sci-fi plot from the '50s, but food irradiation ain't fiction, honey. In fact, Canada allows the process on onions, potatoes, wheat flour, spices and seasonings. Why? Irradiation slows the sprouting, ripening and moulding process so products can sit on shelves longer. In 2002, a battle started brewing when Health Canada was hoping to add ground beef, chicken, shrimp and, strangely, mangoes to the list, and enviro-orgs freaked out. Not only does the process drain some of the vitamins out of food, but gamma radiation creates radioactive waste. Opponents also worry about nasty accidents with the nuclear materials at irradiation facilities and with trucks carrying the materials on public roads. Irradiated foods are supposed to be clearly marked with an international symbol that tells you as much. If more than 10% of the ingredients in a prepackaged product have been irradiated, the label has to list those ingredients. Less than that, and you're in the dark. As for whether Canada's moving ahead with irradiating more food types, Health Canada says it's still under discussion.

Genetic Engineering: Genetically modified organisms (GMOs). You know you're uncomfortable with them, but you're not sure why. No doubt, it's freaky stuff: GMOs are developed in the lab when scientists take genes from one organism, say a jellyfish, and insert them into unrelated species, say a mouse, which is what researchers at Brown University did (don't ask). Okay, so you might not eat mice for dinner, but crops such as soybeans, corn and tomatoes are commonly crossed with bacteria or viruses to improve hardiness, pesticide resistance and drought resistance, or just to make ripe tomatoes less prone to squishing. It's a far cry from old-fashioned hybridization, in which gardeners and farmers crossbreed seeds from different varieties of a single crop to develop produce that is hardier or sweeter or smaller.

Just like the promise of a perfect, healthy child lures us to the idea of designer babies, genetic modification is pushed as the solution to the world's woes. Living in a country with high rates of vitamin A deficiency? No problem, rice can be crossbred with daffodils and bacteria so it's packed with the vitamin. But earth advocates aren't biting. As thoroughly as the government says it tests genetically engineered crops before they are put on the market, critics say it's never thoroughly enough. And GMOs haven't been around long enough for long-term health effects to come to light.

> Living in a country with high rates of vitamin A deficiency? **No problem, rice can be crossbred with daffodils and bacteria so it's packed with the vitamin**

Back in 2000, a report came out that the pollen in Bt corn (the Bt part tells you a crop was crossed with bacteria) wasn't just killing off intended pests, it was killing the larvae of pretty monarch butterflies too. It turns out that the United States Department of Agriculture (USDA) hadn't tested the impact on butterflies or moths that weren't considered a problem to farmers. Oops.

Nature is always up for a fight, and just as viruses seem to get bigger and badder the more antibiotics we take, some herbicide-resistant GMO crops are already proving ineffective against new strains of super-weeds. Researchers are also on the lookout for outbreaks of super-insects that just grow stronger in the face of pesticide-resistant plants.

And like a kid destined for the naughty mat, GMOs never stay put. As with all seeds, they're carried on the wind to neighbouring fields, threatening to contaminate and cross-breed with natural and organic strains. Once you release one of these plants, it's virtually impossible to remove it entirely from the environment.

If you want to know which crackers and veggies were grown without genetic engineering, you're out of luck. Canada decided against mandating the labelling of GMO ingredients, so your guess is as good as mine. But about 75% of processed foods available on shelves and in freezer aisles contain at least one ingredient that's been genetically modified. Greenpeace has put together a thorough guide on which foods are likely to contain geneti-

MONSANTO: THE DARK PRINCE OF THE GMO

You probably can't find a corporation much more maligned by food activists than Monsanto. It is, after all, the company that invented saccharin, was a major producer of aspartame, bovine growth hormones and PCBs and, along with Dow, manufactured the notoriously polluting and destructive herbicide Agent Orange, made famous during the Vietnam War. But perhaps most infamously of all, it's the king of genetically engineered crops. Monsanto controls anywhere from 70% to 100% of the market share of several genetically modified food plants. And hey, since it produces Roundup (the most commonly used weed killer in Canada, both on lawns and fields), its best-selling GMO crops are the Roundup Ready variety, which can basically be sprayed with tons of the potent herbicide without a blade of corn or a soy bean being harmed. I'd need a lawyer if I repeated all the names this company has been called over the years, especially after it sued the pants off

many smaller Canadian and American farmers who either dared save their Roundup Ready seeds for reuse (an ancient farm practice that seems to be against Monsanto rules) or were unlucky enough to have fields downwind from Roundup farms and ended up sprouting Monsanto-patented plants on their farms thanks to pollen and seed drifts.

The bio-tech giant has also gained unwelcome acclaim for pushing terminator seeds— which are essentially sterile and can't be collected and reused. Environmentalists, farmers and politicians around the world worry that the so-called suicide seeds will crossbreed with nearby plants and sterilize crops, an especially devastating possibility for poor farmers in the developing world. Luckily, there's an international moratorium against using and testing this technology in the field (although the Canadian government has been quietly lobbying to overturn it).

cally engineered ingredients and which are in the clear (www.greenpeace.ca/shoppersguide/). Other than that, buying organic is the only way to know for sure that your food was not grown with genetically modified ingredients.

PROCESSING

When the first man boiled a corked bottle of food back in 18th-century Europe, essentially sterilizing it, do you think he had an inkling of the brave new world of processed foods he would eventually spawn? A few decades after the boiled bottle development, the tin can was born, and soon people everywhere were eating foods that had been prepared months, or even years earlier. Okay, so they weren't exactly tasty, but that's nothing artificial-flavouring specialists couldn't clear up.

Artificial Flavours and Colours: A single artificial flavour, such as the fake strawberry essence found in milkshakes, can contain well over 50 ingredients, and complex flavours such as roasted coffee or meat can involve thousands, according to Eric Schlosser's book *Fast Food Nation: The Dark Side of the All-American Meal.* Many of the ingredients are petroleum-derived and come with their own set of environmental ramifications. Even so-called natural flavours and colours can contain the same chemicals as, say, artificial banana flavouring—they just go through a different processing method, says Schlosser. And remember the hoopla about the natural flavouring in McDonald's french fries? Vegetarians were peeved to learn that the fries they'd been chowing down on for years were actually flavoured with beef extract.

Over a dozen artificial colours have already been banned, but that doesn't mean the rest are entirely without controversy. While many, such as FD&C Blue No. 1 and Green No. 3, are no longer coal tar–based, they still come from petroleum. (FD&C, by the way, means the colours are safe for use in food, drugs and cosmetics.)

Some researchers have reported that artificial flavours and colours have a behavioural impact on kids. Scientists in the pediatric neurology department at Yale found that

A VALUE-ADDED PRODUCT?

Ironically, in trade circles, processed foods are often called a value-added product because with each added ingredient and level of packaging more raw materials are needed and more jobs are created. Well, that's one way to look at it, isn't it?

low doses of a mix of food colourings caused hyperactivity in rat pups and could potentially trigger attention deficit disorder. And, of course, these additives are found in multiple combinations in our food—especially if we eat several different processed foods in one sitting. When researchers out of England combined monosodium glutamate (MSG) and brilliant blue or aspartame and quinoline yellow in the lab, they found that the additives stopped nerve cell growth and messed with nerve signalling. The effects were anywhere from four to seven times more pronounced when the additives were combined than when they were consumed on their own.

Preservatives: One of the most infamous groups of additives, these synthetics keep a loaf of bread mysteriously fresh, moist and mould-free for weeks. And while they might be hailed as a great way to cut back on food waste, they're not always entirely benign. There are, of course, genuinely natural preservatives, such as salt, vinegar, lemon and sugar, but a quick glance at an ingredient list tells you that companies who make processed foods rely on much more. The preservative that keeps packaged meats looking perfectly pink and pathogen-free (nitrites or nitrates) can react with the amino acids in protein to form highly carcinogenic nitrosamines. Sulphites have been linked to hives, nausea and difficulty breathing (note that sulphur dioxide, sodium and potassium bisulphite and sodium and potassium metabisulphite are all sulphites). And BHT and BHA may keep fats and oils from going rancid, but they might also contribute to tumours. Is it really worth killing yourself just to eat six-month-old cookies or chips?

Even your choice of refreshments can be tainted with troubling preservatives. When sodium benzoate (used to kill micro-organisms in fruit juices and soft drinks) is mixed with ascorbic acid (vitamin C), as it often is in bevvies, low levels of cancer-causing benzene may be created—the same pollutant that comes coughing out your tailpipe. Health Canada tested 118 samples and found that 80% had no or very low levels of benzene. Four samples had higher-than-accepted levels (including Kool-Aid Jammers and Rose's Cocktail Infusion, a vodka mixer). Health Canada asked them to reformulate their product to eliminate the problem. Some didn't test high enough to get Health Canada's reformulation request but still tested positive. If you want to know how all the products rated, check out Heath Canada's website: www.hc-sc.gc.ca.

Packaging: What goes into a Ding Dong or frozen dinner is one thing; what's wrapped around it is a whole other ball of plastic. There's the sheer volume of waste involved in packaging food in largely non-recyclable plastics, and the fact that it tends to come double-

and triple-wrapped in various shrink wraps, boxes and trays doesn't help matters much. Not when every Canadian is throwing away about a half kilogram of plastic packaging per day, on average, according to the Recycling Council of Ontario. In fact, of what's trashed in urban centres, half by volume comes from packaging.

The situation is even more disastrous when you consider that a good deal of our processed foods come encased in polyvinyl chloride (PVC), which is considered by environmentalists to be the most toxic plastic on the planet, thanks to nasty pollutants such as dioxin that get created in the making and incinerating of the plastic. So why is it so popular?

Every Canadian is throwing away about a half kilogram of plastic packaging per day

Maybe because it's just so damn versatile that you can shape it into hard shells and clear plastic clams, or you can add softeners to it and call it shrink wrap. Problem is, those softeners, called phthalates, have been known to migrate into food. In the late '90s, *Consumer Reports* tested supermarket cheeses wrapped in PVC plastic wrap and found them to have high levels of the plasticizer DEHA, which has been linked developmental problems and birth defects in rats.

7 SIMPLE PACKAGING TIPS

#1 Buy products that don't come with any!

#2 Know your numbers. If you're buying something that comes in plastic, check the bottom for numbers (like #1 and #2) that tell you the plastics are recyclable in your area.

#3 Renewable and recyclable glass is at the head of the class since you're guaranteed it won't leach into your food or drinks.

#4 Buy dry: if you're picking up an ingredient such as chicken broth, the powdered kind goes a lot further than a can of water-filled broth, which gets used up in one meal.

#5 Buy in bulk. Even consider bringing your own container for filling.

#6 Good things come in small packages. For instance, cereals that come in smaller boxes often contain the same amount of, say, muesli, as the bigger boxes, which are just full of air. Compare product weights to be sure.

#7 Keep an eye out for biodegradable corn-based plastic food packaging

Any foods in a tin or aluminum can, such as chickpeas or soda, are exposed to another controversial chemical: hormone-disrupting bisphenol A, used in the plastic resin that lines the inside. Environmental Defence says it can not only leach into food but has been tied to birth defects, reproductive damage and breast and prostate cancer. It's also one of the top ten contaminants found in streams the by the U.S. Geological Survey. Health Canada is poised to re-examine this chem to see if any action should be taken against it.

And you may have thrown out your non-stick pan by now because of health concerns around PFOA (see page 145), but did you know that PFOA also turns up in your food packaging? The non-stick, grease-repellent surface and widespread environmental contaminant is used in products such as microwave popcorn bags and candy wrappers, and it's especially popular at fast-food joints, where it's used in french fry containers, cardboard pizza trays and burger wraps. That may help explain why, even if you've never sautéed in your life, the chemical can be found in 95% of us, according to research by the U.S. Centers for Disease Control. Environment Canada says it's also turning up in much of the wildlife it tests. Many companies—such as Burger King, Frito-Lay, Kellogg, Kraft and most recently McDonald's—have told Ohio Citizen Action that they don't use or have phased out the use of PFOA-coated packaging. For a full list of corporate responses to the PFOA issue, head to: www.ohiocitizen.org.

Palm Oil: Cookies, chocolate bars, crackers, pie crust—if it's processed, it probably contains palm oil, the world's second-largest oil crop after soy. Thanks to their high melting point and cheap price tag, palm oil and palm kernel oil have replaced partially hydrogenated trans fats in many foods. The shortening's popularity has exploded both in Canada and the U.S. since both governments started mandating the labelling of trans fats at the start of 2006. Ironic, really, considering that many companies moved from palm oil to trans fats in the '60s because of the saturated fat scare. The problem is, palm oil isn't just taxing your heart (controversy remains about whether it's actually all that healthy), it's also giving parts of the planet a coronary.

Palm oil doesn't just go into food; it's poured into soaps, creams, detergents, lipstick, gum, candles, animal feed—hell, it's even used as a plasticizer in ultra-toxic PVC (vinyl) and can be found in health store dish detergents. Asian utilities are eyeing the oil for use in "cleaner, greener" biodiesel. Most of it (83%, to be exact) comes from Malaysia and Indonesia, which have over 65,000 square kilometres of palm plantations between them, according to the Center for Science in the Public Interest's 2005 report. One study found that over 40,000 square kilometres of rainforest was lost to oil palm plantations between 1982 and 1999 in Indonesia alone.

> Palm oil isn't just taxing your heart, it's also **giving parts of the planet a coronary**

On the bright side, some companies, including Unilever, have joined up with non-governmental organizations (NGOs) such as the WWF to form the Roundtable on Sustainable Palm Oil. The group is trying to develop environmental standards for palm oil production, and hopes to set up a certification system.

In the meantime, organic palm oil is available. **Spectrum** makes it, but it's hard to find. Check www.spectrumorganics.com. Or you can avoid it altogether—most of the processed foods in health stores don't include it.

FOOD SOLUTIONS

Okay, so all that doom and gloom has made you want to boycott food. Don't pull a Nicole Richie on us and stop eating! There's plenty of hope in the world for people who love a good meal or three a day.

Organic: Some farmers never stopped plowing the land the way their grandparents did. Others have come to it as escapees from mainstream agriculture. And still others are city slickers looking to get their hands dirty and give back to the earth. But organic farming is now big business, and so are its sales—they're jumping about 20% every year, according to Canadian Organic Growers. Back in the day, crunchy-granola types had to hunt pesticide-free produce and packaged foods down in select health stores. Today, mega-grocer Loblaws is now Canada's single largest distributor of organic food, and the sector is worth about $3.1 billion.

But what does organic mean, exactly? It goes way beyond simply being pesticide-free. Sure, an organic tomato will have been grown in soil in which no chemical fertilizers or pesticides have been used for at least three years, but there's more to the story. Special attention is paid to fostering the soil's nutrients. No sewage sludge can be spread on crops (unlike regular crops—yep, human feces is a popular fertilizer in many Canadian municipalities), nor can that tomato be irradiated or fumigated with synthetic preserving agents. It's free of

WHO'S MAKING YOUR GRANOLA?

Ever wonder why your favourite mom-'n'-pop organic cereal is suddenly appearing next to Tony the Tiger and Snap, Crackle and Pop in mainstream supermarket aisles? Well, it ain't because Pa scored a killer deal with the mega-grocers of Canada. Rather, that crunchy granola has been taken in by another, better-connected family—Big Food—but it's all very hush-hush. Nowhere on the box is there any indication of corporate infiltration—no little Kellogg's logo or Kraft insignia—even though as much as **40% of packaged organic foods on health store shelves have been bought out by large American corporations.** Big Food knows its new clientele well enough to recognize that throwing a corporate logo on something like organic baby food might be deter sales.

Many would say that corporate backing just means organic brands are available in more and more stores, to a wider and wider audience. And in major grocery chains there's nothing shameful about big-name brands, so mainstream companies have recently been coming out of the closet and marketing organic foods with their corporate name in big bold letters. Like Kellogg's new line of organic Raisin Bran, Rice Crispies and more.

But while the entrance of mega-retailers such as Loblaws and Wal-Mart onto the organic scene might be applauded, it's also forcing organic growers to drop their prices and sometimes cut corners (see the section on organic milk, page 90). South of the border, the Organic Consumer Association blames the presence of major food corporations in the organics market and in organic trade associations for efforts to water down organic standards in the U.S. Why should we care about American dust-ups? Well, when 90% of our organic food comes from the U.S., their problems become ours.

anything genetically modified, free of hormones and free of fake processing aids and ingredients—basically, it's a tomato born free.

Traditional organic farms don't tend to grow just one crop; instead, they're filled with an array of veggies and livestock, just like old-fashioned ones. The grass-fed livestock are handy at providing free fertilizer (manure), and the free-range chickens are all too happy to eat discarded weeds pulled from the fields (all those fresh greens mean they get sick less too). It's all very symbiotic and is conducted with much less stress on the planet, especially the wildlife and waterways immediately surrounding the farms, than conventional crops. And since organic agriculture tends to be much more labour-intensive, involving hand-weeding and the like (no one said it wasn't back-breaking work), more jobs are created and less fossil fuels are used.

All the bucolic imagery of organic fields might be true for small- to mid-sized farms, but what about the large-scale ones? Big organic farms are less likely to have as much biological diversity and are more often mechanized. But Canadian Organic Growers' executive director, Laura Telford, says there isn't much to fear about larger organic farms. Most are still family-run, and they have bigger budgets that make meeting stringent organic standards easier than it might be for smaller farms. Although the sheer size of organic salad kingpin Earthbound Farm in California was partly blamed for its lack of control in the *E. coli* spinach scandal of 2006. Still, it's important to note that none of Earthbound's organic produce was actually directly tied to the outbreak, only their non-organic greens.

Local Versus Organic: For years, earth-lovers have been telling us, "buy organic, buy organic." But recently, the community's been divided over whether you should really buy organic lettuce from California over non-organic stuff grown 50 kilometres away. Come

WHICH CORPORATIONS ARE HIDING BEHIND YOUR FAVOURITE ORGANIC/NATURAL BRANDS?	
Kellogg's: Kashi (cereal); Morningstar Farms	**Cadbury Schweppes:** Nantucket Organic Nectars
Kraft: Back to Nature (crackers, cookies); Boca Foods (soy "meat" products)	**M&M Mars:** Seeds of Change (pasta sauces, salsas)
Danone: Stonyfield Farm (yogurt)	

THE TOP 10 REASONS TO EAT ORGANIC

#1 You don't have to worry about biting into chemicals with every mouthful.

#2 Organic food doesn't involve poisoning wildlife, workers and waterways.

#3 There's never been a reported case of mad cow disease in organic cattle.

#4 Your meat and eggs are drug-free.

#5 It's the only guarantee that you're not eating genetically modified ingredients.

#6 Your food hasn't been zapped or irradiated.

#7 Organic farms are hotbeds of life, fostering vibrant biodiversity, not sterile fields.

#8 Organic produce is higher in vitamin C and contains 30% more antioxidants.

#9 Eating an organic diet may reduce the levels of pesticides coursing through your body.

#10 Organic farmers can actually make a decent living, unlike most conventional Canadian farmers, whose income is in the red and dropping every year.

winter, Canadians don't have much choice, but what about the rest of the year? Buying locally means fewer dirty fossil fuels went into trucking the food. It also means you're helping to preserve local green space and threatened farmlands close to home. Plus, did you know that the vitamin content in your fruit and veggies diminishes with each passing day after they were picked? Eating food that was grown close to home is one way to make sure you get the most out of every bite.

Eating food that was grown close to home is one way to make sure you get the most out of every bite

Unfortunately, non-organic local farmers also spread petroleum-based fertilizers to boost yields and spray chemical pesticides to keep bugs and weeds at bay. Ideally, you could get both local and organic in one, but lots of major grocery chains buy cheaper American organic produce all year long, rather than supporting Canadian organics when they're in season. Some argue that local farms are just not big enough, and they'd rather buy from one large farm in the southern States than six mid-sized farms near Saskatoon. But that's starting to change. Whole Foods health food chain says it's going to make an effort to support local *and* organic; so is Loblaws. And you should too.

CANADIAN RESTAURANTS SUPPORTING LOCAL FARMERS

After days of eating your own hurried, uninspired dinners, you're looking for a little something different to tease your palette—or at least a restaurant with waiters willing to serve your tired bones. While you're perusing the same old options (Italian? Thai? Chinese?), let me throw a more captivating one your way—Canadian fusion cuisine, sourced with local, organic and seasonal ingredients. A growing number of chefs across the country are realizing that some of the most flavour-packed vegetables, fish and game come from just outside their doors.

Sooke Harbour House, near Victoria, B.C., has the Pacific Ocean at its feet, and its menu (which changes daily) is swimming in tantalizing seafood, including dishes such as local Dungeness crab in lemon thyme butter and trap-caught sable fish prepared with dried cranberries and golden beets.

Michael Stadtlander's rustic **Eigensinn Farm**, nestled in the middle of a magical thatch of forest outside Collingwood, Ontario, was ranked in the top 10 of the planet's best restaurants by London's *Restaurant* magazine. This establishment offers eight- or nine-course meals packed with artfully prepared organic pickings from the restaurant's own farm or that of its neighbours.

Willow on Wascana, in Regina, puts Saskatchewan cuisine on the map. Its mouthwatering dishes, made with local ingredients, include pancetta-wrapped beef, braised bison short ribs and handmade gnocchi with sunflower pesto.

Mukamuk Bistro and Lounge in Banff offers panoramic mountain views while you munch on top-notch Canadian cuisine crafted with local ingredients.

Jamie Kennedy has earned the title of celebrity chef/local organic guru. He crafts award-winning flavours with largely organic, local ingredients at his three Toronto restaurants.

River Café in Calgary serves up the best Canada has to offer with Northwest Territories caribou, Alberta beef, Pacific salmon, local heirloom veggies and foraged munchable flowers—all with a riverside view.

Fleur De Sel in Lunenburg, Nova Scotia, dips into the bounty of Atlantic delights that makes inlanders green with envy—local lobster, oysters and mussels are all on the menu, along with free-range duck and organic arugula salad.

Make sure to tell your grocery manager that you'd like to see more produce that's both pesticide-free and grown close to home. Farmers' markets and organic food boxes are great places to get both (see the Resource Guide at the back for locations near you).

MEAT

Whether your incisors glisten at the sight of a sizzling steak or the thought of a lean roasted chicken breast gets you peckish, there's little question that Canadians love their meat. According to a report by Environmental Defence, cattle numbers have tripled since the '60s and the number of chickens raised for our dinners has quadrupled. And pigs? Those suckers have exploded by 70% in the last decade alone. There's no doubt that we're outnumbered. There are about 15 million beef and dairy cattle, 14 million pigs, 8 million turkeys and a whopping 134 million chickens alive at any one time in Canada. And those animals aren't exactly running around the farmyard like they used to. Factory farms are now the main way to produce meat in this country, crowding staggering numbers of animals into nearly half a million fewer farms than we had back in 1941.

What's the problem? We need to feed ourselves, don't we? Well, the meat industry is vacuum packed with environmental woes. Warning: this is not the best time to be eating a burger.

THE SLOW FOOD MOVEMENT

Tired of rushing through meals that take 30 seconds to prepare, a minute to swallow and aren't even healthy to begin with? About 20 years ago, a small group of gourmets in Italy got together to stand up for real food as McDonald's prepared to move into an old Roman plaza in their city. They issued the Slow Food Manifesto. The gourmets wanted a return to home-cooked meals and two-hour lunches, to food as art and a source of sensual pleasure. In the mid-'90s, followers were encouraged to eat locally grown organic foods and to buy from small-scale artisans and food producers. The movement fostered a return to heritage fruits and vegetables you won't find in the supermarket and ancient family recipes that prepare everything from scratch. Now, over 80,000 people around the globe fed up with the feeding frenzies we call meals have signed on to the eat-slowly-with-friends philosophy.

There are 18 slow food groups, or *convivia*, across Canada. To learn more, check out **www.slowfood.ca**.

Ah, the cross-country road trip. Who hasn't dreamed about packing up and heading out across the continent in search of new sights and sounds? Well, most of our food travels more than we ever do—at least 2,500 kilometres. Factor in all the emissions created by dirty diesel trucks and cargo planes, and we're talking a hell of a lot of climate-changing pollution.

On the first day of spring 2005, Vancouverites Alisa Smith and James MacKinnon moved beyond feeling guilty about their food choices and decided they were going to break the long-distance grub cycle once and for all. For one whole year, they ate and drank only what was grown within 100 miles (or 160 kilometres) of their apartment. And the ground rules were tough. Chicken would have be raised locally, which is easy enough, but it would also have to be fed local feed. The same goes for every ingredient in every loaf of bread and every slice of pie. They quickly realized that items such as sugar ain't a local resource.

Okay, so at the beginning meals were kind of boring (it took some time to find truly regional sources) and involved a lot of potatoes (since wheat was nearly impossible to find within their radius), but they eventually discovered mouth-watering delicacies such as warm Salt Spring brie with ground hazelnuts and frozen wild blueberries, and spring salmon with organic sage butter (being West Coasters, they were pushed off their vegan diet by the proximity of the ocean, full of local seafood). Yes, they found it a little time-consuming to do their own canning and preserving so they'd have enough local supplies come winter. Just getting through the cold season was a feat in itself. But they did it, proving to us all that eating strawberries in January is just plain overrated.

If you're interested in giving the diet a go yourself, if only for a day or a week, head to **www.100milediet.org** (launched by Smith and MacKinnon). Punch in your postal code, and it'll spit out a map of what your 100-mile borders are. The starter guide will give you plenty of useful tips on how to tackle the diet, like freezing local produce in season and planting winter gardens.

Manure: The sheer size of intensive livestock operations means that, for one, they create oceans of manure (enough to fill Toronto's Roger's Centre twice a week, says Environmental Defence). Time to take a mental walk around the lagoons of poop stored on factory farms. But don't inhale. You'll be breathing in toxic gases such as ammonia, hydrogen sulphide and the potent greenhouse gas methane. When the holding tubs break, flood or just plain seep (and they do—almost 4 million litres of hog doo spilled from a Manitoba farm in 2002), we're talking serious pathogenic groundwater contamination. In North Carolina, a 95-million-litre spill into a river killed 10 million fish and closed over 364,000 acres of coastal wetlands to shellfish farming, according to the National Research Defence Council. In Ontario, much smaller-scale cattle manure runoff is thought to be behind the deadly Walkerton *E. coli* disaster of 2000, which killed six people.

Drugs: Regulators have decided that Canadian chickens, lambs and pigs can't legally be given hormones, but our cattle can. Health Canada reps say that's because no data has been submitted to demonstrate that hormones are safe and effective in species other than beef cattle. The growth hormones we use are, sadly, turning up downstream from factory farms and have been found to alter sex-related traits of fish and turtles.

Antibiotics regularly given to all livestock to keep them from getting sick in overcrowded conditions (about half of the antibiotics used in Canada go to livestock and chicken ops) are also turning up in manure, which is in turn sprayed on fields as fertilizer. There are concerns that antibiotic residues in meat could be making humans more antibiotic-resistant. Health Canada, however, says that animals have to test clean before they can be sold to the public as food.

Even if antibiotic residues aren't a concern, Health Canada says over 90% of our exposure to the dangerous pollutant dioxin comes from our food, especially animal fats such as meat, fish, dairy and eggs. The feds say you can limit your exposure by trimming away the fat, or baking instead of frying, but come on, is anyone else freaked out that there are toxic environmental pollutants in our meat to begin with?

Processing Plants: Once animals are trucked to slaughter, a whole other set of problems arise. Meat processing plants are notorious for emitting foul odours, but their pollution problems go way beyond a bad smell. Vast quantities of water are used, not only to rinse down the plant and carcasses, but also to scald chickens in energy-intensive hot water before their feathers are plucked. Some water can be reused, but most of it is just plain nasty—full of blood, manure, fat, feathers, hair and bones. A great deal of water is also used in cooking and canning the meat, and a lot of energy goes into refrigerating the stuff.

Greenhouse Gases: Between all the methane released by flatulent cud-chewers (yes, it's true—gassy livestock account for 18% of the world's greenhouse gases—more than cars, trains and planes!) and the carbon dioxide spewed in the transport of animals to slaughter, from slaughter to supermarket and finally to your dinner table, that lone burger patty creates as much greenhouse gas as a 9.6-kilometre car ride, reports The Green Guide. In fact, according to research by Cornell University's College of Agriculture and Life Sciences prof David Pimental, animal protein swallows eight times more fossil fuels than beans or vegetable proteins.

*That lone burger patty creates as much greenhouse gas as a **9.6-kilometre car ride***

Feed: Livestock need to eat. Trouble is, they eat a lot. In fact, for every kilogram of meat produced, animals are fed about 6 kilograms of plant protein, according to Pimental. What else goes into that meat? Grain-fed beef production sucks back about a 100,000 litres of water for every kilo of beef produced (if you factor in the H_2O needed to grow the grain, feed the cow and process its parts in the packing plant). Talk about a super-wasteful protein source. But are we even giving them a decent diet? Corn fattens cows up nicely, giving them a good marbled cut, but their digestive tracts aren't designed to process it, so they get sick more often (too much corn can lead to ulcers and bacteria associated with sudden death, says research in the journal *Science*) and need more antibiotics. USDA scientists have also found that grain-fed cattle have more *E. coli* in their intestines than grass-fed cows, and that *E. coli* has a nasty way of contaminating cuts of meat and ground beef (not to mention neighbouring spinach farms) when the poor cow gets picked apart at the processing plant.

Of course, that's nothing compared to what happens when you mix a little dead cow into cattle feed. Hello! Did anyone ever consider that cows are vegetarian? You'd go crazy, too, if you were forced to eat your brother for lunch. Sure, the Canadian Food Inspection Agency may have banned cow brains and spinal tissue—and any other parts at high risk of spreading mad cow disease—from cattle feed in 1997 (although they could still be fed dried cow blood, as well as dead chicken and hog bits), but sloppy enforcement and

SUPPORT FOR FARMERS

Are you a farmer, or do you know a farmer who might be ready to make the switch to more sustainable practices? Contact the **Canadian Organic Livestock Association** (www.colabeef.com) or the **Canadian Organic Growers** for tips and support.

How do you persuade someone to go veg when video footage of a chicken factory won't do it? It's damn near impossible if the smell of bacon is wafting by. Try taking him or her to a Chinese vegetarian restaurant. These joints make the most convincing fake beef and pork sautées around. Most meat eaters won't know the difference and will be impressed to taste meat alternatives that go beyond bland tofu.

cross-contamination from other livestock feed mean Canada's mad cow problem ain't going away just yet. (Speaking of which, high-risk cattle parts are finally slated to be removed from all animal feed and pet food in July 2007.)

If you're not into giving up meat entirely, try cutting back on your servings, and buy local organic meat whenever you can. Organic meat is drug-free, and the animals are given organic feed, access to the outdoors and more room to roam on pesticide-free land. Grass-fed animals that are free to munch in farmers' fields are not just happier, they're healthier—and not just in terms of their own sickness rate; they're also more nutritious for us humans to eat. They're lower in saturated fats and higher in omega-3 fatty acids. If your meat is labelled with a vague term such as "natural," make sure to ask your butcher and the grower what that means.

VEGETARIAN

The Union of Concerned Scientists says being a vegetarian is one of the top things you can do for the environment. Not that vegetarians should presume their own eco-righteousness. Beans, the veg-head protein of choice, aren't necessarily all that holy. Brazil, the second-largest soy producer after the U.S., is tearing down rainforests not only for beef (some of our canned and pre-cooked beef comes from there) but for soy. Large farms there have been linked to poor working conditions, slave labour and high levels of pesticide use. And it's not just rainforests that are losing ground. Half of Brazil's soy comes from savannahs once teeming with 90,000 insect species, 550 birds and 150 mammals, including jaguars, that are now being pushed out by soy monoculture, according to the WWF. But—and this is a big but here—tofu lovers, the vast majority of soy is grown for cattle-feed, not human feed. So you're generally off the hook for rainforest destruction.

being a vegetarian is one of the top things you can do for the environment

83

THE TOP 5 REASONS TO GO VEGETARIAN

#1 Meat production requires 10 to 20 times more energy per edible ton than grain production (source: "Eating for the Earth: Meat Production's Environmental Toll" from the 1997 International Conference on Sustainable Urban Food Systems).

#2 One-fifth of the planet's land surface is used for grazing animals, double what goes to growing crops (source: Eating for the Earth).

#3 An area larger than New York state is estimated to be destroyed every year for grazing land (source: World Wildlife Fund).

#4 Over three-quarters of the world's fish stocks are on the verge of collapse (source: Environmental Defence).

#5 You won't be swallowing antibiotics, hormones and dioxin-laced fats.

If you're as uncomfortable with the unknown impacts of playing god with crops, as, oh, all of Europe is, you'll be perturbed to learn that 85% of American soy (and over half the world's) is genetically modified—patented by Monsanto (the notorious biotech company and manufacturer of Agent Orange). To add to the corporate soya plot, chemical giant DuPont owns Solae, which makes the soy protein found in Yves, Smart Deli and Gimme Lean products. Solae makes both GMO-free and genetically modified soy, so be sure to check. (For a full list of Solae products, check out www.protein.com.)

Don't freak—the planet is still better off for your being a veggie lover! To mediate any sins affiliated with the veg diet, always buy organic when you can. You can feel good knowing your protein source, be it chickpeas or tempeh, was grown on a sustainable farm without chemical inputs or genetically modified seeds. Buying from local organic companies is even better, since less fuel is needed for transport.

Health stores are loaded with organic meat alternatives. Beans are the original veg protein of choice, and ambitious boys and girls can even get the dried kind in bulk. Those of us without the foresight to soak stuff overnight get organic canned beans by **Eden** or **Bombay Breeze** in any health store.

Organic tofu and flavoured organic tempeh can be had almost everywhere. Vancouver-based **Green Cuisine** tempeh patties are praised for their tastiness. Speaking of burger patties, **Sol Cuisine** makes organic soy burgers, dogs and ground "meat," as well as organic tofu barbecue ribs. If you're one of those veg-heads who think eating anything that emulates meat is nasty, try nut burgers like those made by Quebec-based **La Soyarie.**

For quick, protein-rich meals, look for frozen tofu vegetable lasagnas, veggie loaves, burritos and the like in the freezer section.

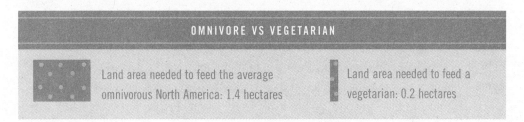

OMNIVORE VS VEGETARIAN

Land area needed to feed the average omnivorous North America: 1.4 hectares

Land area needed to feed a vegetarian: 0.2 hectares

SEAFOOD

Anyone who's been dumped has probably heard the old consolation "There's plenty more fish in the sea." Ah, if only this were still true. We eat over 100 million tons of the poor creatures a year, and that figure keeps climbing as docs tell us to cut back on red meat and stock up on omega fatty acids. Our fish stocks, however, can't keep up.

Wild Fish Stocks: The stats are pretty dismal. According to a report in *Nature* journal, only 10% of large, open-ocean fish are left in the sea. The Marine Sustainability Council says 52% of the world's stocks are being fished at maximum capacity, 24% are overexploited, depleted or recovering and another 21% are "moderately exploited." Environmental Defence says overfishing, habitat damage and pollution mean that 78% of fish stocks are on the verge of collapse. That collapse, warn scientists, is coming mid-century (apolcalypto-style) if we don't get our act together.

Overfishing, habitat damage and pollution mean that 78% of fish stocks are on the verge of collapse

What have we been doing wrong? Well, we basically vacuum the ocean floor by laying down massive weighted nets that scrape up everything in their path, including 1,000-year-old coral and vast quantities of unwanted fish. The undersized, unmarketable or simply accidental bycatch (including dolphins, seals, whales and sea turtles) is tossed overboard, often dead. The UN Food and Agriculture Organization says one in four animals caught as bycatch in fishing equipment dies (about 27 million tons each year). The UN is calling for a ban on bottom trawling in international waters (64% of the planet's oceans fall outside national jurisdictions), saying an immediate moratorium needs to happen if we're going to prevent "irreversible destruction on the high seas." Let's just say the Canadian fishing industry isn't cheerleading the cause, and neither are the feds, but a nationwide poll found that over three-quarters of Canadians support a ban. Jeez, even U.S. president George Bush came out in favour of this no-brainer in the fall of 2006. Tell your MP you want Canada to sign on.

Fish Farming: So if catching wild fish is draining the oceans, farmed fish must be the right choice, no? Well, it depends on how you farm it. Gone are the days when buying farmed salmon was automatically seen as the best way to protect wild breeds from overfishing. Unfortunately, that fatty pink flesh is loaded with way more than just omega-3s. We're talking high levels of dioxins, DDT, flame retardants and seven times the amount of hormone-disrupting PCBs found in wild salmon. (Farmed salmon is fed ground-up fish meal concentrated with toxins.) Oh yeah, and that juicy pink flesh? It's fake. Since farmed salmon is grey and not the lovely hue of wild salmon, artificial colouring is added to their feed.

The salmon farms themselves are ticking off a lot of environmental observers. Just feeding the carnivorous fish involves trawling the seas for enormous quantities of small fish, such as anchovies. In fact, according to the Coastal Alliance for Aquaculture Reform's report "Farmed and Dangerous," it

It takes 3 kilograms of wild fish to grow 1 kilogram of farmed salmon

takes 3 kilograms of wild fish to grow 1 kilogram of farmed salmon. There are 80,000 tons of salmon farmed annually in B.C. alone—you do the math. Overcrowded ocean pens are essentially polluting feces factories and harbouring grounds for diseases such as sea lice. So not only are caged fish pumped full of antibiotics, but 95% of young wild salmon that swim past infected farms while migrating out to sea die, according to a recent University of Alberta study. Escapees also introduce diseases abroad and throw off ecosystems by crowding wild habitat. And watch out for the genetically modified, disease-resistant, fast-growing fish being developed by aquaculture farms. Who knows what would happen if GMO escapees were to mix with wild breeds?

On the other hand, contained systems for farming **tilapia**, **catfish** and even **trout** on land, rather than in water, are seen as an excellent option, eco-wise.

Tuna: All this bad news about salmon came down the pipe right about the time another Canadian favourite was swimming out of favour: tuna. Findings of high mercury content meant lunchtime would never be the same. If I'm eating fresh tuna in, say, sushi or steak form, and I'm a woman of child-bearing age, even the more conservative source, Health Canada, says I shouldn't eat it more than once a month. However, if I'm eating a sandwich with canned light tuna (which is often skipjack tuna), I can have it weekly (though environmentalists suggest monthly is safer). I need to be especially cautious about eating white, or albacore, tuna, which has three times the mercury level of the light stuff. Then again, an investigation by the *Chicago Tribune* found that American tuna companies sometimes use high-mercury yellowfin, not low-mercury skipjack, to make light tuna (6% of the time, according to FDA tests), so light cans aren't always safer. Confused? Who isn't? In 2006, *Consumer Reports* magazine warned pregnant women to stay away from canned tuna altogether.

And you know those reassuring little dolphin-free labels you look for on cans of tuna? Sad to say, Canada isn't enforcing the truthfulness of the "dolphin-friendly" or "dolphin-safe" claims implied by those logos. **RainCoast Trading**–brand canned tuna, however, catches B.C. tuna using hooks and lines, not dolphin-snaring nets. Plus, it tests all its fish for mercury.

Other Ocean Fish: Of course, tuna isn't the only fish drowning in neurotoxic mercury. Thanks to our polluting tendencies, our oceans are full of the stuff, and high levels can be found in Atlantic halibut, king mackerel, sea bass, shark, swordfish and Gulf Coast oysters. Health Canada says mercury levels are so high in shark and swordfish that pregnant women shouldn't eat them more than once a month. And *Consumer Reports* advises pregnant women to steer clear of Chilean sea bass, halibut, American lobster and Spanish mackerel.

Low-mercury but overfished or destructively harvested species such as Atlantic cod (remember the cod ban of the '90s?), Atlantic sole and imported shrimp should be avoided for environmental reasons.

Yes, most shrimp are wild-caught, but more and more are farm-raised, especially Asian shrimp. And you're not safe with imported wild-caught either. Shrimp trawling has the highest bycatch rate of any commercial fishery: 3 to 15 kilograms of unwanted sea animals are caught and trashed for every kilogram of shrimp cocktail. American, or Gulf of Mexico shrimp, are considered better, as this industry is more strictly regulated and the nets are supposedly designed to let sea turtles and other fish escape. Some environmentalists say certain Gulf of Mexico sea turtle populations have been ravaged by shrimp trawlers over the years (though turtle protection has improved over the last decade). Your best, most sustainable bet is always **trap-caught shrimp**, since this method allows fishermen to release 98% of their bycatch alive.

Your best, most sustainable bet is always **trap-caught shrimp**

87

Flagrant disregard for fishing regs and pitiful levels of enforcement are serious problems in many overseas stocks, such as Russian king crab and the oh-so-tasty but oh-so-overfished Chilean sea bass. Turns out policing is hard to carry out in the remote Antarctic waters where the late-breeding bass are caught. Pirate fisherman are netting 10 times what's permitted and are considered totally out of control. **Alaskan king crab** and **European sea bass** are much greener options.

Sustainable Seafood: The Marine Sustainability Council (MSC) has set up an internationally recognized standard that assesses whether a fishery is well-managed and, you guessed it, sustainable. Interestingly enough, the entire commercial stock of **wild Alaskan salmon** has been certified since 2000. Even more surprising, **Wal-Mart USA** announced in 2006 that it plans to source all its wild-caught fresh and frozen fish from the MSC. No word yet on whether Wal-Mart Canada will do the same.

Keeping track of which sea creatures from which coast caught by which methods are more sustainable can be near impossible. For a good pocket-sized (and printable) guide, check out Seafood Watch at www.mbayaq.org/cr/seafoodwatch.asp, or the new Canadian guide put out by several groups including the David Suzuki Foundation, Living Oceans and more. It's called SeaChoice and can be printed off from www.seachoice.org. Just so you know, both focus mainly on environmental sustainability and put little symbols next to fish heavy in mercury or PCBs. Environmental Defense in the U.S. has a website called Oceans Alive (www.oceansalive.org), which focuses on the health concerns associated with each fish and

THE ENDANGERED FISH ALLIANCE

The Endangered Fish Alliance is made up of concerned chefs looking for sustainable options. They make a point of not serving four endangered fish—namely, swordfish, Chilean sea bass, orange roughy and some caviars. Visit their website at **www.endangeredfishalliance.org** to see the full list of member restaurants and caterers across the country, including restos in Alberta, B.C., Nova Scotia and Ontario and caterers in New Brunswick, Saskatchewan, B.C., Ontario and Alberta.

Vancouverites looking for a list of eateries that serve conscience-friendly seafood can head to the Vancouver Aquarium's website (**www.vanaqua.org/conservation/oceanwise**).

even has a handy chart that tells you how many meals a month of, say, bluefin tuna or mahi mahi you should eat if you're a man, women, older child or young child, with big checkmarks down the side letting you know if it's in the "eco-worst" or "eco-best" category. The site also has consumption advisories, recipes and a downloadable pocket seafood selector.

Organic Seafood: If you're looking for organic seafood, good luck. Only two places in the world certify organic fish: Scotland and Ireland. Organic farms in these countries are seen as a bit of a mixed bag: the number of salmon (or cod or trout) per pen is cut in half, they're fed human-grade fish meal, the fake pink dye is banned, but pesticides used to treat sea lice are still allowed (though restricted) and a carcinogenic chlorine-based disinfectant is also permitted. It's better than conventionally farmed salmon, but far from perfect. If you see the organic label on Canadian (or American) fish, you should note that no standards are in place to control the use of the term, so there are no guarantees that what you're eating is actually organic. You can find farmed East Coast antibiotic-free salmon fed organic feed at **Whole Foods Market** stores. (Organic salmon farmers, by the way, often use a natural algae-based pigment to make the flesh pink.) The chain also ensures that all other fruits of the sea it sells are sustainable.

Shellfish: Shellfish lovers of the world rejoice. Farmed oysters, clams and mussels get the thumbs-up from environmentalists, so eat away. What makes them so ecologically sound to farm is that they basically feed themselves by filtering plankton out of the water—in fact, they even filter pollutants from surrounding water as they munch.

Sushi: All this bad news about fish is enough to make any sushi lover cry in her saki. Not only have sashimi fans been told they consume too much mercury-laden tuna and PCB-laced farmed salmon, they've also been blamed for the near extinction of red tuna in the Mediterranean and the stressed sea urchin populations off California. When you head to a sushi restaurant, bring a pocket guide along to help you decide which sashimi is safe to order. Some high-end sushi restaurants, such as Vancouver's **Tojo**, are signing on to the Coastal Alliance for Aquaculture Reform's "Farmed and Dangerous" campaign and saying no to farmed salmon. Talk to the manager of your favourite restaurant and make your desire for sustainable seafood known.

When you head to a sushi restaurant, **bring a pocket guide** along to help you decide which sashimi is safe to order

89

DAIRY

Ads tell us milk does a body good, but does it do much for the planet? Those 1 million dairy cows in Canada produce barns full of manure, just like their meat-producing brothers. Over 20% of dairy ops store solid manure in open piles on the ground, without a roof, and 11% store liquid manure in unlined lagoons. The abundance of poop can lead to serious runoff problems and groundwater pollution. Not good when you factor in the presence of antibiotics, given to cows whose overworked teats are swollen with infection (yes, that means blood and pus).

Controversial bovine growth hormones, designed to boost milk production, are illegal in Canada, but not in the States. Think you're in the clear because all your milk comes from within your home province? Not if you're buying American processed foods that contain milk ingredients, like, say, a frozen pizza. Bovine growth hormones have been clinically linked to increases in mastitis, infertility and lameness in animals. Use of the hormones goes hand in hand with upping levels of antibiotics, since the hormones increase infection rates in cow udders. (Canada does allow antibiotic use in dairy cows, but the milk has to test below maximum residue limits before it gets shipped out to supermarkets.)

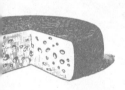

Organic Milk: Even organic milk has not been immune to controversy. In fact, in the U.S., where Wal-Mart is now the largest retailer of organic milk and cartons are flying off the shelves, organic dairy farmers have been accused of watering down standards to keep prices low and quantities flowing. The biggest controversy is the debate over how much time organic dairy cows should graze outside. Thanks to the vagueness of organic standards and lax enforcement, many dairy farms have been certified as organic when they provide little to no grazing time and look more like factory feedlots. The Organic Consumers Association even started a national boycott of a half-dozen dairy companies in the States last summer, while the USDA (which regulates organic standards in the U.S.) was seen as dragging its feet on closing offending loopholes.

SUGAR

They say humans are composed mostly of water, but by now we must be about 40% sugar, given the amount of the white stuff we down. No joke, some of us eat our own body weight a year in hidden and not-so-hidden sugars. Just drinking one soda pop a day means downing half a large mason jar of sugar every week. And many fruit juices and fruity waters contain just as much of the sweetener, despite their healthy image.

We all know sugar's bad for us, and we spend more and more time talking about what it's doing to our kids (elevated rates of obesity), ourselves (kidney stones, type 2 diabetes, heart disease) and our teeth (hello, cavities). But where do these powdery crystals come from? And what kind of environmental footprint does sugar leave?

Sugarcane: Tall stalks of tropical sugarcane are the sweet source behind up to 70% of the world's sugar and 90% of Canada's. A WWF report says sugarcane has probably contributed more to the loss of biodiversity worldwide than any other single crop because so many rainforests have been felled and important wetland habitats destroyed to plant it. Some countries devote half of their land mass to sugarcane. Pretty astounding. Beyond habitat loss, great quantities of unwanted leafy foliage growing on cane stalks are burned off in fires that release vast amounts of greenhouse gases into the atmosphere. Even the polluted waste water discharged from the annual cleaning of sugar mills can have a deadly impact. In the 1995 annual mill cleanup in one region of Bolivia, millions of fish were killed in neighbouring waterways, according to WWF.

Efforts are under way to green up production in spots around the globe. Brazil, the world's leading grower of sugarcane (for both sugar and ethanol), has started taking action to improve the sustainability of its crop. It says it has drastically cut back on the need for water irrigation and uses 50% less fertilizer than Australia's sugarcane growers. Brazil is also at looking at ways to generate energy from sugarcane waste and has banned cane field burning to limit polluting emissions. Of course, buying organic sugar is your greenest option. And fair-trade certified organic sugar? Now that's sweet.

Buying organic sugar is your greenest option. And fair-trade certified organic sugar? Now that's sweet

UNWELCOME INFO FOR VEGANS

Vegetarians will be freaked out to learn that, according the Canadian Sugar Institute, all cane sugar has been—get this—run through a bone char filter. To quote the Institute directly, "Bone char is a carbon filter, derived from dried purified cattle bones." They say no animal traces can be found in the sugar itself, but still, pretty gross.

Chemical Sweeteners: But I don't even eat sugar, you say—I prefer to sweeten my coffee with little yellow and pink packets. Well, take a seat and stay awhile. We need to have a little chat.

Saccharin was the original artificial sweetener, discovered by accident in the late 1800s. Thanks to cancer findings in lab rats, Canada banned the substance in food back in 1977, although you can still buy it in pharmacies. It's required to have a warning label that says continued saccharin use can be "injurious" to your health and shouldn't be used by pregnant women. Why some still insist on buying it, I don't know.

After years of speculation about aspartame's shadowy health impacts, including ties to cancer, lymphoma and leukemia in rats, a recent U.S. study won a lot of good press for concluding that there's no link between cancer and aspartame use among the half-million consumers interviewed. But diet cola junkies shouldn't celebrate just yet. In July 2006, a respected seven-year study by the European Ramazzini Foundation of Oncology and Environmental Sciences concluded that, for a 150-pound person, ingesting four to five 20-ounce (600 mL) diet drinks a day could up your chances of leukemia, lymphoma and other cancers. And that doesn't even factor in all our food sources of the sweetener. Health Canada, on the other hand, still insists it's safe. Even if that's enough to make you sleep peacefully at night, you might want to note that Nutrasweet's aspartame factory south of the border is ranked up there with some of the most polluting facilities in the U.S. It released nearly 329,595 pounds of polluting methanol into Georgia's wastewater system in 2004 and pumped out over 13,000 pounds of methanol into the air, according to EPA files.

WOULD YOU LIKE SOME PESTICIDES WITH YOUR COLA?

We know cola is loaded with sugar and all kinds of questionable ingredients, but you never think you're swallowing pesticides with every thirst-quenching gulp. Well, after a good deal of controversy, several Indian states banned both Coke and Pepsi in 2006, citing the high levels of pesticides found in the soft drinks. Indeed, the Indian not-for-profit Centre for Science and Environment found that Coca-Cola drinks tested across India had pesticide residues an average of 27 times higher than Indian government standards. Some Indian Coke plants had also been accused of draining local water supplies in times of drought and offloading cadmium-contaminated waste onto farmers as free fertilizer.

Don't forget the newest kid on the block, sucralose, which goes by the name Splenda. Ads pump out images of cupcakes and cookies, over which can be heard "It's made from sugar, so it tastes like sugar." But you can't quite call it natural. It is, indeed, produced from sugar, but it's chlorinated to make it low-cal, and activists are concerned about rising levels of toxic cyclohexane (a solvent) emissions from Splenda's growing factory.

High-Fructose Corn Syrup (HFCS): This may be the most common synthetic sweetener hidden in North American foods. Corn is cheaper to grow and make than sugarcane, so it's no wonder that cornstarch-derived syrup is in just about everything we eat. Though it technically comes from corn (a highly sprayed and commonly genetically engineered crop), it's considered synthetic because of all the lab-processing you have to go through to get HFCS. That didn't stop Cadbury Schweppes from labelling 7-UP "100% natural" in 2006, a claim which ruffled a lot of feathers. Of course, with no one policing the widespread abuses of the term natural, who's to stop them? Some research has connected the introduction of HFCS on the market to climbing rates of obesity, but the jury's still out on that one.

Beet Sugar: Sugar derived from beets might sound "alternative" to North American ears, but it's actually the source of 30% to 40% of the world's sugar, according to the WWF. Beet sugar is the main sweetener on the table in Europe, which grows 12 million tons of it — hardly a mom-'n'-pop crop. It's sometimes marketed as ecologically sound, since it's drought-resistant and technically requires less water; nonetheless, it's widely irrigated and is lowering water tables in southern Spain. It's also said to need less chemical inputs than other crops, but the WWF says beet sugar is behind some serious pollution, including contaminated runoff, thanks to high rates of herbicide and pesticide use. If you're choosing a sack of beet sugar at your local health store, make sure it's certified organic so you can avoid the whole ecological mess altogether. FYI, Canada gets about 10% of its sugar from domestically grown sugar beets.

Beet sugar is the main sweetener on the table in Europe, which grows **12 million tons of it**

Sustainable Sugar Alternatives: For real alternatives to destructively farmed sugar or chemical sweeteners, try fair trade **organic cane sugar**. Since sugar can be found in pretty much every fruit, vegetable and grain, there are dozens of types of sweeteners out there, including **barley malt**, **brown rice syrup**, **agave nectar** (which is supposed to be lower on

93

the glycemic index) and **date sugar**. **Wild unpasteurized honey** and **organic crystallized maple sugar** are other tasty ways to satisfy your sugar cravings.

If you're looking for a natural sweetener that's calorie-free, try **stevia**. It comes from the leaves of a Paraguayan and Brazilian shrub and has been used for ages in South America. The ultra-concentrated sweetener takes a little time to get used to (I've yet to convince anyone it tastes good in my cookies), but it doesn't cause tooth decay or affect blood sugar levels. The only thing is, the U.S. FDA isn't convinced it's safe and has been giving the herbal sugar a hard time. Some say it's just protecting the chemical sweetener industry. Either way, you can buy it freely in Canada. **Xylitol**, which traditionally comes from birch tree bark but is more sustainably sourced from GMO- and pesticide-free corn by companies like **Emerald Forest**, is much better for baking. It is also said to fend off cavities and is suitable for diabetics.

CHOCOLATE

Why is it that we often hurt the things we love the most? Oh, sweet chocolate, can you forgive us? You gave us your delicious beans and grew peacefully in the cool shade of the rainforest canopy, surrounded by teams of flittering birds, insects and friendly mammals. Then, sometime between the Aztecs christening you the food of the gods and today, our relationship with you turned more bitter than sweet.

Sun-Grown Cocoa: In the '70s we began moving cocoa trees out of the shelter of the rainforest and onto single-crop farms in the blazing sun. Yields were certainly higher, helping us keep up with the growing demand, but the trees grew stressed and prone to disease. Only hybrid plants fed high levels of chemical fertilizers and pesticides can survive the heat and dryness of open fields. And the shift often involved felling any rainforest in the way—destroying wild habitats and increasing soil erosion and runoff—all to make room for the popular cash crop.

Pesticides: The pesticides used on cocoa plants are often antiquated, extremely hazardous and end up contaminating groundwater and air. Some, such as lindane, a persistent organic pollutant banned in many countries, turned up in every sample of chocolate tested in the late '90s by the U.K.'s Pesticide Action Network.

Child Slavery: Slavery is part of chocolate's dark history, just as it is in the coffee and sugar biz. But it isn't just a blemish of the past. Media exposés a few years ago revealed that forced labour is still very much alive on the cocoa plantations of

DIRTY PESTICIDES IN THE DEVELOPING WORLD

You think we have problems with pesticides in Canada? Consider this: the UN warns that around 30% of the pesticides available in developing countries pose "a serious threat to human health and the environment" and don't meet international standards. Many, such as DDT, have been banned in the developed world, but we're still making them and selling them to farmers in poor countries with shaky enviro regs. To make matters worse, they're often poorly labelled, without warnings, safety info or any mention of the highly hazardous ingredient. A disturbing study by the Institute of Development Policy Analysis found that internationally banned pesticides are being aggressively imported, peddled and marketed in places like Bangladesh (even though they're illegal in that country), to the point that, by the late '90s, sales of outlawed pesticides were triple those of a decade earlier.

West Africa, where 70% of the world's chocolate comes from. According to Save the Children, roughly 200,000 of the 600,000 children working on Ivorian cocoa fields work in dangerous conditions with machetes and pesticides. Many work on family farms, but an estimated 15,000 have been kidnapped or sold into slavery.

Hershey says an International Institute for Tropical Agriculture survey of 2002 found no slaves on the 4,500 farms checked, but the chocolate bar giant acknowledges that conditions need to improve. Kraft's assessment of the survey isn't quite so clear-cut: "while the investigation was inconclusive about the extent of child slavery, it did find that as many as

KNOW YOUR CHOCOLATE LABELS

Certified Organic: Grown without chemical pesticides or synthetic fertilizers, and with special attention paid to water and soil conservation.

Certified Fair-Trade: Farmers and workers paid a fair price; no child, slave or forced labour; workers are free to unionize (check out **www.transfair.ca/en/products**).

Rainforest Alliance–Certified: Chemical pesticides limited through integrated pest management; conservation measures in place for water, soil and wildlife; workers paid the legal minimum wage for that country or higher and have good working conditions.

CAROB

Can't stomach the eco-consequences of chocolate? Or maybe, like me, you're just allergic to the stuff. The carob tree is a hardy, drought-resistant crop native to the Mediterranean that produces what some say is a cocoa-like pod. Okay, so it doesn't really taste much like real chocolate, but it looks like it. Make sure to avoid any carob made with unsustainable palm oil (see page 73). Just as with chocolate, organic carob is best.

300,000 children were exposed to hazardous working conditions." About a year earlier, the chocolate industry signed on to the Harkin-Engel Protocol—a voluntary action plan for monitoring the industry and certifying slave-free chocolate by 2005. Activists say the deadline has come and gone and little progress has been made. But the cocoa biz says it just needs more time and hopes to have half of Ghana and the Ivory Coast up to the standards of the protocol by 2008.

Chocolate manufacturers such as Hershey, Mars and Cadbury have also joined up with government groups, NGOs, researchers and local farmers to develop the Sustainable Tree Crop Program (for coffee, cocoa and cashews). The program endeavours to reduce pesticide use and improve overall farming practices and income levels for growers.

Organic Chocolate: Chocoholics of the world, don't despair! Organic cocoa is grown without toxic chemicals, so noshing on fair-trade organic chocolate is virtually guilt-free! Also look for organic chocolate chips and fair-trade organic cocoa powder for baking and sipping.

COFFEE AND TEA

Maybe it's the cold winters, but we Canadians love our hot beverages. As a nation, we consume 118 million kilograms of roasted coffee beans and over 2 billion litres of tea each year. It's no wonder caffeine has been detected in drinking water in cities big and small. Sure, it might be good to the last drop, but that's a hell of a lot of liquid, with some pretty heavy ecological ramifications.

As a nation, we consume **118 million kilograms** of roasted coffee beans each year

Coffee: People say there's nothing quite as American as a cup of joe and some apple pie. Maybe they're right about the apple pie, but the red berry–covered coffee bush originated in

If you've managed to wean yourself off your caffeine addiction but still like to savour the flavour of a good brew, you're probably well acquainted with the world of decaf. What you might not realize is that, unless otherwise indicated, chemical solvents are used to extract caffeine from the bean. These chemicals include ethyl acetate (found in nail polish remover) and the probable carcinogen methylene chloride (which doesn't break down well in water and can be found in drinking water—gee, wonder why). If the package says Swiss-water decaf, that means water was used to squeeze out the caffeine rather than chems. And if it says naturally decaffeinated, it means the caffeine was extracted either through the Swiss-water method or using carbon dioxide and water.

Ethiopia, not New England. Leave it to 17th- and 18th-century Europeans to turn coffee into a common colonial crop, complete with slave labour and low-paid workers. And the legacy lives on. Up to 25 million families in developing countries worldwide spend long hours each day trimming, weeding and hand-picking coffee beans for about the price of a cup of Tim

KICKING HORSE COFFEE COMPANY

One earth-friendly company stands out for its kick-ass brew and clever sense of humour: **Kicking Horse Coffee (www.kickinghorse coffee.com).** Legend has it the B.C. roastery, started by Elana Rosenfeld and husband, Leo Johnson, began after Elana's mom tossed out the taunt, "What are you two schmucks going to do with your lives? Sell coffee from your garage?" After lots of experimentation and a good sense of marketing, Kicking Horse is now Canada's number one fair-trade organic coffee. The beans, shade-grown under rainforest canopies, are purchased from small co-ops in Central America, then roasted in the remote Kootenay roastery, perched high in Hot Spring Alley. And a garage operation this ain't— Kicking Horse now sells about 11,000 kilograms a week to stores in Canada, the U.S. and Holland. With names like 454 Horse Power, Hoodoo Jo and yes, Kick Ass Coffee, who wouldn't want to try a cup?

Oh yeah, and for a little extra feel-good factor, part of the proceeds go to the Nature Conservancy of Canada's conservation projects. Now that's good 'til the last drop.

KNOW YOUR COFFEE LABELS

Before you start fretting about your next coffee break, rest assured that you can get your caffeine fix without endangering the earth. You just have to learn how to navigate all the mumbo-jumbo that comes with your jumbo latte.

Certified Organic: No chemicals used in the growing or processing; composting done, weeds pulled by hand; shade cover maintained over coffee and companion plants; GMO-free. No criteria for protecting labour standards, even though organic farming is more labour-intensive. Best in combination with the fair-trade label.

Certified Fair-Trade: Grown by small-scale farmers who are fairly paid and are part of an independent, democratic co-op; ecologically sensitive practices in place to ensure product is sustainable and conservation-oriented (most bushes are shade-grown), but not guaranteed to be organic. (Over 500,000 farmers now produce certified fair-trade coffee.)

Shade-Grown: Planted the traditional way, under the forest canopy, which attracts migratory birds.

Bird-Friendly: Shade-grown and certified organic. (The criteria for certification have been developed by the Smithsonian Migratory Bird Center of the National Zoo. With each bag you buy at health stores, 25 cents goes to the Smithsonian's research and conservation programs.)

Rainforest Alliance–Certified: Shade-grown by family farmers using integrated pest management practices (not organic, but reduced pesticide use); trees and native plants planted in any areas not suitable for crops and as buffer zones along rivers and springs; farms hire locally, pay fair wages and ensure access to clean drinking water and facilities.

Green Coffee: Not necessarily eco-friendly—this term just means you roast it yourself. But many companies offer up green beans with heart (fair-trade, bird-friendly and organic) and sell home roasting equipment.

Biodynamic: Take organic coffee, fold in the cycles of the moon and stars, sprinkle in some crystals and complicated rituals and you've got yourself a cup of ultra-holistic biodynamic joe.

Horton's coffee. It would take them three days just to afford a Starbucks grande latte! It's no wonder Global Exchange calls coffee farms "sweatshops in the fields."

Like cocoa, coffee bushes are no longer grown under shaded rainforest canopies; rather, mass deforestation makes way for monoculture coffee plantations in the blazing sun. Sure, such farms produce higher yields, but they do so at a great cost. Out of their moist, cool element, the plants need large amounts of chemical fertilizers. Sun-grown coffee attracts far fewer birds (a natural pest control), so chemical pesticides come into play. Planting coffee bushes in the sun also leads to greater soil erosion, which makes the farms more vulnerable to flooding. Pretty heavy consequences, all for a cup of java.

Tea: The story is very similar on tea plantations. Working conditions are abysmal, and Indian tea pickers average less than two bucks a day. Monoculture tea farms in places such as India have been found to support nearly 50% fewer birds than rainforest-grown tea. Pesticides banned in the West, like DDT, are still being sprayed on tea leaves. One French study found that dozens of green teas from China and Japan contained not just high levels of pesticides, but also of lead. Try reading that in your tea leaves.

Indian tea pickers average **less than two bucks a day**

Big Companies Go Green: NGOs have been pressuring major coffee companies to start selling fair-trade coffee for years now, saying the industry is making mountains off the backs of underpaid farm workers. Starbucks gave in (somewhat) and started selling fair-trade

4 FAB COFFEE AND TEA TIPS

#1 Avoid bleached disposable coffee filters and buy unbleached reusable filters—or spend an extra buck or two on a gold filter that you can wash and reuse everyday.

#2 Buy a couple of portable mugs, one for work or school and one for weekends about town, so you're never without.

#3 Staying at the coffee shop? Ask for a ceramic mug rather than getting a takeout cup.

#4 Minimize your eco-footprint by buying in bulk. Brew that oolong in organic, fair-trade loose-leaf form instead of in bags.

coffee in 2002, and these beans now account for 1.6% of its sales (about 2.2 million kilograms). Starbucks also buys about 30% of its coffee direct from farmers, giving growers a bigger slice of the pie by cutting out middlemen. Fair-trade activists want to see that number climb, and they also want to see the coffee shop start brewing pots of fair-trade java more than just once a month. FYI, three of the Starbucks I stopped in didn't even have fair trade beans on shelves.

FOOD LABELS

You'd think shopping for earth-, body-, and critter-friendly foods would be simple—buy organic. But even conscious shoppers can be confused by all the green labels that crowd the aisles. From cage-free and naturally raised to sustainably harvested and pesticide-free, the options for responsible eating are seemingly endless. It's important to know which terms are government-regulated, which are enforced and which tags can be whipped up by anyone with a brick of tofu and a dream.

Natural: It's hard to believe, considering all the abuse this term has taken, but this label is actually regulated. Who knew? According to the Canadian Food Inspection Agency (CFIA), references to "nature," "Mother Nature," "nature's way" or "natural" in relation to a food product cannot be used if any process has significantly altered any earth-given ingredient. That means the addition of even non-synthetic ingredients such as guar gum, hydrogenated oils, vitamins or treated spring water is a no-no. So how is it that everywhere you look someone's using and abusing the word nature? Bottom line: it's not policed unless you send in a complaint. Go to town, folks. Contact info for the CFIA is in the Resource Guide at the back of this book.

Organic: It may be organic, and then again it may not—if it's not certified, it's impossible to know, since use of the term hasn't historically been regulated. Some small farmers rebel against all the pricey red tape of certification and say their standards are higher anyway. This is an easier sell to trusted customers at, say, local farmers' markets. But again, it's strictly a trust system. Some studies in the U.S. have shown that nearly half the eggs labelled organic without being certified are not organic at all. Unless a product is certified, it's hard to know for sure.

Nearly half the eggs labelled organic without being certified **are not organic at all**

Certified Organic (Canada Organic): There are dozens of certifiers in Canada, so until the feds' new Canada Organic regulation and label are fully phased in you might find a confusing number of logos on grocery shelves certifying to slightly different standards. (Quebec and B.C. are the only provinces that already had their own mandatory systems in place.) But after over a decade of consultations and threats from our trading partners to get rid of our messy voluntary system, Canada is finally ushering in our first ever organic regs, so look for the new "Canada Organic" label with a little maple leaf on it (see www.cog.ca for details).

In general, to qualify for organic certification, farms have to be pesticide-free for three years and must avoid synthetic inputs such as pesticides and antibiotics, as well as the deliberate use of GMOs, while stressing soil-building. Certifiers also tend to have basic stipulations about animal welfare (no caged chickens or rabbits, for instance), although European programs are better than those in Canada and the U.S. on this front. They're also ahead in including labour and social equity clauses.

USDA Organic: This stamp reflects the fact that the U.S. (namely the Department of Agriculture) finally implemented a national organic system in 2002. Trouble is, it created a ceiling, not a floor, and certifiers that might have been more stringent were forced to "harmonize" or drop their standards to get in line with the national program. Some say the USDA system is weaker than the European system and, in some cases, the Canadian system in that it allows substances such as Chilean nitrates on organic crops (making California lettuce much prettier than ours), and farms can have pesticide-sprayed crops on one side and organics on the other. But Canada also allows a couple of substances that the U.S. doesn't. Several attempts to significantly water down USDA regs have been bucked.

100% Certified Organic: You might pay a little more for it, but this is the purest stuff you can find under any certification system. No synthetic inputs can be snuck in, no matter who the certifier.

Pesticide-Free: Sure, it might mean your broccoli hasn't been sprayed with chemicals, which is good, but this label doesn't cover all the other good stuff that comes with organic. The CFIA doesn't really approve of this term because, given all the contaminants in the environment, can

Your best bet is certified organic and fair trade

101

anything ever be pesticide-free? If they spot-test a food item and find out it's not free of pesticides, the farmer can be charged with fraud.

Fair Trade: The certified fair-trade logo ensures that any coffee, chocolate, sugar or whatnot you get from the developing world is made under strong labour standards. The logo often implies that ecologically sensitive practices are encouraged, but it doesn't guarantee it. Your best bet is certified organic *and* fair trade, but these are two expensive logos and not every farm can afford them, which means that not everyone thinks it's so fair. Still, it's the only way to know for sure that what you're buying hasn't been made in the equivalent of a sweatshop.

Biodynamic: Certification standards for this label are similar to those for organic but go one step further by requiring farmers to be in sync with the rhythms of nature and the cosmos and to use specially prepared herbs and minerals in compost and field sprays. Biodynamic farming embraces a philosophy focused on healing the earth; certifiers include Demeter.

GE-Free (or GMO-Free): The feds voted down a law that would have made genetic engineering (GE) labelling mandatory. The CFIA says meat with this label has to be approved by them.

Heirloom or Heritage: Did you know that three-quarters of the world's edible crops have disappeared over the last century? Yep, that's according to the UN Food and Agriculture Organization (FAO), which also says we used to eat about 10,000 different species of food plants and now 90% of the world's diet is down to 120. It seems the food biz didn't like all that variety and whittled it down to a few hardy, easily harvested types with a uniform appearance that could be patented and sold. Heirloom or heritage fruits, vegetables, herbs and even turkeys are those that have been revived from our history. These strains have been around for at least 50 years, and their seeds are pollinated by nature, not man. The term is not regulated.

Grass-fed (or Pastured) Meat: Grass-fed cows are said to be much healthier (the animals get sick less and their meat is more nutritious to the end consumer) than a typical grain-fed cow. In fact, USDA researchers have found that hay- or grass-fed cows are less likely to have *E. coli* in their digestive tracts than grain-fed types (and that's a good thing, considering

E. coli might otherwise contaminate your burger). But there are no federal standards or enforcement mechanisms in place for this label.

Naturally Raised (or Natural) Meat: According to the CFIA, this label should mean the animal was raised without human intervention (i.e., vaccines, hormones or antibiotics). Some health stores use the term on their meat to mean hormone-, antibiotic-, GMO- and animal-by-product-free, as well as free range. But the feed isn't organic.

Omega-3 Eggs: Sure, these eggs are better for your heart, thanks to flax- and vitamin-E-infused diets, but are the hens happy? Omega-3 omelettes are just as likely to come from battery-caged hens as regular old eggs, and they're just as non-organic. (Not to mention the plastic they're wrapped in. What's wrong with paper egg cartons?)

Free-Run (or Cage-Free) Chicken: These cluckers get to run around open-concept barns equipped with wire grid floors, but they have no access to the outdoors. By the way, this is an industry-devised term; no feds oversee the label or inspect the farms.

Free-Range (or Free-Roving) Chicken: These hens get to see the light of day and snack off the land. Not a government regulated term. Only backed up on certified organic eggs.

THE TOP 5 EATING HABITS TO HEAL THE WORLD

#1 Support local growers, be it through farmers' markets, farm-fresh food box deliveries or just keeping your eye out for local labels at the grocery store.

#2 Go vegetarian or reduce meat/dairy intake—meat production uses up to 20 times as much energy as growing grain.

#3 Choose fair-trade coffee, sugar, chocolate and anything else you can find so you can be sure you're not supporting "sweatshops in the fields."

#4 Buy certified organic products to avoid pesticide panic and spare waterways, wildlife and workers from encounters with toxic pesticides.

#5 Pass on resource-intensive, packaging-heavy fast food and heavily processed junk.

Antibiotic- or Hormone-Free Chicken: The CFIA says no poultry can be injected with hormones in this country, so that part of the claim is kind of useless (beef cattle are the only animals that can be treated with growth hormones in Canada). As for antibiotics, the CFIA says even conventional birds shouldn't be shipped to the slaughterhouse until they test clean for drugs. If the product is federally registered, this label will be pre-approved for accuracy. If it's provincially registered, it's open to spot checks or complaint-driven inspections.

Grain-Fed Chicken: This label is meant to signal, "This bird wasn't fed other birds or animals." The feds object to the label, saying the definition is too narrow and doesn't account for supplements such as vitamins or even antibiotics. They prefer the more pointed "animal by-product-free." Policing is the same as for antibiotic-free.

WATER

It's the fastest-growing beverage in Canada. Despite the fact that it flows freely from our taps, Canadians are buying three-quarters of a billion litres of the stuff annually. Yes, from a health perspective we should be happy it's taking sales away from sugar- and caffeine-laden colas. But from an environmental perspective, that's a hell of a lot of plastic for a liquid that once didn't come in any.

Why are we sucking back so much bottled *agua*, anyway, when in some cases it's little more than municipal water cleansed of off-putting odours and the taste of chlorine? Take Dasani, for instance. Coca-Cola, its maker, recently made the shocking admission that the designer water is actually just filtered tap water. Same goes for Aquafina and a quarter of all bottled waters out there. Why, then, you may ask, am I paying $1.50 for it, especially when bottled water is less regulated than tap water? Well, people, we're suckers for a pretty package and some good marketing. And many of us are willing to pay for portability and for the privilege of not having to use

> **By buying bottled water,**
> you're encouraging the industry to commodify a priceless public resource, draining underground aquifers and disrupting ecosystems

water fountains, which have at times been reported to have contamination issues and are harder and harder to come by.

By buying bottled water, you're encouraging the industry to commodify a priceless public resource, draining underground aquifers and disrupting ecosystems. Many places let companies set up shop and take as much water as they want without restriction, and many places in Canada let them take water for free. The Canadian Environmental Law Association says that, even where permits have been granted (Ontario's Ministry of Environment has already given water bottle companies permits to take 18 million litres a day), adequate environmental impact assessments have not been made.

Bottles: Every year, 1.5 million tons of plastic go into making enough bottles to supply our global bottled water habit, according to Sierra Club USA. And all sorts of nasty toxins, such as benzene and ethylene oxide, are emitted during the manufacturing process. Then there's all the petroleum that's needed to create the plastic to begin with (Sierra Club says 1.5 million barrels of oil a year go to manufacturing water bottles).

Granted, water bottles are usually recyclable, but as we know, not everyone recycles. And though you may reuse yours, thinking it's better for the environment, researchers now tell us we shouldn't do so without careful and regular cleansing because bacteria buildup inside the bottles could trigger gastrointestinal illness or even pneumonia. Something about the type of plastic used for water bottles makes them more prone to this.

Recently, reusing water bottles became an even bigger no-no when the media reported that plasticizers actually leach into the water itself. Heat, light and even squeezing the bottle are said to break down the plastic. And the longer water has been sitting in that bottle, either on store shelves or in your trunk or pantry, the worse it gets. Even fresh tap water will be contaminated if it's put into an old bottle. Scientists have argued that this is an urban myth propagated by a student thesis paper and not the findings of peer-reviewed research. Still, the New York–based Natural Resources Defence Council (NRDC) tested 1,000 bottles of 103 brands and concluded that, while most were quite good, some tested positive for arsenic. In an earlier study by the NRDC, six brands tested positive for harmful chemical by-products of chlorination and for the ultra-toxic solvent toluene. A study on Canadian bottled water put

THE TOP 5 REASONS NOT TO BUY BOTTLED WATER

#1 It's often little more than filtered tap water.

#2 The industry drains underground aquifers without sufficient environmental assessment.

#3 Bottled water is less regulated than tap water.

#4 A million and a half tons of polluting plastic is used to make all those damn water bottles.

#5 Plastic bottles could be leaching contaminants into your water.

out by the Institute of Environmental Geochemistry at the University of Heidelberg, Germany, found that disposable PET water bottles (PET, or polyethylene terephthalate, also goes by #1) constantly leach a metallic element called antimony into your water. The longer the water sits in the bottle, the more antimony it has. Polypropelene (#5) bottles didn't have the same problem, but they're not commonly recyclable. (See Appendix: Plastics on page 309 for more.)

The Canadian Bottled Water Association does say you should keep your water bottles out of the sun in a cool place. Health Canada says you should ditch stored bottles after a year.

Polycarbonate Plastic Bottles: For years, the hiker/biker/earthy/sporty set has been turning to shatterproof polycarbonate plastic containers for their hydration needs. But the water hit the fan in the late '90s, when research out of Case Western Reserve University in Cleveland found that polycarbonate plastics can leach low levels of a hormone disrupter called bisphenol A when washed with harsh chemicals. In 2002, Environmental Health Perspectives carried out several studies of its own and found that new bottles also leached bisphenol A; after a few uses, the traces faded, but leaching increased again when the bottles were heated or repeatedly scrubbed.

The plastics people and the bisphenol A lobby point to separate studies demonstrating that the type of polycarbonate used in baby bottles, for instance, doesn't leach. For their part, the Nalgene people say all the studies slamming polycarbonate plastic don't apply to their high-quality, food-grade, American-made polycarbonates (called Lexan), which they say are different from the many other grades of polycarbonates out there, especially cheap imports. Studies still need to be done directly on popular Nalgene bottles to see who's right.

In the meantime, the bottle's in your court, but if you want to avoid polycarbonate plastic bottles, Nalgene and other water bottle manufacturers make opaque non-polycarbonate types that have yet to be hit by controversy.

FYI, water cooler containers—the kind you find in offices and kitchens around the country—are also made of polycarbonate.

Water Filters: If you're concerned about lead in your pipes or pesticide runoff from nearby farms, or you just hate the taste of chlorine, filters can be a good alternative to buying bottled water. (For portability, just fill up a stainless steel mug before you leave the house.) The question is, are you buying the right filter?

Carbon filters vary in price range and quality (generally the more you spend the more it'll filter out). Basic carbon filters like Britas are great for taking that nasty chlorine flavour out of the water and will reduce but not eliminate lead, mercury, copper, cadmium and benzene levels. In the "isn't it ironic?" category, Brita was bought out by, of all companies, Clorox, the maker of cleaning products laden with the very chemical a Brita filters out! Some people have raised questions about whether Brita's styrene-methyl methacrylate copolymer plastic container leaches anything into the water. So far, no real dirt has floated to the surface, and third-party tests by the National Sanitation Foundation found them to be safe.

There are, of course, plenty of alternatives. You just have to be willing to spend a lot more cash. **Reverse osmosis** filters out fluoride, minerals and heavy metals but costs a mint and typically wastes four to nine gallons of water for every gallon filtered. Pollution Probe's water report says **distillers** are best at removing "the largest number of chemicals," plus they work on bacteria, viruses, fluoride, arsenic, heavy metals like lead and even VOCs. The only thing is they're pretty slow and energy-intensive and the machines need to be cleaned often.

It's important to know that, unlike in the U.S., filters aren't regulated in Canada, and some make claims that haven't been substantiated by research. There are three main certifying bodies to look for on filter labels: the CSA, the Underwriters Laboratory and the National Sanitation Foundation (NSF), the best known of the three. Not all certified filters are of equal quality, but these bodies do make sure that any claims made by a filter are accurate, and NSF-certified filters have to meet particularly stringent standards. Before you settle on any particular brand, head to the NSF website (www.nsf.org) and look up the products you've been eyeing. You'll be able to see exactly what each filter is certified to remove.

If you want them to work at all, make sure to care for your filters properly (i.e. change them or clean them regularly, depending on the model).

ALCOHOL

What would summer be without a nice cold beer to air condition our insides, or winter without a glass of red to ward off the cold? And just imagine how glum office parties and frat houses would be without embarrassing quantities of the social lubricant. Even environmentalists get a thirst for the happy juice, though any earthy considerations tend to get checked at the bar door. Sure, you might support your local microbrewery or winery, but does that guarantee you a chemical-free bevvie? Well, fortunately for all you greenies out there, new options keep pouring in.

Wine: Back in the days when grapes were crushed between busy little toes, natural wine was all that was known. Alas, the chemical industry got to wine growers, as it did most other farmers on the planet. Pesticides, herbicides and fungicides are the order of the day, sprayed over vineyards to keep various bugs, weeds and moulds at bay (sorry—that rhyme was entirely accidental). The Pesticide Action Network (PAN) keeps a database of the top 50 pesticides used on wine grapes, several of which are on its bad actor list because they're acutely toxic, groundwater contaminants, carcinogenic or all of the above.

Fear not, wine lovers, organic vintages now abound

In fact, grapes are one of the most heavily sprayed crops around. Pesticide activists not only say the practice is making vineyard workers sick, but also insist there's a link to pesticide use and birth defects among area farmers and non-farmers alike. Traces left in your glass aren't supposed to be harmful, but they're there. A few growers have even turned to genetically modified grapes. The Center for Grapevine Biotechnology is trying to breed a fungus-resistant grape that would need less chemical input, and scientists in Florida have spliced fluorescent jellyfish genes into the mix in the search for a cure for a vine-withering disease. Others are just trying to genetically engineer the best wine. Either way, consumers aren't likely to embrace frankenwine, if they know what they're drinking.

But fear not, wine lovers, organic vintages now abound. On certified vineyards, grapes are fertilized with compost, not petroleum-derived fertilizers, and cover crops such as clover and Queen Anne's lace are grown to attract beneficial bugs. Several international vineyards, such as France's **Château de Caraguilhes** or Italy's **Fasoli Gino**, offer organic wines, as do local wineries such as B.C.'s **Summerhill Pyramid**. Others might not be organic but, like Australia's **Banrock Station**, give back to the earth. Through its wetlands foundation, Banrock funds wildlife and wetland projects in Canada—and pretty much every country in which it's sold, for that matter.

Many wine-growing regions are starting programs to encourage best environmental practices at the area's wineries. As in California, pesticide usage has come down at several Canadian vineyards. **Pelee Island Winery**, for instance, has committed to limited use of "ecologically responsible" pesticide spraying, and has promised to stick with natural island-grown fertilizer and fund local forest restoration efforts.

Up for making your own vino? Some do-it-yourself places offer organic grapes and try to minimize their use of sulphites—be sure to look around in your area. **Feast of Fields** will even ship you a bucket of biodynamic, certified organic juice to get you started (www.feast-of-fields.ca).

Corks: When plastic corks started popping up on the scene, there were rumours that the end of natural cork was near. Getting over our disdain for plastic stoppers, the story went, was all part of giving overharvested, slow-growing cork trees a break.

The rumours were only partly right. Yes, cork harvesting is a slow process (cork trees live to be about 500 years old, and it takes a good 40 years to grow a good layer of harvestable cork), and yes, the end of cork is near, but only, insist environmentalists, if we *stop* buying cork! What? How could this be? Well, the WWF says harvesting cork bark is a sustainable ancient practice that actually keeps the few cork forests in this world (mainly in the

CALIFORNIA'S FETZER

It's always nice to see a big grower go green, especially when it means you can drink a glass or two of vino without an eco-hangover. California-based **Fetzer** first pledged to shift all of its vineyards to organic agriculture practices in 1985, and since then it has become one of the largest certified organic wineries in the world. Its **Bonterra** brand is 100% organic. Even Fetzer's non-organic wines contain about 20% organic grapes (the rest are purchased from other vineyards), and the company is an industry leader in sustainable practices. Fetzer is the only winery that buys 100% renewable energy to power its facilities. Its tractors and trucks run on biodiesel blends. Grapes are irrigated only in very dry hot weather to keep them from burning. Stems and seeds are composted, then spread as natural fertilizer. Fetzer's bottles are made of recycled glass. The labels on their Bonterra line are printed using soy-based inks. Plus, Fetzer pleases vegans by steering clear of (gulp) bull's blood, egg whites and gelatin in its wine, even though the FDA has okayed them as wine additives. I'm feeling warm and fuzzy already, and I haven't even had a glass.

Mediterranean) alive and thriving. Turning to plastic makes them more vulnerable to encroachment by developers. Ad campaigns across Europe are now encouraging wine lovers to say no to plastic stoppers and put a cork in it.

Beer: For all you beer fans out there, sadly the organic selection isn't quite so broad. British Columbia has **NatureLand Organic Lager**, as well as unpasteurized, unfiltered, certified organic beers by **Crannog Ales**. Ontario has **Mill Street Brewery's Original Organic Lager**. Quebec has **La Barberie Blonde Biologique** and **Schoune Blanche**. And that's about it.

Many microbreweries, such as **Muskoka** and **Black Oak**, say their beer's better for you and the world because it's made with "all-natural ingredients," as well as being unpasteurized and preservative- and additive-free. Some avoid killing trees by steering clear of labels, and **Steam Whistle**, for instance, uses an eco-conscious cooling system that draws from deep within Lake Ontario. Is it generally nice to support the local little guy over behemoth beer giants trucking their brew across the country? No doubt. Are microbrewers using organic or GM-free ingredients? Don't assume so unless it's written on the label. One thing is clear: supporting brews made close to home cuts back on the amount of fossil fuels used to get that cold one into your fridge. Same goes for wines.

> **Supporting brews made close to home** cuts back on the amount of fossil fuels used to get that cold one into your fridge

Heineken is the only major non-organic company we came across that says it won't use genetically modified ingredients. The Brewers of Canada tell us that hops and barley are never genetically modified anyway. Wheat and corn (corn syrup is used in the mainstream fermentation process) are a different story.

A small Quebecois brewery called Unibroue fought and won a legal battle with the feds to use a GMO-free label on beer sold in Quebec. The CFIA says it had approved the label only for use in Europe.

Hard Liquor: Martini lovers rejoice—other types of organic booze have started flowing into Canada. Keep your eyes peeled for award-winning **Juniper Green Organic Gin** (made with organic juniper berries, coriander, angelica and savory and distilled from organic grain), as well as organic sake, Scotch and pretty much any booze you can think of. Some, such as **42 Below** vodka, are certified GMO wheat–free. If your local liquor store doesn't carry any organic booze, ask them to start.

KID
STUFF

Wee little creatures enter our lives,
and we do all we can to care for them and shelter them from the world. We put
caustic cleaners out of reach, we install carbon monoxide detectors to pick up on
poisons in the air, and we buy tamper-proof lids to keep them from swallowing what
they shouldn't. But new reports tell us our children's bodies are being inundated
with chemicals we didn't even realize were lurking in our homes.

ENVIRONMENT

We might picture pollutants in the air and in lakes, but never in our worst nightmares do we imagine them lodged in our children's tissue. Well, south of the border, the Centers for Disease Control (CDC) has been testing the urine, blood and saliva of thousands of Americans, including kids, for the presence of toxic chemicals. In their 2005 study, the CDC found that many children had higher levels than adults of stuff like heavy metals and phthalates (the potentially hormone-disrupting chem found in some soft plastics, perfumes and beauty products). Extensive bio-monitoring has yet to happen in Canada (Health Canada is poised to start some time in 2007), but in 2006, Environmental Defence shocked the nation when it tested a small pool of children and their parents in B.C., Ontario, Quebec and New Brunswick. They found an average of 23 chemicals in each child, including carcinogens, hormone disruptors, respiratory toxins and neurotoxins. As in the U.S., levels of certain chemicals were higher in the kids than in the parents. This was the case with non-stick chemicals (found on furniture, carpets, clothing, popcorn bags, fast-food wrappers and coatings on frying pans), brominated flame retardants (found on mattresses, clothing, furniture and carpets) and some insecticides. The children also tested positive for substances such as PCB and DDT that were banned before they were even born!

Speaking of childbirth, the Environmental Working Group out of Washington tested the umbilical cords (collected by the Red Cross) of 10 newborns in 2004 and found an alarming average of 200 industrial chemicals and pollutants in each cord! Overall, they detected a grand total of 287 chemicals, of which 180 are carcinogens, 217 are neurotoxins and 208 cause birth defects in animals—stuff like mercury, fire retardants, pesticides, stain-resistant chemicals, trash incinerator and coal plant emissions, as well as car exhaust pollutants. (Stay tuned for Canadian data on cord blood from Environmental Defence.)

Many of these chemicals keep accumulating in the environment and our bodies, so perhaps it's not surprising that childhood cancers are up 21%, asthma rates are four times higher than they were in the '80s, and birth defects are on the rise, but it is, without a doubt, enough to make a parent mad as hell. We've been unwittingly swaddling our children in fire-retardant PJs and feeding them persistent pollutant–tainted food, and the government hasn't stepped in to do much about it. While we wait

Childhood cancers are up 21%, **asthma** rates are four times higher than they were in the '80s, and **birth defects** are on the rise

Hearing that your child's body is burdened with chemicals we phased out years ago can be incredibly depressing for a parent. Part of the problem is that mothers inadvertently pass part of their toxic load on to their sons and daughters in the womb. Hard to control, but that doesn't mean we should give up the fight. Studies from around the world prove that banning chemicals does lower the level of toxins floating through our bodies over time. The last CDC biomonitoring study showed that removing lead from gasoline, paint and other consumer products has made a huge difference—just 10 years ago, almost 1 in 25 children had worrisome levels of lead in their blood. By 2002, the number had dropped to 1 in 60! And in Sweden, high levels of flame retardants in mother's milk (levels that doubled every five years from 1972 to 1997) quickly dropped after manufacturers voluntarily pulled the nasty family of chemicals from products in the late '90s.

For more info on getting the toxins out of your family, pick up *Raising Healthy Children in a Toxic World: 101 Smart Solutions for Every Family*, by Philip J. Landrigan, M.D., Herbert L. Needleman, M.D. and Mary M. Landrigan, M.P.A.

for them to do something (Health Canada's now embarking on a review of 200 troubling chemicals currently in use), here are some practical and easy ways to green your child's world and make your home chem-free.

PERSONAL CARE PRODUCTS

We know our kids are more delicate than we are, but they're also more sensitive to daily exposures to toxic chemicals. They have more absorbent skin surface for their size than adults and can't eliminate chemicals from their systems as well. Yet nearly every cream, oil and cleanser we introduce to our babies' bodies is loaded with chemicals and artificial scents. And don't ask why nearly every conventional baby product out there, including baby oil, jellies and diaper ointments, is a petroleum industry by-product. As the old saying goes, what's good for the car must be good for the . . . baby?

It makes even less sense when you consider that petrol-based mineral oil and petroleum jelly actually block pores and can irritate rashes. Add ammonia and other skin irritants such as sodium lauryl sulphate, and you have yourself a bottle of baby lotion or cleansing gel. Check out the Environmental Working Group's (EWG) incredibly extensive report on every

While we all had our butts powdered with talcum when we were kids, it's time to break with tradition. Talc may trigger respiratory problems and can be contaminated with asbestos. The National Institutes of Health (NIH) in the U.S. wanted asbestos-tainted talc to be categorized firmly as a known human carcinogen—it was struck down to a probable human carcinogen. The NIH even wanted non-contaminated talc to be officially categorized as a probable carcinogen, but that was vetoed too. Skip the controversy and try plain old cornstarch, rice starch or arrowroot powder instead. The bonus is, you can buy these in bulk. Or get corn-based **Baby Organics** powder. It's talc-free and scented with lavender.

brand of baby cream, oil and wash for details on which products you may want to avoid and why, and which choices are safer (www.ewg.org/reports/skindeep). The Environmental Health Association of Nova Scotia has a more general guide to naughty ingredients and recommended baby products (www.lesstoxicguide.ca)

Personal Care Products Solutions: All this info can bring on postpartum depression, but cheer up—many of the health store brands that make chemical-free stuff for you (see page 6) also make natural products for your tot, like **Weleda**'s almond oil–based baby oil with soothing chamomile and healing antifungal calendula. Pretty **Butterfly Weed Herbal Hug Nappy Rash Ointment** tins also contain antiseptic myrrh and antibacterial lavender.

HEALING CALENDULA

Those pretty marigolds in your garden are hiding a powerful secret. The flowers, also known as calendula, hold potent healing abilities you'll learn to love if you've got a kid in your house or on the way. Creams containing this naturally anti-inflammatory, antifungal, antiviral plant work wonders on your baby's diaper rash (which is why it's so common in health store infant lotions). And big-people creams with the ingredient are great for rubbing on scraped knees after a Little League game or an especially rowdy play session with the neighbour's kids.

Think you can't get by without your drugstore baby shampoo? Try Quebec-based **Druide's Ecological Baby Shampoo**, which is so mild it's "no tears," but instead of chemical ingredients and artificial dyes, it uses organic, biodegradable, fair-trade stuff like hibiscus flower proteins and mango butter. Druide has a whole line of baby gear for bath and nappy time, which you can pick up at most health stores. They even have a little travel kit with mini baby cleaners, shampoos, lotions and oils (www.druide.ca).

CLOTHING

Kids clothes are so damn adorable it's hard to imagine they can be harmful in any way. Luckily, regulations around sleepwear have changed over the years: manufacturers are no longer required to treat their clothing with chemical fire retardants. But you do want to wash all new clothing before you dress your kids in it, because it could have a sheen of wrinkle-resistant formaldehyde. You also want to avoid swaddling your kids in conventional pesticide-heavy cotton, decorated with off-gassing PVC plastic cartoons. (It can be hard to tell whether an article is made with PVC that's been softened with potentially hormone disrupting phthalates, but a strong plastic smell is often a good indication—best to call the company directly if you're unsure.)

Wash all new clothing before you dress your kids in it, because it could have a sheen of wrinkle-resistant formaldehyde

Clothing Solutions: Designers are proving children's clothes can be cute *and* natural. B.C.-based **Sage Creek Canada** carries organic cotton pants and playsuits, and even a Zen yoga collection, including the most darling little kimono (www.sagecreekcanada.com). **T.h.e. Store** (in Vancouver and online at www.t-h-e-store.com) has organic fair-trade cotton tees by **Ecobaby** as well as sleeveless sleepers. Sweatshop-free **American Apparel** offers organic one-pieces and toddler tees online (www.americanapparel.net) and at their stores in Alberta, B.C., Nova Scotia, Ontario and Quebec. **Hankettes** (www.hankettes.com), **Ethic Baby** (www.ethicbaby.ca) and Toronto-based online store **The Baby Shop** (www.thebabyshop.ca) all carry organic baby clothes. For the sassy environmentalist-in-the-making, you can even get organic cotton sleepers, onesies and tees with adorable slogans such as MOTHA SUCKA, FEMINIST and I'M A BREAST MAN (www.grassrootsstore.com). For something a little more colourful with pretty screen printing and designs, check out Vancouver's **Fig Organic Kids Fashion** (www.figkids.com)

DIAPERS

How do you look a baby in the eye and coo, "You're a little environmental menace, aren't you, shmookems?" It's really parents who should be guilt-tripped, considering they're the ones who buy, then toss, 5,000 to 7,000 diapers per child. That's about 1.8 billion disposable diapers a year in Canada, according to the Association for Safe Alternatives in Childbirth. I know, I know, they're oh so convenient, but disposables contain perfumes, potentially asthma-inducing chemicals and plastics such as super-absorbent polyacrylate, the very material that causes toxic shock syndrome in tampon wearers. And, of course, all that wood pulp has to be knocked down (about 250,000 trees go into making the cellulose filling in American diapers every year) and bleached a blinding shade of white, a process that emits nasty toxins.

> disposables contain perfumes, **potentially asthma-inducing** chemicals and plastics such as super-absorbent polyacrylate, the very material that causes toxic shock syndrome in tampon wearers.

Toronto is one of the only municipalities in the country that allows disposable diapers in its composting program, which makes them an earth-friendlier option than in the past, but don't think you're off the hook, T.O. parents. All that plastic just gets separated out, then shipped off to landfill. Only the wood pulp batting gets composted. Yes, green-binning your Pampers is better than nothing, but I have higher aspirations for you, dear reader.

Disposable: What do I suggest? Well, if you can't kick your addiction to disposables, at least switch to greener brands. **Seventh Generation** and **Tushies** are chemical-, fragrance- and chlorine-free and are made with unbleached cotton and wood pulp. You can pick them up at any health store or order them online from **The Baby Shop** (www.thebabyshop.ca).

Reusable: Reusable diapers come with their own eco-baggage—think pesticide-laden cotton and heavy soap, water, bleach and energy use in cleaning—but the benefits far outweigh the full life cycle costs, despite what the disposable diaper people might say. And you don't have to go for the old-fashioned pinned, folded cotton types (though these are the cheapest). New reusables also come with elastic bands and Velcro tabs. Some are made of terry cloth, others of flannel. **Parenting by Nature** is a good online Canadian source for all kinds of cloth nappies (www.parentingbynature.com), but you can also pick them up at most green general stores (such as **Earth's General Store** in Edmonton or **P'lovers** in Halifax—see the Resource Guide at the back for more green general stores),

117

DIAPER WARS

It's difficult for most new parents to imagine a time when toddlers weren't waddling around in disposable diapers, but the first throwaways were poorly designed and didn't really catch on with moms and dads until the late '60s and '70s. Then, as environmental concerns started peaking in the late '80s ('twas the era of the *Exxon Valdez* oil spill and acid rain, after all), eco-activists started pooping on plastic diapers' landfill-clogging record. By the time Earth Day 1990 rolled around, half the U.S. states were looking into either taxing or all-out banning the tossable bum wraps, and diaper service sales started taking off. That's when mainstream diaper corporations launched an aggressive campaign against reusables, attacking cloth types for everything from the pesticides needed to grow cotton to the water pollution involved in washing poo-filled diapers. The cloth biz and environmental orgs fought back with studies of their own proving that cloth diapers used fewer resources than disposable types. A study put out by the diaper service industry even claimed that disposables could potentially harbour the bacteria that cause meningitis and hepatitis. Needless to say, the he-said, she-said continued for a while, but the disposable industry won the public relations battle. Today, though, cloth diapers are making a comeback, with conscious parents trying to cut back on plastic trash by swaddling their babies' butts in biodegradable, reusable fabrics.

which tend to have natural baby sections. Sears and the Bay sell cotton flannel **Kushies** in five-packs both in-store and online.

Only a few brands of reusable diapers are made with extra-green fabrics, and they can be harder to find. **Ecomum** is made with hemp and "green" (or unbleached, undyed) cotton (available at www.grassrootsstore.com). If you've got extra cash, organic cotton is the most eco-friendly choice of all. **Earthy Family** in Calgary (www.earthyfamily.com) and **T.h.e. Store** (www.t-h-e-store.com) offer fitted 100% certified organic cotton nappies with Velcro snaps, as does B.C-based **Hankettes** (www.hankettes.com). Hankettes also has organic wool diaper covers with elasticized legs, organic change pads and pretty much everything baby-related that can be made with organic cotton.

For pails of useful info on cloth diapers, including reviews and tips on overnight diapering, washing and deciding which cloth diaper system is right for you, check out www.cutofcloth.com.

Cleaning Cloth Diapers: To clean diapers, there are two ways to go. Both involve tossing used diapers in a pail (one with a good lid on it to keep odours locked up) until you're ready to wash them, but the wet route means throwing them in a pail that's half-filled with water plus 1/4 cup (50 mL) of baking soda and a 1/4 cup of vinegar (you won't be tempted to use bleach if you use vinegar). The second option is the dry route. The folks at Diaper-Eeze in Toronto say you can dump any solid poop into the toilet, then toss the diaper into your pail and wash a whole pile at once every three days. They also insist that, as long as you're only breastfeeding, the poop shouldn't stain the cloth. (Not sure if there's any scientific research to back this up, but you can conduct your own experiments.)

Bleach and pure detergents such as Ivory Snow will break down your cloth nappies faster

By the way, bleach and pure detergents such as Ivory Snow will break down your cloth nappies faster. Use borax and baking soda or a natural laundry liquid instead. Diapers and diaper covers shouldn't be washed with other clothes.

Open-air drying is always best, but if you must use a dryer, skip the chem-filled fabric softener and toss in 3/4 cup (175 mL) of vinegar in the final rinse. It's easier on the earth and reduces diaper rash.

Diaper Services: If you're too busy or pooped out to clean your own reusables, consider a diaper service such as **Rock-a-Dry Baby Diaper Service & Gifts** in Edmonton, **Diapers Naturally Cotton Diaper Service** in Burnaby, **Tender Touch Diapers** in Winnipeg or **Comfy Cotton Diaper Service** in Toronto. Check your Yellow Pages for contacts and listings in your area. Just note that it can be impossible to find a service that doesn't use harsh bleach. I contacted a dozen services across Canada, and they all used the stuff.

Wipes: Many moms would smack me if I tried to take away their disposable baby wipes, so let's compromise. While you're at home, why not try the old damp-cloth method? When you're out and about, bring some unscented, alcohol- and chlorine-free **Seventh Generation Baby Wipes** with you. Like everything else mentioned here, you can pick them up at most health stores and green general stores. They're moistened with aloe vera, vitamin E and water and, unlike other wipes, aren't chlorine-bleached, so the manufacturing process didn't create super-toxic dioxins. You can also buy reusable organic cotton wipes at www.grassrootsstore.com or www.hankettes.com.

Before Tabitha Tucker became pregnant, being zealously earth-conscious was not at the top of her list of priorities. The former women's shelter coordinator and her husband, Chris Strashok, were, she recalls, "minimal recyclers" at best. But the moment little baby Terran was born, their eyes opened to the sea of chemicals and disposable products that surround infants in our culture, and they became instant environmentalists. They ran out to buy cloth diapers from the only store in Calgary that sold them, but once the first pail of soiled bum-wraps was full, it hit them that they had no clue how to wash them. Tabitha scoured the web for solutions, but the answers only led to more questions about issues beyond reusable diapering. Wouldn't it be nice, thought the pair, to have all this info in one place. By the fall of 2002, **Earthy Family** was born. Now it's one of the rare sources in Canada of unbleached certified organic cloth diapers grown and sewn by work-at-home moms in the U.S. (as well as baby shampoos, diaper ointments and personal care products for the whole family). Earthy Family also rounds up natural remedies to breastfeeding problems, tips on avoiding environmental toxins during pregnancy, articles on gardening with children and recipes for diaper wipes, as well as an electronic cookbook on baking with whole foods for health-conscious families. Basically, Earthy Family fills the info gap, offering up a centralized place to get helpful tips on raising Canadian kids the old-fashioned way (**www.earthyfamily.com**).

BABY BOTTLES

If you can't use nature's best nursing device—the female breast—then you should know that standard amber-coloured rubber nipples may be contaminated with low levels of carcinogenic nitrosamines. Best to replace them with clear silicone nipples, which also last longer. As for the bottle, *Consumer Reports* found that small amounts of hormone-disrupting bisphenol A can potentially leach from hard polycarbonate plastic (#7 on the bottom) when it's heated or after prolonged use. The makers of baby bottles say they use a higher-quality polycarbonate that doesn't leach. But glass bottles are guaranteed to be made from a non-toxic, inert renewable resource and are generally shatter- and heat-resistant. If your toddler likes to whip his or her bottle onto your ceramic floor, you can also get non-leaching, recyclable polyethylene (#1, #2 or less-commonly recycled #4 and #5). **Gerber**, **Rubbermaid** and **Evenflo** all make bottles with the better plastics. Evenflo also makes harder-to-find glass ones (call 937-773-3971 or special order through Toys R' Us or Hudson's Bay). (See Appendix: Plastics, page 309, to learn more about the numbers on plastics.)

FOOD

What we put *in* our babies' bodies is even more important than what we slather on their bottoms. Young children tend to eat a lot of only a few types of food (you try eating nothing but banana and carrot purée) even after they move beyond their milk habit, so it's important to pay close attention to what we spoon into their mouths.

Baby Food: If your child is in the mushy fruit and veg stage, be aware that many conventional baby foods have tested positive for several different pesticides that are considered probable human carcinogens, neurotoxins and endocrine disrupters (punch in "baby food" at www.ewg.org for more info). The fact that babies tend to eat way more of a few foods doesn't help.

PREPPING FOR PREGNANCY: GETTING THE TOXINS OUT EARLY

What's best for your children after they're born is also best when they're in the womb. Moms can pass on hundreds of chemicals to their unborn babies, so it's a good idea to start phasing out the hidden toxins lurking in your life when you're planning a pregnancy, or at the very least when you find out your pregnant. Here are a few tips to giving your unborn baby a head start in life:

Say goodbye to tuna: canned albacore, fresh tuna and swordfish are high in neurotoxic mercury, which can be harmful to your babe-to-be.

Pass on pesticides: home pesticide use on lawns and indoor bugs is one of the main reasons biomonitoring studies are finding pesticides in our bodies.

Eat lean: animal fats store persistent chemicals such as PCB, so it's best to cut them out and choose fat-free milk and lean cuts of meat.

Embrace stains: stain-resistant coatings on older furniture and carpets are full of persistent PFOs that are building up in our bodies (see page 206 for more info).

Work clean: any woman working with powerful chemicals at her job should consider asking for a position change while she's pregnant. Hair stylists, for instance, should say no to chemically dyeing and perming. The children of hair dressers in a large 20-year-long Swedish study were found to have higher rates of birth defects, cleft palettes and spina bifida. Even heavy use of hairspray was linked to lower birth weights.

To add insult to injury, all the nutrients in most jarred foods have been boiled and pasteurized away. What's the point, when it's so easy to make your own? Just steam some peeled apples, peas, yams or whatnot (ripe bananas and pears don't need steaming) and toss them in the food processor or blender. You can even make a huge batch and pour extras into ice cube trays for freezing. Toss the frozen cubes into large phthalate-free baggie, (all **Ziploc** and **Glad** products are phthalate-free), then defrost them in the fridge or on the counter. Homemade baby food is much cheaper than store-bought stuff, and it's far healthier, especially if the foods you use are local and organic. If your produce is not organic, make sure to clean it well with a natural fruit wash before you cook it (the jury is still out on these, but for more info on cleaning fruits and vegetables see page 65).

Look at what your kids eat and drink the most of and consider switching to organic for those first

If you don't have time to make your own baby food, health stores and even grocery stores are stocked with certified organic bottled brands such as **Healthy Time** and **Earth's Best**. Both also make wheat-free organic teething biscuits, cereal, applesauce, cookies—pretty much everything your kids like to eat. Even **Heinz** and **Gerber** make organic baby food now.

Big Kid Food: It would be great if you could afford to feed your family nothing but organic food, but hey, it's not cheap or always locally available. Still, buy as much of it as you can, as often as you can. Many of the persistent chemicals used on crops 30 years ago are still in our bodies and our children's bodies to this day. It's best to remove as many potential sources as soon as possible.

Look at what your kids eat and drink the most of—such as milk and juice—and consider switching to organic for at least those. Organic milk isn't much more expensive than regular. Dry organic goods such as cereal and cookies and produce such as bananas and carrots are also quite affordable. It's the organic red peppers that'll kill your budget, but you can build up to those. FYI, buying organic is the only way to be sure that what you're eating doesn't contain genetically modified ingredients.

Also be aware that 94% to 99% of our exposure to persistent organic pollutants such as PCB comes from our food, especially fatty stuff like dairy, fish, fatty meat and even breast milk, according to Environmental Defence. The medical and environmental communities agree that, despite the presence of contaminants in breast milk, it's still more nutritious and provides more immune-building antibodies for your child than formula. But you might want to limit your child's intake of red meat, fatty fish such as farmed

THE TOP ORGANIC KIDDIE FOODS TO SPEND YOUR MONEY ON

#1 All bottled baby food (purées may contain pesticides).

#2 Apples, peaches, pears, nectarines, imported grapes, cherries and berries.

#3 Spinach, potatoes, bell peppers and celery.

#4 Meat, eggs and dairy.

#5 Anything else you can afford to buy. (Conventional broccoli and cereal might not have much pesticide residue on them, but that doesn't mean wildlife, waterways and workers didn't suffer from being doused in chemicals.)

salmon (which has also been found to have brominated fire retardants), tuna (especially canned white albacore and fresh tuna, which are high in mercury) and other fatty foods. (See Food for Thought.)

BABY'S ROOM

Besides Lamaze classes and diaper shopping, one of the first things parents work on when they find out they're pregnant is the baby's room. The main concern tends to be whether to paint it blue or pink, or go Switzerland-neutral with yellow. But as we put all that blood, sweat and panic into fixing up the nursery, we don't really think about all the chemicals we're carting in.

Cribs: This is where we rest our babes so they can be safe and snuggly through the night, so we tend to look for cribs that meet safety standards and won't let our kids fall off the side. But what's it made of? Composite woods are bound together using formaldehyde, which off-gasses smog and asthma-inducing volatile organic compounds (VOCs) long after we assemble it. Same goes for all the other pressed wooden furniture we buy for the room.

It's best to get unfinished solid wood that you can finish yourself with natural hemp or linseed oils. **IKEA** sells some cribs, cabinets, change tables and high chairs from farmed trees, rather than pillaging from natural forests. And all of their pressed woods are essentially formaldehyde-free. The cool thing is that a lot of their baby furniture is multi-functional, adding to the longevity of the products. Cribs can be converted into junior beds, and change tables can turn into big people's tables or shelves.

Mattresses: Knowing what's in your baby's mattress is enough to give any parent bad dreams. Conventional mattresses are stuffed with polyurethane foam treated with fire-retardant chemicals (while some of the most persistent brominated fire retardants are being phased out, that doesn't mean they're not still on the market), as well as antibacterial and stain-repelling chems. Rip open the plastic wrapping when you get it home and you can just smell the fumes coming off it. Make sure to air it out for several weeks before you plop your baby down on it. You might even want to put a tightly woven dust mite–proof cotton barrier cloth between your baby and the mattress, especially if the mattress comes coated in vinyl, which could off-gas plasticizing chemicals. Better yet, invest in organic bedding made with natural fibres such as cotton and naturally fire- and water-resistant wool. **T.h.e. Store**, **Grassroots** and **Sage Creek** all carry organic crib mattresses, and T.h.e. Store and Grassroots carry wool moisture pads, organic sheets and barrier cloths. **Willow Natural Home** out of Nelson, B.C., has the works in ecological baby bedding, including organic kids' pillows, crib shams and comforters (www.willownaturalhome.com).

If you're worried about your kid peeing on the mattress every night, don't—I repeat, *do not*—get a vinyl mattress cover. If you can't find a vinyl-free crib cover, just buy clear plastic polypropylene sheeting used for house painting and wrap that like a flat sheet around the mattress. Better yet, buy a wool puddle pad from a company like **Natura** (www.naturaworld.com). They also make crib duvets, crib mattresses and more. (See page 159 for more on mattresses and bedrooms.)

Paint: See page 207 for info on paint.

Carpeting: The natural choice for flooring seems to be soft, cushy carpeting your rugrats won't scrape their knees on, but wall-to-wall types are made with petrochemicals, and while the industry has greatly greened itself over the years, VOCs still off-gas from new carpets. Carpets have also been known to trap allergens such as dust mites. Cushy cork, fast-growing bamboo and wood flooring certified by the Forest Stewardship Council (FSC) are all sustainable options. If you want to soften up the room, throw down a vegetable-dyed organic hemp rug in sage green or Oregon grape (www.rawganique.com). (See pages 199 and 203 for more info on flooring and carpeting.)

Looking for an earth-friendly place to register for your baby shower? Natural baby stores are popping up across the country, but not too many offer formal gift registries. Ontario-based **Parenting by Nature** lets you register for funky BabyHawk Mei Tai Asian baby carriers, cloth diapers, cute baby shoes, natural lotions, soft organic teddies and plenty of stuff for mommy (**www. parentingbynature.com**). At **Ethic Baby** you can sign up for little organic outfits and bamboo baby gifts. It might also be worth asking your local green general store or fave online baby store if they're able to set up a registry for you and your wee one on the way.

Hunting for prezzies for the baby to be? **The Baby Shop** makes it easy with their natural gift baskets. Some are stuffed with organic baby food, others organic bath gear. T.O.-based **www.thinkgreenstore.com** has them too.

TOYS

We all love to find the perfect gift for the tots in our lives, the kind that secures you the title of "cool aunt" or "hip dad." Trouble is, most of the items on their wish lists are loaded with the types of toxins you don't want them playing with.

Plastics: Action figures and dolls are often moulded from that eco-villain PVC, considered the worst of all plastics. They might also contain lead and cadmium stabilizers, but it's impossible to tell just by looking at them. In the late '90s, Greenpeace found that 20% of PVC toys contained lead. Health Canada conceded that might be true but said the vast majority did not have "extractable lead that exceeded the international standard." Translation: not a lot of lead could be chewed or sucked out by young ones. Health Canada says it still monitors children's PVC toys for lead and cadmium.

If it's a soft, squishy toy destined to be drooled on and chewed by the youngest ones in your circle, the PVC was likely softened with potentially hormone-disrupting or carcinogenic phthalates, which have a nasty habit of off-gassing into the air. Even plain old modelling clay can be made with PVC, and it left phthalates on the hands of kids that played with it, according to *The Green Guide*'s toy report. Many will tell you the jury's still out on the plasticizer's toxicity, but Canada has prohibited its use in soothers and teethers, and the E.U. banned it altogether. Back in 1999, toy giant Mattel (maker of Barbie and Fisher-Price toys) announced it would be phasing out PVC and phthalates in toys for kids under three (but not for those four and up).

OUTDOOR PLAY SETS

If you've got a wooden outdoor play set that's more than a couple of years old (made in 2003 or before), chances are it's constructed with pressure-treated chromated copper arsenated (CCA) wood. Same goes for our gazebos, fences and decks. Sure, the wood is weather-resistant, but that arsenic leaches into the soil over time, and CCA wood has now been banned for any-thing residential, including play sets, picnic tables and boardwalks.

Health Canada isn't telling us to rip out our old backyard sets, but they are warning parents to make sure their little ones wash their hands thoroughly when they're done playing on CCA wood sets and in surrounding soil. Even though arsenic is really, really bad for us (it's a known human carcinogen), Health Canada says CCA wood doesn't pose any "unreasonable risks to public health" and anyone that's worried should just paint the play set with an oil-based semi-transparent coating once a year. But

Environmental Defence Canada tested 24 play-ground structures and surrounding soil for arsenic in Vancouver, Montreal, Toronto, Halifax, Edmonton, Winnipeg and Ottawa in 2003 and found that half of them were twice as high as federal guidelines (one was 12 times higher). Many municipalities across North America have since torn arsenic-laced playgrounds down (for the full report, see **www.environmental defence.ca/reports/arsenic.htm**).

If you choose to get rid of yours, whatever you do, don't toss the dismantled wood in a fire—you don't want to be inhaling that stuff. Treat it as toxic waste and bring it your munici-pal hazardous waste depot. For an arsenic home testing kit, head to **www.ewg.org/reports/ poisonwoodrivals/orderform.php**.

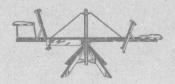

Brio and **Chicco** toys are fully PVC- and phthalate-free. **Lego** and **IKEA** toys are also PVC-free. For a full report grading toy makers on their PVC use, check out www.greenpeace.org/usa/news/2003-toy-report-card.

Stuffed Animals: It ain't just plastics that can spoil playtime. Teddy bears are stuffed with either synthetic petroleum-based fills or pesticide-drenched cottons. Many toys, including teddy, are sprayed with brominated fire retardants, the very kind turning up in breast milk. Eesh! Better to get all-natural kinds made with organic fibres, wool batting, recycled fabrics or tofu—yes, tofu. **Tofu Bear** and his buddies **SOYnia Bunny** and **Little Edamame Bear**

(Ed for short) are ultra-soft snugglers made with patented Soysilk. These cashmere-like plushies are woven from the waste created in the manufacture of tofu and are petroleum-free and biodegradable (www.tofubear.com).

Wood: Wooden toys look so old-fashioned, you just assume they must be good for the planet. But even a carved choo-choo train can be made with varnishes and paints high in air-polluting VOCs. Plus, you wouldn't want your kids' playhouse to be chopped from old-growth trees that provide habitat for other kids (like baby bears or baby baboons), now would you? Look for wooden toys and games crafted from sustainably harvested woods such as **rubber** or **bamboo** and sealed with non-toxic finishes.

Packaging: Don't even get me started on all the freakin' packaging that quadruples the size of the actual toy and ends up in landfills, a serious problem when you realize that Canadians spend just over $1.4 billion on toys annually. Look for toys with minimal packaging. Who needs a giant, oversized box for a toy half its size?

Look for toys with minimal packaging. Who needs a giant, oversized box for a toy half its size?

These boxes only take up more room on the truck, so more emission-spewing trips are needed to haul them to you. By making the packaging a touch smaller on a private-label

Look for toys with minimal packaging. Who needs a giant, oversized box for a toy half its size?

GREAT GREEN KIDS BOOKS

Spark lifelong interest in the powers of Mother Nature with books like *Exploring the Night Sky* and *Do Tornadoes Really Twist?* Bright, big, colourful books on bugs, birds or bears are great for younger children. And no budding environmentalist's library is complete without Dr. Seuss's *The Lorax*—it's a moving tale about the regretful Once-ler who long ago chopped down all the beautiful Truffula Trees in the land for profit. Don't worry: it's got a hopeful twist. For more hands-on inspiration, *Earth Book for Kids: Activities to Help Heal the Environment* talks about stuff like acid rain (and gives tips on testing your own rain for acid), as well as pesticides, endangered wildlife, water conservation and more. In the creative realm, *EcoArt! Earth-Friendly Art & Craft Experiences for 3- to 9-Year-Olds* suggests projects for twigs, weeds and pebbles, and gives info on recycling and composting. *Earth-Friendly Crafts for Kids: 50 Awesome Things to Make with Recycled Stuff* is another good book for smoggy days when you want to entertain the young 'uns inside.

brand of toys, Wal-Mart says it'll need 497 fewer freight containers and will save $2.4 million per year in freight costs, 3,800 trees and over 1,000 barrels of oil. Not bad. No word yet on Wal-Mart working to improve labour conditions in their supply factories around the world.

Eco-Friendly Toys: While earth-conscious toys aren't exactly taking the malls by storm, there is a decent selection out there if you know where to look. Many smaller toy stores carry all sorts of cool products. Look for handcrafted toxin-free Audubon Society–endorsed stuffed great horned owls, trumpeter swans and yellow-rumped warblers that put out authentic bird calls when you squeeze 'em (www.wildrepublic.com) or natural rubber lizards and dolphins made by Rep Pals. Plan Toys makes great dollhouses, boats, instruments and whole cities with wood from trees that no longer produce rubber (www.plantoys.com). And they're coated with a non-toxic finish. HaPe makes a cool line of memory, strategy and creative games from sustainable bamboo: young tots can balance monkeys in a tree, while older kids can fiddle with trapezoids (www.hapetoys.com/Bamboo.asp). Haba is another respected line of non-toxic wooden toys you can find in toy shops.

If you're willing to shop online, you'll find all kinds of cool stuff. Eco Toy Town has a truly inspiring collection of earth-friendly toys, including handmade multicultural dolls with hemp skin, recycled plastic innards and backpacks containing the seed of a tree, vegetable or flower waiting to be planted. They have a crate of stuffed vegetable teddy bears made of organic cotton, hemp Frisbees, garden flower and leaf presses and all kinds of cool co-operative board games (www.ecotoytown.com).

The Magic Cabin is another amazing website that makes me want to be a kid again (www.magiccabin.com). They have all sorts of whimsical eco-friendly toys made with natural or recycled materials, such as a recycled-tire horse swing, jungle safari play sets made of rubber wood, silk dress-up costumes, nature study kits, organic stuffed blossom babies with musical leaf beds, build-your-own-birdhouse kits, travel toys, outdoor toys, beach toys, instruments—you name it (note that not everything on this site is earth-friendly, so read product details carefully).

Eco-artware.com has the cutest little piglets, penguins, ducklings and elephants, which they call sweater critters (www.eco-artware.com). They're made of old wool sweaters and stuffed with shredded second-hand polyester. Too cute.

Toronto-based **Grassroots** carries soft toys stuffed with organic cotton, including a bunny, a doggy and a turtle—all with embroidered eyes for safety. You can brighten up bath time with a funny reclining rubber frog or a rubber ducky—both made of natural rubber, hand-painted with non-toxic paint. The store also carries a selection of toys for older kids, such as super-cool solar-powered car and windmill model kits and board games made from natural and recycled materials. These are feel-good games based on saving the earth co-operatively, rather than stealing property, sinking battleships and generally beating the crap out of your competitor (www.grassrootsstore.com).

Since sweatshops plague the toy biz as much as the clothing biz, there's one good way to ensure your gifts aren't bringing misery to others or to the earth: buy fair trade. **Ten Thousand Villages** carries wooden puzzles made by disadvantaged Sri Lankan youth using fast-growing plantation-grown wood and lead- and toxin-free paints. Or get a lovely cloth doll from Peru made with natural unbleached and vegetable-dyed cotton, a cheery stuffed cotton fish mobile to hang over your baby's crib, ornate kites, chess sets and more.

You can also troll through local guild shops, craft stores and galleries for handcrafted toys made by artisans in your area. The Canadian Crafts Federation has a link to all the provincial craft associations, who in turn have listings of craft shows (www.canadiancraftsfederation.ca). Of course, if you buy local, less fossil fuel is used in transport, and craftspeople often have an eye towards using less toxic sealants and natural materials. But ask questions to make sure materials were sourced sustainably!

SCHOOL

You'd think our institutions of learning would be exemplary role models for the thousands of kids who pass through their hallowed corridors. And yes, they might preach about the 3Rs and the perils facing endangered critters, but the reality is, when it comes to green issues,

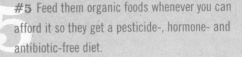

THE TOP 10 ENVIRONMENTALLY FRIENDLY THINGS YOU CAN DO FOR YOUR CHILDREN

#1 Walk or bike your kids to school or, if that's not feasible, ride your bikes on weekends—a family that bikes together saves the planet together!

#2 Keep them inside on smog-alert days (going for a car ride when there's a smog alert on is a big no-no!) And be honest: explain how pollution from cars, smokestacks and leaving the lights on makes it hard to breathe!

#3 Make sure their toys are PVC-free—you don't want them breathing in off-gassing plastic softeners.

#4 Show them that less is more: don't reward them by showering them with toys—the planet doesn't need the resource extraction, chemical pollution and landfill clogging that comes with making and eventually trashing toys.

#5 Feed them organic foods whenever you can afford it so they get a pesticide-, hormone- and antibiotic-free diet.

#6 Say no to high-fat, high-sugar, chemical-laden processed foods—there are plenty of natural alternatives, even for packaged kids' snacks.

#7 Use natural shampoos, creams and soaps: what you put on your tot's body is just as important as what you put in it.

#8 Create a non-toxic nursery or kids' room, full of earth-loving children's books.

#9 Resist the urge to swaddle your babe in landfill-clogging disposable diapers. If cloth is out of the question, get unbleached, chlorine-free throw-away diapers.

#10 Teach them to love nature. Take them to the park, on little hikes, or for picnics in conservation centres, where there are often all sorts of earth-friendly educational activities for young 'uns.

most schools need to be sent to detention. Sure, they talk about nourishing young minds, but they then poison them by spraying deadly pesticides on the grounds and mopping hormone-disrupting chemicals on the floors.

Whether you're a college kid trying to turn your campus on to solar power, a high-schooler hoping to get your team into organic shorts, a parent lobbying to get the poisons out of your tot's play area or a concerned teacher, you *can* convince your school to go green. You just need to get organized.

Pesticides: Toddlers crawl on it, teenagers get tackled face first onto it and college kids sit on it cross-legged as they chat about their upcoming philosophy exam and cute TAs. Grassy schoolyards see a lot of activity, so no matter how old the students (and teachers!) are, toxic pesticides shouldn't be sprayed on school grounds. Many are linked to cancer, neuro-logical damage and developmental problems. But the youngest are the most vulnerable since their organs can't easily eliminate toxins from their systems and their brains and nerv-ous systems are still developing. Whether used outside to keep grass bug-free or inside to keep ants and roaches under control, pesticides are a bad idea.

After several incidents of toxic pesticides such as Roundup wafting into school vents, kids swallowing insecticide granules and fumigants making students sick, Americans were kicking around a bill (the School Environment Protection Act) that would force schools to notify parents when pesticides were used on school property, but the bill just didn't have enough votes. No national effort is under way in Canada, although several municipalities have already banned the cosmetic use of pesticides within their borders. If your school falls outside these zones, you'll have to contact your school and/or your school board directly. Ask about their pesticide policy, demand that students and parents be notified before bug-killing chems are used and press them to establish an integrated pest management policy that looks at minimizing toxic chemicals or cutting them out entirely.

Recycling and Waste: No doubt, kids are messy, but Waste Reduction Week Canada says high schools generate about 16 kilograms of trash per student each and every week. Multiply that by the 5 million elementary and middle-school kids in the country, and we're talking 80,000 tons a week! If you're a teacher or a high-school or middle-school student and want to figure out how much your classroom's churn-ing out, just pull out some gloves and a scale and get digging through the trash. Figure out

High schools generate about **16 kilograms of trash** per student each and every week

131

IS YOUR SCHOOL MAKING TOO MUCH WASTE?

Is the cafeteria handing out disposable cutlery and plates? Make sure reusable forks and crockery are promoted.

Are there recycling bins in every class and hallway?

Is your school composting? Organize food scrap bins in the cafeteria and build a composter outside. You can spread all the highly nutritious soil it generates on school grounds. Teachers can even work with the class to build a composter from scratch (**www.wrwcanada.com/ 12_composters.htm**).

Are groundskeepers composting grass clippings? If not, the best thing to do is to just leave them on the grass, where they'll quickly break down, rather then carting them to landfill. For help on greening your school grounds, including funding for native trees and heirloom veggies, contact Evergreen (**www.evergreen.ca**), which has already funded the greening of over 560 schools.

Are printers and photocopiers loaded with 100% recycled paper, high in post-consumer content?

Are printer cartridges being recycled?

what your school is tossing unnecessarily and change it. University kids could try this tactic, but it might take while to canvas a whole campus. If your college isn't recycling, start a campus-wide campaign to instigate change. Try to ban hard-to-recycle plastics, like polystyrene, from your cafeteria. Set up a Swap Room, like University of Toronto's, where students can bring old computers, desks, and pretty much anything they want to unload that other students would be all too happy to have.

If you're packing a lunch for yourself or your kid, make sure to toss it into a reusable lunch bag or box. And instead of buying pre-packaged snacks, which tend to come in non-recyclable landfill-clogging wrapping, purchase crackers, trail mix or carrots in bulk and throw a handful into a small plastic food container.

Energy Use: In the spring of 2006, England's education secretary announced that all schools must become more carbon-neutral by 2020 and should be "models of energy efficiency and renewable energy." On top of that, the education secretary asked that schools serve up healthy, local and sustainable food and beverages, prepared on-site. Wow. If only we had a national mandate for that here. But why wait around when you can take action

Does your school cafeteria use fresh, local ingredients? Fat chance, right? It probably serves more frozen fries and greasy burgers than anything else. You might have trouble convincing your school to spend more cash on organic stuff, but you may be able to persuade them to cook locally. A fresh salad bar in the spring and fall could be good way to get students to eat more veggies. Look into setting up a farm-to-school program and an organic food garden on school property. For tools and tips, order FoodShare's report "Salad Bars in Schools: A Fresh Approach to Lunch" and download the Center for Ecoliteracy's "Rethinking School Lunch Guide" from **http://ecoliteracy.org**.

now to make sure your own school is cutting back on excess energy use? It'll save your school money: one out of every four dollars schools spend on electricity is needlessly wasted on inefficient boilers and leaving lights on, according to the U.S. Department of Energy.

Cleaning: You've heard of teachers cleaning kids mouths out with soap but this is ridiculous. Petrochemicals, bleaches and caustic solvents found in cleaning products—especially

TIPS TO HELP YOUR SCHOOL SAVE ON ELECTRICITY COSTS

#1 Make sure programmable thermostats are set to 25°C in the summer and 21°C in the winter.

#2 Be light bright: switch to ultra-efficient compact fluorescents.

#3 Post signs above monitors and switches reminding students to switch off computers and lights at lunch and recess. Consider installing motion sensors or timers on lights.

#4 Get schooled on the benefits of upgrading computers: Energy Star models can save up to $55 a year in energy and about 135 kilograms of carbon dioxide emissions each.

For more tips, see the U.S. Department of Energy site: **www.eere.energy.gov/buildings/info/schools**.

the powerful industrial types used in schools—have been linked to asthma, hormone disruption and allergies. How bad can they be? Well, in July of 1987, a fairly young (40-year-old) school janitor collapsed and later died after cleaning a bathroom floor with a product that contained butyl cellosolve (an ingredient still used in professional cleaners today) without any ventilation. The school fought it, but worker's comp ruled that it was indeed the chemicals that killed him, according to *Art Hazard News*.

Let's get real: your school's not likely to switch to baking soda and vinegar, and buying small consumer-sized cleaners from health stores isn't really an option for large schools with volume demands. Instead, give them a list of eco-friendly institutional cleaning products, such as Ontario-based **Eco-Max**'s scent-free multi-purpose cleaner, free of smog-inducing VOCs and made of biodegradable, renewable ingredients (available at www.eco-max.ca).

E-groups: Getting your school to embrace the greener way can be about as easy as getting a class full of five year olds to sit still. It's even harder when you're just one person, so join forces with a group of like-principled people. If you're in university, look into whether an environmental campus group is already up and running. The national Sierra Youth Coalition runs the Sustainable Campuses Project, with wings in every region of the country, to unite students who care about climate change, campus sustainability and other big-picture issues. Plus, the coalition links students to eco-groups in universities across Canada.

High-schoolers and middle-schoolers can form an environmental club with the help of a geography or earth sciences teacher. Start by assessing your school's impact on the earth by measuring its ecological footprint (learn how at www.globalfootprints.org). Then pick an area in which you think your school is slacking. Do your homework on the issue before meeting with school staff and making your pitch. Just because you're young doesn't mean they won't listen to you. Tons of kids across Canada have convinced their schools to buy

SCHOOL BUSES

School buses may be the ultimate form of car-pooling, but they also choke out tons of sooty diesel emissions linked to smog and increased asthma rates. Not to mention all the idling they do as they wait for tardy students. Encourage your kids to walk or bike to school—if they can get their friends to join them they'll not only be having fun, but they'll be getting great exercise and helping the environment to boot!

sweatshop-free uniforms, for instance. For tips on organizing your own campaign, check out Maquila Solidarity Network's action guide "How to Become a No Sweat School" (www.maquilasolidarity.org or www.studentsagainstsweatshops.org).

If the PTA isn't interested, concerned parents can start their own coalitions with other green moms and dads who want formaldehyde-free desks in the classrooms and organic milk and local salad greens in the cafeteria. Some school boards already have parent environment networks—be sure to ask. Just like the kids, you need to do your homework before you talk to school staff. Draft a policy you'd like to see in place, and once you've met, work together on coming up with a written action plan.

GOOD WEBSITES TO HELP YOU GREEN YOUR SCHOOL

Waste Reduction Week Canada: This organization is responsible for, surprise, Waste Reduction Week, held every October. Its site has all sorts of great resources geared towards teachers, including extensive waste reduction planning kits, homework and activities (**www.wrwcanada.com**).

Go Green Initiative (U.S.): Started by a PTA prez, this org also focuses on waste reduction in schools. Its site includes planning guides, budget worksheets and a PR kit (**www.gogreeninitiative.org**).

Alliance to Save Energy's Green Schools Program (U.S.): This site has tips that will help get your school's energy consumption down by 5% to 15% (**www.ase.org/section/program/greenschl**).

School Supplies: Whether you're in your last year of high school or plugging away at your Ph.D., you can bet that there are millions of students across the country just like you buying copious amounts of correction fluids, plastic binders and lily-white ancient-forest-filled notebooks every August and September. And I'd wager that few have considered the ecological ramifications of losing yet another pencil. More than 14 billion of the damn things are manufactured every year, not to mention all the highlighters, pens, and crayons that students go through on an annual basis.

Paper Mate makes **EarthWrite**-branded pencils using 100% recycled content. **Frogfile**, out of Bowan Island, B.C., sells slick recycled plastic pens with non-toxic ink, as well as birch/beech wood pens made with industry leftovers (www.frogfile.com). Toronto-based

Grassroots also sells cool pens made of sustainable wood and refillable corn-based bioplastic instead of petroleum products (www.grassrootsstore.com). FYI, refillable pens or pencils are generally better than single-use ones.

For paper, look for 100% post-consumer, acid- and chlorine-free lined notebooks. If you prefer the flexibility of loose-leaf, Frogfile sells a cool binder made of recycled chipboard and cloth binding, another made of unused or defective circuit boards and yet another slick and sturdy one made of old tires. For printing, look for 100% post-consumer paper. Mainstream shops such as Grand & Toy, Staples/Business Depot and Office Depot are now carrying some. If your local store doesn't, be sure to request it. Note that Weyerhaeuser has been slammed by the Rainforest Action Network and Forest Ethics for destructive forestry practices.

As for markers and highlighters, I'd tell you to give them up cold turkey, but I have to concede that I was a highlighter junky in undergrad. If you're a slave to the yellow wand, at least look for the refillable water-based type so you're not tossing out a non-recyclable plastic marker every two weeks.

Last but not least, you need something to carry your gear to class in. Both Frogfile and

---

THE SEEDS FOUNDATION

Hey teach, looking for tools to tell your kids about our personal and societal responsibility to care for the environment? That's the very mission of the SEEDS Foundation (www.seeds foundation.ca). The organization has put together education resources on climate change, a bird conservation challenge and a nifty water conservation challenge. But it's perhaps best known for its Green School program for elementary and junior high students, which teaches kids to take action to help the planet both at school and at home. The Green School kit comes with special materials such as trophies, certificates, banners, a hallway progress chart and an environmental log book with tips on setting up classroom environmental action reps, PA announcements and more. The more projects your school takes on, the better its score. Over 8,000 elementary schools across the country have already gone through the program. Some schools, such as Mapleton in St. Andrews, Manitoba; Selkirk in Whitehorse, NWT; and Haldane in Chase, B.C., were really gung-ho about saving the planet and completed over 2,000 greening projects through SEEDS. Forget A's, top grades here get Earth awards. Now we're talkin'.

BE AN ANCIENT FOREST—FRIENDLY SCHOOL

Is your school clear-cutting Canada's 10,000-year-old boreal forest with every piece of paper students and teachers use to print? With a soccer field's worth of trees being knocked down every two seconds around the globe, we need to know whether our centres of learning are doing all they can to protect Canada's precious resource. Make sure your school is buying paper products, including tissue and toilet paper, with a high recycled content. For more info, including a shopper's guide to ancient forest–friendly paper products, check out **www.greenpeace.ca**.

U.S.-based **Green Earth Office Supplies** (www.greenearthofficesupply.com) sell 100% post-consumer recycled rubber school bags and messenger bags, as well as every green school supply you could dream of. (FYI, some **Mountain Equipment Co-op** stores across Canada will repair backpacks, for a fee.) You can also go the used route and check out your neighbourhood army surplus store or second-hand shop.

> some Mountain Equipment Co-op stores across Canada **will repair backpacks,** for a fee

LICE

A lice alert's been issued, and your little ones have started scratching. Now what? Once the bugs strike, most people run to the drugstore for a bottle of any louse-killing drops or shampoo they can find, but beware: those are dripping with nasty chemical pesticides.

Three types of over-the-counter topical treatments are common in Canada. One contains pyrethrins, derived from chrysanthemum blossoms, which aren't so bad. Those allergic to ragweed, however, could have a reaction to them.

The second kind, permethrin, isn't even allowed on bug-repellent clothing for campers in Canada. So why are we rubbing this possible carcinogen and suspected hormone disrupter on our childrens' heads?

If you think that's bad, open door number three. Lindane, a neurotoxin from the same family of chemical pesticides as DDT, has been banned for agricultural use in over 50 countries! Canada has been slagged for still allowing it on a limited number of crops, as well as on people's scalps. The U.S. Environmental Protection Agency recently banned lindane except as a treatment for head lice, which has pissed off both children's advocates and environmentalists. Health

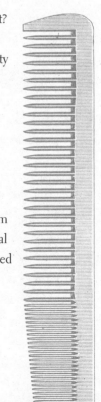

Canada says infants, children under six, pregnant and nursing women and elderly people with a history of seizures should not use products containing lindane (unless their doctors okay it). Do you get the feeling it's toxic?

To make matters worse, lice attacks are a bit like bad horror movie sequels: they keep coming back, even when you use the strong stuff. Some lice are reported to be resistant to all three products.

Instead of committing yourself to chemical bath after chemical bath, douse your house with **Lice Squad**'s all-natural enzyme-based green house cleaner (www.licesquad.com). It works on fleas and bedbugs too. Lots of schools and camps actually turn to the Lice Squad. The company makes highly touted natural enzyme-based drops and mousses called Nitpickers Secret and Not Nice to Lice.

The Canadian Pediatric Society cites an Israeli study that had success killing lice with a product called **Hair Clean 1-2-3**, a spray containing coconut oil, anise oil and ylang-ylang oil (www.quantumhealth.com).

Some home remedies recommend covering your head in a thick layer of petroleum jelly, olive oil or mayonnaise overnight. Unfortunately, these treatments won't do much but make you never want to eat mayonnaise again. Tea tree oil is often prescribed in alt circles, but the astringent can be pretty drying and hard on the skin with prolonged use.

No matter what, you'll never completely get rid of lice unless you remove the nits (lice eggs) near the scalp, so you'll need a good nit comb and a lot of patience. To prevent spread or recontamination, make sure to wash all your clothing, bedding and towels in hot water.

PETS

We cuddle and, yes, even clothe them like they're our furry children and tend to think of pets as one of the family, but in the process we're turning the poor things into nature's outlaws. With all the plastic bags used for poop-and-scoop and kitty litter that we toss every week, flea control chems and not-so-earth-conscious edibles, our pets are becoming little eco-monsters. Luckily, there any many ways to get Mittens back to her natural roots.

Litter: Let's start with the back end. Whether in a box, cage or backyard, all animals do it. In fact, roughly 200,000 tons of pet waste (including litter, cage chips, etc) are trashed every year in this country. Many of us fill our feline "powder rooms" with chemically-scented, non-biodegradable clays that hog landfill space. Unless, of course, your municipality accepts kitty litter in its municipal composting program—and few do. Toronto is one of the exceptions. And if you flush it because the label says you can, don't be fooled into thinking it just disappears. It ends up being filtered out at the water treatment plant and sent to landfill.

As convenient as it seems, the clumping kind is the worst for your dear Fluffy. (If it clumps in the box, it can clump in his belly and make him sick, an especially dangerous scenario for kittens.) Most clay litters, clumping or not, kick up silica dust, which can cause respiratory problems in both cats and humans. (Pregnant women should not change litter at all to avoid potential exposure to parasites.)

Pregnant women should not change litter at all to avoid potential exposure to parasites

There are ways to bring balance back to your litter box. **MewsPrint** and **Yesterday's News** are made of recycled paper pellets. For the scoopable variety, try corn-based **World's Best Cat Litter**. **Swheat Scoop** is flushable and biodegradable, as well as clay-, chemical- and fragrance-free, and can even be added to home composters once scooped. President's Choice **PC Green Twice As Absorbent Clumping Cat Litter** is made of 96% processed corn cob (the other 4% consists of "fragrance" and a mysterious proprietary "de-dusting agent"). Hamster and bunny owners should look for cage liners made of recycled or reclaimed wood, such as **CareFresh**. These products are available at most pet stores.

Poop and Scoop: Dog lovers go through a lot of plastic bags in their lifetime. If you're walking your pooch three times daily and he's got an active digestive system and lives to be, say, 16, that's 17,520 bags worth! Now, doesn't it seem silly to put perfectly biodegradable dog poop into a bag that takes over 100 years to break down? Make scooping more earth-friendly with biodegradable and compostable bags. **Bio Bag**'s Pooper bags take only 40 days to break down in a good compost environment (www.biobag.ca). You can use these bags when you scoop out your kitty litter too.

Cleaning: Need to clean up an accident without resorting to noxious chemicals? **Nature Clean** makes a pet odour and stain remover spray, as does **Earth Friendly**. **Zeolite** is a non-toxic, negatively charged mineral that absorbs barn-sized odours, so it should work for your critter. If Maggie got herself a little dirty in the process and needs a bath, look for an all-natural pet shampoo made without unpronounceable chemicals and synthetic fragrances.

139

Food: Of course, our loyal friends need to eat. Mine reminds me of this within hours of his last meal. Trouble is, most conventional pet food brands are loaded with additives and preservatives and support the bottom (read "rancid") end of the not-so-earth- or animal-friendly meat industry. If you see the word "by-product" in your ingredient list, it's basically telling you that your pet is getting all those bits humans wouldn't touch. The food could even include 4-D animals: dead, diseased, dying or disabled, as well as restaurant grease. Sadly, euthanized shelter pets can also make the cut. In fact, the National Animal Control Association in the U.S. has a policy that states: "Dead animal disposal can include cremation facilities, landfill burial, or rendering" (as in meat rendering plants). Ick.

> **If you see the word "by-product"** in your ingredient list, it's basically telling you that your pet is getting all those bits humans wouldn't touch

"Meat meal" is basically mysterious odds and ends that have been stripped of their fat and water content, but if it's got a specific animal attached to it (like lamb meal or chicken meal), *The Green Guide*'s pet product report says it's not quite as bad.

Pet lovers might be a little disturbed to know that pet food is often tested on animals. And that doesn't mean they gave it to a few happy free-roaming pets to see if they liked the flavour—no, we're talking about dogs confined to cages in research labs. PETA has a list of which companies steer clear of such testing, but it's American, so it might not cover all of our Canuck brands. If you're curious, call up a pet food company and ask if they test their products on animals; if they say they don't, ask if their policy against testing applies to sub-contracted labs.

Several mainstream pet food makers are hopping on the alt health bandwagon and marketing their lack of dyes or the addition of antioxidants. It's a good start, but there are better options. In fact, there are too many to name! But here are a few. **Karma**'s at the top with its 95% organic pet food (it even has organic free-range chicken and organic kamut! Find a local source at www.karmaorganic.com). **Wellness** is loaded with veggies and human-grade meat. **Wysong** and **Solid Gold** are other good brands.

Natural pet food is so hot right now that even celebrities have infiltrated the world of kibble (see **Paul Newman's Own Organics** and **Dick Van Patten's Natural Balance Pet Foods**, both of which have respectable ingredient lists). Even the bigger pet store chains carry a slew of premium alt-meals now. Just make sure to read labels carefully and look for the purest ingredient lists.

If you have the time, you can design your pet's menu from scratch. It's the best way to know what's actually in your dog or cat's food bowl and can be exceptionally nutritious if you do it right. You'll need a good cookbook to get started, but don't reach for just any old one filled with cute pet photos and unhealthy or excessively elaborate recipes (I mean, are dogs really meant to eat macaroni and cheese?). *Dr. Pitcairn's New Complete Guide to Natural Health for Dogs and Cats* has some great homemade diet suggestions for pets, as well as tips on tending to your pet naturally.

Fleas: As soon as you see your pet scratching that hard, you know you're done for. But you don't want to reach for commercial flea collars and powders because they're loaded with potent pesticides that actually poison many animals and can be toxic to your kids. Take organophosphates, for instance. This old-school family of pesticides (which includes chlorpyrifos, malathion and diazinon) is designed to mess with insect nervous systems, and—wouldn't you know it—they also have the potential to damage the nervous systems of our pets, triggering seizures, twitching and in some cases death.

Even more common are collars, sprays, dips, spot treatments and shampoos containing pyrethrins, which can be especially toxic for cats. Yes, some may be derived from chrysanthemum blossoms, but synthetic versions called pyrethroids (including permethrin) ain't natural. (See page 137 for more on permethrin.)

No surprise, then, that most vets have moved away from both types of flea control systems. They now tend to focus on newer-generation products such as Advantage and Revolution. Veterinarians and the product manufacturers swear by their safety and insist they won't harm a hair on your pet's head. But even though they're considered less toxic, you'll still find plenty of pet owners who insist their dog or cat's sudden vomiting and shaking came on right after such flea treatments. Something to keep in mind.

So what's a flea-infested owner to do? First, bathe your pet in mild soapy water to drown any existing fleas. You can also sprinkle Muffy or Buster with all-natural **diatomaceous earth** (fine white powdery fossilized algae that grinds away at the fleas' exoskeleton). Vacuum your house thoroughly and often, even daily, to remove eggs, larvae and adults, making sure to vacuum furniture (both under and over), baseboards and cracks and crevices. Throw some diatomaceous earth or borax in the vacuum bag to kill any eggs and sprinkle some around your house, as well, under rugs and furniture.

But don't stop at your pet and your living room. Those fleas are coming in from some-where, and you might as well fend them off as best as you can in your backyard. Sprinkle diatomaceous earth everywhere and release microscopic nematodes, which prey on flea lar-vae and pupae (pick up nematodes at garden supply stores).

You can order natural flea-repelling shampoos and sprays, as well as remedies, from www.onlynaturalpet.com if you can't find any at your local pet store.

Natural Health: Watching our pets struggle with illness or injury is painful for puppy lovers and feline fiends alike. But there are alternatives to conventional vets and their high-potency pharma treatments: a growing list of practitioners are dedicated to holistic animal care.

You can use the herbal home remedies that keep our own bodies humming to help furry companions back to health. Boost weakened immune systems by adding fresh crushed garlic (for dogs *not* cats), echinacea and powdered vitamin C to your pet's food. For older animals, stir in other antioxidants such as liquid vitamin E and grape seed extract. Stave off digestive difficulties and boost nutrient absorption by sprinkling probiotics on their dinner. Squeezing in capsules of salmon or herring oil can soothe itchy skin and dandruff.

When more complicated illness arises, alt vets can prescribe homeopathic and herbal remedies and offer chiropractic adjustments. Some even provide animal-friendly acupunc-ture to treat sore hips, stubborn urinary tract trouble and seizures.

To fill a pet's prescription, you can find a slew of natural remedies specially formulated for animals at some pet stores. But beware: they are often merely marked-up versions of human herbs. If you opt to treat your tabby with self-prescribed human health store goods, make sure to contact your vet first to find out which dosage is best.

WHERE THE HEART IS

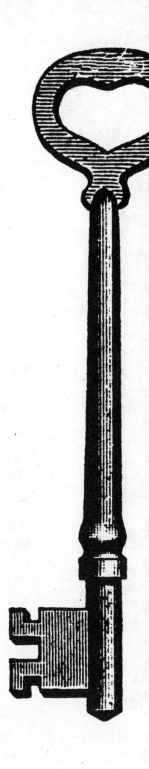

There's no place like home.

The damn cliché is such a truism we even weave it into doormats and cowboy songs. It is, after all, where your family is (even if it's just you and the cat), along with your cushy couch and the remote. Too bad home is also where the toxins are. Yes, lurking in your cozy abode are some serious pollutants that can make the indoor air quality in a house worse than a smog alert day. They're hiding in your cookware, cleaning products, coffee table and candles. They're even building up in household dust (which is a problem when you dust as infrequently as I've been known to) and settling into your tissues.

Now, stop thinking about how our houses impact us and consider how what we do between those four walls weighs on the world. Those long showers, the loads of warm-water laundry, the blazing lights left on at all hours of the day—they all consume gobs of polluting electricity and precious water resources we can't afford to waste. Let's not forget that the planet is also our home. You don't want me to have to use another tired catchphrase—you know the one about how you can never go home again.

KITCHEN

Some sort of instinctual pull must draw us close to our food source—hence, the tendency for house parties to turn into kitchen parties (I've conducted my own scientific studies on this one) and for kitchens to trump comfy family rooms as the centre of activity in many homes. Even if you can't cook to save your life, and toast and fried eggs are as creative as you get, you need to know how to get sizzling, get clean and get out with the least damage to your stomach and the planet.

Cookware and Bakeware: Ever charred the bottom of your non-stick pan? Who hasn't? The problem is, you're not just offending your taste buds: overheated non-stick-coated pans can release toxic fumes that'll literally kill a canary if you have one in your kitchen. Teflon says such high-temperature burning doesn't happen under normal circumstances, and the stuff is perfectly safe otherwise. Nonetheless, 95% of humans have the chemical in our bloodstreams. It turns out PFOA, the compound used to manufacture the coatings, beats out nasty pesticides like DDT when it comes to indestructibility in the ecosystem (what an honour). Quite disconcerting when you consider that nearly a dozen studies have tied it to thyroid damage and a scientific advisory panel to the U.S. Environmental Protection Agency (EPA) concluded in January 2006 that PFOA is a "likely human carcinogen."

95% of humans have the chemical tied to non-stick surfaces **in our bloodstreams**

Sadly, we've surrounded ourselves with it, putting it on cookware, burger wrappers, popcorn bags, french fry cartons and candy packaging. And even though polar bears have never made muffins or fried eggs, the chemical is turning up in their systems—and in most other wildlife—at alarming levels.

The EPA has recently asked major corporate manufacturers of the substance to phase out 90% of their usage by 2010 and to ditch the compound entirely by 2015. Health Canada has banned the import of new versions of chemicals in the same family, but old stuff is still allowed. So while the government hasn't told us with any clarity to ditch our non-stick woks, whisks, colanders and waffle irons, environmentalists are saying there's no better time than the present to remove the chemical from your life, since every molecule you get in your system will be with you for life.

Unfortunately, cities don't have special programs in place for the safe disposal of non-stick cookware. But you can always mail it to the federal health minister's office with a little note that says, "Phase out PFOA today."

Cookware Solutions: If you're not up to the role of human guinea pig, you might want to switch to **stainless steel**. It's a little stickier, but much safer. Just add a little more cooking oil. **Cast iron skillets** (made, in part, of recycled scrap iron, filtered of contaminants) are another sound choice—plus, a little iron in your diet is actually good for you! Keep it rust-free by seasoning it with coconut oil or another oil high in saturated fat.

If you've got a wallet full of cash and are willing to spend it on your cookware, **lightweight titanium** is a good option. Some pans are pure titanium with non-stick titanium dioxide surfaces; these are considered non-toxic. Others are titanium-coated aluminum. But take note that some titanium pans out there get their non-stick surface from the same chemicals used in Teflon. Talk about sneaky! Make sure to read the fine print and the FAQ (frequently asked questions) section of corporate websites.

Copper and aluminum are great heat conductors, so they warm up quickly and save you energy, but because of health concerns, aluminum and copper pots should always be coated with stainless steel (a little copper isn't bad for you, says Health Canada, but too much of it can be poisonous, and safe daily exposure doses haven't really been determined).

Glass is a great renewable source and is valued by natural medical practitioners and people with enviro-sensitivities because it's inert and is perfect for stovetop cooking or baking.

Bakeware Solutions: Glass and cast iron aren't exactly on the table for anyone with a penchant for muffin-mixing. And most of the stuff on the market is coated with non-stick chemicals. Those little paper muffin cup liners might create a barrier between your cranberry muffin and the tin, but they tend to be made with bleached virgin paper, and they're disposable—tsk, tsk.

So what is a conscious baker to do? Well, you have a few options. **Ceramics** are popular for bakeware, although you have to make sure the glaze is lead-free (see sidebar for more info). **Stainless steel cake moulds and tart dishes** do exist, but they can be hard to find unless you head online. And **silicone** isn't just for *Baywatch* babes. Nope, this non-toxic, manmade fusion of silicon (basically sand) and oxygen is now being moulded into muffin trays, sheets, bread pans and even oven mitts. It looks kind of freaky, as manufacturers tend add bright dyes to it, but I've yet to dig up any dirt on this stuff. It's available pretty much anywhere that sells bakeware. Silicone/fibreglass-blended baking sheets such as Silpat are also safe.

Perhaps the earthiest option for the oven is **stone bakeware**. Stone bakeware is a lot like your ceramic mug, but the clay is cooked at a higher temperature, making it stronger, chip-resistant, watertight and oven-safe. The good stuff is unglazed and is the same colour as terra cotta. But like anything that's mined, clay isn't without environmental repercussions, especially in developing countries such as India, where clay mining has been accused of draining water tables and polluting the air. **Pampered Chef**'s line of high-quality stonewear is made with more sustainable American clay, and it comes with a three-year unconditional guarantee, so even if you drop and crack it, they'll give you a new one (www.pamperedchef.com). Plus, after you cook on its porous surface once or twice with a fatty food, it becomes naturally non-stick for life.

Aluminum Foil, Baking Trays and Cans: We put everything from beans to beer in aluminum cans, and traces can be found in items such as baking powder, antacids, buffered aspirin and hemorrhoid meds. We consume about 10 milligrams of aluminum a day, and most of that comes from food, says Health Canada, adding that less than 1% is actually

LEAD IN THE KITCHEN

Think crappy baking skills are behind your lead-heavy muffins? Check your bakeware: the glaze on ceramic bakeware and cookware tends to contain lead, as does old china and—surprise, surprise—lead crystal (which most of us know as just crystal—you know, the sparkly stuff you're afraid to break). Canadian regulations limit lead content in glassware and glazes on ceramics used in preparing, serving or storing food, but it's still in there. You might want to ditch dishes that are heavily scratched or chipped.

Health Canada says acidic foods such as fruit juice, wine and pickles boost lead leaching. Come on, doesn't everyone use their crystal glassware for wine? To be fair, Health Canada says the amount of lead that leaches into your wine over the course of a dinner still falls under maximum limits, but if you kept it in a crystal decanter for a few weeks you'd be sucking back over 100 times the accepted levels—not to mention rancid wine.

Older china and imported ceramics have been a source of lead poisoning, so beware. Health Canada says you shouldn't serve up any food on lead tableware to children or pregnant women, and you should soak new crystal in vinegar for a day and rinse before using.

Fair-trade lead-free dishes are available at Ten Thousand Villages locations. CorningWare ceramic bakeware is also lead-free. If you're uncertain, just ask.

absorbed by the body. Pots and pans give us 1 or 2 milligrams daily. Foil, I imagine, accounts for much less, unless you're baking off it at every meal and sucking on the stuff.

Aluminum has been tied to Alzheimer's, Lou Gehrig's and Parkinson's, as well as anemia and glucose intolerance. So, should you stop using aluminum foil and trays? Health Canada says, "Studies have shown that the amount of aluminum that leaches from aluminum cookware and aluminum foil into food is generally negligible." Did anyone else catch the word "generally" in there? Leafy foods and acidic ones such as citrus and tomatoes absorb the most, says Health Canada. And the longer food is stored or simmered in aluminum, the more of the metal it'll suck up.

As for the planet's health, well, as you'd predict, mining aluminum (or bauxite ore) ain't pretty: vegetation is stripped, habitat lost, soil eroded. Since aluminum smelting is so damn energy-intensive, smelters are often situated near cheap and dirty power sources—coal and destructive dam projects. And aluminum production gives as much as it takes, emitting about 95 million tons of greenhouse gases industry-wide in 2005 and dumping massive amounts of caustic waste.

Aluminum Solutions: The good news is that aluminum foil sheets and containers are 100% recyclable, but not every municipality accepts them, so ask. Most accept foil trays, though. Aluminum is actually the most recycled metal on earth, and the industry says a third of all aluminum in use comes from recycled sources. Environmental Defence, by the way, advises the use of tin foil over plastic wrap any day. You can boost your green factor by getting 100% recycled foil, called **If You Care**, at some health stores or online (www.ifyoucare.com). Ninety-five percent less energy goes into making the Scandinavian import than non-recycled foil. That's true for all recycled aluminum products, so all you urban myth circulators trashing the recycling of aluminum cans saying it takes more energy to recycle them than it does to make new ones are flat-out wrong.

> The good news is that **aluminum foil sheets and containers are 100% recyclable,** but not every municipality accepts them, so ask

Plastic Wrap: Can you imagine the excitement in 1950s homes when Dow first introduced the ultra-clingy polyvinylidene chloride (PVDC) film, Saran Wrap? It stuck to everything: bowls, pots and especially itself. The stuff even had patriotic roots, having first been sprayed on fighter planes during the war to protect them against salty sea spray.

For years, most plastic wrap was either PVDC or PVC. And, as I've said before, PVC is considered the most toxic of plastics. It can emit dangerous dioxins when being made and during incineration. On its own, it's quite rigid, so softening chemicals called phthalates are added to make it nice and pliable so you can stretch it across your bowl of leftover pancake batter. As much as a third of PVC and 10% of PVDC wrap can be made up of the potentially hormone-disrupting plasticizers, which have been found to drift into food. In fact, in the late '90s, *Consumer Reports* tested various grocery-store cheeses and found that those that came in manufacturer's plastic wrapping or individually wrapped slices tested negative, but those wrapped in PVC cling wrap had very high levels of the plasticizer DEHA (found to cause developmental problems in rats).

Plastic Wrap Solutions: You can't tell from the packaging, but major manufacturers such as **Glad** and **Saran** have switched to much less controversial low-density polyethylene (or LDPE), which is less clingy but phthalate-free. If you're unsure about your brand of choice, call the company info line. **Saran Premium Wrap** is now also chlorine-free as part of "the company's commitment to use more environmentally responsible ingredients in our products."

PVC can emit dangerous dioxins when being made and during incineration

Even if you're using less environmentally damaging plastics such as LDPE, note that all plastics have eco-ramifications (they all come from petroleum, for starters). Plus, they don't really biodegrade, and plastic wrap isn't recyclable (see page 309 for more on plastics). So try to find alternatives whenever possible. A piece of fruit sliced in half can be put, cut side down, on a plate (and sprinkled with lemon juice to prevent it from browning). Plates can also be used to cover bowls or other dishes. **Tupperware**, **Gladware** and **Ziploc** containers, which are phthalate- and PVC-free, are better than plastic wrap, since they can be washed and reused. **Pyrex**, **IKEA** and **Crate and Barrel** carry all kinds of glass storage containers in different shapes and sizes, so there's no excuse. It's time to break the cling-wrap habit, folks, because it *is* just a habit.

Refrigerators: No one wants to dole out cash for new appliances, but older models can really hold your energy bills hostage. If you're in the market for a new fridge, the Energy Star label is an easy indicator that what you're buying is more energy-efficient. A fridge with this label uses 40% less energy than conventional models sold in 2001—a good thing, considering that 20% of your energy bills go to keeping your milk cold and your ice frozen. A third of us also have a second fridge that's about 20 years old tucked away in the basement or garage. These babies are serious power-leachers and should be turned in to the conservation police. Some municipalities will even pay you money to do so.

Ovens: Like to slave over a hot stove? When it comes to ovens, gas ranges are more efficient than electric, but neither come with Energy Star ratings. Certainly the use of natural gas is cleaner, in terms of greenhouse gases, than getting your electric power from a coal plant. When you're shopping for a new oven, you can determine which one is the best bet by comparing the amount of kilowatts used per year, listed on the EnerGuide sticker. (This is different from the Energy Star label. It simply tells you how many kilowatts an appliance uses, whereas Energy Star puts its seal only on something that's more energy-efficient.)

High-tech electric ovens without coils are generally more efficient than the old-fashioned type, but they can take longer to heat up. The Office of Energy Efficiency says spending a little more on self-cleaning ovens (because of the extra insulation in them) or convection ovens (because they cook foods faster) will save you money in the long run, thanks to energy saving.

Microwave Ovens: No matter how often we use these things, we're never totally comfortable with them (you can tell by the way people take four paces back after they press "start"). Despite their omnipresence in North American kitchens, controversy still clings to microwaves. The official line is that the radiation is non-ionizing (which means it's not related to the cancer-causing ionizing radiation used in X-rays), but a tiny amount of radiation is indeed emitted from these machines. It falls below national safety standards, but it still freaks some people out. To avoid leaks, make sure the door's seal and hinges aren't damaged or dirty. And keep anyone with an older-generation pacemaker away from old microwaves. The electromagnetic field emitted could trip them up. No joke. The shielded design of modern pacemakers and microwaves is said to prevent this startling side effect.

Government websites insist that microwaving does not affect the nutrient content of food, and many studies concur with that statement, but a handful of others demonstrate just the opposite. A study out of Stanford U found that microwaving frozen breast milk drastically diminishes the amount of infection-fighting agents naturally present in mother's milk. Another out of Japan in the late '90s concluded that microwaving zaps the vitamin B_{12} content of food. A more recent study, published in the *Journal of the Science of Food and*

THE TOP 10 ENERGY-SAVING COOKING TIPS

#1 If you're baking in ceramic or glass, you can reduce the oven temperature by 25°F (20°C) and still cook the food in the same amount of time (these materials conduct and retain heat better than metal).

#2 Keep your metal burners clean so they reflect heat better. (Same goes for your refrigerator coils and cooling your food, by the by.)

#3 Make sure to match pan size to the element you're cooking on. A small pot on a large burner is just wasting energy. And small burners use less energy.

#4 Who says pasta needs to cook at a raging boil for 15 straight minutes? The package instructions for Tinkada rice noodles tell you to cook them for 1 or 2 minutes in boiling water, then turn off the stove and cover the pot for 20 minutes. It only takes 5 minutes longer, and saves energy. You can do this with basically any pasta—just test it after 15 minutes until you figure out the timing for your particular brand of penne or linguine.

#5 Keep a lid on it (your cooking, that is). You're just letting all that heat escape otherwise, unless, of course, it's integral to the recipe, like a reduction sauce.

#6 Smaller is always better: Think toaster oven over electric oven and hand-held blender over food processor.

#7 Human power obviously burns much cleaner than electricity, so consider a manual coffee grinder, a hand beater and a plain old knife over fancy plug-in gadgets.

#8 Rice cookers and slow cookers (Crock-Pots), are much more efficient at whipping up your dinner than stovetop methods. Just make sure you stick to Teflon-free models and look for those with stainless steel interiors.

#9 If you're cooking with frozen food, make sure to thaw it first (unless otherwise indicated); it'll take longer to cook that fish or whatnot if it's still half-frozen.

#10 Curiosity kills your electrical bills. Keep your oven door closed as much as possible while you're cooking. Peeking inside causes at least 20% of the heat to escape, and the poor oven has to waste energy warming itself up again.

You think you're doing a good thing by saving your old yogurt and margarine tubs and using them to store food, and you are. But whatever you do, do not heat leftovers stored in old plastic tubs in the microwave. The plastics will leach into your grub! Same goes for takeout containers. Transfer the food to a microwave-safe dish, or better yet, throw it in the toaster oven or a frying pan to get it sizzling again.

Agriculture in 2003, found that microwaves nuke out 97% of the flavonoids in broccoli. So even though microwaving your food is more energy-efficient than cooking it in the oven (75% more, according to the Ontario Ministry of Energy), that's not enough to convince most environmentalists and health nuts that using the contraptions is a wise idea.

Dishwashers: Ever wondered what's more water-intensive, hand-washing or dishwashing? Most of us would guess that anything done by hand (and is so damn time-consuming) would win this battle, but researchers at the University of Bonn in Germany decided to settle the bet once and for all with cold hard science. And guess what? Modern dishwashers prevailed, using half the energy, one-sixth the water and less soap, to boot. Not sure who the winner would be if they compared hand-washing to an old dishwasher from the '80s. New Energy Star–qualified types, by the way, use 25% less energy than basic models.

Ever wondered what's more water-intensive, hand-washing or dishwashing?

DISHWASHER TIPS

#1 Sure, scrape food off your dish before you toss it in the dishwasher, but there's no need for all this crazy double-washing business. If your dishwasher can't clean a layer of gravy off your plate, you need a new dishwasher.

#2 If you have an air-dry button, use it: your dishes will dry just as well without a blast of heat (and you'll use 20% less energy overall). It just takes a little longer. If your machine doesn't have an air-dry option, no biggie—just open the door after the final rinse.

#3 Don't start your dishwasher until it's full. No wasteful half-loads!

No matter how you wash your dishes, get low-flow aerators for your taps. And if you are your own dishwasher, turn the water off while you lather up or, if you've got a whole whack of dishes to catch up on, fill one sink for washing and one sink for rinsing. Might as well save water anywhere you can, especially knowing about 20% of the water used in your house is used in the kitchen, and most of it goes into washing dishes.

WATER WISE

To calculate how much water your house is wasting, both indoors and out, visit www.h2ouse.net.

BATHROOM

Ever had the water cut off to your bathroom? Panic tends to set in fairly quickly. No showers, no flushing, no washing your hands. Did I mention no flushing? We're in there many times a day and take all that free-flowing water for granted. Typical Canadians! And that water might come cheap to homeowners (Canadians pay some of the lowest water bills in the world, which is partly why we're so wasteful with it), but filtering it and piping it to you costs your municipality quite a bit. Environment Canada says the cost of maintaining (including repairing and upgrading) municipal water treatment and sewage systems across the country over the next 10 years should be about $23 billion dollars. The average $27 water bill we pay monthly hardly covers it.

Showers: I'm not about to ask major water hogs to go cold turkey and shower with the water off right out of the gates, but if you're taking 20, 30, 40 minutes or more in there you need to reassess. Every minute you stand there, you're spraying yourself with 15 to 30 litres of water. A five- to eight-minute shower is ideal, but I'd even take 15 from you one-hour shower junkies. Set an egg timer to keep yourself on track.

No matter how long you're in there, a handy dandy **low-flow shower head** will decrease the amount of water you use. If your shower can fill a 2-litre jug with water in under 10 seconds, you need a new head. Look for one that uses no more than 11 litres per minute. You'll save money not only on your

If your shower can fill a 2-litre jug with water in under 10 seconds, you need a new head

153

water bill, but on your electricity bill too—that water doesn't just heat itself. And if you are up for turning off the water as you lather up, install a shower adaptor you flick on and off without having to reset the water pressure and temperature.

Shower Curtains: Of course, the longer you're in the shower, the longer you're exposed to your shower curtain, and if your curtain or liner is vinyl, it may be off-gassing potentially hormone-disrupting phthalates. Vinyl (or PVC) is a nasty polluter from birth right through to its final resting place in a municipal incinerator, so it's something you definitely want to avoid. To make matters worse, chemical fungicides are often added to make the curtain more mildew-resistant. And *still* they get gross, and since they're hard to clean we just toss 'em and buy a new one.

Even fabric curtains can be coated with water-repellent non-stick coating, made using persistent contaminants that have been found in most of our bloodstreams and in a shocking amount of wildlife, so what's an eco-sensitive bather to do? Well, you can find **hemp shower curtains** online. And, really, if hemp was good enough for most of the world's sails for centuries, it should be good enough to withstand a measly shower. Rawganique.com sells naturally antifungal organic hemp shower curtains under $100. If you're crafty, you can buy hemp fabric by the metre at hemp shops and sew one yourself. Those of you with a little more cash saved up should check out B.C.-based **Hankettes**, which offers organic cotton canvas shower curtains in natural or hand-dyed purple or brown with locally handmade wooden buttons (www.hankettes.com).

On the cheaper side, **IKEA's plastic shower curtains** look like the vinyl types you find everywhere, but they're actually made of polyethylene vinyl acetate (PEVA). It's still vinyl, but without the chlorine, which is the part that creates dangerous dioxins during manufacturing and incineration.

You can also install a **shower door** or **sliding enclosure**. They last forever, you can clean 'em to your heart's content, and they won't let water spill all over your bathroom floor.

Baths: A typical bath uses about 75 litres of hot water (double if you've got a big tub), while a five-minute shower with an efficient shower head uses about half that. I'm not saying you shouldn't bathe. Just make it a special treat, as opposed to an everyday event. If you're addicted to frequent baths, wash your sins away by filling the tub only one-quarter full.

Heavy soakers should note that tub-time can be seriously dangerous. It's not just that

THAT DRIPPING FAUCET

This ain't no drop it the bucket. A dripping tap can fill 55 one-litre water bottles a day. If you let it go unattended, you could be wasting over 20,000 litres a year! Can't seem to tighten it yourself? Call a plumber or professional handy-man or -woman to do the job. While you're at it, install a new water-saving aerator on your faucet. Every drop counts.

you might fall asleep in there—if your tub is old, there's a good chance you're soaking in lead. For over a century, the neurotoxin has been added to porcelain enamel, and both new and old bathroom fixtures (from sinks to tubs) may leach the substance, but older bathtubs that have been scrubbed with abrasive cleansers for years leach the most. According to one sample, 62% of porcelain tubs were leaching the stuff! If you're nervous about potential exposure, some hardware stores carry household lead-testing kits, or you can get one online at www.leadinspector.com. If your tub tests positive, resurfacing it should eliminate your exposure to the neuro-toxin. You can do it yourself with a tub refinishing kit, available at hardware

If you're addicted to frequent baths, wash your sins away by filling the tub only one-quarter full

stores, or call in a pro. Just look in the Yellow Pages under "bathtub refinishing." If you have a newer acrylic bathtub or acrylic tub liner to cover an old porcelain tub, you should be safe.

Towels: Next time you're in the market for new towels, skip the pesticide-heavy cotton type tied to child labour abuses in Egypt and invest in unbleached, undyed cotton or 100% organic towels, dyed with low-impact vegetable dyes. **Hankettes** makes organic cotton towel sets, plus bath mitts, face cloths and pretty much anything else they could dream of (www.hankettes.com). You can also order some through **Willow Natural Home** in Nelson, B.C. (www.willownaturalhome.com), **Grassroots** in Toronto (www.grassrootsstore.com) or **Earthshine Natural Living Concepts** in Calgary (www.earthshine.ca). Or check the green general stores near you. If you're looking for something other than beige, California-based **Native Organic Cotton** sells towels and bathrobes made of 100% certified organic U.S.-grown cotton, woven in earth tones created with colour-grown fibre ("colour-grown" means they use a cotton plant that naturally grows in sage or brown hues, with no added dyes). Check out their website at www.nativeorganic.com.

Toilets: Up to 65% of indoor water use happens in the bathroom, according the feds. And about a third of that goes right down the toilet with every flush—as much as 20 litres per flush with old loos. Not sure what your toilet's sucking back with each round? Just check the back of the bowl, in front of the tank: there should be a label there telling you how many litres per flush it uses (e.g., 10 lpf). If your house was built after 1996, it should have a **low-flow unit** built in; otherwise, you're shit out of luck (couldn't resist that one). Of course, you can wander over to your neighbourhood hardware store and buy one for about $100. These units use less than 6 litres of water per flush, which is great (your municipality might even have a rebate program in place, so ask). You'll save at least 13,000 litres year and about $50. You can even get a fancy **dual-flush toilet**, which uses more water to swallow up solid waste than it does mellow yellow.

If you're renting or don't have the cash for a new loo just yet, pick up a cheap **toilet tank dam** or water-saving bag for a toonie or two. Even a weighted plastic bottle in the tank will do. But no bricks, please—they break down and can screw up your plumbing.

LEAKY TOILET?

Water bills suspiciously higher than usual? You've probably sprung a leak without knowing it. So how do you know if your toilet's tanking? Well, do you have to jiggle the handle to make it stop running? Does it sound like a creek is babbling in your bathroom? Ever seem like there's a phantom flusher in your house? Even if it's doing none of the above, you could still have a silent leak. **Find out by putting a small amount of food colouring in the tank, then wait 20 minutes. If you see colour in the bowl, you're leakin', darlin',** Time to call a plumber. You're wasting about 2,800 litres a month!

Toilet Paper: We all buy it and, sure, most of us prefer the feel of extra-cushy three-ply, the kind that's "cottony" soft, but is it really worth flushing bleached-out ancient forests down the toilet on a daily basis?

How much damage can a little square of tissue really do? you ask. Well, over 700,000 tons of disposable tissue products are tossed in Canada every year, including facial tissues and paper towels. The average person goes through about

The average person goes through about 100 rolls of TP a year, according to Greenpeace. **That's a good 5 kilometres' worth**

100 rolls of TP a year, according to Greenpeace. That's a good 5 kilometres' worth if you were to roll it out. And if you multiply that by a nation of 32 million, we're talking about 3.2 billion rolls, or 160 million kilometres, not to mention the emission of thousands of kilograms of nasty air and water pollutants during manufacture (such as the deadly dioxins released in the chlorination process). Even if you think that's exaggerating and we use only half as much, that's still 1.6 billion rolls, any way you tear it.

Then there's all the stuff we export: 300,000 tons of tossable tissue products go to the U.S. every year. Most of that is coming from virgin wood sources, such as Canada's treasured boreal forest.

And wouldn't you know it, the same chemical that's causing so much controversy in the world of reusable water bottles and ceramic dental fillers is turning up in toilet paper. Yep, bisphenol A and three other chemical compounds that mimic female sex hormones are used in paper production. Researchers in the department of waste management at a university in Dresden, Germany, found that not only did both recycled and non-recycled bathroom tissues test positive for the chems, but they're a significant source of estrogenic emissions to wastewater. They concluded that tainted toilet paper could contaminate the sewage sludge many municipalities treat and spread on farmers' fields (yes, Canadian municipalities too).

For those of you wondering who the worst offenders are when it comes to chopping down old-growth forests, Procter & Gamble (maker of Charmin TP and Puffs facial tissue) and Kimberly-Clark (maker of Kleenex and Cottenelle) top Greenpeace's list of culprits. According to the Kimberly-Clark's sustainability report, less than 29% of its fibres comes from recycled fibres, and that, says Greenpeace, tends to go to commercial versions of their toilet paper, available to offices, schools, and so on. Kimberley-Clark says its practices are sustainable, and that it has indeed worked to protect old-growth forests. For more on the he said/she said, check out http://kleercut.net/en/ResponsetoKC.

Toilet Paper Solutions: You wanna hear the good news? If each household in Canada switched just one roll of the virgin bleached stuff with one roll of the recycled kind, we'd save almost 48,000 thousand trees and prevent 4,500 kilograms of the air and water pollution that comes from making it. One roll. Just imagine what would happen if we replaced a dozen rolls, or shifted over to recycled tissue altogether.

Several brands contain some degree of recycled material, but read the fine print and look for a high level of post-consumer content (minimum 80%). Some good brands are **Seventh Generation** (available at health stores), **Fiesta** (available at many corner stores) and

HANKETTES

Back before disposable tissues, a cloth handkerchief was up everyone's sleeve. In fact, its replacement, Kleenex facial tissues, had trouble catching on until 1926, when they were peddled under the catchy new slogan "Don't carry a cold in your pocket." Wouldn't you know it, germphobia took hold, and 80 years later, the thought of a reusable cloth hanky makes most of us wince.

Enter Lesley Roberts. The Vancouverite's hay fever allergies were so bad that she went through a box of tissues a day, which was making her feel a tad guilty. She thought about sewing her own cotton hankies, but it wasn't until one night when she was lying awake in bed that inspiration struck. She tossed off her sheets, grabbed some scissors and some junk cardboard and started fashioning the first-ever tissue box designed to store reusable cloth tissues. Soon enough, she started selling organic cotton flannel hankies that pulled out from a cardboard box, just like the throwaway kind—except in this case, you keep the box and use it as a handy home dispenser for your washable tissues. Now her company, Hankettes, gets all its cotton from an organic co-operative of growers in Texas and North Carolina. Her small team cuts, sews and packages all its own products in B.C.'s countryside. And they not only make hankies in all sizes, they also offer tea towels, cloths, napkins, diaper wipes, bath mitts—pretty much anything that'll get consumers away from single-use items (**www.hankettes.com**).

Still cringing over the whole cloth nose-blowing thing? Consider this: **if every household in North America switched one box of tossable paper tissues for one box of cloth ones, we'd save over 2 million trees from the chop.**

PC Green (available wherever President's Choice products are sold). None of these use chemical bleaches in their whitening process, which is another key feature to look for. Elemental Chlorine–Free labels, by the way, tell you the paper was made without chlorine gas in a process that creates less emissions but could still release dioxins into the environment. Look for products labelled Process Chlorine Free, as the ones above are.

When it comes to facial tissue, there are even fewer eco-options. Even Kleenex's website says the only thing recycled about its facial tissue is the cardboard carton. **Seventh Generation** and, more recently, **Cascades** are really the only brands that get the thumbs-up from Greenpeace's eco-shopper's guide. It turns out that few of us are willing to part with the extra softness that comes from blowing your schnozz with virgin forest.

BEDROOM

Ah, the bedroom. It's a corner of the home full of pleasurable possibilities, and at the top of our list is getting a good, sound sleep. Most of us spend about a third of our lives nestled in bed. (I'm a mess without my nine hours. I never could figure out you kooky people who survive on four.) But all that time sandwiched between blankets and mattresses can get you tossing and turning when you consider what they're made of.

Pillow and Comforter: We all need a place to rest our heads, but our pillows and comforters are likely stuffed with either petroleum-based polyester fillers (who knew a night's rest could contribute to our dependence on fossil fuels?) or down. We tend to imagine fluffy feathers falling naturally from plump, happy birds as they waddle around sunny barns, shedding their winter insulation. I hate to burst any bubbles, but you should know that down feathers are forcefully plucked from geese, chicken or ducks either before or after they're slaughtered. The feathers are then sterilized with formaldehyde, bleached and sprayed with chemical anti-allergens. Not so idyllic after all. Note: plucking birds while they're alive causes them considerable pain and distress.

Pillow and Comforter Solutions: IKEA makes a point of not using down and feathers from living birds; instead, its pillows and comforters are made with by-products from the poultry biz. You can also go for **100% organic cotton fill pillows**, which are slightly heavier and firmer. **Organic wool fill** is fluffier. Plus, it's naturally resistant to dust mites and mildew, so it's great for anyone with allergies (see page 32 for more on organic wool). **Natural rubber** (either shredded or moulded) is another great option for those with asthma or allergies, as it's naturally dust-resistant and hypoallergenic. Others swear by pillows stuffed with **buckwheat husks**, but they're not exactly cushy. You can pick up any of these pillows in many green general stores or online at Canadian sites such as **Willow Natural Home** (www.willownaturalhome.com) or **Grassroots** (www.grassrootsstore.com). (Check the Resource Guide at the back of the book for green general store names and addresses.)

For comforters, toasty and breathable organic wool in an organic cotton casing is an excellent choice. **Euphoria** organic wool comforters or duvets, available at www.allergybuyersclub.com, are handmade in Canada using organic cotton outer shells and lightweight certified organic lambswool on the inside. **Allergy Buyers Club** also offers silk-filled and silk-encased comforters, as well as some stuffed with alpaca wool. Many green general stores also stock comforters.

159

Sheets: You know you want soft sheets with a high thread count but betcha don't want to be wrapping yourself in a pesticide-drenched crop. Sure, cotton is natural, but this water-hogging plant is also the proud recipient of 25% of the world's insecticides—chemicals that inevitably end up contaminating local groundwater and making both workers and wildlife sick. And over half of all American cotton is grown from genetically engineered seeds. Then it's bleached with chlorine, soaked in chemical dyes and sprayed with a wrinkle-resistant permanent-press chemical finish, likely formaldehyde. Washing your sheets before you use them will eliminate about 60% of that formaldehyde, according to one study. But even a few visits to the washing machine won't get rid of it completely. It's best to skip on iron-free promises—a little crinkling won't kill anyone.

> Over half of all American cotton is grown from **genetically engineered seeds**

Sheet Solutions: Pesticides, chemicals and human rights abuses (see sidebar opposite) not something you want to get twisted up in each night? I don't blame you. Wrap yourself in 100% organic cotton bed linens, free of bleaches and dyes. Green general stores in your area are likely to carry them. If there's nothing near you, you'll have to head online. A good Canadian source is **T.h.e. Store** (the initials stand for Total Home Environment), which carries organic linens in natural or white (www.t-h-e-store.com) or www.earthshine.ca. **Indika Organics**, out of the U.S., sells a high-end environmental bedding line made of vegetable-dyed Peruvian cotton, but it doesn't come cheap. Indika also offers beautiful hemp and bamboo duvet covers and shams (www.indikaorganics.com). **Coyuchi**'s bedding gets its hues in part from naturally coloured cotton strains from Latin America (www.coyuchiorganic.com), but you can get full sets for a better price at **Native Organic Cotton**, which uses low-impact dyes (www.nativeorganic.com). Organic hemp sheets (said to be surprisingly soft), organic flax linen and organic cotton bedding are available from **Rawganique.com** for a pretty penny. Your best bet might be sustainable bamboo sheet sets from www.bedbathandbeyond.com for under $100!

Mattresses: Now for what hugs your frame night after night, even when your love life fails you. We tend to choose a mattress based on whether we prefer firmness or deep, cushiony comfort. But while you're dreaming away, your polyurethane-foam-stuffed padding is off-gassing air-polluting volatile organic compounds (VOCs). Something's got to be sprayed on that ultra-flammable foam to keep it from bursting into flames every time a fool smokes in

We fawn over luxurious Egyptian cotton sheets and pay a mint for them.

Unfortunately, the one million children working Egyptian cotton fields don't get to see much of that money. Human Rights Watch says young cotton pickers, hired seasonally to remove leafworm infestations from leaves because they're just the right height, work 11-hour days, seven days a week, in 40°C heat. And all the children surveyed reported being beaten by their foreman. Egypt developed child labour laws in 1996, but Human Rights Watch says the laws aren't being enforced. On a positive note, Egypt has been successful at reducing the amount of pesticides it uses on cotton and has banned a few really bad ones. Still, doesn't really wash away their sins, now does it?

bed. But does it have to be super-persistent fire-retardant chemicals known as PBDEs? Environment Canada considers the whole PBDE family toxic, and the mattress industry has voluntarily opted to phase it out, but mattresses with PBDEs are still in stores (see page 315 for more on PBDEs).

Salespeople also try to sell you on stain-resistant finishes, but note that these can be made with chemicals from the same dodgy family behind non-stick frying pans. The maker of Stainguard, 3M, phased out its most persistent ingredient (PFOS) by the end of 2002 and insists that its modified recipe has a "low risk" of accumulating in the food chain.

> Stain-resistant finishes can be made with chemicals from the **same dodgy family** behind non-stick frying pans

Although modern furniture designers seem to be trying to make it impossible for us to use traditional box spring frames, many of us are still partial to them. But less expensive ones made of plywood or particleboard often contain off-gassing formaldehyde. And was the wood sustainably harvested? To be sure, ask if it's been certified by the Forest Stewardship Council (FSC).

Mattress Solutions: IKEA says all of its box springs use FSC-approved wood. Plus, IKEA particleboard is all formaldehyde-free, and their mattresses are free of PBDE. Or you can skip the box and coil thing altogether and opt for natural rubber. It's a nice, springy, supportive base for organic cotton and wool mattresses, and you can choose the level of firmness you prefer. You can also get traditional spring-based types made with organic cotton and wool (wool, by the way, is naturally fire-retardant). Ottawa-based

161

WHEN YOU CAN'T AFFORD THE VERY BEST

While going organic is the ideal, let's face it: many of us can't afford all this stuff. There's nothing wrong with sticking with your old sheets. But if you're in the market for new bedding, try buying one piece at a time. And if you're really stuck for cash, another good option comes from second-hand stores. You can rest assured (Get it? Rest? Oh, the fun never ends) that any wrinkle-retardants and chemical sprays are long gone after years of use. And with a good washing (it's okay to use hot water just this once), they're as good as new—or better, depending on how you look at it. Many second-hand stores sell sheets, pillowcases and mattresses. If you're nervous about what could be lurking in a used (or new) mattress, get an organic barrier-cloth mattress cover (available at any of the stores that sell eco-mattresses). They're so finely woven that bacteria, mould and dust mites can't get through. They're also available for pillows and are a good idea for anyone with dust allergies, even on brand new organic beds.

Obasan is a good Canadian online source for high-calibre mattress alternatives, comforters, pillows and infant bedding (www.obasan.ca), as are **T.h.e. Store**, **Grassroots** and **Willow Natural Home**, all mentioned above. **Eco Bedroom** (www.ecobedroom.com) has a good selection of alternative mattresses, as well as conventional cotton mattresses flame-retarded with non-toxic borate, which passes the federal cigarette smouldering tests. It also carries organic baby mattresses, futons, comforters, pillows and more (see page 124 for more on children's bedding).

DONATING OLD MATTRESSES

Got an old mattress you want to kick to the curb? Many companies, such as Sleep Country, will pick it up and donate it to charity when you're buying a new one from them. Or you can call your local homeless shelter, women's shelter or Salvation Army and ask if they'd like it. You can sleep soundly, knowing you're giving your mattress a second life and giving someone else a much-needed place to rest.

FURNITURE

Nomads must not have had much furniture. I mean, really, worrying about shelves and dining-room tables would have seriously slowed them down as they chased antelope and buffalo across the countryside. Of course, to this day, furniture still weighs us down (anyone who has ever tried to move a pullout couch knows they weren't designed to be lifted up five flights of stairs). But we all accumulate it, and that collection of coffee tables, couches and ottomans somehow makes our home what it is: ours. Too bad all that stuff isn't just creating atmosphere—it's poisoning it with fumes and deforesting the planet.

Foam: Let's start with that pillowy couch you're sitting on. The soft, cushy part tends to come from foam—polyurethane foam, to be exact. Polyurethane itself isn't the greenest thing on the planet. Making it creates toxic by-products such as toluene and ozone-stripping CFCs. But it's hard to find a sofa that isn't stuffed with this stuff.

An additive that is more avoidable, however, is the flame-retardants. It seems that foam is quick to catch on fire, so for decades furniture makers have been turning to a PBDE known as penta to put a stop to that. The thing is, PBDEs don't just stay put in our couches. They're in the dust from decaying foam that fills our homes (the Environmental Working Group found them in every home sampled), and Environment Canada says they turn up virtually everywhere they test (air, water, land, Arctic seals). These chemicals (tied to thyroid and developmental problems in lab animals) are considered persistent, bioaccumulating toxins—which means they build up in our fatty tissues and stay there. Perhaps scariest of all is that they're turning up in human breast milk—an upsetting fact considering that babies exposed in the womb and through breastfeeding are purportedly most at risk from the troubling health effects. The E.U. has already banned penta, and California, Hawaii and Maine have all moved to do the same. Canada is in the midst of phasing it out, but you can still buy furniture treated with the stuff, so don't forget to ask. **IKEA** furniture, by the way, has been PBDE-free since 2002.

Many foam makers and ottoman stuffers are now turning to fire retardants that haven't yet been found toxic to humans. But you never know. Better to stay away from foam if you can afford to go the natural route. Back in the day, coaches used to be stuffed with **natural latex**, and green furniture makers are turning to the tree-tapped substance again to fill their sofas. There's plenty of selection if you're willing to shop online from American retailers and cough up a little coin (see page 165). Just ask what kind of fill they use.

Wood: Wood is natural, renewable and biodegradable, but that doesn't make that bookcase soft on the earth. Indeed, wood furniture in general is teeming with toxins. It's coated in varnishes, glues, waxes and paints that release smog-inducing, lung-irritating VOCs. Pressed woods such as particleboard, fiberboard and even some plywood are often major culprits. Although the industry has reduced emissions by 80% over the last couple of decades, VOCs such as formaldehyde are still out there causing headaches, allergic reactions and nausea in unsuspecting home-dwellers. Worse yet, furniture can off-gas noxious vapours for years!

When hunting for wooden furniture, beware of particleboard posing as the real thing. Increasingly convincing veneers might dupe you into thinking you're buying maple when you're actually buying sawdust and resin glued together. These are only okay if you find stuff that's formaldehyde-free and made from non-virgin wood sources. When in doubt, ask.

Then there's the whole deforestation factor. According to Greenpeace, most Canadian lumber comes from ancient forest systems such as the boreal. So that lovely coffee table in your living room might be the last incarnation of a 100-year-old tree. What can you do to avoid this? Look for wood products that are old growth–free. The

That lovely coffee table in your living room might be the last incarnation of a 100-year-old tree

FSC label is trustworthy, but FSC-certified furniture is hard to come by. **IKEA** is likely your most convenient inexpensive source. Only about 20% of its wood furniture comes with the FSC stamp. (IKEA also uses virtually formaldehyde-free finishes.) Just remember, the logo isn't always visible, so once again it's best to ask.

FAST FACTS ON WOOD

Canada has 17 million hectares of FSC-certified forest.

Over 20% of the world's FSC-certified forests are in right here in Canada.

Only 10% of our managed forests are FSC-certified.

Since April 2005, the area of FSC-certified forest in Canada has tripled.

(source: Forest Stewardship Council Canada)

Green Furniture: Green Culture has perhaps the biggest selection of enlightened furniture online (including bedroom, dining and kids' sets) but they're not yet 100% eco-friendly. Be sure to read the fine print (www.eco-furniture.com). Seattle-based **Greener Lifestyles** has slickly designed fair-trade couches, armchairs, dinner tables and more made with FSC-certified, low-VOC finishes and natural latex fill (www.greenerlifestyles.com). Some high-end Canuck furniture designers offer FSC woods as well. Vancouver-based **Ornamentum Furniture** takes minimalism up a notch with their certified wood designs for the dining room, living room and boudoir (www.ornamentum.bc.ca). **Frank Smith** is another quality collection with FSC-certified wood and strawboard options (www.franksmith.ca). For the home office, **Knoll's** offers FSC-certified and low-VOC or VOC-free furniture. For a full list of FSC-certified wood retailers and products, head to www.fsccanada.org.

Another option is **sustainable bamboo**. **Crate and Barrel** has a line of bamboo bedroom furniture. And if you decide to turn away from wood altogether, Quebec-based **CNI Furniture** has an eco-line of about 125 über-sexy chairs, coffee tables, nightstands and lamps made of coconut shells and vines, corn cobs, dried pods and banana fibres (call 450-674-1669 for a list of retailers in your area).

> **slickly designed** fair-trade couches, armchairs, dinner tables made with FSC-certified, **low VOC finishes** and **natural latex** fill

Recycled: Overall, furniture that uses **reclaimed wood** (from old barns, homes or naturally felled trees) or **post-consumer waste** (such as cork, wheat straw or sunflower husks) is the greenest way to go, but it's harder to find in Canada. Online green directories such as U.S.-based www.ecobusinesslinks.com can give you a vision of what's out there. And you might be able to find woodworkers and furniture makers near you who use these materials to build dining room tables, chairs and more. You can get beautiful reclaimed wood stuff from Toronto-based **Hardware** (www.hardwareinteriors.com), FSC-certified **Vintage Woodcraft** (www.vintagewoodcraft.com) and Washington state's **Alan Vogels's Time Warped Furniture** (www.alanvogelfurniture.com), but these places aren't set up to order from online.

Let's not forget about **antiques**. Not only are they fun to hunt, this is furniture recycling at its finest! Don't think you're doomed to doilies and your grandmother's tacky side tables. There are lots of eras and styles to pick from, including American primitive, art deco, Victorian, early Canadiana. If exotics are more your thing, you can get stunning antique cabinets, armoires and tables from the

Far East and South Asia that will make your place pop. Sure, they've travelled a ways to get here, but it's better than buying a brand new teak table. Also keep in mind that many antique dealers sell refurbished stuff and even make new furniture with reclaimed barn doors or whatnot.

If all this is out of your price range, look through the classified ads or go to BuyandSell.com or Usedcanada.ca for stuff like second-hand computer desks, kitchen gear, couches and more. **Craig's List** (www.craigslist.com), **kijiji.ca and Freecycle.org** are other must-see sites.

ELECTRONICS

Not to romanticize the past, but back in the day, electronics were made to last several years—decades, even! Sure, they're cheaper now, but they might as well be disposable at the rate you have to replace them. Natural Resources Canada estimates that Canadians dump more than 272,000 tons of computer equipment, phones, TVs, stereos and small appliances in landfills each and

Electronic gadgets are teeming with toxic heavy metals and chemicals

every year. Between 1992 and 2000, Canadians ditched enough computers to fill 953 Olympic-sized swimming pools, says Environment Canada. To make matters worse, all those gadgets are teeming with toxic heavy metals and chemicals, such as the nasty endocrine-disrupting fire retardants found in outer plastic casings and circuit boards, the 50 grams of mercury in your flat screen and the 2 to 4 pounds of lead in traditional cathode ray tube TVs. Environment Canada says computers alone are responsible for about out 1.1 tons of mercury, 4.4 tons of cadmium and 4,750 tons of lead in the trash. And consumer electronics as a whole contribute 40% of all the lead found in landfills. Bottom line: it's time to think twice about kicking your old gear to the curb.

Recycling: If you've squeezed the last drop of life from your gadgets, or you just can't get by without a larger-capacity computer, there are many places you can bring your old electronics for recycling. First of all, if you have an old laptop or PC you want to get rid of, get in touch with **Computers for Schools**. The Industry Canada program refurbishes over 100,000 old computers a year and donates them to schools, libraries and not-for-profit learning orgs across the country. In fact, they've already given away about 650,000! Plus, they'll give you a charitable tax receipt. Check their website for provincial contacts (http://cfs-ope.ic.gc.ca). **ReBOOT Canada** is a non-profit that will fix your old computer or printer, then hand it over to other deserving charities, or recycle it properly if it's beyond help. It has locations in nearly every province (www.rebootcanada.ca).

More and more computer companies, such as **Apple**, **Hewlett-Packard** and **Dell**, have take-back programs of their own. Dell will take your old one even if you don't buy a new one from them. Plus, they'll recycle other computer-related stuff. For instance, you can send Dell your keyboard, mouse, monitors and printers. Hewlett-Packard picks up printers, scanners, fax machines, desktop servers, monitors and handheld devices, as well as cables, mice and keyboards.

For other electronics, call your municipality to ask whether it takes back old tech. Many do or will put you in touch with local companies or organizations that do. Unfortunately, the feds aren't into passing mandatory national extended producer responsibility regulations (extended producer responsibility means manufacturers take responsibility for the full life cycle of their products by, for instance, funding national recycling programs), but they're working with the industry to develop uniform standards that each province can implement through Electronics Product Stewardship Canada, if they so choose. Saskatchewan has recently given the green light to starting an electronics stewardship system called SWEEP (Saskatchewan Waste Electronics Equipment Program). Ontario has a program in the works, as does B.C. And Alberta is at the front of the pack, having recycled 142,429 computer monitors, 70,487 printers, and 63,711 TVs between the time the program started in October 2004 and July 2006. That's over 7,000 tons of e-waste saved from landfill! Under their system, consumers fork out a couple of extra bucks to cover the cost of recycling when they buy a product, and they can drop off old gear at over 100 collection sites across the province, free of charge.

If you're stockpiling dusty computers, VCRs and beta cams like most Canadians, you might as well sit tight until programs arrive in your area. Hey, if you've been hanging on to that black-and-white TV this long, what's another year or two?

Buying New: Now for tips on shopping for new tech. One problem with most household electronics is that they're phantom power users. They're actually still on, in standby mode, when you turn them off, wasting a surprising amount of electricity to power all those little lights, timers and clocks. Natural Resources Canada blames "leaking electricity" from electronics and smaller appliances, combined with the fact that households own more of the damn things, for the 4% increase in residential energy use over the last decade. TVs, VCRs and cable boxes are the worst culprits, but stereo systems are almost as bad.

BAMBOO CASING

In the cool, can't-wait-till-it-hits-Canada category, keep your eyes peeled for bamboo-encased computer monitors, keyboards, mice and iPod cases. If you know any Japanese beyond "sashimi" and "arigato," you can try ordering them online. Although English should get you by on the Play Engine site in the U.K., where you can now order a lead-free flatscreen LCD TV framed with bamboo, as well as bamboo flat-screen computer monitor, keyboard, even a bamboo mouse (**www.playengine.co.uk**).

To curb all that leaky power, look for the Energy Star label on everything from DVD players and TVs to computers and major appliances. To earn the government logo, goods must use a minimal amount of energy when off, so, for instance, an Energy Star DVD player must consume no more than 3 watts of power—75% less than conventional models. Note that the label isn't always on the outer packaging, so it's best to ask, but most new computers are Energy Star–approved. In fact, if you wander around any electronics store you'll find that most new TVs, DVD players and VCRs also come with the label. FYI, the seal of approval doesn't tell you anything about how efficient your set is when it's on.

So how do products match up when they're actually in use? Unfortunately, there's no real labelling system in place to help you with this, which really bites because most power is consumed when electronics are in active mode, not standby mode. But in general, VHS players, even the new ones, consume more energy than DVD players. And since your computer uses less power than your TV, watching films or downloaded television shows on your desktop or laptop is a greener choice, especially compared to new-fangled big-screen TV sets. The bigger and sharper the image, the more juice your set needs to deliver it. A 32-inch liquid crystal high-definition television (LCD HDTV), for instance, can suck back nearly 400 kilowatt hours per year, nearly double that of an older analog screen of the same size. And a 50-inch plasma HDTV can drink up well over three times as much as that analog one. It's certainly enough to make your hydro bills jump. Is it really worth seeing the pores on your favourite starlet's nose? For a full breakdown of how much power each model sucks, punch "TV" in the search engine of www.nrdc.org.

To be fair, newer plasmas are improving as manufacturers reduce active mode power consumption, and non-HDTV LCDs use the same amount of power as regular analog sets. Still, Canadians bought almost 200,000 energy-hogging HDTVs in 2002 alone, according to a market research report by Euromonitor.

As for computers, laptops aren't just lighter, they use much less power than desktop models. Yep, the typical laptop draws about 30 watts of electricity, while bulkier desktop models use about 120. Flat-screen LCD monitors for desktop computers will lessen your energy consumption.

Laptops aren't just lighter, they use much less power than desktop models

Beyond basic energy use, few companies recycle more than 2% of their products. **Hewlett-Packard** (HP) was ranked number one in a 2003 computer report card put out by the Computer TakeBack Campaign (a new updated report card is coming out, so check their website for details: www.computertakeback.com). HP was one of the first companies that worked with consumers and government to take back aging gear and deal with it in an environmentally friendly way. Dell rose to second place after getting a failing grade in 2002. It stopped using American prison labour, initiated a recycling program and publicly supports producer take-back regulations, unlike most of the electronics industry, which is vocally against them. Euro-based NEC is also credited with rapidly phasing out toxins and using a high level of recycled content.

MUSIC GEAR

Clunky 8-tracks and toxic vinyl might be history, but are we any better off today with all the digital music devices we own now? Tapes (yes, some people still have these) and CDs are relatively bulky and tend to collect dust in our basements when we're tired of them. And if we trash unwanted or scratched CDs (and DVDs), the polycarbonate plastic and aluminum don't biodegrade and will release nasty fumes if they're incinerated by your municipality. **MP3 players and iPods, on the other hand, can hold thousands of songs in the palm of your hand, so create a lot less waste.** The problem is that they contain all the same toxic crap that every other electronic item on the market does, but they tend to die even faster, meaning kids are chucking and buying new iPods and MP3 players way too often. Ask about corporate take-back recycling policies before you buy. Apple has one in place for its iPod, and Dell has one for its Pocket DJs, so make sure to use them. Unless you're listening to tunes on a corn-based CD, the digital route just might squeak out as the greener option.

But even companies with an A on the take-back report card have been in detention with Greenpeace for years over the presence of toxic chemicals in their products. And a detailed report by the TakeBack Campaign and Clean Production Action in 2004 found persistent brominated fire retardants in the dust swiped from 16 computers in museums and university labs across the U.S. The good news is, in 2006 Dell promised to phase out any remaining persistent brominated fire retardants and toxic PVC plastics by 2009, then HP vowed to remove the last of its troubling fire retardants and PVC components by 2007 (it had already removed PVC from all products, except cables and wiring). Both were at the top of Greenpeace International's 2006 *Guide to Greener Electronics*, with **Dell** tied with **Nokia** for first. But HP slipped in the ranking when it was discovered that an HP laptop contained a type of fire retardant (deca) it claimed to have stopped using years before. Very sneaky.

Nokia, by the way, is leading the way in wiping out harmful chemicals from its product line, having gone PVC-free by the end of 2005 and totally PBDE-free by 2007. Sony Ericsson's doing pretty well when it comes to phasing out the worst chems, but it's slacking in terms of take-back programs. Samsung and Sony have phased out some toxins on some products, but recycling could be more widespread around the globe (Sony does have a voluntary take-back program in North America, though). Panasonic, Toshiba and Motorola have been dragging at the back of the pack. Apple, which markets itself as a progressive, creative brand, has been perhaps the biggest disappointment, getting only 2.7 out of 10 for failing to give concrete dates for phasing out PVC and making no commitments to phase out toxic fire retardants. The Greenpeace guide is updated every three months, so check back at www.greenpeace.org.

The efforts these companies are making to reduce toxins are especially important considering that many so-called recyclers are really just shipping your hazardous e-waste to

RECYCLING CDS, DVDS AND TAPES

If you think someone else might put your Wham collection to better use, why not give it, along with all your unwanted CDs, DVDs and tapes, a second life by dropping it off at Goodwill or Value Village? Used CD shops will buy your old CDs or DVDs. But if no one wants them because they're scratched or full of unwanted data, you can send old CDs, DVDs, jewel cases, cassette and VHS tapes to U.S.-based GreenDisk, where they're reincarnated into new jewel cases, rewritable CDs or soft shell cases for CDs and DVDs (**www.greendisk.com**).

developing nations with flimsy enviro laws. An estimated 50% to 80% of American electronic waste (according to the Worldwatch Institute) is being dismantled without any safety protection for workers or environmental safeguards. It happens with Canadian waste, too, even though we've signed international conventions saying we would never export our toxic trash. Electronics Product Stewardship Canada has drafted a qualification program to address the growing problem.

Batteries: If you have a dusty battery drawer somewhere in your home, good for you—you've taken an important step towards keeping a good chunk of household hazardous waste from landfill. Still, many of the 150 million batteries purchased every year in Canada end up in the dump. Thankfully, mercury (used to prevent corrosion and increase shelf life) was largely phased out of the mini power logs back in 1996, so we've reduced the amount of mercury entering the waste stream from a scary 75 tons in 1968 to less than 1 ton a year now, according to the Recycling Council of Ontario. Even so, roughly 35% of the mercury in the Canuck environment and 50% to 70% of the heavy metals found in landfills come from household batteries. Sheesh!

Manufacturers may say you can simply trash alkaline and lithium batteries at will, but that doesn't mean you should—especially if you're buying cheapie imported batteries, which may still contain mercury. Instead, bring your old batteries to your hazardous waste depot.

Now, what to do with those rechargeables that just won't charge any more, no matter how hard you try? Thanks to an industry-sponsored program that was originally designed to keep nickel cadmium out of the waste stream (it's a cumulative toxin to plants, animals and humans alike, as well as a known human carcinogen), there are thousands of locations where you can bring your old rechargeable batteries (nickel cadmium or not) from cellular or cordless phones, power tools or camcorders. Just stop by your neighbourhood Zellers, Radio Shack, Canadian Tire, Home Depot, Mountain Equipment Co-op or phone stores, or call 1-800-8-BATTERY for the collection site nearest you. The Source by Circuit City also has a battery rebuild program that revives your dying cordless phone or laptop batteries.

One rechargeable can replace up to **300 single-use batteries**

Once you're rid of your old ones, might I be so bold as to suggest that you never buy single-use batteries again? That's right, never—or as close to never as you can get. There's really no need to buy the disposable type when there are plenty of excellent rechargeable alternatives to choose from. And one rechargeable can replace up to 300 single-use batteries!

Yes, it's true, a battery is a battery, and the metal extraction process used to make the bloody things involves everything from habitat destruction to air and water pollution. But **Rayovac** and **Pure Energy** rechargeables are more eco-friendly because they don't contain cadmium, don't leak electricity when not in use and don't continue to receive an electric current once fully charged. Pure Energy is the only brand that comes with the Eco-Logo (the tag of approval of the federal Environmental Choice program).

And who needs dirty coal or nuke power to charge your gadgets when you can run your batteries on the sun's rays! Solar panels now come built into cool-looking backpacks, camera bags and laptop messenger bags. Look for them at www.grassrootsstore.com, which also sells plain solar battery chargers. You can get wind-up and solar-powered cellphone chargers at www.windupradio.com.

POWERING YOUR COMPUTER WITH WIND

Offset those dirty carbon emissions created to run your computer by funding a little wind power. Thirty-nine dollars will buy enough wind energy to power your desktop for three years, and $16 will do the same for your laptop. Then you can go back to whiling away your life playing online video games with a green conscience (http://pembina.org/wind).

CAMERAS

Weighing in at 50 kilograms, the first daguerrotype camera was not for the masses. Now everyone and their kid has one (you can even buy a SpongeBob SquarePants version). But that doesn't mean they're non-toxic.

Both digital and traditional point-and-shoots can contain dangerous components such as lead, cadmium and mercury in their lenses, sensors and displays. Most companies have switched to lead-free solder in recent years and are moving to phase out harmful heavy metals. But detailed reports of emissions reductions and eco-initiatives don't always give you the full picture. Film and digital camera maker Kodak, for instance, has long been embroiled in a battle with eco-activists regarding methylene chloride and toxic dioxin pollution around its industrial park in Albany, New York.

As for who's the greenest of them all—digital or traditional film—it's time to assess.

Film: Conventional camera users may have cursed the mounds of film wasted over the years because of low light, blinking kids or severed heads (yes, Mom, I know you didn't mean to photograph us from the nose down). But what about the eco-implications of processing all those shots? Fortunately, the volume of chemicals needed to print Grandma's birthday party pics has dropped from just under 2 litres to 90 millilitres since 1968, a whopping 96% reduction, according to *E Magazine*'s Earth Talk. Nonetheless, those chemicals still add up.

Of most concern to municipal water treatment folks is silver. As nice as it is around your neck, it's actually a pollutant when in water. And silver is found in the film itself, then is transferred to photo-processing water. Most commercial mini-labs have silver recovery machines. The metal is refined and recycled into things like jewellery (back to the pretty type of silver). The rest of the chems in the processing stew are said to be non-toxic and largely biodegradable in municipal water treatment plants (although sewer overflows might mean some end up in lakes and streams—a very bad thing).

If you're one of those dinosaurs with a home darkroom, don't think you can just dump your chemicals down the drain (though most of you do—shame on you!). You should be keeping your used chemicals in jugs and calling up a silver recovery company such as Environmental Control Systems (which has locations across the country)—they'll pick them up for proper disposal for an annual fee. Just look up "silver recovery" in the Yellow Pages.

> The volume of chemicals needed to print **Grandma's birthday party pics** has dropped a whopping 96% since 1968

All you tofu-heads out there might be grossed out to learn that film is made using a gelatin base (the collagen in cow or pig bones, hooves and connective tissue). If you're a hardcore vegan, this might be enough to make you drop your old camera and switch to digital.

Digital: Beyond being hoof-free, how does digital measure up? Well, traditionally these cams have been serious battery hogs. But technology has been advancing in leaps and bounds, so almost all new digies use rechargeable batteries and chew through them much less quickly than models from two or three years ago. At this moment, **Sony Cyber-Shots** are said to be, on average, twice as efficient as other brands, but at the rate of camera tech evolution, this info might already be obsolete. (Just kidding. Er, maybe not.)

While printing digital images doesn't involve the same chemical bath as film, inks are still used to print those pics. Most are water-based, but some pigments contain toxic heavy metals and polluting VOCs. (**Epson** says its inks are VOC- and heavy metal–free.) And they

There's something about photos that make us feel guilty for wanting to toss them. But hey, maybe you have valid reasons to destroy all proof that your ex ever existed, or perhaps you're hoping to erase any hard copy images of you with a mullet. Either way, I don't judge. Just know that your prints can't be tossed in your recycling bin, thanks to the chemical coating on the paper. That's not to say you can't run them through a shredder or throw darts at them before you junk them.

can also be printed on Energy Star–certified ink jet printers, available at camera stores or pretty much anywhere you'd buy office equipment. Make sure to refill or recycle your old ink cartridges.

But let's get real. Digital cams have the upper hand ecologically because most people don't bother printing 95% of their pictures. Sure, some would say, "Well, you're sucking up computer power to look at those images." But the truth is, we all have computers anyway, and few of us bought them just to upload digital shots of our dogs rolling in the neighbour's flower beds.

The main downside to digital is partly our own fault: people keep buying new cameras all the damn time when it's really not necessary. Don't be lured by promos telling you to trade in your old digie within the year for discounts on a jazzier model. Only buy what you need. If you're primarily shooting family pics and printing standard 4-by-6 images, you don't need more than 4 or 5 megapixels (6 max). The more pixels and added features your camera has, the more batteries it sucks up. And you'll save power by turning off the digital screen that lets you see what you're shooting. I know, I know, that's half the reason you like digital—I'm just saying.

Disposable: If you look at nothing but the electronics, single-use cameras are considered the greenest option of all. Yes, it's counterintuitive, but despite being called "disposable," they're actually returned to the manufacturer and their parts are either ground down and remoulded or simply reused about 10 times. In fact, they have the highest recycling rate of any consumer product. Fuji says it has a recycling rate of 110% (the extra 10% comes from people bringing in cameras they bought on vacation in other countries). And Kodak says 90% of the camera, by weight, is reused.

> If you look at nothing but the electronics, single-use cameras are considered the **greenest option of all**

CELLPHONES

Let's take a quiet moment to look within. Now, ask yourself just how many cellphones you've owned in your lifetime. Go ahead, count 'em. Don't forget that time when you accidentally dropped it in the toilet, or when it fell out of your bag who knows where. Some us can go back to the time before camera phones and Blackberries, back to when they called them car phones and you needed a briefcase just to fit the battery. No matter what the reason, most cell users get a new one every year and a half or so. That's a hell of a lot of waste, considering about half of us have one.

Ask yourself just how many cellphones you've owned in your lifetime

Sure they're small, but they pack a punch: they're full of lead, brominated fire retardants, nickel, cadmium—all kinds of fun stuff that accumulates in our tissues. Then there's the whole brain cancer controversy tied to the frequencies these babies give off. Various studies have found that rat brain cells have died and gene expressions have been altered when exposed to cellphone radiation. Interestingly, independent studies have been way more likely to find physiological impacts than industry-funded ones. In 2005, the head of the Public Health Agency of Canada cautioned Canadians to moderate their cellphone use until concerns about the long-term effects are ironed out.

Going back to the toxins lurking in the hardware, Europe and Japan are at the fore in setting up stricter manufacturing standards. Canada's not making too many federal moves on this front (although we are phasing out some brominated fire retardants), but many companies are starting to remove certain chemicals no matter where in the world they sell the phone. All new **Sony Ericsson** phones are free of PVC and brominated fire retardants; the same goes for **Nokia**. **LG** products will be PVC-free by 2008. Motorola's lagging at the back of the pack, according to Greenpeace's electronics report.

Get over your fear of commitment and cozy into a long-term relationship with the phone you already have. Don't just ditch it when a younger, slimmer, sexier model tempts you. And if you do move on, or it dies off, make sure to give it away. Non-profit Rechargeable Battery Recycling Corporation's Call2Recycle program has cellphone drop-off recycling boxes at many Canadian Tire, Home Depot, Sears, Circuit City and Bell World outlets (for locations near you, check out www.rbrc.org/call2recycle/dropoff/index.php). Pitch-In Canada, a non-profit org, has a cellphone collection program that pays $1 a pop to groups engaged in fundraising drives (www.pitch-in.ca).

LIGHTING

Afraid of the shadows? You'd have to assume our whole nation is, considering our obsession with lighting every corner of our homes, offices and malls as brightly as possible. In fact, 20% of our household energy bills are spent on keeping those bulbs lit.

The question is, if you're leaving a room for five minutes, is it better to leave a light on or turn if off? The truth is (and you might want to cover your kids' ears at this point, or those of anyone who's a gluttonous light-leaver-on-er), the more you turn a light on and off, the shorter its life span. That said, regular bulbs should always be turned off as soon as they're not needed, as they're super-wasteful and inefficient. On the other hand, if we're talking fluorescent lights, many agree it's worth turning them off only if you're leaving the room for more than 15 minutes, as they take more energy to start up.

Bottom line, for every kilowatt hour of electricity you waste (a single 100-watt bulb left on for 10 hours uses a kilowatt), power plants release nearly 700 grams of climate-changing CO_2 into the air. Not to mention all the other pollutants being choked out of the stacks. If that fact doesn't convince the family to be responsible with its light usage, tape pictures of coal plants billowing toxic clouds next to the light switch. Maybe that'll work. If you want to know what you're wasting in cash, check out the energy calculator at www.hydroonenetworks.com/en/efficiency/. Of course, there comes a time when we all need light in our life. So which ones should you get?

Incandescent: Regular incandescent lights haven't changed much since Edison's time—they're still incredibly inefficient. In fact, only 5% to 10% of the electricity they consume is emitted as light; the rest is wasted as heat. So-called long-lasting incandescent bulbs are just lights that put out less output, or lumens. They'd lose against compact fluorescent lights (see below) any day.

Halogen: Halogen lighting was hailed as top of the line in the '80s and '90s. These fancy incandescents still rock if you want sleek, modern ambience and high-quality light, but the coolest part is that they use up to 40% less energy than their plain incandescent cousins, according to Canada's Office of Energy Efficiency. Plus, they last a long time (about 3,000 hours). The downside is that these babies are fire hazards (you can fry an egg on the tall torchiere types found in student apartments everywhere), and they're not as efficient as compact fluorescents. Get a pro to install in-ceiling types.

Compact Flourescent: Compact fluorescent light bulbs (CFLs) are definitely the greenest way to go. Sure, they've got the word "fluorescent" in their name, but they're nothing like the nasty office lighting that flickers overhead, giving you headaches. In fact, the light they give off is fairly comparable to that of regular bulbs if you buy the right ones (see "The Right Hue for You," below). Yes, they cost more up front, but the price has come down, and they use two thirds less energy and last 10 times longer than incandescents. And with all the energy you'll save, you can expect to cut the lighting portion of your bill in half.

CFLs aren't angels—they contain a millimetre-wide pinch of mercury—or about 5 to 10 milligrams' worth (as compared to the 25 milligrams in watch batteries and 500 in silver dental fillings, says the Office of Energy Efficiency). It's the nature of fluorescents. But before you get freaked out and swear them off forever, consider this: your super-energy-efficient CFLs contain much less mercury than what's spewing out of the coal-fired power plants that power your regular, inefficient bulbs.

Philips is recognized industry-wide for having the lowest mercury content in its CFLs (the Philips Marathon 16-watt, said to last five years, is available at stores such as Home Depot and Staples). But while other companies do have slightly higher mercury levels, they're not considered high enough to be dangerous.

Make sure to read labels, as each light promises to last a different amount of time. **Globe CFLs** last up to 5,000 hours. **Greenlite CFLs** should keep shining for up to 10,000

THE RIGHT HUE FOR YOU

Maybe you've already brought home a CFL and thought, "Damn, I'm not a fan of the light it gives off." Don't despair: you're not stuck with one option. Different CFLs give off different types of light. And although they have improved over the years, you may not be crazy about all of them. Some are warm, some bluish, some remind you of sitting in a cubicle. That's because of something called colour temperature: the lower the colour temperature, the warmer the light.

To give you an idea of what's out there, you can often choose between 2,700K (if you're wondering what the K stands for, it's a unit of heat measurement called Kelvin), 4,100K and 6,500K bulbs. **The closest to the yellowy glow of regular incandescent bulbs is 2,700K.** The higher the number, the whiter, cooler and bluer the light. FYI, most "daylight" bulbs are about 6,500K.

One 100-watt bulb gives off more light than four 25-watt bulbs (it's actually closer to that of six 25-watters). Better to use one stronger bulb than 6 weak ones.

According to Environment Canada, if every house in Canada switched just one regular incandescent bulb to a CFL model with an Energy Star label, we'd save over $73 million in energy bills and stop almost 400,000 tons of greenhouse gas emissions from choking out of electrical generators—that's basically the same as taking 66,000 cars of the road!

hours, as will **Pur Lites**. Overall, an easy rule is to look for the Energy Star symbol, which points the way to most of the best CFLs and guarantees that your light uses 75% less power than regular bulbs.

Full-spectrum lights are either CFLs or incandescents that are said to emit all colours in the visible spectrum. They've also been credited with fighting everything from tooth decay to cancer. Yes, that's a little far-fetched, and some call them full-on fakes, but many people insist that they help with seasonal affective disorder (SAD). **Teldon** makes full-spectrum light bulbs that last up to 10,000 hours.

Natural-spectrum lights are supposed to most resemble sunlight. They filter out the yellows and greens that would be in regular lighting (so they tend to look bluish, which never feels all that natural to me). Note that natural-spectrum lights aren't always compact fluorescents; those that aren't don't save any more energy than regular lights, but they can last a good long time. **Seventh Generation** makes some that last about 3,500 hours (four times longer than ordinary bulbs, but not as long as CFLs). Flicker-free **Verilux** natural-spectrums last up to 5,000 hours and come with a three-year warranty.

Dimming a light by just 10% doubles the bulb's life

Ambient Lighting: If you've got a chandelier or some fixtures in which CFLs just won't work, at least use the minimum amount of wattage possible. If you're trying to create ambience over, say, a dining-room table, it's better to have six 15-watt bulbs in your chandelier than six 60-watters. And make sure you have a dimmer switch. Dimming a light by just 10% doubles the bulb's life. It's important to note that you can't use dimmer switches with 95% of CFL bulbs. Put a regular CFL on a dimmer switch and it'll flicker or hum and shorten its life, but you shouldn't have a problem if you buy good-quality CFLs labelled as dimmable

(Philips makes some). Chandelier owners take note: chandelier-sized CFLs are now available (yay!), but are pretty bright and aren't yet dimmable.

The other option is to pick up three-way CFL bulbs with low, medium and high settings. Of course, you'll need three-way lamp fixtures for them to work. Or skip the fixtures altogether and just burn some (petroleum-free) candles. Much more romantic.

Disposal: Over 300 million light bulbs and tubes are purchased each year in Canada— and, no matter how long they last, they eventually end up in the trash. But because of their mercury content, do not, I repeat, *do not* throw your CFLs or any fluorescent lights out with

---

LIGHTING TIPS

#1 Get motion sensors for outdoor lights. Even if one gets triggered 10 times a night for five minutes, that's way better than leaving it on from nightfall to sunrise.

#2 Use targeted lighting (such as a desk lamp) when you're reading or doing the crossword.

#3 Some lamp shades and fixtures are light leaches: they soak up all the bulb's rays and leave you in the dark, wasting precious wattage. Choose lighter-coloured lamp shades.

---

your regular garbage. When they burn out (and trust me, it doesn't happen very often— these babies can last five years or more) take them to a household hazardous waste depot for safe disposal or recycling (they can even reuse the mercury). You don't want that toxin leaching out in landfill and contaminating surrounding areas.

If one happens to break in your home, don't panic: the tiny amount of mercury shouldn't make you sick. Don't vacuum the mess (you don't want mercury dust being kicked up or leaching from the bag into the air), just sweep it up and wipe the area with a damp paper towel, then put it all in a plastic bag and bring it to your haz-mat waste depot as you would your burnt-out CFLs.

Candles: Light up a few candles, take a couple of deep breaths and let a day's worth of stress melt away while you're saving a little on electricity, right? Well, I wouldn't inhale too deeply knowing those candles are emitting nasty pollutants such as benzene, formaldehyde, soot and lead. Indeed, most candles are made of paraffin, a totally unromantic

179

waste product of the petroleum industry. Some can actually emit black soot made up of polluting polyaromatic hydrocarbons, according to the EPA. That soot is created during incomplete combustion of carbon-containing fuel. You can tell whether your candle is creating excess amounts of this indoor air pollution, known as ghosting or fogging, by checking for dark, oily deposits that are impossible to wash off around electrical outlets, appliances, vertical blinds and walls. As yummy as they can smell, highly scented candles or candles that are soft to the touch are often a culprit. That includes aromatic candles billed as "aromatherapy." (The Canadian Federation of Aromatherapy says a quality candle containing high-grade aromatherapy oils will give off scent for only a few moments.)

Keeping wicks trimmed (yes, there's a reason why candle labels tell us to do this!) and away from drafts helps reduce soot emissions. Obviously, staying away from scented and gelatinous petroleum candles is a good idea too. (And if oily black soot isn't enough of a reason for you, artificially scented candles can also give off potentially hormone-disrupting phthalates.)

Even if a black cloud hasn't descended upon your pad, there's still a chance that your favourite candles are made with dangerously high levels of lead, especially if they were purchased from the dollar store or made in China. The toxic compound is placed in paper or cotton wicks because it's thought to make candles burn more slowly and evenly. A recent study found that one leaded candle-burning session a week can send enough lead into your home's atmosphere to raise a child's blood lead count above federally accepted levels and increase chances of behavioural and learning problems. Eek!

Canada has yet to institute a ban on lead candles, but Health Canada says one is in the works. In the meantime, consider chucking any candles that puff black soot when you snuff them, and note that tea lights, pillar candles and candles that create wax puddles are more likely to contain lead. Health Canada says you can test your wick by peeling apart any fibre in the wick and seeing if it has a metallic core. If it does, rub it on white paper—if you see a grey smudge, it's probably lead. If it tests positive, toss it. North American–made candles generally don't contain lead. **IKEA** candles are also lead-free.

Alternative Candles: Set the mood without filling the air with fumes. Long-lasting **beeswax** is said to actually clean the air by releasing calming negative ions that cling to dust, making particles heavy so they fall (of course, you kick them up again when you walk around, but still, kind of a cool thing). They might be pricier, but be sure to buy 100% beeswax candles—there are lots of watered-downed versions on the market that are mixed with paraffin or bleached.

Then there are **veggie-based candles** made from soy. They burn clean, long and bright, and their manufacturers say that dollar-per-hour, they're actually cheaper than paraffin.

CLEANING

Decades of marketing have taught us that your house isn't clean unless you can see a bald man reflected in your floors and your children can eat off your garbage can lid. And, of course, those grimy dishes, tubs and toilets have to sparkle with one easy stroke.

As a result, we've got cupboards stocked with toxic soups (full of chemical whiteners, colorants, perfumes, smog-making VOCs and harmful petroleum-based chemicals) that are often the most dangerous products in our homes. They're major contributors to indoor air pollution (which can, shockingly, be anywhere from two to 100 times higher than outdoor air). Anyone with asthma or chemical sensitivities can tell you just how harmful these products can be to your health, but what about the ecosystem's?

Chemical Cleansers: Sure, many of the ingredients in chemical cleansers break down into harmless substances, but others make it through the water treatment process to wreak havoc on our waterways. Some surfactants (the stuff that makes them sudsy and spread well) used in degreasers, disinfectants and general cleaners break down into hormone-disrupting agents that have been shown to feminize fish. And nearly 70% of American streams tested positive for this stuff!

It's hard to tell which bottle or spray is better or worse, since most labels don't list any ingredients at all. But there are some clues. Products with the word "warning" could make you really sick but won't kill you. "Caution" means slightly toxic. Stay away from anything labelled "danger," "poison" or "corrosive"—they're the most toxic.

The ecological nightmare is only compounded when you factor in the growing trend towards disposable cleaning wipes, mops and dusters, which are clogging our landfills unnecessarily. Stop the insanity, people! We didn't need these before, and we don't need them now.

Of course, no discussion of modern cleaning agents is complete unless we face up to our addiction to antibacterial . . . er, everything. Please, let it go! Exposure to household germs isn't a bad thing, In fact, it bolsters our immunity to them. But it is bad when those bug-fighting ingredients, such as triclosan, make their way into 58% of our streams, as well as into breast milk.

Disposable cleaning wipes, mops and dusters are clogging our landfills unnecessarily

WHAT DO YOU MEAN, IT'S "BIODEGRADABLE?"

If there's one term that companies toss around to get a little eco-cred for their products, it's this one. The word "biodegradable" is about as abused as the term "natural." The insinuation is that whatever you purchased will fully break down and return to nature after you chuck it. Back in 1989, seven U.S. states sued the maker of Hefty garbage bags for saying that some of its bags would biodegrade when, in fact, they only partially degraded (into plastic bits) in direct sunlight, and not at all in landfill. In the U.S., the Federal Trade Commission has issued guidelines for how the term should be used and has taken action against several companies that made misleading or flat-out false biodegradability claims. No one even pretends to police the term in Canada.

That means you're on your own, sheriff. **Read labels carefully**. Look for certification symbols and details about biodegradability testing standards, and do your research. If a product sports the word "biodegradable," call the company and ask what it means. Has the product passed any particular tests? Under what conditions does the product degrade (in full sun or in dark, airless landfill piles)? And just how long does it take to return to Mother Nature's warm embrace? Four hundred years is not a good answer. Not that the makers will tell you much.

Don't be duped by tricky wording. Many mainstream cleaning products say they contain "biodegradable ingredients" or "biodegradable surfactants" (surfactants make things sudsy and rinse "clean"). Some even offer up valuable testing codes (like OECD #301d), indicating they're proven to break down quickly in water. But what about the rest of the ingredients? And keep in mind that being biodegradable doesn't necessarily make an ingredient eco-friendly. **DDT, for instance, often breaks down into two compounds that, according to** *E Magazine*, **are more toxic than DDT itself.**

However, there are lots of great companies out there that are happy to come clean and tell you right on the label how long it takes their product to break down. **Nature Clean** makes bleaches, soaps, shampoos and toilet bowl cleaners (available at most health stores and even some grocery stores), 99% of which biodegrade within 28 days. Quebec-based **Druide** uses the same standard for its line of personal-care products.

Even super-biodegradable products such as **Campsuds** should never be used directly in rivers or lakes, where they could harm fish. Soap up at least 60 metres away from fresh water and bury your wash and rinse water in a hole 15 centimetres deep. According to Campsuds maker Sierra Dawn, the soil's bacteria will completely and safely biodegrade the detergent.

And don't be a sucker. It may smell like green apples or have an orange on the label, but that doesn't mean it's any more natural. In fact, some citrus-containing degreasers were also found to have the nasty surfactants mentioned earlier.

All-Purpose Cleaning: If you're looking for a good, all-natural, truly eco-friendly all-purpose cleaner but want the ease of the ready-to-spray types, there's plenty of choice out there. Health stores are stocked with a variety of natural cleaners by companies such as **Seventh Generation, Ecover, Nature Clean** and **Simply Clean. Citra-Solv** has a good orange-scented all-purpose kitchen degreaser. By far the most effective non-toxic green cleaner I've come across is B.C.-based **Pink Solution**. This stuff has lifted five-year-old carpet stains, shower mould, baked-on oven grime, rust and can be diluted to clean windows, pets and more (www.pinksolution.ca).

Or make your own by tossing one part vinegar to one part water in a spray bottle. You can add a few drops of essential oil if you want to mask the vinegar scent. In tandem, a vinegar-dampened sponge and tossing down a sprinkle of salt make a good all-purpose grease-cutting scouring agent. Really, you just need to pick up a copy of *Organic Housekeeping* by Ellen Sandbeck—it's loaded with tons of practical green cleaning tips and recipes for homemade cleaners designed for every single dirt scenario in your home.

If you must banish bacteria, try **Benefect Disinfectant Spray**—it's 100% plant-based, with no added dyes or fragrances. And it kills 99% of germs naturally (see page 11 for more info on antibacterial personal care products).

Or bypass cleaning products altogether with the **Blue Wonder** cloth. Its patented microfibre knit (half polyester, half nylon) is ultra-absorbent and antibacterial, and it magically enables you to clean windows, sinks, stoves, pots, TVs and pretty much any surface you can think of without cleaners (www.bluewondercloth.com). Lots of people who have to avoid mainstream cleaning products because of chemical sensitivities swear by it. **Mabu** makes a similar all-purpose, naturally bacteria-resistant cloth from vegetable cellulose pulp.

Windows: As for getting windows, mirrors and glass surfaces sparkly, be aware that you're inhaling a fine mist of the lung-irritant ammonia with every squeeze of the nozzle. Windex Multi-Task with Vinegar and its outdoor version don't actually contain ammonia, but all conventional window cleaners contain chemical detergents, surfactants and perfumes.

183

RECIPE FOR WINDOW CLEANER

In a spray bottle, combine:
1/4 cup (50 mL) vinegar
1/2 tsp (2 mL) natural dish detergent
2 cups (500 mL) water

(Don't be fooled by newer pseudo-natural lavender and orange types.) Some window cleaners even contain nerve-damaging Butyl Cellosolve. FYI, **Nature Clean**'s natural glass and window cleaner did a good job in home tests.

Toilet and Bathroom Cleaners: Freud would say our culture has some serious potty-shame issues. We keep whatever it is we do in there behind locked doors, then regularly douse the room in enough bleach, artificial fragrances and harsh disinfectants to throw any CSI off the trail. It's important to keep your *salle de bain* clean, but do you really need to eat off your toilet? Yes, you say, my two-year-old niece just might lick the bowl. But do you want her licking highly caustic chemicals?

Pretty much every bathroom product comes with the "cleaning power" of chlorine bleach. Too bad chlorine is a hazardous air pollutant and can react with chemicals in the environment to form dioxin, a particularly nasty hormone disrupter that builds up in our tissues. Then there are all the corrosive ingredients in toilet bowl cleaners, some of the most toxic in your house, which can burn your eyes, skin and lungs. And did I mention the smog-inducing VOCs that evaporate into the air? Avoid toilet cleaners with Teflon in them.

You definitely don't need to be flushing non-stick coatings into our waterways to end up accumulating in the bodies of wild animals and humans. To add insult to injury, we're all buying landfill-clogging disposable toilet wands, pre-filled with bleach, to do our dirty work.

Calcium stains will come off

if you drop a 1,000-milligram tablet of

vitamin C into the bowl overnight

Even for tough jobs, you can pour in 1 cup (250 mL) of borax and 1/4 cup (50 mL) of vinegar, let it sit for a few hours, then scrub. Calcium stains will come off if you drop a 1,000-milligram tablet of vitamin C (yes, the kind you take for a cold) into the bowl overnight. If you want a ready-made toilet cleaner, and are stuck on the blue dye type, at least reach for an otherwise green version such as **Seventh Generation**. It even smells like fresh peppermint. **Ecover** makes a potent pine-scented one.

As for the rest of the bathroom, there are two kinds of people in this world: spray shooters and cream users. Fans of a good lathery spray will like **Nature Clean's Tile and Bath Spray**, but **Earth Friendly Creamy Cleanser** is a good one for anyone who prefers non-spritz products. For areas where you don't want a lot of bubbles, such as countertops and toilet seats, **Simply Clean's Super Cleaner** and **Eco-Max**'s bathroom spray were a hit. (Available at health stores.)

Instead of buying a scouring powder for your tub, try sprinkling on baking powder or straight borax powder and rubbing with a damp sponge. Plain vinegar is a good basic bath cleaner. To get rid of built-up soap scum, just rub straight vinegar (heating it up first helps) on your shower door or tub, wait five minutes, then rinse. Got mildew problems? Pull out an old toothbrush, dip it in a paste of borax and water and go to town. You can also try putting

IS THERE A GREEN VERSION OF DRANO?

Stuck with a little lagoon full of hair and debris that just won't drain properly? It's enough to make any eco-head entertain the idea of pouring—gasp!—a toxic clog-clearing product down the sink. But wait—before you turn to acids and industrial lye, which can seriously harm your health, the wastewater stream and PVC pipes, there are alternatives.

For less serious jams, it's always worth trying the old baking-soda-and-vinegar combo. Pour some baking soda and 1 cup (250 mL) of vinegar into the drain, wait 15 minutes while it fizzles and pops, then pour in a kettle of boiling water. Do this several times, until the clog clears.

For tougher situations, try 1 cup (250 mL) of washing soda (a stronger relative of baking soda that you can find it in the laundry section of your grocery store or any health store), followed by 3

cups (750 mL) of boiling water. Again, repeat until you break on through to the other side. Just don't overdo it if you have PVC pipes.

All-natural enzyme- and bacteria-based cleaners, such as **Citra-Drain** (available at health stores), eat away at hard-core clogs. Let it sit for several hours, then flush with water. Simple plungers and plumber's snakes can also work well. **One-Second Plumber** (from Canadian Tire) uses air pressure to drive clogs through the line. Each canister works 24 times. They're good for both sinks, toilets and tubs. Another good chem-free option is **Drain King**. It attaches to your garden hose and creates a hard-core water flush. Could be messy, though.

To avoid future sink jams, get yourself a metal strainer that fits over your drain and do monthly, even weekly, baking soda sessions.

What's this? A promise to kill 99.99% of germs on a health store cleanser? There must be a catch. Some sort of hidden chemical. Surprise—there isn't. Canadian-made **Nature Clean's All-Natural Household Disinfectant** wipes out as close as you can get to 100% of bacteria such as salmonella and staph (as well as mould, mildew and funguses such as athlete's foot) without harsh bleach, persistent triclosan or any other chemical disinfectant. Instead, it relies on the bug-fighting power of one of my favourite herbs: thyme. Spray it on washroom doorknobs, countertops, diaper pails, you name it. Okay, so it smells pretty strongly of thyme, but isn't that better than some artificial scent whipped up by chemists?

several drops of antifungal grapefruit seed extract (available at health stores) in a little water and let it penetrate.

Ellen Sandbeck, the author of *Organic Housekeeping*, says if you towel or squeegee your shower dry every time you use it, you'll only have to clean it every few weeks. My mother has long sworn by this technique (she also patented cleaning the shower while you're taking one). No matter what, it's always best to whip out your sponge after a shower has taken place—all that heat and steam loosens up the dirt.

Oven Cleaners: You know they're bad for you because of the skull and crossbones on the label. And the warnings don't lie: noxious foaming oven cleaners are full of lye and corrosive sodium hydroxide. But they can easily be replaced with non-toxic alternatives that you leave on for a few hours, such as **Nature Clean Oven & Barbecue Cleaner**. After testing all the natural options, my favourite was plain old baking soda and time (and my oven grit was really baked on—it had never been cleaned!) Try slathering the charred surface with a mix of baking soda and hot water and let it soak in overnight. The next day, scrub with a soapy abrasive sponge. The gunk should just slip off.

Dishwashing Detergent: Sure, yours is soft on hands, but what's it doing to the planet? Most conventional dishwashing liquids and powders are petroleum-based. Some even contain hormone disrupters. And while most laundry detergents and dish soaps stopped using ecosystem-disrupting phosphates years ago, some dishwasher detergents still contain them, so be sure to check.

Ecover, **Nature Clean**, **Earth Friendly**, **Citra-Solv** and **Seventh Generation** all make great, largely chem-free dishwashing soaps. One small, completely unscientific study found that Ecover's suds cut through grease the best, and it's also my personal fave. Nature Clean's all-purpose unscented cleaner suds up well on dishes, plus it can be used to clean the rest of your house. You can even wash your fruit with this stuff.

For natural automatic dishwasher detergents, Ecover beat out the rest, and powders in general seemed more effective at getting the grime off than gels.

Wood Polish: Furniture polishing sprays might not have the same notorious ozone-destroying CFCs they used to back in the day, but they still contain air pollutants that fill your home with fumes. And lots of them have ingredients, such as phenol, that have ties to cancer. Why risk it, when you can buy all-natural furniture polish from the health store or make your own with a simple mix of 1 cup (250 mL) of olive oil and a squirt of lemon?

LAUNDRY

Let's be honest. Laundry is one of those chores few of us like to do—especially if you have to schlep bags of dirty socks to a gritty old laundromat every week. But you can make the experience much less irritating for the earth and your skin if you dump those mainstream cleansers at the curb.

REDUCE YOUR PACKAGING

Buy in bulk whenever possible. To conserve packaging, look for brands that let you refill their bottles (such as **Nature Clean**) and concentrated formulas that you dilute at home.

Laundry Detergents: If you believe advertisers, the hills are alive with the smell of laundry. In fact, they've somehow bottled the scent of spring, sunshine and tropical breezes. In truth, your laundry detergent is probably the farthest thing from nature in your pantry. Most of the laundry products at mainstream shops are filled with artificial dyes, clingy perfumes and petroleum-based chemicals that can build up in our bodies and our water systems. Some are carcinogens; some, like the phthalates in those "summer fresh" perfumes, contain potential hormone disruptors; others emit vapours that can cause headaches, dizziness and vomiting (many people can't even walk down the laundry aisle in grocery stores without getting sick). It's hard to know what's in there for sure, since companies aren't required to list ingredients, but those that are advertised ain't good. Like bleach. Sure, it makes your whites whiter, but it's also highly caustic, burns the hell out of your skin and poisons thousands of children a year. It's also a hazardous air pollutant and can create nasty dioxins.

Laundry Detergent Solutions: Thankfully, there's a slew of legitimately non-toxic, cruelty- and chemical-free products out there. Just beware of greenwashing. Even the big boys offer perfume-free lines these days, which are indeed better for the scent-sensitive, but they don't make your suds chem-free. And note that "phosphate-free" labels are pretty meaningless, considering that all major manufacturers eliminated the ecology-disrupting mineral from their powdered products back in the mid-'90s.

But there are lots of genuinely green laundry soaps out there, and your local health store should carry a wide variety. Many supermarkets also carry at least one. Of the nine I've tried, Quebec's **Biovert** got tough stains out the best, but I couldn't find an unscented version. **Ecover** is a good all-around laundry soap with lightly scented and unscented options.

Hanging clothes to dry in sunlight is the cheapest whitener on the market

Soap Factory Laundry Miracle did equally well. Toronto-made **Nature Clean** is great because some health stores let you refill your old bottles.

Want to whiten your whites without resorting to toxic bleach? All sorts of bleach alternatives, in liquid and powder form, are carried by mainstream and health shops. Those with a mild base of hydrogen peroxide are the greenest bet. Of course, hanging clothes to dry in sunlight is the cheapest whitener on the market.

Eco-adventurers willing to try something a little off the beaten path might pick up those mysterious laundry balls or discs available at health stores. These electrically charged or magnetized pucks are said to soften water, dramatically reducing the need for soap. Plus, they claim to work for up to 700 loads. But beware: the Federal Trade Commission in the U.S. Bureau of Consumer Protection says they're bogus.

HOMEMADE LAUNDRY POWDER

Make your own laundry powder with 1 cup (250 mL) of soap flakes, 1/2 cup (125 mL) of washing soda (not the same as baking soda) and 1/2 cup (125 mL) of borax, all of which should be available in the laundry aisle of grocery and health stores.

What's the big difference? Well, in the world of cleaning products, a lot. The word "soap" is generally tied to products that use natural ingredients, such as animal fat–based soap flakes. The official definition of "detergent," according to the EPA, refers to synthetic cleaners. The main drawback to soaps is that they'll form soap scum in hard water (as you've probably experienced in your shower). They might leave a layer of residue on your clothing, too, although I've never had a problem with this. But the situation isn't totally black and white now that earth-friendly companies have developed detergents made from plant-based surfactants (which make a laundry cleaner penetrate, lather and spread). Confused? If you're buying a detergent just make sure the label clearly says it's made from plant materials instead of chemicals.

Stain Removers: It's amazing how frantic we get around stains. Down goes a little Shiraz or salsa, and the party stops. Suddenly, everyone thinks they're an expert and starts yelling out random tips on how to get that giant splotch off your favourite top.

That's if you catch it quickly. Even worse are those mystery stains you only notice when you do your laundry a week after you wore the damn thing. And if you're as klutzy as I am, you wonder how you can make oil stains fashionable, since they're on nearly everything you own.

Stay away from oh-so-handy disposable stain-removing laundry wipes and pens. The world doesn't need the extra trash. And do you really need to waste power and batteries on those weird ultrasonic vibrating stain-removing machines (Tide makes one) that come with throwaway pads and chem-based cleaners? Also keep in mind that do-it-yourself solutions aren't automatically earth-friendly. My god, Martha Stewart's website recommends pouring lighter fluid on mustard and grass stains!

Did you know that washing machines are at their most energy-efficient when they're packed with a full load?

Front loading machines use about 40% less water and 50% less energy than top loaders, according the Canada's Office of Energy Efficiency. And compared to a 1994 model, a new Energy Star model can save you over a $100 a year in hydro bills. Plus, these guys spin out more water than others during the spin cycle, so you can reduce your drying time. Save even more power by washing in cold water and do your part to prevent global warming while getting the stink out of your hockey socks.

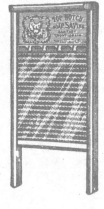

What's the point, when there are perfectly natural, ecologically sound solutions? Natural stain-removing gels by companies such as **Ecover** and **Nature Clean** work pretty well overall. Eco-safe bleaches (made of hydrogen peroxide) do a decent job on wine stains. But my all-around fave is the basic stain bar that several companies, such as **Simply Clean**, make. It's like a natural Magic Eraser! But it's not vegetarian—the bars are often made with tallow.

Dryers: Let's clear the air and get one thing straight: first and foremost, hang-dry what you can. About a third of your household's energy use goes to tossing your T-shirts around with hot air. But if you need your undies dry in a hurry, or your municipality has banned clothes-lines (yes, this really happens), there are ways to green up your drying habits.

For one, you could get a new clothes dryer. The average new dryer will save you about 300 kilowatts a year in energy over 1984 models—that's enough to run your dryer about 150 times! Look for the one with the lowest number on the little EnerGuide tag at the store—that tells you how many kilowatt-hours the machine is estimated to use per year.

Also, set your dryer on its lowest setting. And don't automatically turn the dial to 60 minutes. Your clothes can often dry in much less time. Start with 30 or 40 minutes and remove your clothes before they're bone-dry. Synthetics often dry after 10. If you've got a moisture sensor built into your dryer make sure to use it so you don't keep tumbling long after your shorts have been baked.

Fabric Softeners: Next on the list: toss your fabric softeners—both liquids and dryer sheets. Sure, the fruity scent clings to your jeans long after you've washed them, but so do all the other chemicals. Not good when you're talking about chems like chloroform, a probable human carcinogen, and benzyl acetate, a suspected kidney, liver and respiratory toxicant. One study even found that fabric softeners gave off the hazardous air pollutant toluene. Plus, dryer sheets aren't recyclable.

MAKE SURE TO CLEAN YOUR LINT TRAP

If the prospect of your house burning down due to a clogged lint screen hasn't already scared you into action, perhaps the knowledge that an uncleaned screen sucks money out of your pocket on a daily basis might persuade you. In fact, cleaning your lint filter could save you up to 40 bucks a year in energy costs, since clogs can increase energy use by about a third.

Everyone's been there. You're wearing a cute skirt or a kicky pair of pants, thinking, "Damn, I look good," then, suddenly, you feel it coming on. The cling. Panic sets in as you realize that within minutes your Sunday best will be hugging your body like bad plastic wrap. In such moments, we all dream of having a can of Static Guard in our purse, but what's in that stuff anyway?

Turns out it's got humidity-loving chemicals such as dimethyl ditallow ammonium chloride (what a mouthful!), which is toxic to fish and algae and isn't readily biodegradable. It also has chloromethane (which breaks down very slowly in air) and lots of petroleum-based ingredients such as butane, propane and isopropanol.

When you're being menaced by the cling, reach up under your outfit and brush the inside of the fabric with a metal hanger. Sounds bizarre, but it just might get you out of a staticky situation.

Remember, you can also avoid static by pulling your clothes out of the dryer before they're fully cooked or using nature's clothes dryer—the clothes line.

Fabric softener solvents are especially harmful if exposed to heat (um, isn't that what dryers are all about?). A study published in *Consumer Reports* found that using a liquid softener on terry cloth, fleece and velour made the fabrics seven times more flammable! Pretty scary.

Liquid softener addicts should turn to all-natural options such as **Ecover, Simply Clean** or **Seventh Generation**. A reusable chemical-free dryer cloth such as the **Static Eliminator** is another cool option. It combats static remarkably well and lasts for up to 500 loads. You can pick these up in health stores and some hardware stores. Beware of

HOMEMADE FABRIC SOFTENER

Up to trying a home brew? Add some baking soda to your water-filled washing machine (before filling it with clothes), then pour in 1 cup (250 mL) of vinegar during the rinse cycle. Missed that oh-so-brief window? **Just pour some vinegar on a damp cloth and toss it in the dryer.** Don't worry, you won't smell like salt and vinegar chips, and it'll keep static cling at bay. "But I don't want to give up my spring-fresh scent," you say. Not to worry—you can create your own aromatic blend by adding 10 drops of an essential oil to your green liquid softener (if you bought the unscented type) or that damp cloth destined for the dryer.

reusable spiky laundry balls you pop in the dryer to soften your shirts—most are made with that problematic plastic PVC and could be offgasing harmful plastic softeners onto your clothes.

Dry Cleaning: About 80% of dry cleaners use the super-toxic chemical tetracholorethylene, otherwise known as perchloroethylene, a.k.a. perc. Sure, perc is a great dissolver of dirt and oil. It's just a shame that it's so damn bad for us. In fact, the chem is classified as a possible carcinogen and is considered acutely toxic to wildlife and fish. This is particularly worrisome since perc is now a major groundwater contaminant, thanks to improper disposal procedures. Of course, it doesn't help that federal disposal regs are not really enforced. But even if a cleaner is discarding chems properly, the substance is still vented into the air. Environment Canada regulations have required dry cleaners to phase out wasteful old-generation machines and reduce perc use and emissions by 70% by 2005 (the department is still assessing whether that goal was reached). Parts of California have banned the use of perc altogether.

Need more disturbing info to turn you off your dry cleaning habit? Turns out food that spends one hour in a car with dry-cleaned clothes (like, say, a bag full of groceries) absorbs elevated levels of perc. Not so appetizing, is it?

"But what about my closet full of dry clean only tags?" you cry. Well, for one, don't believe the hype. Many say "dry clean" or "dry clean only," but most of these garments can be handwashed in cool water with gentle, natural soap—especially most synthetics, blends and wool. Silk is tricky because it might shrink, and rayon can shrivel up; best to test a small swatch.

Don't believe the tag. Many say "dry clean" or "dry clean only," but most of these garments can be handwashed in cool water with gentle, natural soap

If you're dead set on hiring a pro, there are a number of greener cleaners around. Just note that cleaners who call themselves perc-free might use something just as toxic, like petroleum hydrocarbon, which is considered a hazardous air pollutant and smog-inducing VOC. A silicone-based process called GreenEarth is also somewhat controversial. The U.S. EPA considers it a sound alternative to other ozone-depleting chems but one study tied extremely high exposures of the solvent to cancer in labs rats. The silicone lobby argues the study was taken out of context and 30 other studies prove it's perfectly safe. Anyway, if you're into checking it out, you can track down GreenEarth dry cleaner across Canada at www.greenearthcleaningcanada.com.

FYI: Dry cleaners listed as green on the Canadian Centre for Pollution Prevention website (www.c2p2online.com) are part of the federally funded Green Clean Project but might still be using perc. They could be classified as "green" for practices such as reusing hangers and plastic bags (speaking of which, make sure to bring your wire hangers back, people), or may be in the process of phasing out perc but haven't yet. It's best to ask.

Wet cleaners are a greener and more common alternative. They use specially formulated detergents, water and often computer-controlled machines, and can accommodate most dry clean only garments. Supposedly, that includes wedding gowns, wool suits, silks, leather, comforters and rayon. Of course, wet cleaning is not entirely holy, since the process can release soap surfactants and bleaches into the sewers, though these solutions are purportedly biodegradable.

Take note that some dry cleaners will tell you they "wet clean" when all they're doing is washing your clothes in a regular old machine and charging you extra for it.

AIR PURIFIERS

Forget televised outdoor air quality alerts. Your nose and your lungs will tell you when the air in your home just ain't cutting it. Whether winter's got your windows shut tight (and the air in your pad is about as fresh as your woolly socks after a heavy round of shovelling), or summer's pollen- and smog-heavy winds leave you gasping, most of us are breathing in all sorts of irritating indoor air pollutants, including animal dander, dust and mould. That's no surprise. But when Clean Production Action got seven U.S. environmental groups to test the vacuum cleaner dust in 70 homes, they found endocrine-disrupting compounds, carcinogens and bioaccumulating toxins such as fire retardants, phthalates and pesticides (even DDT) in the dust of pretty much every home tested (for the "Sick of Dust" report, see www.safer-products.org).

It can be impossible to rid your home of this stuff entirely, especially if the source of those pollutants (your furniture, your electronics, your lead blinds) remains, but you can get rid of a sizable amount of dust by simply, yes, dusting your home with a damp cloth and vacuuming regularly. In fact, anyone with serious allergies should be doing this daily. You can even get vacuum cleaners with HEPA filters built in (see www.allergyconsumerreview.com for suggestions).

For most people, that should be good enough. However, if you have allergies, are chemically sensitive or just want the air in your home to be as pure as possible, you might consider

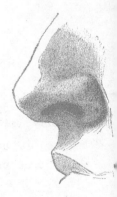

getting a room or whole-house air filter. Before you panic and run out to buy one, you need to know what you're doing. Consult Allergy Consumer Review and Air Purifiers America to see what would work best for you: **HEPA filters** or **carbon filters**.

Negative ionizers, by the way, are generally bad news. The American Lung Association says harmful particulates that have been ionized by these electronic air filters have a better chance of sticking to your lungs.

For those of you with forced air, *Consumer Reports* says a cheapie furnace filter such as **3M Filtrete Allergen filter** (available at Canadian Tire) should do just fine to control airborne dust, pet hair and dander. Make sure to change these every few months.

PEST CONTROL

We're not the only creatures that like to scurry inside when the air gets brisk and the leaves start falling. October through February is peak time for rodent infestations, not to mention all those squirrels, raccoons and birds that like to nest under our roofs. While it may be tempting to reach for that can of Raid or rat poison, remember that's a definite ecological no-no that can make everyone in your home sick, not just the invaders. So what's a bug-weary, beleaguered homemaker to do?

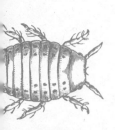

Physical Fortifications: No matter what your pest, you've gotta start by battening down the hatches. Any breach in your fort is an invitation to miniature outsiders looking for a warm place to call home. Seal up any cracks or gaps around baseboards, cupboards, vents, electrical outlets and pipes (mice can squeeze through a hole the size of a dime). Perforated and sheet metal, concrete and wire mesh hardware cloth are all rodent-resistant. A good caulking job should keep ants out. Weatherstripping under doors is another must.

Leaky taps and toilets are like rivers of fresh water for all sorts of pests—get them fixed! Food in your cupboards should be kept in airtight plastic or metal containers or sealed bags. Casually folding the cellophane down over your crackers ain't good enough, people.

> Any breach in your fort is an invitation to miniature outsiders looking for **a warm place to call home**

Vacuum often, clean your kitchen daily, and make sure to sweep under, around and, yes, even behind your appliances frequently. (I know this is tough if you're usually as nonchalant about cleaning as I am, but you're at war, kids, take it seriously!)

Animals: If you're already stuck with unwanted furry guests, stay away from poison powders and sprays, which kill the mouse over either days or minutes by making it bleed to death internally, attacking its nervous system or some kind of horrific death. Plus, these can and do make your pets and curious young kids sick too.

Traps are your best bet. Be sure to get the cruelty-free kind. Glue traps are just plain evil, since they tear a strip off the poor thing's skin as it tries to escape. Instead, use food to lure the whiskered scramblers to live traps. But you'll be defeating the point of these if you let a little mouse die of dehydration in your basement. Check the traps often and release any captives several kilometres from your home, or they'll be back. Reusable **Tin Cat** live traps (available at Canadian Tire and Home Hardware) can hold up to about thirty mice, but the more traps you have going the better.

Kitchen Bugs: Some mainstream bug killers list benign boric acid (borax) as their active ingredient, but they don't tell you that the (non-listed) so-called passive or inert ingredients, which make up 95% of the product, can actually be quite toxic. The group Beyond Pesticides says more than 200 "inert" chemicals are actually hazardous air and water pollutants. Here in Canada, the feds have issued a warning against buying Miraculous Insecticide Chalk and Cockroach Sweeper, as they may contain illegal pesticides and traces of lead.

If roaches have taken over your kitchen New York–style, a powdery trail of **sugar and baking soda** (50/50) is said to kill them in a couple of weeks, according to Golden Harvest Organics' tip sheet on pest control (www.ghorganics.com).

Some techniques can be used on multiple creepy crawlies. Try sprinkling straight non-toxic borax (which you can buy for a few bucks in the laundry section of your grocery store) on cracks, garbage cans and under appliances to kill roaches, water bugs, silverfish, fleas, ants, millipedes—pretty much anything that crawls. Please note, though, that borax shouldn't be swallowed by anything or anyone you don't want to make ill.

Vacuuming is a great non-toxic way to suck up roaches, wasps and ants. Most will suffocate in the bag, but to be sure, you should soak the bag in soapy water or freeze it for 24 hours (um, yeah, I know, I wouldn't want those things in my freezer either).

Diatomaceous earth is a handy all-natural, non-toxic substance (made of crushed marine fossils) to keep around the house, and it won't harm pets. It kills off all sorts of wigglers, such as earwigs, roaches, ants and fleas. Sprinkle it around cracks, crevices, baseboards, under appliances and above kitchen cabinets, and roaches, for instance, should be dead within two weeks. Put some in your vacuum bag too.

195

Keep a spray bottle full of **soapy water** on hand to spritz ants, roaches and other bugs. This surprisingly lethal cocktail even works on garden pests.

Moths: Is your favourite wool sweater riddled with mysterious holes? You've got a moth problem, honey. Whatever you do, do not use mothballs. Not only do they stink up your clothes, but they're made of toxic volatile compounds associated with serious health problems, including liver and neural damage and cancer. Even moth-repellent blocks labelled cedar or lavender may contain the main toxin found in mothballs. Instead, try all-natural **herbal moth bars**, made with essential oils and eco-wax, available at some health stores.

> ## PEST CONTROLLERS
>
> If you're not into doing all of this yourself, check the Yellow Pages for an eco-friendly pest controller, such as **Evergreen Pest Control** in Ottawa. Unfortunately, not every town has one just yet, so if you can't find one near you, make sure to look for a company that uses integrated pest management techniques and is willing to try less-toxic and cruelty-free steps first.

Moths do their dirty work in the summer, when our wool clothes are hidden in dark drawers, so lay your woollens out in the sun every so often to kill any sun-loathing larvae. Before you store your wools, try washing them with eucalyptus-filled **Eucalan**. Its ingredients are generally plant-derived, though it does contain some synthetics. And if you think you've got a moth infestation in your sweater, stick it in the freezer in a plastic bag for a few days. That'll kill the larvae off and keep your top looking peachy keen.

If the winged things are sprouting up in your pantry, you've got a whole other type of moth. Ditch any sack of flour or rice you may have had sitting open in the cupboard, wash everything down well then be sure keep any new supplies in sealed plastic or metallic containers.

HOME
IMPROVEMENT

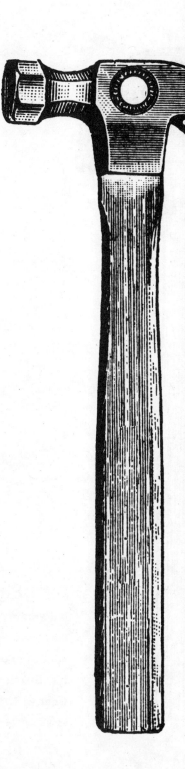

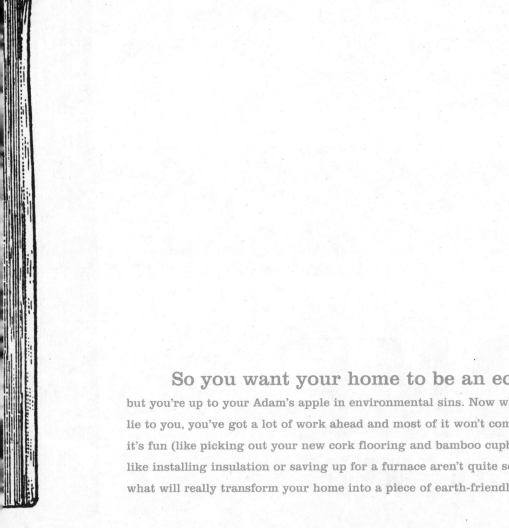

So you want your home to be an eco paradise

but you're up to your Adam's apple in environmental sins. Now what? Well, I won't lie to you, you've got a lot of work ahead and most of it won't come cheap. Some of it's fun (like picking out your new cork flooring and bamboo cupboards) others, like installing insulation or saving up for a furnace aren't quite so sexy but they're what will really transform your home into a piece of earth-friendly heaven.

RENOVATIONS

Those of you lucky enough to have green one-stop-shop home stores in your area, such as the Healthiest Home and Building Supplies in Calgary, Ottawa and soon Toronto (www.thehealthiesthome.com), take advantage. You'll find a lot of green home improvement products there. The rest of the country isn't quite so lucky, but you can always shop online and browse local home stores, which might carry some of these options. The truth is, there's a serious lack of solid distribution across Canada for some of this stuff. If you want to see these products in your area, tell the manager of your local home reno store. They will special-order some for you. And if they get enough requests, they might start carrying them in the store.

For a full list of green reno products certified under Environment Canada's EcoLogo program, including insulation, low-VOC (volatile organic compound) paints and finishes and building materials, check out www.environmentalchoice.com. **AFM Safecoat** makes great adhesives, sealants, caulking and more that are low-VOC and free of bad stuff such as formaldehyde, ammonia, acetone and phthalates. And don't forget to check out www.fsccanada.org/findwoodproducts.htm for a directory of certified wood products (about 100 building material suppliers are now certified by the Forest Stewardship Council).

FLOORING

Starting from the ground up, you've got lots of options for what falls beneath your feet. More and more flooring stores are carrying **cork**, which can be harvested without damaging the tree. There were some rumours flying around about cork supplies running low because

THE ENVIRONMENTAL CHOICE ECOLOGO PROGRAM

You might have spotted the EcoLogo seal on purchases in recent years. So what is it, exactly? Well, EcoLogo is a green labelling program set up by Environment Canada's Environmental Choice program and run by a company called TerraChoice. It's been around since 1988, but it's popping up on more and more products, including construction materials, cleaning supplies, household goods and garden stuff, as well as office, automotive and agricultural products. Each product has been independently audited to ensure that it meets certain green criteria, which are as diverse as the products themselves. For a full directory of EcoLogo products, as well as the standards they were held to, check out **www.environmentalchoice.com**.

the trees couldn't keep up with demand, but enviro-orgs such as the World Wildlife Fund (WWF) say that precious Mediterranean cork forests, and the endangered animals that dwell in them, will actually be threatened if we don't continue to buy cork!

Bamboo is another beautiful and increasingly widespread eco-flooring choice. Why is it so sustainable? Well, it's not actually a tree, and it grows so fast it's almost a weed. Don't want to steal food from the mouths of panda bears? **Silkroad Flooring** carries EcoLogo-certified bamboo flooring, plywood and veneers made from a type of bamboo that isn't a food source or habitat for the super-rare bears (www.silkroadflooring.com).

Reclaimed wood, taken from lake floors, riverbeds and old barns, not only saves a new tree from the chop but it revives a little piece of history in your living room. But buyer beware. When I looked into a few sources of vintage wood flooring, it soon became clear that "vintage" was more of a look than a reality. Most flooring with this name was really new wood that was distressed to make it look old. Ask to be sure.

You can also get flooring made out of trees axed because of storm damage, disease, safety concerns and construction projects. It's often called **rescued wood**. **Urban Tree Salvage** (www.urbantreesalvage.com) and **Canadian Heritage Timber Company** (www.canadianheritagetimber.com) sell flooring made of this stuff. Canadian Heritage also sells the reclaimed kind.

Once upon a time, before the vinyl invasion, linoleum actually came from natural sources. **Natural linoleum** is making a comeback, often going by the name **Marmoleum**. The all-natural extra-tough flooring is made of pine resins, flax and, yes, linseed oil (hence the "lin" in linoleum).

FSC-certified wood flooring is also a good option.

GREEN RENO WEBSITES

www.greenhomeguide.com: This site, which promises "Unbiased reviews and advice from professionals and homeowners like you," also has an inspiring directory of green home services and product retailers across the U.S., which is extremely useful if you're willing to shop online or cross the border.

www.designinggreen.com: Yay! A Canadian directory of over 1,000 green building and design products and services! The Virtual Sample Room, as it's called, was founded by multiple partners, including Environment Canada and Canada Mortgage and Housing Corporation.

CABINETS

We all need these miniature doors to cover up our mismatched plate and beer stein collections, but you want to stay away from anything made of pressed sawdust and wood shavings, such as medium-density fibreboard (MDF) and particleboard. They sound eco-friendly because they use up by-products from the wood-cutting process, but they actually use up to 80% virgin tree content, according to Green Seal. Plus, all that sawdust is bound together with the probable human carcinogen formaldehyde, which off-gases air-polluting, headache-inducing fumes into your home. So avoid MDF and particleboard unless you know they're formaldehyde-free, as **IKEA**'s cabinetry is.

Better still are **strawboard or wheatboard cabinets**. Made of compressed waste straw or wheat, they're basically bio-based particleboard, or MDF, made without formaldehyde and often finished with a pretty veneer of sustainable wood certified by the Forest Stewardship Council (FSC). **The Healthiest Home** (www.thehealthiesthome.com) sells some. For more FSC-certified wood products, see www.fsccanada.org/findwoodproducts.htm. **Bamboo** is also a sexy sustainable option for cabinets.

Make sure to ask for water-based finishes, low-VOC stains or paints, or natural oils. Better yet, get them unfinished and stain them yourself.

THE PVC DEBATE

When it comes to home reno stuff, PVC is in virtually everything: pipes, windows, flooring, horizontal blinds, fake leather couches. Trouble is, the building block of PVC, vinyl chloride, not only is a known carcinogen, but also creates dangerous dioxins (which accumulate in our tissues and the environment) in the manufacturing process and when incinerated at low temperatures (like in crappy municipal incinerators). The additives alone, such as potentially hormone-disruptive and carcinogenic phthalates added to make the hard plastic soft, are super-controversial. Then there are all the heavy metals, such as lead and cadmium, used to stabilize the plastic (hence the lead in vinyl blinds).

The industry, of course, says vinyl is completely safe, the dangers are exaggerated, and it's cleaned up its practices since its dirtier days. Enviro-groups don't buy any of it, and a couple of years back they demanded that the U.S. Green Building Council take a stand against the vinyl building materials that make up over half of all vinyl purchases. (FYI, many green homes are built with energy-efficient vinyl windows, and some argue that the energy savings they offer are worth the price tag.) The council looked into it for two years and came out with a draft statement. Its conclusions disappointed many anti-PVCers, who said the council ignored important studies and used poor source material and questionable methodology. Architects/Designers/Planners for Social Responsibility protested that most of the scientific literature scanned came from industry sources.

Either way, many companies have already started phasing it out, and entire municipalities have been making moves on this front. Just last year, Seattle decided to ditch plans to install 34,000 feet of PVC drainage pipes, instead using high-density polyethylene (HDPE) pipes. The move reflects the city's 2002 resolution to reduce or wipe out the purchase of any products with persistent bioaccumulative toxins (PBTs), including PVC. San Fran also has an ordinance mandating that all city departments stay away from PVC plastic whenever possible.

If you want to get into the nitty-gritty of vinyl-less building materials, head to **www.healthybuilding.net/pvc/alternatives.html**.

COUNTERS AND BACKSPLASHES

There are all kinds of fancy, though hard-to-find options out there for redoing your counters. **Canadian granite, recycled glass terrazzo** and **bamboo** all win green points (order through **The Healthiest Home** or check your local fine home store). Manitoba-based **Avanti** is developing counter tops made from hemp fibres and urethane (www.avantipolymers.com).

If you're willing to shop out of the States, **Eleek** makes slick metallic counter tiles out of 100% recycled aluminum (www.eleekinc.com). For backsplashes and bathrooms, **recycled glass tiles** are a gorgeous way to get use out of old bottles. Available at The Healthiest Home, or search on Treehugger.com.

CARPETS

Remember the plush, shagadelic carpeting of the '70s? Or the wall-to-wall craze of the '80s? Back then, hardwood lost out to carpets, whose soft, padded texture was considered ideal for kids and nice on the feet. Then people started talking about the dark side of carpeting, not only how it's made with polluting petrochemicals, but also how it traps allergens such as dust mites and can create problems for asthmatic children, and how all sorts of mystery fumes off-gas from its fibres.

For its part, the industry says carpets do trap allergens, but in a good way, keeping them from being airborne, especially if you vacuum with a good vacuum once or twice a week. (Obviously, carpets aren't for lazy people). But researchers haven't been convinced. One environmental engineer told *New Scientist* magazine that the dust trapped by carpets contains heavy metals, pesticides and persistent fire retardants. And you'd have to vacuum 25 times a week for several weeks to bring the level of those contaminants below safety standards. One Johns Hopkins University prof has said that the thicker your carpet pile, the deeper your chemical contamination (if you're set on getting a carpet or rug, get one with a low pile). Another study, out of the University of Southern California in the '90s, found DDT imbedded in a quarter of the carpets they tested. Tests by the U.S. EPA have corroborated the presence of up to 10 pesticides deeply embedded in carpet fibres. Most of these scientists suggest that, at the very least, you make sure shoes (which can carry pollutants on their soles) are always checked at your front door.

You'd have to vacuum 25 times a week for several weeks to bring the level of contaminants below safety standards

Chemicals: What about the chemical fumes said to come off the carpeting itself? The industry says air-polluting, lung-irritating, smog-inducing VOCs dissipate within 48 to 72 hours. The Canadian Carpet Institute says they should be gone within a week, after which your floor covering is "essentially" VOC-free. The industry also insists that its carpets are formaldehyde-free. Maybe so, but *Environmental Building News* has reported that VOCs—from, say, painting your house—can get trapped in carpet fibres and will continue to be

203

released into the atmosphere over time. And if your carpet has been tacked down with solvent-based glues, you can factor in even more VOCs rising from your flooring.

Synthetic Carpets: No doubt the carpet industry has done some serious revamping over the last few years to spruce up its green cred. But carpets are still made mostly of petroleum-based fibres that require a massive amount of energy and water to make, not to mention all the hazardous air pollutants and VOCs released in the process. Turning those fibres into carpeting involves another huge influx of energy and water—about 23,000 BTUs of energy and 10.1 gallons of water per square yard (according to an excellent report by Green Seal that's chock full of good info cited throughout this section), although these figures are an improvement over the past. Between 1995 and 2002, Nova Scotia–based Crossley Carpets, for instance, cut water usage by 27%, internal waste going to landfill by 47%, electric power use by 17% and fossil fuel use by 31%.

Nylon carpeting is considered the most durable, but there's no good way to spin the fact that making nylon produces the poison gas hydrogen cyanide, as well as carcinogenic benzene, air-polluting chems and all sorts of nasty toxins. The good news is that nylon 6 is recyclable, and manufacturers such as **Interface**, **Mohawk** and **Shaw** include up to 50% recycled content in some products. At the head of the class is **Milliken's Earth Squares**, which are made with 100% refurbished post-consumer nylon. Milliken was also the first company to send zero waste to landfills and go PVC-free.

While polypropylene and polyester (PET) rugs are more environmentally friendly to produce, they aren't as durable, and you can't recycle them when you're done with them. But **Beaulieu**, **Mohawk** and **Talisman** all produce PET lines made of 100% recycled pop bottles, which is very cool. It's nice to see cola finally doing some good.

Backing: Like so many things in life, what you see is never what you get. Over half of a carpet's weight comes from the backing. And while the carpets themselves might be getting somewhat more ecologically responsible, almost all of the plastics used as carpet backing are linked to serious eco-problems. Above all, stay away from PVC backing; although it's recyclable, it contains phthalates that might off-gas harmful fumes throughout the life of the carpet.

Almost all of the plastics used as carpet backing are linked to serious eco-problems

Plus, it releases persistent toxins when it's incinerated after you trash the carpet. Synthetic rubber is also made with a toxic brew. And popular polyurethane backings use a nasty chemical that can make workers really sick (though it isn't supposed to be harmful in a finished product).

Wool and jute backings are, of course, good natural alternatives, but wouldn't you know it, they're nearly impossible to find. Shaw has a carpet cushioning called BioBalance, made by Dow, with 16% soy oil. There's no mention of whether that's pesticide-free soy, but either way it's better than the alternative, since the bean is renewable, unlike petrol-based plastic. Still, the backing is mostly just polyurethane.

Sealers: Glues, seam sealers and removable carpet padding can all give off smog-inducing, lung irritating VOCs, but the glues are probably the worst offenders. Adhesives aren't used in home installations as extensively as they are in commercial spaces, but if any glues will be used in your home, make sure to ask the person laying your carpet to use water-based, low-VOC ones. Peel-and-stick carpet squares also minimize the amount of glue used on-site, although they do get their stick from somewhere.

Recycling Carpets: In an effort to clean up their image, many manufacturers now have take-back programs. That's good news, because a hell of a lot of carpeting is landfilled ever year (2 million tons are junked annually in the U.S. alone). Don't worry, they don't expect you to rip up your wall-to-wall and cart it to them. When you buy a new carpet, installers will take your old one away and recycle it. Some manufacturers, such as **Milliken**, make old carpets into new ones. Milliken even goes so far as to provide a written guarantee that your carpet will be recycled when you're through with it. Others, such as **DuPont**, melt old carpets down and turn them into car parts, sound proofing and all kinds of nifty things.

You can actually lease carpet tiles from **Interface**, a company made famous in the Canadian documentary *The Corporation* for changing its policies and championing environmental reform. If tiles get worn down in high-traffic areas, no problem, Interface will replace them. That's so much better than having to ditch a whole carpet! The **InterfaceFLOR** brand is actually, in part, made from corn, and the **Terra** line is 36% recycled.

Carpet Solutions: Looking for some guidance, maybe a nice label that tells you the carpet you're about to buy won't put out harmful emissions? The U.S. Carpet and Rug Institute has developed an indoor air–quality testing program that is also followed by Canadian carpet manufacturers. Rugs that meet its emissions standards have a Green Label logo on the back

For years, consumers have reached for carpets that come with extra stain protection. Hell, who wouldn't want something that promises to keep dirt, food and life stains from sinking into your rug? Scotchguard has long been the king of stain-resistant surfaces, but back in 2000 its manufacturer, 3M, quietly phased out production of its original recipe. Turns out the main chemical in Scotchguard, PFOS, is shockingly persistent. It's been found in children and adults, in blood banks, polar bears, dolphins, birds—you name it, they've got it. And Scotchguard records indicate that 3M knew about this sticky side effect for decades. The substance's extreme prevalence is even more upsetting when you look at the data tying it to liver tumours and learn that PFOS has killed off rat pups exposed in utero, even second-generation ones that hadn't been directly exposed.

While the company might have phased PFOS out, it's still using fluorochemicals to make its trademark Scotchguard products, but it swears these aren't so bad. To quote 3M: "3M's 'next generation' formulation has low potential to bioaccumulate, low toxicity and minimal to no environmental impact." Notice they haven't said there's no chance that these will build up in your blood, just a low chance. Hmm. Either way, any Scotchguard-treated product purchased in 2002 or earlier would contain the original persistent eco-toxins. You might consider pulling the rug out from your under your feet, and pronto.

(for more details and a list of compliant products, check out www.carpet-rug.com). However, one green building expert I spoke to dissed the industry-run program, calling it greenwashing.

The Green Label Plus program is much more hard-core; even the carpet industry says the Plus program uses "the most stringent criteria," while the regular Green Label, well, not so much. Green Plus also analyzes carpets for "chemicals of concern" (which aren't otherwise tested for) and tests for them every year. It makes sure carpets meet California's stringent indoor air–quality standards for low-emitting commercial settings. The catch is, the testing isn't available to homeowners, but only to builders, architects and the like for use in school and office settings. You might want to call the carpet institute and ask why.

If you'd rather avoid petroleum-based synthetics altogether, **plant-based jute, seagrass and sisal rugs** are available at most carpet stores. FYI, wall-to-wall sisal is usually synthetic—the real stuff is tough to install wall-to-wall. Rawganique.com offers certified organic European **hemp area and throw rugs** tinted with low-impact dyes in pretty colours such as ocean blue, Oregon grape and sage green.

Wool carpets are available pretty much everywhere, but finding ones that are free of chemical treatments and harsh moth-proofers is almost impossible. You pretty much have to head online. **Nature's Carpet** sells undyed or vegetable-dyed organic wool area rugs and carpeting (www.naturescarpet.com), as do **Eco Choices** (www.ecochoices.com) and **Earth Weave** (www.earthweave.com).

Lots of rugs are now essentially machine-made, and while we might ooh and ah over rarer (and pricier) hand-woven ones, they have been tied to terrible working conditions, long hours and child labour. But even machine-made ones have been linked to sweatshops. The **Rugmark** label tells you your rug was made in India, Pakistan or Nepal without the use of child labour; children were instead given access to schooling. For a list of Canadian retailers that carry Rugmark products, head to www.rugmark.org.

Some fair-trade shops carry hand-knotted rugs made by worker co-ops that were paid a fair price. **Ten Thousand Villages** locations across Canada, for instance, have traditional Oriental designs made in Pakistan, as well as more modern geometric styles woven in Nepal, all of them 100% pure wool or silk-and-wool blends. Some of the rugs are dyed using natural pigments, but not all of them, so be sure to ask.

PAINT

Itching to liven up your digs with a fresh coat of paint? Fortunately, the days of slapping liquid lead onto our walls vanished with the '70s, but today's colour concoctions are still a chemical soup. There are thousands of chemicals that can be used in the mix, including carcinogenic or neurotoxic stuff such as toluene, formaldehyde and benzene.

As a rule, alkyd- or oil-based paints are much more toxic than water-based ones. According to the Union of Concerned Scientists, they contain up to 60% VOCs, which send polluting smog- and headache-inducing fumes into the atmosphere (not to mention your lungs). Plus, the oil part is a petroleum product. But just because latex paints are water-based, don't assume that they're great eco-saviours. They're not made with natural latex (or rubber) tapped from a tree; they're made with acrylic—a petroleum-derived plastic. And they still contain up to 10% VOCs. However, most paint suppliers, even mainstream ones such as **Benjamin Moore** (www.benjaminmoore.ca), **Color Your World** (www.coloryourworld.com) and **General Paint** (www.generalpaint.com), now carry lines of low-VOC and even no-VOC paints and finishes. Just ask. (By the way, so-called low-odour oil paints aren't any more eco-friendly—they just have masking agents so they don't smell so bad.)

Note that low-VOC wall paints are generally limited to flat, eggshell and semi-gloss finishes in whites and soft pastels. Brighter, shinier colours require petrochemicals, which give off more VOCs. Plus, it's important to realize that VOC-free doesn't mean chemical-free. Some products are still loaded with harsh mildew-fighting fungicides and biocides (a preservative found in most commercial paints). You won't know unless you ask.

Paint Solutions: Farrow & Ball is a U.K. company that offers a high-quality clay-based line, free of VOCs, biocides, fungicides and ammonia. And rather than chemical dyes, natural mineral tints are ground into its products to produce 130 beautiful colours. It has only one Canadian location (in Toronto), but you can order online at www.farrow-ball.com, and they'll send you colour charts and sample pots.

> **Brighter, shinier colours require petrochemicals, which give off more VOCs**

For entirely natural paints, try **Eco-House** products, which are particularly suited to use on concrete, stucco and new drywall (www.eco-house.com). The New Brunswick company tapped into the German concept of using liquid quartz minerals as a base for its extra-durable silica dispersion paint. It works well on both interior and exterior surfaces. Plus, it's naturally antibacterial and solvent-free.

Wood stains can, of course, be just as toxic as wall paint, but there are eco-friendly alternatives out there. Canadian-made **Hempola** is made of—you guessed it!—hemp, available through health stores or online at www.hempola.com. Eco-House also makes all-natural wood finishes, as does AFM Safecoat (www.afmsafecoat.com).

Least toxic of all is **milk paint**, which has been around since the Stone Age (okay, more

LEAD WALLS

If you live in an old house and suspect that your walls are painted with lead, get a lead testing kit from your local hardware store or online (www.leadinspector.com), especially if you have small children who might end up playing with flaking paint. Even small amounts of lead dust are dangerous to infants and young children, says Health Canada. If your home was built after 1980, the insides should be fine, but exterior paint might still have contained lead. If your house is pretty new—as in post-1992— you're in the clear inside and out. If you do find lead, don't disturb it without professional help. You don't want to be kicking up any toxic dust. And if you're worried about your own lead levels, ask your doctor to test your blood.

like ancient Egypt). The modern variety is still a natural, non-toxic stain perfect for antiquing furniture. It can even be used on plaster, drywall or stucco. And no, it won't sour on your walls (although it does kind of smell like milk when you first put it on). It's basically made of powdered milk protein, lime and mineral pigments, and it's perfect for nurseries and for anyone with multiple chemical sensitivities. Beware, though, of anyone who mixes milk proteins with formaldehyde or synthetic plastics such as acrylic and calls it milk paint. You can sometimes find milk paint at furniture restoration shops, or you can buy it online from **The Old Fashioned Milk Paint Company** (www.milkpaint.com). If you're a bit more ambitious and want to get into pioneer mode, you can make your own (punch "milk paint" in the search box at www.canadianhomeworkshop.com for recipes).

Paint Clean-Up: No one wants to rinse chemicals down the drain, but in general, municipalities say you can wash water-based latex paint out of brushes and rollers in the sink. Just try to wipe off as much paint as you can first, preferably using newspaper. Never, ever, *ever* pour paint down a street gutter or into a storm drain. Storm sewers are generally connected to the nearest body of water, so you could be killing off fish. Plus, paint thinners and strippers are flammable, so you could be contributing to a nasty sewer fire. You should never pour solvents down your own pipes for the same reason.

Oil paint is a whole other ballgame—one where the players can get dizzy, nauseous and headachy from the fumes. It should never be rinsed into your sink. (The whole oil-and-water thing wouldn't work out well for you, cleaning-wise, anyway.) Again, wipe off as much paint as you can using newspaper, then soak your brushes in thinner and wipe them with a rag. To condition brushes, soak them in diluted shampoo, then rinse and dry handle end up.

Keep in mind that paint thinner can be reused. Just let the paint settle to the bottom and reuse the clear stuff on top. You can filter it or pour off the clear liquid into a labelled jar with a tight lid. Take the leftover paint sludge to one of your municipality's household hazardous waste depots.

Keep in mind that paint thinner can be reused

If you're halting your paint job partway through, you can wrap soiled paint brushes, rollers—hell, the whole tray—in a plastic bag for a few days to keep them from drying up. (I once left a painting task unfinished in this way for two weeks with no troubles since it was pretty well sealed—hey, I'm a busy girl. Who has time to do two coats around the trim?) That way, you keep the chems you pour down the drain to a minimum.

If you're thinking of peeling paint off furniture or walls, try to avoid super toxic chemical strippers. Use elbow grease and get sanding instead. Unless, of course, you're dealing with lead paint. I said it before, I'll say it again: call a pro for help.

For lead-free situations, you can also try making a thick paste of washing soda (available at health stores and some supermarkets) and water. Spread it on the surface you want to paint and leave it on for several hours, misting it with water now and then, then rinse it off and strip. (Thanks to **Care 2 Make a Difference**, a great website full of homemade solutions and articles, for the idea: **www.care2.com**.)

WALLPAPER

Wallpaper may add a lovely textured marble finish to your living room and animated bears to your nursery, but you need to know that this roll-up stuff ain't pretty for the planet. In fact, it's made of one of the most reviled plastics around: vinyl (or PVC). Vinyl creates dangerous dioxins in the manufacturing process and is then softened with potentially hormone disrupting phthalates that can offgas into the air. It's all-around bad, bad, bad. Plus, if you apply it in a high-moisture area, you're trapping humidity and welcoming mould. And did I mention that wallpaper glues emit smoggy VOCs? Even low-VOC kinds contain irritating chemicals such as methyl formate.

But fear not, earth-friendly options abound, made of actual paper, bamboo, cloth, sisal, dried grasses (a.k.a. grasscloth), even cork in all kinds of beautiful and interesting designs. Your local paint store might even carry books full of this stuff, so be sure to ask. **Treehugger** showcases a wild selection of green wallcoverings (www.treehugger.com/files/interiors/ wallcoverings). Just think how great it would be to have walls decked in old phone book fibres when conversation starts to lull at your next dinner party.

HEATING

It's hard to appreciate Canadians winters when you don't have a warm, welcoming pad to come home to. Signs of severe heat deficiency include hovering over your oven for warmth, fear of removing clothing and a paralyzing phobia of getting out of bed in the morning. Don't let this illness take over your life. You *can* make your home both warm and energy-efficient.

Thermostat: Getting a programmable thermostat is an important first step. You can set it so that your furnace kick-starts in the morning before you get up, cools down when you're gone and warms up again before you come home from work. You can get a good one for upwards of $70, and it'll easily pay for itself within a year. Energy Star–qualified thermostats have four temperature and time settings and should save you about 10% on your power bills.

Furnace: If you're a homeowner and your furnace is more than 20 years old, suck it up and sink your cash in a new one. Buying a modern furnace will save you money in the long run, since they're about 20% to 30% more efficient. Look for the Energy Star label when you're shopping. And ask if your municipality or province offers rebates on energy-saving furnaces.

Ask if your municipality or province offers **rebates on energy-saving furnaces**

While natural gas is pushed as the clean energy choice, it's still a polluting fossil fuel. However, it does burn cleaner than oil or coal, so of the mainstream energy options it's your best bet.

Whatever you do, stay away from baseboard heaters. They're super-cheap in terms of initial payout, but anyone who's lived with them knows they do little to warm your pad and hike your power bills like there's no tomorrow.

If you can afford the $10,000 to $20,000 investment, consider a **geothermal heat pump**. It warms your home by tapping into the stable temps below the frost line (about 12.5°C). These systems are more efficient then any top-of-the-line gas furnace and will cut your energy

GREEN RENO BOOKS

Natural Remodeling for the Not-So-Green House:
Bringing Your Home into Harmony with Nature
by Carol Venolia and Kelly Lerner (part of the
Natural Home & Garden series)

The New Ecological Home:
A Complete Guide to Green Building Options
by Dan Chiras (part of the Chelsea Green Guides
for Homeowners series)

Eco Deco:
Chic Ecological Design Using Recycled Materials
by Stewart Walton

Green Remodeling:
Changing the World One Room at a Time
by David R. Johnston and Kim Master

costs by up to two-thirds (you still need a regular furnace to kick in the difference). Plus, some systems double as central air conditioners in the summer, so it's like getting two major appliances in one (see page 218 for more geothermal cooling systems).

FURNACE MAINTENANCE

Furnace filters should be replaced or, if you have washable ones, rinsed out, every three months at the very least, though once a month is ideal. This will come as a shock to the vast majority of us who thought an annual filter change was all that was needed. Sorry, kids. Dirt buildup here will mean your furnace can't do its job as well. When my filter was first cleaned after I moved into a new apartment, so much wind started blowing through the vents that curtains began to billow, and the place grew warm for the first time. You also want to make sure you call in a pro for an annual furnace checkup to make sure your system is running safely and at peak efficiency.

Space Heaters: If you're renting or simply can't afford major furnace repairs or replacements, portable space heaters can seem like the only way to warm your home. Trouble is, they're pretty inefficient and will run up your hydro bills. Maybe that's why there aren't any models certified by Energy Star.

Space heaters powered by a combo of electricity and natural gas or kerosene emit dangerous carbon monoxide and sulphur dioxides either into your living room (if they're unvented) or into the great outdoors (if they're vented). The first will kill you, the second will kill the planet. Electric radiant heaters are supposed to be more energy-efficient, and since they don't use fuel they don't emit any nasty fumes, but they only warm the person they're pointed at, not the room.

Weatherstripping: This is your cheapest defence against frigid outside air, so listen up: it's extremely important to fill any and all holes and cracks around windows, doors, baseboards and plumbing fixtures with caulking or weatherstripping (removable strips of plastic designed to seal in your window frame, available at any hardware store). A surprising amount of cold air gushes in from these poorly insulated areas. Just put your hand over a light socket and you'll feel it. Holding a smoking incense stick in front of these areas can help you see drafts more readily.

Sitting around ye old hearth before a roaring fire seems like such an ancient practice it can't be bad for you, right? Unfortunately, burning wood emits climate-changing greenhouse gases such as carbon dioxide, carbon monoxide and other smog-forming pollutants that deteriorate the air quality both inside and outside your home (and you thought that was just the smell of winter). In fact, residential fires are responsible for 25% of the particulate matter in Canada's air pollution, 15% of smog-inducing VOCs and 10% of carbon monoxide emissions, according to Environment Canada. Even smaller towns can get clouds of brown haze over them when wood burning is at its peak. Plus, inhaling this stuff can aggravate health problems such as angina, asthma and bronchitis, and several of the compounds coming out of that fire are nasty carcinogens (like dioxins, formaldehyde and benzene).

If split wood has been well "seasoned" (dried in the sun) and cut to the correct length (see **www.woodheat.org** for details), toxic smoke is reduced. But you'll only really cut back on emissions if you get an **advanced combustion wood stove** or fireplace. These burn 90% cleaner than older models and use a third less wood. They even re-burn smoke to create heat.

You can also fuel your fire with **sustainably harvested firewood**. Some chains, such as Whole Foods, carry FSC-certified wood (although, as of yet, there is no indication of this on the packaging). Or pick up some **Java Logs**, made of recycled coffee grounds, wood and vegetable by-products, available at many grocery and hardware stores. They emit about 10 times less carbon monoxide and six times less particulate matter than firewood. Fake logs, by the way, should be burned only in traditional fire places, not wood stoves. If you'd rather skip the whole messy burning log thing altogether, natural gas fireplaces are a cleaner option, but some can be extremely inefficient. A bad one can generate carbon monoxide and really degrade your indoor air quality (not to mention pollute the planet unnecessarily). Make sure to get an energy-efficient one with an annual efficiency rating of about 70%.

Windows: Though your windows let in warming sunlight, they also have the potential to leak about 25% of your home's heat. If you've weatherstripped all you can and they still sap warmth, you have a few options. For one, you can get cheap insulating shrink wrap. Canadian Tire offers energy conservation kits that come with window film, caulking foam and sealing liquid—not particularly eco-friendly ingredient-wise but helpful in this context.

#1 Apply low-E film to regular windows. It's very handy, though scratchable.

#2 Well-sealed exterior or interior storm windows will taper your heat loss by 25% to 50%.

#3 Leave south- and west-facing windows uncovered during the day so you can soak in as much sunlight as possible. It's free heat!

#4 If you have any radiators or south-facing windows, make sure they're clean—dirt and dust absorb heat, robbing you of precious warmth.

Also, insulating **honeycomb** or **cellular curtains** actually keep the heat in and cool out. Double- or triple-celled models are best and are available at most blinds stores. **Window quilts** are the most insulating window covering on the market; they fold or roll down at night to create a good seal, but they're far from fashionable.

When you've got the funds, look for windows with low-E (for emissivity, which is the ability of a surface to emit warmth) films. Their thin metal coating (don't worry, it's invisible—you're not buying tin-foil-lined panes here) keeps the heat inside in the winter and outside in the summer. Make sure to look for the Energy Star label when you're browsing for windows, skylights and doors. For a useful Canadian map to help you determine which Energy Star climate zone you're in and which type of Energy Star window you should buy as a result, head to www.allweatherwindows.com. The site also has a directory of dealers across Canada. Home Depot carries them, and Sears will special-order them for you after sending a consultant to your home.

COOLING

On extra-sticky summer days, do you ever wish you were small enough to put a lawn chair in your fridge and just chill out in there? Okay, maybe I'm the only one. But come on, if you've lived without air conditioning, you've no doubt stuck your head in the freezer for one brief, blissful moment and thought, "Man, this is heaven." Of course, it's clearly no long-term solution, so let's get realistic.

Windows: If you're going to try to stay away from energy-hogging air conditioners, you've got to get strategic. Leave your windows open at night and shut them in the morning before it gets warm. They'll seal in the cooler air, but only if you draw all the blinds, too.

Up to 40% of heat comes in through your windows. Outdoor shutters and awnings keep the sun's rays from touching the glass, but almost any old blind will do the trick. **Cellular** or **honeycomb blinds** are better than most. **Sheerweave sun control roller shades** allow you to see outside but keep out up 95% of the sun's rays. Whatever you do, stay far away from plastic blinds made of toxic PVC or vinyl. The stuff is bad, bad, bad for the environment and has historically been found to contain lead (especially naughty if you have kids).

Fans: Moving air across your skin is the key to keeping cool, so get yourself some good fans. They use 90% less electricity than air conditioners. But not all fans are alike. Energy Star ceiling fans move air up to 20% more efficiently than standard ones. Some, like aerodynamic **Turbo-Aire high-velocity cooling fans** (available at Home Depot and Canadian Tire), deliver 100% more air and are 300% more energy-

> **Fans use 90% less electricity than air conditioners**

8 GREAT TIPS FOR KEEPING YOUR HOUSE COOL IN JULY

#1 Use low-energy fans to keep air circulating.

#2 Plant a cooling garden and trees to shield your house from the sun.

#3 Keep your shades drawn. Those rays are cooking your home, and if you've got a/c, you're forcing it to work extra hard

#4 Install awnings over your windows to keep the sun from hitting the glass.

#5 About to redo your roof? Choose light-coloured tiles or roofing materials. Dark roofs absorb more heat.

#6 Install a radiant barrier (a thin sheet of aluminum, often lined with craft paper or cardboard) inside your roof to help reduce cooling bills.

#7 Invest in high-quality low-E windows. A typical double-paned window allows about 75% of the sun's heat into your home. But good-quality windows will seal out the sweltering heat of the summer.

#8 Use energy-efficient compact fluorescent bulbs—regular incandescent bulbs give off more heat.

efficient than others with the same size motor. The 12-inch one consumes less power than a 100-watt bulb. Pretty impressive.

Reversible window fans (available at Home Hardware and Canadian Tire) are great because, if you have a couple of them, you can adjust them to pull air from one window and push it out another, creating a much-needed cross-current.

While not as popular in Canada as they are in the States, **whole-house fan systems** are fantastic at sending cooling gusts of air throughout your entire house. They actually suck air from outside your windows and pull it through your home up into a vented attic. They're ideal for use at night or in the early morning and can really lower the temperature of your house in a hurry, drawing cool air onto stuffy top floors. If your summers don't get too, too hot, you can use them in place of air conditioning, or you can use one in conjunction with a/c to cut back on energy costs. They use about one-tenth as much power as air conditioners do. Unfortunately, they're pretty hard to find in Canada. You'll have to head to U.S. sites (www.housecooler.com, www.airvent.com, www.quietcoolfan.com) or stop in at any hardware store on a trip south.

Air Conditioners: No matter how many fans you run, the escalating heat of Canadian summers is enough to make many eco-lovers cave and buy—gasp!—an air conditioner. The number of households that purchased the energy suckers jumped nearly 25% between 1990 and 2003. Why? The combination of warmer-than-average summers (hello, climate change!), population growth and the fact that we're getting, well, soft. Yes, it's true, I said it: we're terrified of breaking a sweat and enjoying the seasons in all their glory. Canadians are fortifying their homes and cranking the a/c all summer long regardless of the outdoor temperature! Try only turning it on when you really need it to stave off heat exhaustion or to sleep and let windows and fans carry in cooling breezes otherwise. As you'd expect, the provinces with the hottest summers (Quebec, Ontario and Manitoba) upped their share more than others.

A/C DISPOSAL

If you've decided to get rid of your window a/c, don't toss it with your regular trash. The toxic cooling fluids inside can contaminate landfills, leach into the environment and mess up local groundwater. Call your municipality about proper disposal. They should have hazardous waste depots where you can drop off your old unit. Stores like Home Depot have also been known to offer rebates on new, more efficient models if you bring in your old clunker. Be sure to inquire.

If you're considering an a/c unit, this is one of the only times I'll tell you not to buy used. Newer models are much more energy-efficient, especially those certified by Energy Star. Energy Star room/window units use at least 10% less energy than other new models. And Energy Star central air systems use about 20% less power. Maybe that doesn't sound like much savings, but think of it this way: for every kilowatt hour of electricity you save, you stop the release of nearly 700 grams of polluting carbon dioxide from local power plants. It adds up quickly when you consider that the average air-conditioned home uses about 1,400 kilowatts per month in a typical summer.

Also look for the Energuide sticker when you're shopping. It's not a seal of approval like the Energy Star label (although both are government-run), it just tells you the energy efficiency ratio (or EER) or each unit. The higher the number, the more efficient the machine. The Ministry of Natural Resources publishes a useful printable guide to picking out the right air conditioner for you, complete with an Energuide directory of room air conditioner models (http://oee.nrcan.gc.ca/publications/equipment/roomaircond). It'll even break down the rough operating costs for each unit.

Carrier and **Bryant** are two of the only air conditioning manufacturers that use the chlorine-free refrigerant Puron. While the rest cut out notorious ozone-destroying CFCs a long time ago, the coolant fluid they now use still has some impact on the ozone layer.

Make sure to buy the right unit for your space. There's no need for one that can cool

IF YOU ALREADY OWN AN AIR CONDITIONER

#1 Set your thermostat to 25°C and program it so it turns on an hour before you get home.

#2 Clean your filter at least once a season to make sure it's working efficiently.

#3 Make sure windows are sealed properly to prevent hot air from coming in. This is especially important for the window the a/c is in—those crappy adjustable accordion sides that come with some units won't cut it for most windows.

#4 If your central a/c isn't working well, or if the coils freeze over, you could have a coolant fluid leak. Call a repairperson immediately. Not only is your unit not running efficiently, but you're dripping out harmful greenhouse gases that contribute to climate change.

#5 Have your central a/c unit inspected periodically by a professional.

1,000 square feet when your bedroom is only 200 square feet. And don't be an energy pig. Turn it off (or at the very least raise the temperature) if you're leaving a room or your house for more than four hours. Can't bear the thought of coming home to a warm pad? A **programmable thermostat** (available at Canadian Tire and Home Depot) can set the a/c to start chilling your space about an hour before you get home. It's a handy tool that'll keep you cool while saving you money and energy.

Geothermal Systems: While we're sizzling above ground, a few feet down the soil is cool as a cucumber (about 12.5°C). You can tap into that by drawing the cool air into your home through the liquid-filled coils of a geothermal system. And these systems magically reverse themselves in the winter, so when it's –5°C outside, they'll draw warmth from the earth's crust below the frost line (your furnace kicks in the difference). Geothermal systems can reduce energy consumption by 25% to 75% for serious long-term savings. Depending on the type of system you get and the size of your house, they can cost anywhere from $10,000 to $20,000 upfront—but you'll recover that cash in five to 12 years. For a directory of geothermal contractors and more info on the topic, visit the Earth Energy Society of Canada website at (www.earthenergy.ca).

> Geothermal systems can reduce energy consumption by 25% to 75% for **serious long-term savings**

INSULATION

There's no doubt that a good layer of insulation has the power to keep energy from escaping through your walls and roof. And while some say the energy savings involved in well-installed insulation offsets the not-so-eco-friendly materials used to make it, if you can afford it, it's best to support products that are green through and through.

Skip old-school, greenhouse-gas-emitting polyurethane foam, which is also treated with PBDEs (ultra-persistent fire retardants, some of which are being phased out but are still on the market). Instead, go for **blown-in cellulose**, made with recycled paper (**Thermo-Cell's Weathershield Insulation** is actually certified by the feds Environmental Choice program). If done right, it'll keep cold air at bay better than fibreglass, and it takes up to a quarter of the energy to manufacture, according to Ecology Action's Green Building Materials Guide. But it can be pretty dusty, so make sure it's well sealed into the wall.

Air Krete is a blown-in brand that's considered non-toxic (it's made of a type of formaldehyde-free cement), and it doesn't have the same dust problem that cellulose has

Got a boring, flat roof that's just sitting there drawing heat into your home? Why not turn it into a vibrant green setting, full of sun-loving plants that soak up the hot rays and keep them from heating up your pad? Environment Canada says that a typical one-storey building with about 10 centimetres of grass growing on its roof cuts its cooling needs by 25%. You could also copy endangered habitats by planting native butterfly gardens or drought-tolerant prairie gardens. You can even plant veggies up there to supply yourself with fresh food (you can't get any more local than that).

Green roofs do the air good by filtering out particles and converting carbon dioxide emissions into fresh, clean oxygen, and they're good for local lakes and rivers because they sop up rain and prevent storm sewer overflows. Rooftop rain barrels can collect the water needed for more water-intensive green roof designs, but some don't even need watering once the greenery is established.

But before you start throwing dirt down, you have to make sure that your roof is structurally sound. Then you need a waterproof barrier, a root barrier, a drainage layer . . . you know what? You need a professional. Call up a roof contractor with green roof experience; they'll help you get started, even if you want to do your own landscaping. Green Roofs for Healthy Cities has contractors listed on its website (**www.greenroofs.org**). And pick up *Planting Green Roofs and Living Walls*, by Nigel Dunnett and Noël Kingsbury, for some good tips.

(www.airkrete.com). And while I just dissed polyurethane foam, there's one that's actually made in part with soybean oil: **BioBase 501** was voted one of the top 10 eco-friendly building supplies by BuildingGreen.com in 2003, emits very few VOCs and is extremely fire retardant. Plus, it's actually cheaper than polyurethane foam (www.biobased.net).

But if you'd rather avoid these blown-in types, which require professional installation, there's a new product on the block that's been featured in *Newsweek* and elsewhere. Made of recycled denim, **Bonded Logic**'s non-toxic panels are fire-treated with benign borax (the same stuff used as a green cleaner) and can be easily cut with a sharp utility knife (www.bondedlogic.com).

Was the insulation in your home installed before the mid-'80s? Is it made with **vermiculite** (a mineral)? Beware: it may contain carcinogenic asbestos fibres. Health Canada says if that's the case you shouldn't let kids play in the attic, or even go into the attic without a respirator mask, plus you should seal all cracks in your walls. Don't remove or disturb this stuff without calling in a pro. I mean it.

GREEN ENERGY

It wasn't long ago that "living off the grid" implied that your home was made of logs and was located in some remote wooded location. Now, even concrete dwellers can unplug from the coal/nuke/hydro grid with a few solar panels strapped to the roof of a semi-detached, and maybe a wind turbine or two. Or you can get really earthy and dig into the soil beneath your house, drawing from the stable temperatures just a few feet underground when the weather outdoors gets a little chilly or sweaty for your taste (for info on this option, see Geothermal Systems, page 218).

Whether you decide to go for solar or wind power, you'll first have to do an energy load assessment of your home to figure out how many kilowatts you use on average (see www.nspower.ca/energy_efficiency/energy_calculator/). And before you buy panels or a turbine, most companies stress that you should make your abode as energy-efficient as it can be and invest in energy-efficient Energy Star appliances.

Don't forget to look into rebates in your home province and municipality at http://incentivesandrebates.ca. Some cities and provinces will even give you cash back if your home energy operation makes more power than you use. Call your local hydro company to find out. Also pick up a copy of $mart Power: An Urban Guide to Renewable Energy and Efficiency or The Renewable Energy Handbook for Homeowners: The Complete Step-by-Step Guide to Making (and Selling) Your Own Power from the Sun, Wind and Water, both by William H. Kemp.

Solar Energy: If you're thinking of venturing beyond solar-powered garden lanterns and want to harness the sun's rays to power your home, you need to do a little homework. Typical solar panels are actually photovoltaic (PV) systems—they convert sunlight directly into electricity. You can buy basic PV modules from places like Canadian Tire and install them yourself—but that's not something I'd recommend, as it can get kind of complicated. You generally have to put in an extra two-way hydro meter (it costs several hundred dollars) and power cut-off switch (which prevents you from killing the people working on power lines on your street) and ask an electrician for a final stamp of approval. Unless you're qualified to compete on *The Apprentice: Home Improvement Edition*, you might want to call someone to do it for you. For a full list of solar retailers across Canada, check out www.solarbuzz.com/CompanyListings/Canada.htm.

Costs vary depending on how much of your home you want to power. **Autonomous systems** are completely independent from the grid. This type is generally more popular in

ECO-LABELLED HOMES

Shopping for a new home? Sure, they tend to be more energy-efficient than creaky old houses, but that doesn't make them earth-friendly. Keep an eye out for the following green labels:

Energy Star: Homes with this label are 40% more efficient than current building codes. They come with Energy Star appliances, better draft-proofing and insulation, and more efficient heating, cooling and windows.

R-2000: These homes are about 30% more efficient than non-R-2000 homes. Energy-efficient windows and doors, water-saving fixtures and extra insulation are all par for the course, as with Energy Star. But the R-2000 label goes a little bit beyond Energy Star homes by calling for EcoLogo-approved paints, varnishes and finishes and low-VOC cabinets to reduce indoor air pollutants. For more on the program and links to R-2000 homes near you, go to http://r2000.chba.ca.

LEED: This green rating system (LEED stands for Leadership in Energy and Environmental Design), developed by the U.S. Green Building Council, goes far beyond the two other labels. It sets the bar for leading-edge eco-design, construction and building use, and either silver, gold or platinum ratings are awarded based on a point system. To date, it's been geared more towards buildings, and a growing number of condo developers are getting LEED-certified. But a LEED rating system for homes is currently being developed. For more info, head to the Canadian Green Building Council's site, at **www.cagbc.org**.

cottage country with minimal electrical needs. **Hybrid systems** are also off-grid but combine solar panels with wind turbines or some sort of generator. The most common and financially palatable system for urbanites is **grid-connected**, meaning you still fuel your home with some regular hydro-, nuke- and coal-fired power, but you reduce your overall reliance on dirty energy. You can get more or fewer panels depending on your budget, but one company said solar power generally averages out to about $12 per watt, fully installed. Really, it's impossible to estimate price without knowing how much energy you suck back daily. The bigger, and more wasteful, your household is, the more you'll have to cough up.

If you're not ready to commit to the whole-roof concept, consider a **solar-heated hot water system**, or "thermal solar heating." Since a quarter of your home's energy goes to keeping your showers steamy and your clothes and dishes clean, switching to solar can really make a dent in your energy bills. You can get one pretty cheap. But if you spend a little more, you can buy a vacuum tube model, which is four to five times more efficient at capturing heat energy in the winter. Pool owners can also install solar-powered water heaters for a couple grand.

> A quarter of your home's energy goes to **keeping your showers steamy and your clothes and dishes clean**

The Canadian Solar Industries Association has a helpful website teeming, or should I say beaming, with useful information on all of these options: www.cansia.ca.

Wind Energy: Leashing wind energy can be a little trickier, especially if you live in an urban centre. You could face height restrictions, and you definitely need a permit from your

---

MONEY FOR ENVIRONMENTAL RENOVATIONS

Canada Mortgage and Housing Corporation (CMHC) offers a 10% refund on its mortgage loan insurance premium for homeowners who borrow money to build or buy an energy-efficient home or renovate an existing one.

To find out about incentives and rebates in your home province for all things green— eco-renovations, Energy Star appliances, solar panels, etc.—head to **http://incentivesandrebates.ca/**.

If you dream of being nature-powered but don't have the cash to outfit your house with turbines and solar panels, you might want to look into buying renewable energy from someone who does.

Green Power Certificates: Organizations such as the **Pembina Institute** sell Wind Power Certificates to offset the electricity used by your home and all the pollution emissions that come with it. Note that this option means you're going "carbon neutral," but you're still going to get an electricity bill from your utility. Think of it this way: you can get carbon offsets to compensate for the carbon dioxide emissions created by your flight to Mexico, but that doesn't mean you're going to literally be flying a biodiesel solar-powered plane.

Bundled Green Power: With this option, you can replace your regular utility provider and its bills with a green power retailer. They don't come and put solar panels on your house, and they can't run a direct power line between you and their wind turbines 200 kilometres away, but for every kilowatt of energy you use, you'll put your money towards funding renewable energy, in the form of wind, solar or certified low-impact hydro power (hydro power that's often less than 30 megawatts and ensures that the passage of fish is facilitated, that dams aren't built on

fragile ecosystems or where salmon spawn and so on). You tend to pay a little more a month, but you'll have a clear conscience and will be helping to clean the air.

So far, Alberta, eastern B.C., Nova Scotia, P.E.I. and Ontario are the only provinces that have local green power retailers. Some are run through provincial power corporations, such as **SaskPower's Green Power** program, which for about $2.50 per 100 kilowatt block allows residents to tap into the utility's own wind farms, as well as wind power it buys from others. Others, such as **Bullfrog Power** in Ontario, are green energy retailers. They buy power from wind farmers (20%) and low-impact hydro farmers (80%), then sell it to you. They've been criticized for being middlemen who make a cut, but, hey, no one else in Ontario was offering consumers the option to buy renewable energy before these guys stepped in. See Green Energy Suppliers on page 320 for contact info in your region.

Pollution Probe has put out a great guide to all this information and offers details on what green power certificates and bundled green power options are available in your province (see **www.pollutionprobe.org/whatwedo/ greenpower/consumerguide/**).

municipality's building department. Again, a pro can sort this out for you. A small, 1,000-watt turbine itself will cost a few grand, plus the tower, parts and installation.

Turbines are great in the darker months, when solar panels aren't so productive. Plus, the cooler months are exactly when the wind picks up and turbines come into play. For a step-by-step planning guide and helpful info on setting up your own wind turbine, check out www.smallwindenergy.ca. And don't forget that, depending on what province you live in, you might be able to sell any extra power back to your utility company.

OUTDOOR LIVING

There's something to be said

for climatic deprivation. Suffering through sleet, snow and cold, spitting skies half
the year makes wearing flip-flops and sitting on a patio that much more pleasurable (although tell me that in the thick of February and I'll clock you on the nose).
Canadians may know how to make the best of bleak winters, but come cottage
season, we dig up our flower beds and fire up the barbecue like it's our last day
on earth. We also treat the planet like there's no tomorrow. Come on now—our
summers need not be defined by gas-guzzling lawn mowers, pesticide-drenched
gardens and coal-fired grills. We're so much better than that.

GARDEN AND LAWN CARE

Nothin' like working the soil and breathing in all that fresh oxygen to reconnect us with the earth underneath our feet and help us forget about the 9 to 5. Whether you've got a patch of grass, a sprawling acre of gardens or a wee balcony, there's a jungle of options out there for the eco-conscious gardener. But reaching for a bag of synthetic soil, fertilizer or pesticide could banish you from the Garden of Eden.

Fertilizers: Fertilizer ads promise bigger, fuller flowers in greener, lusher gardens. As tempting as the offer is, stay away from all the synthetic Miracle-Gro types and chemically boosted soils that dominate garden centres. They can burn plant roots, throw off natural soil structure and run off your lawn and pollute groundwater. Many have petroleum-derived ingredients and actually strip soil of its ability to retain and release nutrients over time (no wonder you feel like you need to add more and more of the stuff).

Perhaps the best gift you can give your garden is to spread a layer of nutrient-rich **organic compost** instead. You can either make your own (see page 231) or pick up a few bags from your local garden centre (which might be a mix of composted manure, leaves, bark and the like). It'll also suppress weed growth, especially if you try a no-till approach to your plots, where you don't turn up your dirt every spring. (Tilling is said to disrupt the ecology of soil.)

If you want to give trees, shrubs or plants an added boost, look for all-natural fertilizers made from kelp and fish meal, worm castings or other non-chemical substances (although some might say it's best to leave the fish in the sea). **Terracycle** sells a certified organic, odour-free squirtable liquid worm poop fertilizer in reused soda bottles (available at Home Depot and Zellers). Five cents from each bottle mailed into the company is donated to the Nature Conservancy or the charity of your choice. A little **molasses** in your water is great for sweetening tomatoes (trust me, you've never had tomatoes this tasty).

> Look for all-natural fertilizers made from **kelp and fish meal, worm castings** or other non-chemical substances

HOMEMADE FERTILIZER

Make your own all-purpose fertilizer by adding 1 teaspoon (5 mL) of molasses, 1 tablespoon (15 mL) of liquid kelp and 2 tablespoons (25 mL) of fish fertilizer per 2 quarts (2 L) of water, then sprinkle away.

A good **corn gluten fertilizer** will even fend off pesky procreating weeds before they start. Plus, unlike petrochemical-based ones, natural fertilizers actually boost your soil's nutrient-retaining properties.

For the lowdown on all the different basic organic fertilizers, plus info on making your own with ingredients you grew yourself (such as comfrey and nettle), see www. the-organic-gardener.com. You can get an even more detailed breakdown of organic fertilizers at www.basic-info-4-organic-fertilizers.com.

Not sure what your soil needs? A soil test will tell you its pH and organic matter content so you can figure out what nutrients you should feed it. *Canadian Gardening* mag has a good list of provincial and private labs that will do the testing (www.canadiangardening.com/ cg_soiltesting.shtml), or look up soil testing in the Yellow Pages.

ORGANIC IMPOSTERS

The way the organic label is thrown around garden centres you'd think you were shopping at Whole Foods. Alas, don't be mislead into thinking that it means your fertilizer is anything close to certified organic standards. It generally implies that it came from natural sources but that's not always the case. In fact, it can contain synthetic urea, synthetic versions of plant nutrients and human sewage sludge, none of which would fly on a real organic farm. Look for ingredients you recognize, like corn, fish and seaweed.

Pesticides and Herbicides: What if you've nourished your soil properly, but you're already infested with weeds? Well, join the club. But before you resort to potent herbicides, consider this: a few weeds won't kill you; toxic pesticides will. Home pesticide use is often fingered for the presence of pesticides in humans, and those chemicals are considered especially dangerous for young children, who also happen to spend more time rolling around on the grass than we do. The pesticide most commonly used on Canadian lawns, 2,4-D, is linked to elevated rates of non-Hodgkin's lymphoma and prostate cancer. Herbicides also wash off our lawns and gardens in the rain and end up contaminating groundwater and local waterways (Sierra Club of Canada says over 90% of 2,4-D used eventually ends up in water).

A few weeds won't kill you; toxic pesticides will

Still, two-thirds of Canadians use chemical pesticides on their lawns and gardens to keep weeds and bugs at bay. But that's starting to change now that one in four of us live in municipalities that are banning the cosmetic use of chemical pesticides (including Halifax, Vancouver and Toronto, as well as the whole province of Quebec). Even if yours hasn't, stay away from chemical weed killers and make your peace with the pesky greens. I mean, really—if the Canadian Cancer Society, the Learning Disabilities Association of Canada and the Canadian Association of Physicians for the Environment all urge you not to use the stuff, why would you?

Natural Weed and Pest Control: A healthy lawn will sprout fewer of the wily suckers. Sprinkle a little topsoil on your grass and throw down some low-maintenance **rye** or fine **fescue grass** seeds instead of water-sucking Kentucky bluegrass. Overseeding and mowing high (so you leave about 2.5" to 3" of grass) keeps weeds at bay. Leave any grass clippings on your lawn (unless there's over a centimetre of the stuff, in which case, add it to your flower beds or compost pile); clippings break down into valuable nitrogen and make it harder for weeds to grow. Aerating your lawn with one of those rolling aerator thingies, aerator shoes or a pitchfork will also let it breathe and help nutrients and water reach its roots. For a great cartoon-illustrated guide to going chem-free, pick up *How to Get Your Lawn and Garden Off Drugs: A Basic Guide to Pesticide-Free Gardening in North America,* by Carole Rubin.

HOMEMADE HERBICIDE

Still freaked out by weeds? Remove them by hand before they go to seed. Or, to kill off those growing on garden paths or between patio blocks, spray a homebrew of gin or vodka and water on weeds (carefully avoiding other plants). Straight vinegar also works. Cola gone flat? Pour it on your weeds instead of down the sink. That'll kill them within a week.

As for pests, you can go medieval on their ass without reaching for harsh chemicals. In fact, it's always best to fight fire with fire. Set a bag of **native ladybugs** (not the invasive Asian type) free in your garden to keep aphids under control (make sure to spread them out properly, though, if you want them to be effective). A bag of **praying mantis eggs** will do the same and will nix whitefly, too. Spreading microscopic **nemotodes** will get rid of beetle grubs in your grass. And while they might creep you out, **bats** eat a hell of a lot of insects. Pick up a bat box at your hardware store to keep these helpful bug-munchers around. **Birds** also eat bugs, so put out a birdhouse or feeder to draw them to your yard.

NATURAL INSECTICIDAL SOAP

Natural insecticidal soap controls all sorts of bugs on fruit, flowers and veggies. Make your own by combining 1 tablespoon (15 mL) of natural dishwashing soap with 1 gallon (4 L) of water. Pour some into a spray bottle and go to town. Crushed garlic steeped in warm water will work on bigger bugs. *You Grow Girl: The Groundbreaking Guide to Gardening*, by Gayla Trail, has tons of great gardening tips (especially for the urban gardener), including a list of natural insecticides that are safe enough to eat (**www.yougrowgirl.com/garden**).

For a listing of good bugs versus bad bugs, and to learn which good bugs will help you get rid of the bad ones, see **The Bug Lady** (www.thebuglady.ca). The site even sells beneficial bugs by the bag, so you can get your gnats, spider mites and thrips under control in a jiffy.

What about bigger garden munchers, such as rabbits? I have to confess that I'm biased on this front as I've had three pet rabbits, so I don't really get why anyone would want to discourage these fuzzy creatures from frolicking in their yards. But if they're tearing up your lettuce patch, then plant marigolds near their favourite foods and sprinkle pepper around after every rainfall.

THE BUG LADY

Growing up in Northern Ontario, Jessica Dawe was always playing with bugs. But it was still the era when high-school counsellors were pushing girls to be either secretaries or nurses, and Jessica wasn't interested in either. It wasn't until a few years after she dropped out of high school that she discovered horticulture by accident. "The idea of using bugs fascinated me," says Jessica about figuring out that you could use good bugs to control bad bugs. "It seemed to be a no-brainer—why use a chemical when the solution had been evolving for thousands of years and was sitting right out in the landscape?" Now B.C.'s bug lady is busy trying to banish people's fears about tossing a bag of ground beetles into their gardens to munch on annoying grubs, slugs and snails. She's also propagating the idea that a healthy, diverse garden can attract more of these bug trappers naturally, so you don't have to resort to toxic pesticides. Imagine that—nature keeping itself in balance without chemical intervention! Visit Jessica's website at **www.thebuglady.ca**.

Mulching: We've all heard that spreading mulch on your garden is a good thing when it comes to cutting back on water use. But did you know that wood chip mulch can breed what's called "shotgun" or "artillery" fungi, pesky wood-rot fungi that shoot tar-like spores? (They can even spread to your house—talk about a scary B-movie plot!) And since wood-based mulches steal nitrogen from the soil as they decay, they can slow the growth of older plants and even starve new ones to death, not to mention attract fire ants and termites. Dyed mulch (what the hell is it dyed with, anyway?) is supposed to be even worse for young plants.

So what are you supposed to cover your soil with to help it retain water? Compost! Yes, according to Ohio State researchers, 5 centimetres of compost is just as effective as 5 centimetres of wood chips at keeping weeds at bay, but much healthier for your plants. If you don't make your own (see below), head to a garden centre. Leaves and lawn clippings also make good mulch.

COMMUNITY GARDENS

Got garden envy? Most urbanites don't have much space to cultivate. If you lack a yard, or your balcony potting just ain't satisfying your need to dig up weeds, look into helping out around your local community garden. Many hold weekly work bees, as well as monthly workshops on eco-gardening topics.

Composting: If an apple rots in a landfill, does anybody cry? Well, avid composters do. Once you've seen what food scraps and yard waste can turn into—beautiful, nutrient-rich soil—there's no going back, baby. About a third of what we throw away and truck to landfill is food scraps. Talk about a waste!

More and more municipalities are starting composting programs by handing out bins and getting citizens to collect kitchen scraps to boost waste diversion rates. And it's working. But what if

> About a third of what we **throw away and truck to landfill** is food scraps

your town hasn't picked up on this yet, or if you want to create your own nourishing compost for your garden? This is where home composting comes into play. Just buy a bin from your local hardware store or garden centre (either a rotating one, a regular plastic one with a lid and air holes or a wooden one), place it on a level spot in a corner of your yard, then start feeding it equal layers of green stuff (food scraps, coffee grounds, tea bags, houseplants) and brown stuff (dry grass clippings, dry leaves, straw, a few wood chips). You'll want to keep

PLANT-A-ROW GROW-A-ROW

If the idea of eating homegrown cauliflower or kale yet again is greeted by a chorus of moans and groans in your house, you know you're growing too much of a good thing. Most of us try to hand out any extras to family and neighbours, but back in 1986 Winnipegers Ron and Eunice O'Donavan had a novel idea. That summer, they had grown a bumper crop of potatoes—way more than their family could stomach. So they decided to donate the extras (two 35-kilogram bags of spuds) to a local community centre that was feeding the needy. But it wasn't until early October that Ron was mulling over the potato donation and said to his wife, "I wonder if we could get other gardeners to grow a row." Soon Ron, who had worked for the city's parks department for years, teamed up with a new food bank

called Winnipeg Harvest, and a great partnership was born. Twenty years later, over 1 million kilograms of fresh produce grown in backyards across Winnipeg were donated to the food bank through the Plant-A-Row Grow-A-Row program. And the concept hasn't stopped there. In fact, the Grow-a-Row idea caught on in nearly every province from coast to coast, and south of the border, as well.

Keep the concept in bloom and grow an extra row of your own. For a list of participating communities and information on the program, head to **www.growarow.org**. If no one else is doing it in your town, why not start a campaign? For a food bank near you, visit the Canadian Association of Food Banks' website at **www.cafb-acba.ca**.

meat and fish, dairy products, peanut butter and fats out (unless you're planning on throwing a raccoon party). Diseased plants, cat litter and troublesome weeds (such as crabgrass) should be left out too.

Everyone seems to recommend a different way to build the compost pile, but here's one way to go: put down a layer of twigs or coarse material, then a 5- to 10-centimetre layer of browns, followed by a 5- to 10-centimetre layer of greens, then a thin layer of soil. Continue alternating layers, stir it up every couple of weeks, and you should have good compost within a few months. One thing is for sure: if you have too much of one layer or another, you'll end up with weird smells or no compost. For troubleshooting tips, see the Composting Council of Canada's site at www.compost.org.

Indoor Composting: Apartment dwellers without municipal composting programs can do their own pint-sized composting indoors. How? Okay, now, don't freak—the key to indoor composting is worms, specifically red wigglers. Yes, vermiculture sounds kind of creepy-crawly for the house, but don't worry: they stay in their bins. Plus, worms eat half their weight in food, then poop it out into valuable odour-free worm manure called castings. Just think, people pay good money for this stuff in quality garden supply stores (one B.C. company calls its nutrient-dense casting product Black Gold) and you'll be getting it for free. You can mix your finished compost with sand and potting soil in equal parts for indoor pots. If you make too much, just give it away as a hostess gift. For more details on vermiculture see www.gardenguides.com/articles/worms.htm.

Worms eat half their weight in food, then poop it out into valuable odour-free worm manure called castings

Native Plants: If you want a truly eco-friendly garden, roll up your sleeves and plant some indigenous or native flowers, shrubs and grasses. The eco org Evergreen has an excellent province by province guide to which trees, shrubs, grasses, wildflowers, vines, ferns and aquatic plants are legit locals (www.evergreen.ca/nativeplants). Those that are truly indigenous to your eco-system are extra-hardy because they're already adapted to your area's conditions, and tend to need less water, pest controls and overall fussing then plants that originate in other climates. They'll also help keep the local ecosystem happy, like the **elderberry shrub**, which provides food and shelter for many songbirdies, or the much-need **milkweed** for monarchs.

Heritage Plants: Go from garden centre to garden centre and you'll see pretty much the same plants—hydrangeas, petunias, geraniums—that all look like they came from the same mother. The truth is that there's little genetic variety left in the world of flowers and garden veggies. It's all been whittled down to the few that fly off shelves. Genetically modified seeds, hybridized plants, flowers grown in dyed water are all common. This is where heritage plants step in to fill a void of authenticity. Heritage or heirloom gardening is kind of like planting antiques. Essentially, they're grown from strains that are at least 50 years

NOT SO NATIVE Beware of dodgy labeling. "Wildflower" seed mixes may grow wild somewhere, but likely not in Canada (in fact, some wildflower weeds are actually noxious in your area).

old, they're non-hybridized (so they haven't been cross-bred, like most modern plants) and they're open pollinated (which means you can save their seeds and replant them from year to year). **Seeds of Diversity** holds an annual exchange that allows its members (a mishmash of hobby gardeners, farmers, agricultural historians and researchers) from across the country to get free heirloom, native and organic seeds for the price of a postage stamp. Not a bad deal.

Lawn Mowers: The smell of cut grass just screams summertime, doesn't it? Trouble is, much of what we're inhaling contributes to the smoggy haze that makes the hotter months so taxing on the lungs. "Oh, but it's just a little lawn mower, how bad can it be?" Pretty bad. Running a two-stroke gas-powered mower for one hour can puff out as much pollution as driving a new car for 550 kilometres, according to Ontario's environment ministry. Multiply that by the 2.7 million Canadians mowing their lawns every weekend in the summer, and we're sucking back 150 million litres of gasoline a year, says the Clean Air Foundation. Throw in all the leaf blowers and weed whackers firing up in yards across the country, and we're talking a hell of a lot of pollution.

Cleaner electric options are 90% less polluting. You can also get rechargeable types, so you're not bound by a cord. Even four-stroke mowers are more efficient (70% more) and choke out less smog-inducing fumes than two-strokes. Needless to say, manual mowers that run on push-power are the greenest of all.

Running a two-stroke gas-powered mower for one hour can puff out as much pollution as driving a new car for 550 kilometres

Mow Down Pollution, run by the Clean Air Foundation, is the largest dirty mower take-back program in the country (www.mowdownpollution.ca). The program lets Canadians turn in old gas mowers and trimmers at all Home Depot locations in the spring. You get instant rebates of up to 100 bucks on cleaner machines. And any steel or aluminum on your old contraption is recycled. Since 2001, over 12,000 mowers and trimmers have been turned in, saving 240 tons of greenhouse gas and smog-forming emissions from filling the summer air.

WATER

Canadian water use goes up by 50% in the summer. Even the greenest of the green use extra H_2O to keep themselves and their yards from wilting. You just have to be smart about it—especially when there's a water advisory on.

GREY WATER ON THE GARDEN

Canadians love to toss water around like we're H$_2$O millionaires. In fact, according to the Organisation for Economic Co-operation and Development (OECD), **we're the second-highest per capita water users in the world, soaking up 4,400 litres each per day** when you factor in our home, farm and industrial uses of the precious resource. Wouldn't you know it, those of us who pay a flat rate use 457 litres a day, while those of us who pay for each drop use about 269, according to Environment Canada.

Why wash all that grey water (used water from non-toilet sources) down into the sewers when we could be capturing it and putting it on our gardens? It can be as basic as putting a big bowl in your sink as you rinse out lettuce or coffee mugs or placing a bucket in your shower.

(Little bits of food and natural soaps are perfectly acceptable to living greens. Just keep in mind that you don't want to be pouring chlorine or even eco-cleaner borax on your poor plants.)

Grey water gadgets, like the one made by B.C.-based **Envirosink (www.envirosink.com)**, allow you to pour any water captured in your sink into a funnel that connects to a storage tank. They're great for saving that water you waste when you're waiting for it to warm up or cool down, rinsing produce or washing dishes. You can use the stored water on your garden or send it to your toilet. You can also get more complicated systems with filters, pumps and piping from every room that uses water. Best to mull it over with the experts: **http://greywater.net/**.

Sprinklers: Try to water early in the morning or in the evening to stop the water from evaporating in the hot sun. Forego the urge to sprinkle frequently; instead, water deeply once a week. If your soil is constantly moist, plant roots will never spread (as they should if they're going to gather moisture well). And resist the temptation to pull out the hose at the sight of plants wilting in the midday sun—plants often send water to their roots during scorchers to prevent evaporation. Relax. They'll send it back up when it cools. If they don't, water them in the evening. If you're dealing with newly planted trees or shrubs, they do need to be watered more often than usual until their roots settle in.

Canadian water use goes up by 50% in the summer

Rainwater: Any rain that trickles from the sky can be saved and used on your garden. Ask your municipality if it has a downspout disconnection program. If not, call a handyman (or woman) to do it for you, or do it yourself, so that your downspout can collect any rainwater

A hose is a hose is a hose, right? Actually, no. Most cheapie hoses are made of that nasty plastic PVC, and many have been stabilized with lead. In 2003, Consumer Reports tested 16 brands of hoses and found that several leached unsafe levels of lead into water. The mag advised people to stick with hoses that are labelled "safe for drinking" on the packaging. And while leaky soaker hoses or drip irrigation systems can be way more efficient than old-fashioned sprinklers, that's only true if they're used right. Water loamy soil with these for 30 to 40 minutes once a week, sandy soil more and clay soil less. Burying the hose under your mulch will help prevent water from evaporating.

that funnels off your roof. Pick up a rain barrel with a fine screen to keep bugs out (wouldn't want to it to become a mosquito brothel, now would you?), then use the water you collect on your plants. Warm rainwater is easier on plants than ice-cold chlorinated hose water, anyway.

Water-Smart Plants: Logic tells you to avoid planting water-intensive flowers, which means steering clear of flower I.D. tags that say "keep moist" and sticking to the ones that say "water weekly" or "let dry between watering." Yet lots of people end up watering drought-resistant types more than other species! Why? Well, these xerophyte plants can survive dry spells, but do they look good trying? Not always, according to a horticulture myth site posted by a prof at Washington State U. In fact, some will shed leaves or won't flower unless they get lots of liquids; as a result, well-intentioned people end up using more water than they would have on run-of-the-mill landscape plants. Do your research.

Grass is perhaps one of the biggest backyard water-suckers. In fact, the average suburban lawn sucks up about 45,500 litres of water every summer in Canada, according to Go for Green (www.goforgreen.ca/gardening). But it doesn't have to be that way. Our problem is, we all plant one strain of super-thirsty grass that needs tons of water and chemical inputs to look happy and "healthy": Kentucky bluegrass. You (and the planet) would be much better off if you planted some **low-maintenance fescues** or **perennial rye grasses**. Don't worry: your backyard won't look like a field of wheat. These breeds are even used on sports fields and golf courses, so relax—your lawn can still be as green as your neighbours'.

PATIOS AND BALCONIES

If you've ever lived in an apartment with no outdoor access, you know just how much a patio, balcony or even a well-placed fire escape means to a person. The access to fresh air, the sun kissing your face, maybe an encounter with a butterfly or a bird—in my case, even nightly visits by a family of raccoons living in my neighbour's roof were treasured after I moved from a dark basement apartment. Of course, once we have such a space, we have to fill it with stuff—pots, patio furniture, a barbecue, those fancy lights you string outside—all of which have environmental ramifications.

Pots: Just because something is filled with earth, next to earth or "of the earth" (think clay, metal or wood) doesn't mean it's earth-friendly. Take terra cotta, for instance. This mainstay of the flowerpot world is made of seemingly benign clay. "What could be wrong with clay?" you ask. "It's been sculpted by potters and artisans since the beginning of time." Well, like anything we mine commercially (including those cute tin planters), clay comes with plenty of eco-implications, especially in certain parts of the world. Indiscriminate mining of the stuff in areas of India has dried up local wells (leading to severe drinking water shortages), and paddy fields, once wetland habitats for plants and animals, are being dug up and dried out for the mouldable mud. Also, beware of planting edibles in glazed terra cotta. The finish could contain lead that can leach into your dinner.

Fake terra cotta and other plastic pots aren't great, either. Most are made with polyethylene

THOSE PATIO LANTERNS

Oh, those patio lanterns—they're so quintessentially Canadian that Kim Mitchell had to sing a song about them (and we're subjected to hearing it again and again every summer until the end of time). No Canadian summer is complete without them. Luckily, they're perfectly compatible with your decked-out eco-garden—if you get the right kind.

Old-school strings of mini incandescent lights are fairly wasteful when you compare them to the LED kind. If you can't find LED patio lights, just grab your Christmas set (the outdoor kind) and string them up around your patio umbrella or deck rail. **But who needs electric lights at all when the sun can keep your yard lit long into the night?** Solar-powered deck, garden and shed lights are all available at Canadian Tire, as is a sun-fuelled canvas umbrella whose LED lights twinkle come nightfall.

(a relative of the pop bottle), which, according to Greenpeace's pyramid of plastics, isn't too bad. But like all plastics, they're petroleum-based and contain chemical UV stabilizers. Cheap plastic planters can easily crack, as can low-grade terra cotta, so it's best to invest in better-quality containers that you won't have to replace every spring.

So what should you plant your petunias in? Start by hitting second-hand stores, flea markets and garage sales, where you'll find plenty of weird and wonderful retro containers. And think outside the pot. Old boots, wooden crates and vintage suitcases make great planters. You can also get fibrous pots made out of **recycled cardboard** from any local garden centre (speaking of which, try to shop for plants sold in cardboard over those sold in non-recyclable plastic). Pick up baskets made of fast-growing, sustainable **bamboo**. Fair-trade shops tend to have all kinds of planters made of **ceramic** or **wicker**, crafted by worker co-ops with an eye towards sustainable materials.

Patio Furniture: Need a place to sit? Pretty, naturally weather-resistant exotic woods such as teak are all the rage these days, but they're often overharvested, deforesting tropical countries. Rainforest Relief is pressuring retailers such as Wal-Mart, Pottery Barn and Linens-n-Things to stop selling any patio furniture made of teak, nyatoh, kapur, balau, jatoba, garapera, ipê and other tropical woods that are in high demand for their exotic look. The group's campaign has already pushed Martha Stewart and Crate and

> **Naturally weather-resistant bamboo is an exotic option that's actually sustainable, since bamboo grows so damn fast**

Barrel to stop using nyatoh wood. **IKEA**, by the way, only uses tropical woods that have been certified by an org such as the Forest Stewardship Council (FSC). Naturally weather-resistant bamboo is an exotic option that's actually sustainable, since **bamboo** grows so damn fast. You can often find great handmade bamboo chairs, tables and loungers at fair-trade shops.

Woods that aren't naturally weather-resistant are sealed with petroleum-based finishes that off-gas powerful air-polluting volatile organic compounds (VOCs). And plastic furniture

---

THE FOREST STEWARDSHIP COUNCIL

Choose wood furniture sourced closer to home and certified by the FSC. Ask local woodworkers if they use certified wood for their patio chairs; you'll be surprised by how many do. If they don't, give them the FSC website (**www.fsccanada.org**).

is, again, plastic—made of either polyethylene or PVC (vinyl). Polyethylene is considered much more benign than vinyl, which has all kinds of nasty enviro baggage. But both types tend to break suddenly after a couple of years, giving Grandpa a mini heart attack at your backyard barbecue. (Don't feel bad, the pricier plastics would have cracked, too.)

For durability and class-appeal, **wrought iron** is great, since it lasts forever. So how 'bout this: we'll forgive the not-so-forgivable eco-legacy iron ore mining has given the planet as long as you promise to keep your wrought iron patio furniture forever. If your grandkids don't want it when you pass on, antique stores will surely jump at it.

Rustic outdoor furniture made from **willow branches** is in the clear because the branches are fast-growing and usually hand-collected in small quantities, says the Wise Guide to sustainable products (www.worldwise.com/wiseguide.html). Plus, they don't need any sealants, since they still have their bark. What about wicker? First of all, you've gotta know your terminology. Wicker refers very generally to pliable twigs; **rattan** specifically refers to a climbing palm plant. Wicker is often made using rattan, which is fine, since it's considered renewable, but make sure you're not getting the type that's coated with harsh chemical sealants. Stay away from fake petroleum-based plastic wicker.

Natural materials aren't the only eco-options in town: you can get patio furniture made from **recycled plastic**. It's not only super sturdy, it's low-maintenance too, and it's available in all shapes and sizes. Just know that it can be pretty expensive. (You can order Canadian-made recycled plastic Muskoka chairs, footstools, tables and five-piece sets online from www.crplastics.com).

PATIO CUSHIONS

Need to soften your seat? Many patio cushions are Teflon-coated to deflect rain and stains. But let me tell you, the great outdoors needs less non-stick chemicals, not more—Teflon's building block, PFOA, is already concentrating in the tissues of wildlife and humans. Look for cushions made of untreated natural fibres that you put away when it rains.

Decking and Fencing: Until recently, lumber intended for outdoor use (known as pressure-treated wood) was treated with chromium and arsenic (actually chromated copper arsenate, or CCA), and some of those toxin-leachers could still be on shelves. Several towns have ripped out playgrounds built with this kind of wood after realizing that it leaches quite readily into surrounding soil (especially sandy soil, and especially when exposed to sunlight, which is, like, all the time). If your flower beds are framed with arsenic-laced pressure-treated wood, the toxins could make their way into your veggie patch too. (If you decide to toss your old wood, make sure to bring it to your local hazardous waste depot. Call your municipality for details).

Alternative pressure-treated woods are already on the market. But the U.S. Environmental Protection Agency says little research has been done on the environmental impact of ACQ and copper azole, for instance. Borate-treated lumber is less toxic, but some say you shouldn't use it outdoors.

The best option for decking and anywhere wood touches soil, especially if you are to build, say, an above-ground veggie garden or child's sandbox, is **cedar**. The natural oils in cedar mean no sealants or chem treatments are needed.

Crafty boys and girls willing to sweat to improve their yard can buy deck tiles, deck boards and two-by-fours made entirely of **recycled plastic**, which is durable and rot- and corrosion-proof (check out the stuff made by www.renewresources.com). **Trex** sells fencing, decking, railing systems and benches made of recycled plastic grocery bags, reclaimed pallet wrap and waste wood (www.trex.com.) **Home Depot** sells "wood" made of recycled plastic and wood fibres, as well as FSC-certified lumber, fencing and deck tiles.

If you can't afford cedar or recycled lumber, and you do need to treat your fence, deck or what have you, get an **all-natural finishing oil**, or a plant- and mineral-based wood treatment by **Lifetime Wood Treatment**, out of B.C. (www.valhalco.com).

BARBECUES

Given the hellish temperature of many kitchens come summer, there's no way we could make it through without an outdoor grill. You can only have so many salads (unless you're on the raw food diet), so it's either that or packaging-heavy takeout, and barbecuing is definitely the greener way to go. Especially if you do it right.

Charcoal and wood send soot and smog-inducing carbon monoxide into the air

Hibachis: Anyone with a deep yearning for mesquite or a super-low budget knows the allure of the hibachi. Unfortunately, the most wallet-friendly option is also the dirtiest. Charcoal and wood send soot and smog-inducing carbon monoxide into the air. That applies to both lump charcoal (which is basically unprocessed charred wood) and the pillow-shaped

Got a chunky, gunky grill caked with last June's basting sauce? Skip the toxic chem-based cleaners. **Nature Clean** and **Simply Clean** make all-natural barbecue sprays. You can also make your own scrubbing paste with baking soda and water that you apply with one of those wire BBQ brushes. Give the grill a good scrubbing then wipe with a wet cloth.

briquettes (made of scrap wood and sawdust). The briquettes may contain coal dust or hidden chems left over from the scrap wood, and the lump kind contributes to deforestation. You just can't win.

Whole Foods, if you've got one near you, carries its own "365" brand of hardwood charcoal, which uses scrap wood from the furniture biz but is purportedly free of additives, coal, chems or fillers. Or think tropical and get some **coconut shell charcoal**. Though hard to find, this stuff burns without smoke, odour or harmful emissions (you can order it online at www.barbecuesgalore.ca).

Grills: Another problem with cheapie barbecues, whether they burn charcoal or propane, is the grill itself. More often than not, low-grade models use chrome-coated aluminum, which chips easily, leaving you with a bare aluminum cooking surface. Not good for the brain cells. You're safer with a **cast iron** or **stainless steel** grill. The **porcelain-coated** kind, which is quite common, is also good.

If dishes are out of the question at that backyard bash or picnic, make sure to pick up biodegradable/compostable disposable plates, cups and even cutlery, as well as napkins or paper towels made with high post-consumer recycled content from your local health store. If it doesn't carry them, ask the manager to order some (businesses, festivals and stores can contact GreenShift at **www.greenshift.ca** to order bio-plastic cups, bowls and more). Or order some yourself from **www.worldcentric.org** or **www.frogfile.com**. You can even bury these in your garden when you're done with them and let them decompose.

No matter what type you buy, more and more Qs come with removable grill-top or grill-side trays, rib racks, baskets and roasting pans coated with a non-stick surface. Sure, your fish fillets and mini potatoes will slide off the fire without much trouble, but is that really worth it when you know those non-stick chemicals are turning up in polar bears and breast milk everywhere? Plus, burning some of these chems at high temps has been found to release toxic fumes. And really, who hasn't burned food on the barbecue?

Fuel: In terms of fuel sources, your cleanest, most energy-efficient bet is either **natural gas** or **liquid propane** (which is extracted from natural gas). In fact, backyard 'cuing with either of these is more efficient than cooking in your kitchen oven, which takes forever to preheat. Don't get me wrong—natural gas is no saint (think offshore drilling and piping through traditional native lands), but I've yet to encounter a barbie that runs on vegetable oil. An electric barbecue run on solar panels would definitely win the green ribbon at the country fair. There are funky **solar cookers** on the market, but they don't give you the flame-roasted effect. However, advocates swear these metallic contraptions cook a mean casserole and bake some fine cookies in about the same time as your regular oven, if it's sunny out, and a little longer if it's partly cloudy. If you're interested in checking them out, head to www.solarcooking.ca. Solaroven.net even sells a solar hybrid oven you can plug in if the sun goes away. Or make your own with a little foil and plans from http://solarhaven.org/SolarCooking.htm.

GETTING AROUND

Remember when people had to travel everywhere on horseback and hop in a canoe just to get from Montreal to Toronto or Vancouver to Victoria? Yeah, me neither, but our modern need for speed makes us cringe at how long it must have taken for anyone to get anywhere. We've relegated our hikes, canoes and equine friends to leisure activities, things we drive 100 kilometres out of town to go do. For our real life, we've got an elaborate network of planes, trains and automobiles to get us where we want in a hurry, with a web of paved roads, rails and invisible air routes to guide the way. Now you can lower the roof on your convertible and scream "Eat my dust, world!" at 150 kilometres an hour (or rather, "Eat the cloud of particulate matter and greenhouse gases that billows behind me"). Love 'em or hate 'em, modern means of getting around are here to stay—you've just got to know how to pick 'em to make the best of life's nutty journey.

CARS

Maybe it's something about the vastness of the land or the crappiness of the winters that makes us want to get around in climate-controlled bubbles, but whatever it is, Canadians love their cars. Over 18 million vehicles are registered in this country, and in a three-month period in 2005 alone they travelled a whopping 88.6 billion kilometres, says StatsCan.

If you already own a car, you have to look deep inside and get all Montel Williams meets David Suzuki on yourself. Ask yourself, Do I really need to drive as much as I do? Can I take transit or bike to work? Can I even afford to drive at the rate gas prices are skyrocketing?

Exhaust: Wanna know what's chokin' out your tailpipe? Probably not, but pull over and let's talk. The average car produces between 10,000 and 12,000 pounds of climate-changing, globe-warming carbon dioxide every year. Canadians tend to buy smaller cars than our southern neighbours, but we still cough up plenty of asthma-inducing, smog-breeding junk. Here's how the 2004 model of one of the country's most popular cars, the Toyota Corolla, stacks up (based on 12,500 miles a year, or 20,000 km): On top of the 7,000 pounds of carbon dioxide, it spews about 300 pounds of carbon monoxide, 15 pounds of nitrous oxides and 7 pounds of hydrocarbons, many of which are toxic carcinogens and nerve damagers. All combined, they contribute to respiratory infections, ground-level ozone (a.k.a. smog), and climate change. Not good.

> The average car produces between 10,000 and 12,000 pounds of climate-changing, globe-warming carbon dioxide every year

Mining and Metals: Your car's environmental record doesn't just hinge on its tailpipe. There's a hell of a lot of mining going on (with a quarry-full of eco-implications) just to dig up enough steel, aluminum and dozens of other metals to make all those cars. Thirty-five percent of all iron mined in the U.S., for example, goes to the auto biz, according to Environmental Defense's Green Car Report. Then there are all the toxic innards, like the mercury switches in pre-2003 North American–made cars and imports from the '90s (thanks to the sloppy recycling of old vehicles, these switches are one of the largest sources of hazardous mercury pollution in Canada). Lead starter batteries, according to the Clean Car Campaign, account for the majority of the world's current lead pollution.

Chemicals: Oh, and that new car smell? That's partly the scent of chemical phthalates used to soften PVC plastics in the dashboard, door panels and weather strips. We inhale them every time we get in our cars—talk about indoor air pollution. And, scary but true, these chemicals break down even faster in the hot sun. The plastics industry says phthalates are safe, but Canada has already banned the softener in baby toys, and California classified some as "reproductive toxicants." Hyundai was found to have by far the highest levels of phthalates collected from its windshield. Mercedes had the highest number of PBDEs—the toxic family of persistent flame retardants found in farmed salmon and breast milk.

Volvo has banned the use of several PBDEs and phthalates in its cars. **Honda**, **Toyota** and to some degree **Nissan** are in the midst of reducing and replacing PVC parts. And in accordance with the much-praised End of Life Vehicle directive out of Europe, pretty much every car manufacturer has agreed to phase out lead, mercury and cadmium from all their cars, even outside of Europe, to make them more easily recycled and less toxic in their afterlife. For more info and details on how different cars rank in terms of their indoor air pollution, check out "Toxic at Any Speed" at www.ecocenter.org.

Petroleum: If aliens were watching us from outer space, do you think they'd call the planet "Earth"? Doubt it. Given how the human race revolves around the black goopy stuff we dig out of the earth's crust, we'd be known as Slick, Sludge or Black Gold. And dig for it, we do—in the rainforest, on the ocean floor, in wildlife reserves and in all sorts of ecologically sensitive regions. We knock through wildlands to build roads to remote regions and leave toxic legacies where poorly stored waste water from drilling leaches into surrounding waterways, polluting rivers, lakes, streams and local citizens. A prime example can be found in an ongoing class action lawsuit representing 30,000 largely indigenous Ecuadorians that claims Texaco dumped 70 billion litres of waste products into the local environment throughout the '70s and '80s. The region in question is still appallingly contaminated, say activists, despite Texaco's remediation efforts a decade ago. About 2.5 million acres of rainforest were purportedly lost to contamination and drilling.

Then there's the type of oil mining you see in Canada, where more energy goes into extracting and refining petroleum from the tar sands than the oil produces. In the process, Sierra Club of Canada says tar sand oil creates two and half times more greenhouse gases than conventional gasoline. In fact, Alberta's oil and gas sector is responsible for making the province the biggest greenhouse gas polluter in the country, according to a 2006 David Suzuki Foundation report. Canada's 21 operational oil refineries are also big polluters, emitting all sorts of volatile organic compounds (VOCs), including carcinogenic benzene, as well as smog-inducing sulphur dioxide, nitrogen oxides and carbon monoxide. You don't want to live downwind from one of these babies.

More energy goes into extracting and refining petroleum from the tar sands **than the oil produces**

Of course, all that oil has to be shipped to its destinations. The life-smothering devastation that strikes the seas every time there's an oil spill on tankers or off-shore drilling sites is enough to make any dolphin-lover weep. In 2005, there were 21 accidental oil spills that leaked under 700 tons and three that were over that volume. If you think the *Exxon Valdez* made a heartbreaking mess sliming the coast of Alaska with 37,000 tons back in 1989, you'll cringe when you realize it was actually one of the smallest of the major oil spills of the last 30 years (in 35th place), according to International Tanker Owners Pollution Federation Limited. A devastating 63,000 tons spilled off the coast of Spain in 2002, and 1991 was particularly bad, with 260,000 tons dumped near Angola and 144,000 off the coast of Italy. The industry has been painfully slow to take any preventative action. Shipping companies have until 2015 to phase out vulnerable single-hulled ships in European and American waters, but by 2003, only half of the planet's tanker fleets had converted to double hulls.

Finally, let's not forget the ecological ramifications tied to waging war in the name of oil (not that this happens, of course—wars are fought for freedom and democracy). Oil fires, often set as acts of sabotage in conflict zones, come with their own special legacy. According to the World Watch Institute, the fires set in Kuwait by Iraqi soldiers in the first Gulf War released a ghastly 500 million tons of carbon dioxide into the air, poisoning crops, livestock and water supplies far and wide. The country is still recovering to this day.

Buying a Car: If you still feel you need to buy a car, consider getting joint custody rather than buying one all to yourself. If you don't need it every day, look into auto sharing programs near you, which allow you to pay as you drive. They're popping up all over the country. And don't forget to carpool. What's the point of three colleagues driving to work from the same part of town in three separate cars? Many highways even have special car-pooling lanes to encourage the practice.

When buying, think small. The smaller the car, the lighter it'll be, the less earthly resources went into it and the less fuel you'll need to use. Unless you're hauling cargo up snowy mountain faces, ditch the four-wheel or all-wheel drive—it'll just suck up more fuel (up to 10% more, in fact). Power windows, seats and mirrors all draw more power and add weight to the car. At the dealership, look for the EnerGuide sticker in all new vehicles. It'll tell you the car's highway and city fuel consumption rating, and the estimated cost of gas for a year.

I know, I know, you want names. Everyone and his car-loving uncle puts out a list of the greenest rides, but perhaps the most trusted source is the American Council for an Energy-Efficient Economy (ACEEE), which publishes *Green Book: The Environmental Guide to Cars and Trucks* (available online at www.greenercars.com). The ACEEE assesses automakers for fuel economy and emissions, factors in the pollution from manufacturing the car and producing and distributing the fuel, then tosses in pollution from the car's tailpipe and evaluates the health problems caused by each pollutant. The group even accounts for the power plant pollution created by plug-in cars. On a scale from 0 to 100, the greenest car of 2006 got a 57. Actually two did: the **Honda Insight** and the **Honda Civic GX**, which, interestingly enough, beat out the **Civic Hybrid** for overall eco-ness. The 2006 list of the "meanest" vehicles for the environment was topped by the Dodge Ram, which scored a dismal 12.

The *Green Book* provides rankings for all vehicle types, so you can look up the greenest compact pickup or mid-size wagon. If you're buying a used car, check the *Green Book* to see how older models fare and pick up a copy of *Consumer Reports* for its view on the most reliable second-hand cars.

Toyota and **Honda** produce some of the greenest cars on the market to date. American cars, on the other hand, are accused of falling at the back of the eco-pack. According to Environmental Defense in the U.S., vehicles produced by the Big Three automakers—DaimlerChrysler, GM and Ford—spew way more carbon dioxide every year than the largest

Toyota and Honda produce some of the greenest cars on the market to date

power company in the States (which includes nearly 60 coal-burning power plants). Ford, in particular, has faced an onslaught of attacks from environmentalists for churning out the biggest gas guzzlers with the lowest overall fuel efficiency (getting fewer kilometres per litre than the Model T!), but it gained some cred when it promised to turn half of its fleet into hybrids by the year 2010. Then, six months later, in the summer of 2006, it dropped that pledge like a hot potato. Instead, it promised to double the number of cars it makes that run on alternative fuels, such as ethanol blend E-85 and biodiesel (see page 252). The move's considered a cop-out because these fuels are barely available to consumers.

Hybrids: The modern hybrid hit the streets in 1999 with the introduction of the **Honda Insight**, but it was largely ignored by most of the population until the price of gas went

through the roof. These cool new vehicles cross electric motors with gasoline engines to bring you better fuel efficiency—well, most of them, anyway. The Honda Insight gets the most kilometres per litre of all the hybrids, edging out the **Toyota Prius**. But most cars, hybrid or not, don't get quite as many kilometres per litre as advertised. And beware of poser hybrids, like the 2006 Honda Accord Hybrid, Toyota Highlander and Lexus RX330, which use the energy generated from the battery for extra power and peppy acceleration, not fuel savings.

Depending on where you live, you might be eligible for some government incentives if you purchase a hybrid. Ontario has recently doubled the rebate for these cars, so you can now get up to $2,000 back, which is also what B.C. offers. P.E.I. drivers win the prize with a $3,000 rebate. Everyone else is pretty much out of luck, so keep bugging your MPPs for change on this front.

Most cars, hybrid or not, don't get quite as many kilometres per litre as advertised

If you're thinking of buying a used hybrid, find out if the warranty has expired and, if not, if it covers the battery and if it's transferable. It's a good idea to ask whether the battery has been changed. Be aware that it generally needs to be replaced after about eight years—and that's when most warranties expire. Replacing it will cost you a few grand.

Car Heaven: Jalopy, clunker, K-car—whatever you call it, do us a favour and get it off the road. Sure, not everyone can afford to run out and buy a hybrid, but just trading in your rattletrap for a newer, cleaner used car will give the planet a bit of a break. Environment

Need to rent a car for a week or the weekend? Discount Car and Truck Rentals has started renting hybrids, namely the **Toyota Prius** and hybrid **Ford Focus**. If it costs a little more, just think—you'll easily make up the difference with all the gas you save! If a hybrid isn't available, rent a **Honda Civic** or any of the fuel-efficient vehicles listed on **www.greenercars.com**.

Canada says pre-1988 vehicles are responsible for 50% of road emissions (and they only make up 10 to 15% of cars!). When it's time to put her down, look into scrapping incentives in your area, especially if you live in an urban centre. The Scrap-It program out of Richmond, B.C., will give you $1,000 towards hybrid wheels, up to $500 towards a bike and lots of other cash incentives. Edmonton, Calgary and Toronto all call their versions Car Heaven and offer free tows, a tax receipt and a chance to win prizes. Fredericton will give you credit towards a new or newer car, a one-year bus pass or a bike and helmet.

Auto Maintenance: Need an oil change? Canadians dump abut 275 million litres of used motor oil every year. That's seven times more than the *Exxon Valdez* spill. Much of that could be reused, but isn't. Look for re-refined oil, like **Tech-2000** or Zellers' **Autoprix**. If you change your own oil, ask your municipality what you should do with it. Many will take it, as long as it's in a clean, leak-proof container.

> Canadians dump abut 275 million litres of used motor oil every year. **That's seven times more than the *Exxon Valdez* spill**

As for cleaning products, there's absolutely no need to resort to chemicals. Make your own non-toxic car cleaners with all-natural ingredients (1/4 cup (50 mL) liquid castile soap and hot water will do as a body wash; a vinegar and water blend works on windows). **Blue Wonder** cleaning cloths claim they can handle the inside and outside of your car without added products. And even if you're using the most biodegradable of suds, water advocates and many municipalities recommend bringing your car to an automated car wash where water is recycled and properly treated before it's dumped into sewers. It's much better than letting your soapy water drip down your driveway, rinsing chemicals into nearby waterways. If you insist on doing it yourself, suds up on a grassy surface (often called a lawn) to reduce runoff.

THE TOP 10 TIPS FOR SMART DRIVING

#1 Slow down. You'll use 20% more fuel driving at 120 kilometres an hour than if you stick to the highway speed limit. Dropping down from 100 to 90 kph will save an additional 10%.

#2 Chill out. Jackrabbit starts, rapid acceleration and aggressive driving use up to 40% more fuel than following the speed limit.

#3 Stay cool—by rolling down the windows, that is. Switching on the a/c ups your fuel needs by 20% in the city.

#4 Pump up. Proper tire pressure can reduce your greenhouse gas emissions by an eighth of a ton a year. Cold temps can decrease air pressure in your tires, so get your gauge out more often in winter.

#5 Carpool!

#6 Don't tire yourself out. Heavily treaded snow tires suck back more fuel than all-season tires. Unless you live in serious snow country, there's no need for them. If you're in the market for new tires, Michelin Energy MXV4 passenger tires (available at Canadian Tire) are the only explicitly fuel-efficient tires I know of. You'll use 5% less fuel and significantly reduce emissions.

#7 Use your feet. Leave your car at home if you're just going to grab a carton of milk around the corner. If you're running around doing errands, walk between stores rather than moving the car three blocks. This is especially important come winter, when engines burn 50% more fuel on short trips than in summer.

#8 Get moving. Newer, computer-controlled engines don't need to warm up for more than 30 seconds. Yes, we know that contradicts what most automakers tell us, but the Office of Energy Efficiency says the best way to warm your car is to drive it.

#9 Dump out your trunk. Driving around with golf clubs in winter and a bag of salt in summer only weighs down your car and uses more fuel.

#10 Get out of your car and hop on a bus, subway, train or bike!

ALTERNATIVE FUELS

It seems like there are a million and one ways you can fill 'er up these days, at least if you're following prototype cars. But in terms of what's available on the street as we speak, there are only a few alt routes to tank up.

Diesel: Diesel's got a dirty rep, but it's actually more fuel-efficient than gas and, as such, emits less carbon dioxide. A year ago, I would have told you that it's ultimately dirtier than gasoline since it's less refined and emits more sooty particulate matter (kind of obvious when you stand behind an idling tractor trailer). But Canada has recently aligned itself with new American regs that mandate the introduction of cleaner diesel. The diesel currently at the pumps has 97% less polluting sulphur than the old stuff. Nonetheless, more crude oil is used to make diesel than to make gasoline, and petroleum's always a bad thing, so diesel will never get two green thumbs up.

Biodiesel: The silver lining is that any diesel engine can run on biodiesel blends. The biodiesel fuels you'll find at rare pumps tend to come in blends of 5% to 20% agriculturally grown soy or other biological matter and 95% to 80% regular diesel, so they still pollute, but not as much. Vegan alert: in place of soy, tallow is sometimes used. Supposedly, most new diesel engines can run on biodiesel without converting anything. Just ask.

Any diesel engine can run on biodiesel blends

WHERE TO TANK UP

Pretty much every international oil company has a record of nasty spills and/or exploiting countries in the developing world. But when you have to tank up, both Greenpeace and Sierra Club of Canada advise steering clear of Esso. The company may have spent over $1.2 billion to finally reduce the notoriously high sulphur content of its gas and diesel (reducing smog-causing properties by over 90%), but it's still maligned by enviros for dragging its feet on the matter, for denying that fossil fuels contribute to climate change and for running ads in the U.S. condemning the Kyoto Protocol. Your best bet is **Sunoco**, which is the leader in ethanol use and the only oil company to sign the CERES principles for environmentally sound business practices. And don't overfill your tank! Even small spills contribute to pollution.

Straight Vegetable Oil (SVO): If you dream of pouring a bottle of canola oil or filtered deep-fryer grease from a local burger joint into your diesel tank, you need a straight vegetable oil (SVO) conversion kit; otherwise, you'll end up mucking everything up (to put it technically). You basically need a separate hose and a tank and oil warming system, which will cost up to $1,500.

Ethanol: Even regular cars can fill up on blended wheat- or corn-based ethanol gasoline. E-10 is 10% ethanol and is available at over 1,000 service stations across Canada. It's said to reduce your greenhouse gas emissions, in part because the plant actually sucks up carbon dioxide as it grows on farmers' fields before it's processed into gasoline. About a dozen cars, including some Chrysler minivans, Ford Explorers and the Sebring sedan, can now run on an 85% ethanol blend called E-85. Since you need more of the stuff to power your car, manufacturers make E-85 models with larger fuel tanks. Trouble is, E-85 fuel is nearly impossible to find at this point.

FYI: Getting your gasoline-blended fuel from the fields, be it corn or soy, comes with a whole other set of problems. Both crops are largely genetically modified, loaded with pesticides and petroleum-fertilizers. In fact, renowned scientists such as Cornell's David Pimental say making corn-based ethanol uses way more energy than it creates, just like the tar sands oil of Alberta. The Canadian industry is supposedly working on alternatives, including making ethanol from agro residues such as straw, corn stalks and forestry leftovers. We'll have to wait and see who wins at the pumps.

Natural Gas and Propane: You might have seen delivery trucks, taxis and commercial vehicles powered by natural gas or propane. Both are fossil fuels, just like gas or diesel, and digging them out and piping them to us comes with heavy environmental implications, but both burn cleaner, produce fewer toxic pollutants and up to 20% less global warming emissions over their life cycles, and cost less (30% to 40% less). Plus, they're sourced locally (from Canada's north) rather than overseas. They're not perfect, but they're an option. Conventional gas cars can be converted to run on the stuff for about $4,000 to $6,000, but they don't burn the fuel quite as cleanly as factory-made types. For places to refuel on natural gas, check out www.ngvontario.com; for propane, see www.propanegas.ca.

MOTORCYCLES AND SCOOTERS

Ever daydream about hitting the open road on a badass cruiser? Sure, the gas tank may be tiny and you might get more kilometres per litre from your two-wheeler, but according to Environment Canada, most motorcycles expel 10 times more carbon monoxide and 14 times more polluting hydrocarbon than the average car.

"How can this be?" you cry. Well, cars are subject to much more stringent regulations than either scooters or motorbikes. And most bike makers have been slow to clean up their acts.

Scooters can actually be the worst option— even more polluting for their size than large diesel trucks

New models of motorcycles and scooters should have pollution-curbing catalytic converters, which can cut hydrocarbon emissions by 60%. Fuel injection systems and oxygen sensors also help with emission reduction. Trouble is, most people take off catalytic converters and emissions canisters after they get their ride home because they think it weighs down the bike. But you would never do such a thing, now would you?

Whether you're opting for a scooter or a hog, steer clear of smaller two-stroke engines. Without getting into all the nitty-gritty, two-stroke engines are lighter and relatively peppy, but they're completely unregulated and are literally the dirtiest things on wheels. We're talking the same inefficient, highly polluting types of engines you find in lawn mowers, jet skis and snowmobiles. Although nearly every motorcycle now has a four-stroke, far fewer scooters have made the switch. So scooters, while cute and super-fuel-efficient, can actually be the worst option—even more polluting for their size than large diesel trucks! Unless you get one of the four-stroke types, such as the **Vespa ET4** (last I checked, Vespa was testing prototypes of gas-electric hybrids, so keep an eye out). All new **Honda** scooters and motorbikes are also four-stroke. And keep an eye out for the zero-emissions fuel cell–powered hybrid scooters trickling onto the market.

If you already have a scooter or cruiser and want to ease its eco-burden, you can switch to biodiesel in a flash if it's got a diesel engine.

TAKE PUBLIC TRANSIT TO WORK

One public bus full of passengers takes roughly 40 cars off the road in rush hour, saving 168 tons of greenhouse gases and 70,000 litres of gasoline, according to Environment Canada.

Just remember, pure biodiesel will solidify in the cold, so unless you have some sort of engine heater and heated parking space, use it in warm weather only. Biodiesel blends shouldn't be a problem.

BICYCLES

Something happens to many of us between our early tricycle days and adulthood that makes us shun our two-wheeled friends. Sure 50% of Canadian households have at least one adult bike in the garage, but are you actually riding it? According to the World Watch Institute, choosing to bike a 6-kilometre round trip instead of driving it keeps 7 kilograms of pollutants out of the air, including carbon dioxide, carbon monoxide and nitrous oxides. Plus, it'll save you a hell of a lot of money in fuel (and transit passes).

DEVINCI BIKES

Though bikes do have the greenest rep as a way of getting around town, most are coated with toxic spray paints loaded with polluting VOCs. Not **Cycles Devinci** out of Saguenay, Quebec. The company joined the federal government's Enviroclub program (**www.enviroclub.ca**), designed to help small and medium-sized manufacturers become more eco-friendly. Thanks to new painting systems recommended by Enviroclub, the company ditched its wasteful high-volume, low-pressure spray process. Now, its solvent use is down a whopping 80% (from 33.5 to 6.4 grams of paint per bike), and Devinci uses a third less paint, cutting nasty VOC emissions dramatically. Stick that in your Tour de France trophies, Lance.

It seems people are finally starting to clue in to its advantages: in 2005, bikes outsold cars in the U.S. for the first time since the oil embargo of the early '70s, and more North Americans are biking to work than ever. Nothing like paying a fortune at the pumps to get people pedalling again. And did you know that 100 bikes can be built with the same amount of energy and resources it takes to build one mid-sized car?

Buying used is a great, cheap way to give bikes a second life. If that's still too costly for you, some cities have cool bike sharing programs or ways you can earn free wheels. **Freewheels** in Montreal will give you a bike if you donate four hours of your time at its bike repair shop. **The Purple and Yellow Bike Project** lets you access its fleet of bicycles on the UBC campus if you sign up for a key.

Bikes outsold cars in the U.S. for the first time since the oil embargo of the early '70s

Okay, so you live in Montreal and you have to go to Toronto for a wedding next weekend. Environmentally speaking, should you do the five-hour drive or take the one-hour flight? The average car produces about 250 grams of carbon dioxide per kilometre, while a plane chokes out about 150 grams of the greenhouse gas per person per kilometre, so you might initially say, "Aha, I'm better off flying." Not so fast. Don't forget that the plane might be only a third full, but it still has to lug those 80 empty seats. And once you factor in the round-trip cab ride to and from the airport in both cities, especially if you're idling for an hour in traffic on both ends . . . All in all, driving such a short haul is definitely the greener option, but it's far from the greenest. A train will take you from core to core in four hours flat with no green guilt. If you do opt to drive, make sure to carpool.

AIRPLANES

Who doesn't love the feeling you get when you're high in the air on a plane, heading for somewhere, anywhere different? Well, aviaphobes, who find nothing but fear in the friendly skies. Or business travellers who spend more time with flight attendants than their kids. But for most people flying is kind of magical. Too bad that stuff coming out of the engines isn't fairy dust. Indeed, for each flight, over 150 grams of carbon dioxide is spewed into the atmosphere per person per kilometre. It's actually the fastest growing source of greenhouse gas emissions in the world!

Airlines: There's no list out there rating the greenest airlines. But many are taking on environmental goals and posting eco-commitments online. For instance, Japan's **JAL Group** has adopted a green purchasing policy (which means any purchases it makes should be environmentally friendly—electric forklifts, a natural gas fleet, 100% recycled paper for JAL magazine), and it washes and reuses plastic cutlery. **Singapore Airlines**, **Finnair** and Scandanavia's **SAS** have all ditched disposable cutlery and serve food in washable crockery. And pretty much every airline is using the high price of fuel as an excuse to go green by cutting back on the amount of weight on board.

Green Tags: No matter what, air travel is never environmentally friendly, and many eco-heads (especially in Europe) have sworn off it. That's easier said than done in a giant country like Canada with miles of ocean on three sides. But there is one thing you can do to assuage your guilt and ease your impact: get green tags. With green tags, you offset the carbon your flight creates by supporting renewable energy or planting trees for anywhere from $5 to $150 per flight. If you have to fly for work, ask your employer to foot the green tag bill. Just know that all tags are not created equal—nor are they judged equally by environmentalists. Planting a dozen trees to neutralize your flight might seem wonderfully idealistic, but eco-heads dis it as an impermanent solution (those trees may be chopped down) and point out that trees take ages to mature to the point where they absorb significant amounts of carbon from the atmosphere.

To gauge your emissions, check out carbon flight calculators like those at **Green My Flight** (www.greenmyflight.com), a for-profit offshoot of the Vancouver-based Uniglobe Travel Agency. Green My Flight is the first service to be certified by the feds Environmental Choice program (the EcoLogo label is normally affixed to products). In this case, a minimum of 80% of your cash will go towards turbines. Not-for-profit **Offsetters** is another Canadian flight emissions

If you have to fly for work, ask your employer to foot the green tag bill

HOW MUCH CARBON DIOXIDE IS MY FLIGHT EMITTING?

Toronto–Montreal: 182 kilograms
Vancouver–Edmonton: 205 kilograms
Winnipeg–Quebec City: 489 kilograms
Calgary–Ottawa: 632 kilograms
Regina–Moncton: 635 kilograms
Victoria–Halifax: 970 kilograms

You think you feel guilty about your abundant frequent flyer points? The founders of super-popular budget travel series Rough Guides and Lonely Planet feel awful about all the plane-hopping they've done in a lifetime as über-successful travel writers/publishers, not to mention all the flights they've indirectly, or not so indirectly, encouraged readers to take. Both say they're going to buy credits from carbon-offsetting org **Climate Care** to neutralize the emissions created by their jet-setting staff. Rough Guides will issue global warming warnings and list alternative forms of transport (you know, like the train). It's even putting out a *Rough Guide to Climate Change.*

neutralizing program (www.offsetters.com). A minimum of 80% of your money goes to greenhouse gas–saving projects such as installing efficient lighting in households in South Africa and efficient cooking stoves in Bangladesh. Calgary-based **Pembina Institute**, a non-profit NGO, uses carbon offsets kind of like a fundraising tool. Half the cash from your purchase of green credits to offset your cruise or flight goes toward Pembina's respected environmental research and half to an actual wind farm.

Why not give your cash directly to renewable energy suppliers to make sure it goes to the right cause? That way, you can choose to fund a project close to home. The only thing is they might not be set up with convenient flight calculators like the other sites. Environmental Defence lists green power sources across the country at www.environmentaldefence.ca/aveda/action.htm. Still, flying less is your most earth-friendly option.

CHEMS ON A PLANE

Not all pollution happens outside the aircraft. In fact Aruba, Cuba, Grand Cayman, Barbados, Jamaica, India, Australia and several other countries require routine "disinsection" on inbound flights, often *while* you're on board. That means they're spraying you with insecticides to make sure no bugs disembark with you!

Some airlines, like, Air Canada and Air Transat, notify passengers right before they spray, but others like Canjet and Skyservice don't. Your best to check with the airline before buying your ticket about where and when they spray and whether they do it with you on board.

TOURISM

See the world, they said. So you do. Whether you're saving up your pennies for a six-month backpacking adventure in the Far East or figuring out how to get as far away as possible from your desk job with your week's vacation, we all need to break away from our daily lives and see what life is like over yonder. But what we see as a perfect vacation setting can mean just the opposite for locals. We wish away the rain; they call it a drought. We see refreshing swimming pools and green golf courses; they witness a major divesting of precious water sources. Even as the locals are fighting over loaves of bread in countries on the verge of economic collapse, the ripest crops in the land are trucked to hotels to make sure we visitors are well-fed. Yes, foreign dollars are wanted, and no, no one's saying you have to stay home for the rest of your life, but it's important to realize some of the impacts of our wandering ways.

Cruises: Cruises are known for their gluttony and extravagance (I mean, really, is a skating rink necessary aboard a boat?), so maybe it's not surprising that they're also extremely wasteful. According to the international eco org Oceana, average cruise ships produce about 10,000 kilos of garbage, 100,000 litres of sewage, and up to 130 kilos of toxic chemicals (dry cleaning fluid, photo processing chems) each and every day. In the winter of 2006, the International Council of Cruise Lines and Conservation International announced

> Cruise ships produce about **10,000 kilos** of garbage, **100,000 litres** of sewage, and up to **130 kilos** of toxic chemicals

that sensitive marine areas (including coral reefs, shellfish growing areas and protected areas) would be incorporated into navigational charts as "no wastewater discharge" zones. Industry reps say they also voluntarily treat all sewage and discharge when ships are within 4 nautical miles of shore. But what about other areas? Canadian laws don't prevent sewage discharges at all. Plus, environmentalists maintain that even treated wastewater fails to meet federal standards. Not a carnival for aquatic life.

Water Usage: Even if you're not cruisin' on water, you're probably going through way too much of it, be it for pools, golf courses, water parks or even in showers and toilets (many hotels have thousands of guest rooms—when you think about it, that's a hell of a lot of flushing). France, Greece, Italy and Spain have already lost half of their original wetlands, in large part because of tourist activities, according to a report by the World Wildlife Fund (WWF). The report points out that tourists and tourist facilities in the Mediterranean suck up four times more water than locals. In dry regions, this can be a real problem.

Souvenirs: When you're out and about in the world, ensure that whatever shopping you do isn't leaving a dent in the local ecosystems as well as your wallet. Trinkets and carvings made from elephant tusks may be legal in the country you're visiting (as they are in Hong Kong or South Africa), but you may need special permits to export them, and you definitely aren't allowed to bring them into Canada. You can get pretty coral jewellery, shells or sea sponges from many vendors in the Caribbean, but keep in mind that you're making an ecologically unwelcome purchase. If you spot a giant clam shell on the shores of the Philippines, leave it be. And even if your eco-hotel is engaged in protecting sea turtles on the beach, souvenir kiosks are often all too willing to target these endangered creatures for their attractive shells. Also, stay away from carvings made from endangered woods like rosewood, ebony or African blackwood.

Thinking of getting a nice shahtoosh shawl on your travels in India? What harm could come from wool, right? Well, three of these highly endangered Tibetan antelopes are killed for their underwool in the making of just one shawl, according to wildlife trade monitoring network, TRAFFIC (a joint program of the WWF and IUCN—the World Conservation Union).

Wherever you plan to go in the world, the old adage "Take nothing but photographs, leave nothing but footprints" should be your mantra.

Ecotourism: In recent years there's been an explosion of interest in ecotourism. Often the label is casually affixed to any excursion that involves seeing trees, wild animals—any form of nature, really. There's usually a caravan of SUVs involved that truck well-meaning tourists into pristine locations considered untouched by the masses. Sound magical? The problem is, as wildlife activists will tell you, such areas should remain untouched; daily carloads of people disturb wildlife and degrade fragile ecosystems. It's gotten so bad on certain trails in Peru and Nepal that they've been nicknamed "Coca-Cola trail" and "toilet paper trail."

It's gotten so bad on certain trails in Peru and Nepal that they've been nicknamed "Coca-Cola trail" and "toilet paper trail"

So, whether you're planning an adventure in Canada or around the world, how do you know if you're picking a responsible tour operator? Ask the tour company for its environmental and social policies. A group that discusses conservation and ecosystem education is more likely to be an ecotour company, rather than a plain old adventure or nature tour company. Ecotours should include local and indigenous communities in the planning, develop-

You don't have to leave the country to check into an ecologically inspired room for the night. **Aurum Lodge** is a wilderness retreat at the base of the Alberta Rockies. It was built without impinging on sensitive areas. The lodge has solar hot water heating and composting toilets, and in-floor heating that can run on solar collectors on sunny days. Not too far away, in downtown Banff, is the **Banff Park Lodge**. It's a good deal bigger and more luxurious, but it's also the first independent hotel to earn four green leaves as part of the Audubon Green Leaf Eco-Rating Program for environmental best practices. The **Monterey Inn Resort** in Ottawa says it's the first company in Canada to go carbon-neutral by planting enough trees (about 5,000) to offset its production of greenhouse gases. **Chanterelle Country Inn and Cottages**, a 150-acre property on Cape Breton's Cabot Trail, in Nova Scotia, was designed with the chemically sensitive in mind: only organic fragrance-free cleaning products and soaps are used, and its restaurant features "Cape Breton Fresh" organic local cuisine. It won the 2005 Sustainable Tourism Award from Nova Scotia's tourism association. Even some ultra-slick hotels (you know the kind of place that could be in *Wallpaper* magazine) are going green. Just wait to see the **Shangri-La Hotel** opening in Vancouver in 2008. If you're up for classic luxury, the **Fairmont Hotel** chain literally wrote the book on greening the hotel biz (it's called the The Green Partnership Guide). Its Chateau Lake Louise location, for instance, gets 40% of its power from renewable sources. For a directory of every Green Leaf–rated hotel in Canada, check out **www.terrachoice.com** (properties listed are rated from one to five eco-stars, or leaves). The "Green" Hotels Association also lists ecologically minded places to hang your hat (**www.greenhotels.com**).

ment and operation (you don't want all the money leaving the country)—ask whether local guides are used. And ecotours should allow only small groups. Prod them about whether any of the tour fee goes to local conservation groups.

It might seem a little unsavoury, but the International Ecotourism Society suggests that you ask your hotel how it disposes of its waste and sewage. It's a huge problem, even in ecotourism meccas such as Costa Rica. Sewage runoff can wreak havoc on coral reefs, as well as on all sorts of flora and fauna in local lakes and rivers—wherever the dumping occurs.

Germany's To Do! Awards are a highly reputable measure of sound ecotourism models. Check www.to-do-contest.org for inspiring award winners. Green Globe 21 is a green certification body that supposedly does on-site visits, but note that hotels with a Green Globe Affiliate stamp haven't necessarily taken any action to improve their property. All the stamp signals is that the hotel has paid a certain amount to Green Globe, that it's aware of its environmental problems and that it hopes to improve—but it doesn't have to prove that it will.

IT'S ALL FUN AND
GAMES

Do you get through trying Mondays

by dreaming of your week off in the woods? Do you break away from it all on weekends to cut fresh powder down a snowy slope? Perhaps you bliss out on a yoga mat to burn off a little stress. Now I bet you're thinking, "Here comes Ms. Buzz Kill, ready to ruin my fun. Do I really have to worry about the ecological ramifications of my one joy in life?" Relax. I know there's no coming between you and your favourite source of pleasure. Just know that there's a dark side to everything—but if the biggest shopping season of the year can be turned into an earthy event, even your golf game can get greener.

SPORTS

Most athletes well aware of how the environment impacts them—smog, for instance, can make biking a bummer and an unusually warm winter can make snow sports a no-go. However, few enthusiasts think about the ecological ramifications their fave hockey arena, pool or ski hill has on the earth, despite all the chemical use, energy consumption and habitat destruction that may be involved. It's time for a pep talk on how to improve our game.

Water Machines: Canada is blessed with so much fresh water, it's no wonder we've turned our lakes, oceans and even rivers into giant amusement parks of sorts. Some water sports, like the quintessentially Canadian art of gliding across the skin of a lake in a carved-out canoe, are perfectly sustainable; others, not so much. Take Jet Skis. The California Air Resource Board says a day of jet skiing releases as many pollutants as driving a car about 223,000 kilometres! The Earth Island Institute reports that Jet Ski pollution actually causes chromosomal damage in fish.

A day of jet skiing releases as many pollutants as driving a car about 223,000 kilometres

Ultra-polluting two-stroke engines power the vast majority of motorboats in this country, which affects you, water skiers and wakeboarders. Investing in four-stroke boats, Jet Skis and personal watercrafts makes an enormous difference, ecologically speaking, since they put out 97% less airborne pollution than the two-strokes. But however many strokes they have, they still make a hell of a lot of noise, and they're still bound to piss off the shore-bound.

Swimming: Swimming, of course, emits zero emissions when you're just flapping your arms around in a lake or ocean, but factor in the impact of heating and chlorinating pools, and you've got a whole other story. When chlorine mixes with carbon-containing material like leaves, bugs, dirt and skin flakes (yum), toxic trihalomethanes such as carcinogenic chloroform can form. Belgian researchers found that young kids who swam regularly in chlorinated pools had increased risks of asthma. Canadian researchers studied competitive swimmers and found that they too had increased risks.

But don't panic, backstroke enthusiasts! There are **chlorine-free pool systems** out there that use UV light, ozone (popular in Europe) and even hydrogen peroxide. You can also get **salinated pools**, but these cost a mint.

Still, pools require a lot of water to fill, which isn't great during water advisories, and they need frequent topping up in really hot, dry weather. Plus, many of us refuse to swim in anything below 25°C, so wasteful hot water heaters come into play. If you already own a pool, you can offset some of this by getting a good solar blanket (not the PVC kind) and a solar hot water heater (see www.cansia.ca/pools.asp for info). The rest of you, don't dig your own, just visit a community pool.

Golf: They call golf courses "greens" but there's nothing green about these bad boys other than the grass. To carve courses out of the natural landscape, acres of forests, wetlands and wild habitats are often cleared. They're then replaced with non-native grasses that are drenched in pesticides and so much water that rural water tables are lowered and nearby creeks and streams contaminated. I'm not kidding, the average American golf course uses about 300,000 litres of water per day—yes, I said per day.

But all that's starting to change. Instead of clearing pristine lands to put up a course, a surprising number of planners are reclaiming contaminated sites, capping them, then building greens over them. The city of Kingston, Ontario, built a nine-hole course and recreation centre over an old landfill. The **Coquitlam** dump in Vancouver is now home to putting enthusiasts. And Edmonton's **Riverside** club was built on an old coal mine.

> The average American golf course uses about
> ## 300,000 litres of water per day

More progressive courses certified by the likes of the GreenLinks Eco-Rating Program are reining in their bad behaviour. Some, like **Kedron Dells** near Oshawa, Ontario, spray pesticides only as required rather than every 10 days, water only at night to prevent wasteful evaporation and cut their grass less often, among other things. **Banff Springs Golf Course** and the **Glen Arbour Golf Club** in Nova Scotia have been similarly certified under the Audubon Cooperative Sanctuary System. In P.E.I., provincial courses are joining British sustainability efforts led by the Royal Ancient Golf Club of St. Andrews that call for using much less water, planting drought-resistant grasses, slashing back pesticide use and substituting recycled glass sand for real sand in bunkers. Shouldn't this be par for the course everywhere?

Ball Sports: Nearly gone are the days when balls were made of natural rubber. Soccer balls, basketballs and volleyballs are mostly made of that eco outlaw PVC. Polyurethane is still toxic but not quite so bad. Real leather is no saint, but at least it eventually breaks down. There's also been plenty of scandal around soccer balls, in particular, being stitched by 10 year olds. You can play with a clear conscience if you order certified fair-trade soccer balls, volleyballs and rugby balls through **Y Focus** in Ottawa (http://yfocus.ncf.ca/fairtrade/).

Yoga: Even the ancient Indian art of stretching yourself into a pretzel is not immune to modern eco-problems. I-am-one-with-the-universe yoga bunnies tend to have no idea that most of the mats they tote to class are made of what Greenpeace calls the most ecologically harmful plastic on the planet— PVC. Sure, many of these mats are "100% closed-cell," and manufacturers tell us no chemicals should escape the plastic surface. But come on, you can smell the fumes coming off those pretty pink, purple and blue things. You're probably inhaling the chemical softeners, phthalates, that make those mats so squishy. The industry insists phthalates are safe, but some of the softeners have been tied to hormone disruption and cancer.

> Most mats are made of what Greenpeace calls the **most ecologically harmful plastic on the planet—PVC**

Vancouver original **lululemon** (with stores in B.C., Alberta, Saskatchewan, Manitoba, Ontario and Quebec) carries only PVC- and chloride-free mats made with a biodegradable and compostable material (see page 34). They also have soy fabric T-shirts. Online retailer **Epic Green** sells fair-trade mats made of natural jute backed with natural rubber so they don't slip around (www.epicgreen.com). You can also get 100% organic hemp mats from Rawganique.com, but these don't have much grip or traction.

Skiing and Snowboarding: Multiply the soil erosion that can happen at a popular sledding spot by a thousand and add super-wasteful snow-makers, glaring lights and heated chair lifts, and you've got yourself a ski hill. Besides the fact that every new resort or run destroys many animals' homes, snow-makers can divert valuable water from local streams, and bio-accumulative snow-hardening chemicals end up polluting soil and water.

Some resorts are trying to green up their act, especially since slope-lovers are realizing the impact global warming is having on their favourite activity. Keep Winter Cool warns skiers and snowboarders that climate change could mean fewer ski days, less real snow, more snow guns, wetter seasons—even fewer mountains (http://keepwintercool.org). The U.S. National Ski Area Association's Sustainable Slopes charter acknowledges that greenhouse gases are a real threat to the industry so it lobbies government to take broader action and encourages members to cut their emissions (through energy, water and waste conservation). In B.C., **Whistler Blackcomb, Panorama Mountain Village** and **Mount Washington Alpine Resort** have all signed on to the challenge, as have **Ski Wentworth** in Nova Scotia, **Blue Mountain** in Ontario and Quebec's **Tremblant, Mont Orford** and **Mont Ste-Marie.**

So far, Canadian hills haven't gone as enviro as some U.S. hills that power their chair lifts with wind turbines. **Aspen**, Colorado, has the industry's largest system of solar panels and has reduced its annual carbon dioxide emissions by about 1 million kilograms.

In 2006, B.C.'s **Whistler Blackcomb** scored one of six silver National Ski Area Association (NSAA) medals for its top-notch recycling program/composting system (which now diverts 60% of the hill's landfill waste). Plus, Whistler residents are looking into ground-source heat pumps and biodiesel, and are ditching propane in favour of cleaner natural gas to fuel the area.

For details on which hills have been helping to conserve local wildlife, which have eco-friendly snow-makers and which have water- and energy-saving initiatives, check out www.nsaa.org/nsaa/environment/the_greenroom. Keep in mind, though, that the NSAA did come in 10th on a list of America's worst greenwashers because their Sustainable Slopes Program doesn't put poor performers on probation or have third-party audits. If you're planning on crossing the border for a little winter holidaying, American slopes are perhaps most honestly and scathingly reviewed by the Ski Area Citizen's Coalition (www.skiareacitizens.com).

By the way, the ski hills within Banff National Park (**Lake Louise**, **Sunshine Village** and **Mount Norquay**) are the only hills on the continent in a UNESCO World Heritage site, so they face pretty stiff environmental restrictions.

If you're a fan of cross-country skiing, you can glide in peace, knowing you're doing much less damage to the ecosystem, though trails shouldn't go through known feeding areas or nesting or breeding grounds. Conservation areas and provincial parks can be great places to ski and often offer other winter activities such as snowshoeing (which is super-low-impact) and ice

> If you're a fan of cross-country skiing, you can glide in peace, knowing **you're doing much less damage to the ecosystem**

SUSTAINABLE SNOWBOARDS

Dude, you totally need to get a snowboard made from sustainably harvested materials, like anything by **Arbor bamboo boards** (for Canadian retailers, see **www.arborsports.com**). Seriously gnarly **Venture** snowboards are made in a wind-powered Colorado factory of wood certified by the Forest Stewardship Council. You can even get yours with organic hemp or cotton top sheets to help cut back on the use of plastics and solvents (order online at **www.venturesnowboards.com** or stop by Northern Hemisphere if you're in Whitehorse). A cheaper, but always sustainable option is to carve some slopes on a second-hand board.

| WAXING |

Instead of priming your skis or board with petro-chemical wax, which can wind up in ground-water, get 100% biodegradable soy-based Bio-Glide wax at **www.welovesoy.com/bioglide.html**.

skating at frozen lakes. Canada Trails lists about 500 cross-country ski trails across the country (www.canadatrails.ca).

Ice Skating and Curling: Sorry, but I have to go after Canada's two national pastimes. There are about 2,200 ice rinks and 1,300 curling rinks in Canada, most of which are blindingly wasteful in terms of their lighting and cooling systems, using about 1 billion kilowatt hours of energy per year—that's about 15 billion pounds of CO_2 emissions. Natural Resources Canada says switching to new refrigeration technology could cut energy consumption by 40%, and integrating a new heating, ventilation and a/c system at the same time could slash bills by 60%. Though it's impossible to get concrete numbers, many rinks have taken on energy-efficiency retrofit measures. You can't know for sure unless you ask your rink.

But the penalty-worthy behaviour goes beyond power usage. Poorly maintained ice resurfacers spew carbon monoxide, nitrogen dioxide and other fumes into the poorly ventilated buildings—enough to trigger asthma and respiratory infections in kids putting in heavy ice time. Electric Zambonis are available, but aren't widely used, mostly because of their high price tag.

Snowmobiles: These monsters generate as much pollution in one hour as a late-model car does in a year! But if that's not enough to convince your cousin to get off his Ski-Doo, make sure he's riding one with a more efficient four-stroke engine rather than a two-stroke.

CAMPING

The crackling fire, the starry sky, peeing in the woods—it's enough to dupe you into thinking you're one with nature. Alas, just because your tent is green, that doesn't mean you are. In fact, camp supply stores will tell you that most of their goods are far from eco-friendly. Seems a tad hypocritical, really, considering how much campers love the outdoors.

Gear and Tents: Most of the waterproof synthetic stuff is made with toxic solvents that emit polluting volatile organic compounds (VOCs) and dioxins in production. Lots of backpacks (and even sleeping bags, such as Marmot's old Pinnacle Gossamer bags) are coated with Teflon, which is made with a super-persistent chemical, PFOA, found in rivers and bloodstreams everywhere (new Pinnacle bag shells are made of nylon and silicone). Whatever isn't coated with Teflon is made with its sister chem, PTFE, found in Gore-Tex. We're surrounded! Now, that's not to say you should toss out your old Gore-Tex gear. W.L. Gore and Associates (the maker of Gore-Tex fabric) says PTFE is so "stable" it won't leach or off-gas in landfills. (See page 30 for more on Gore-Tex.)

A lesser evil is nylon waterproofed with silicone, neither of which seems to ruffle as many eco-feathers as Gore-Tex and Teflon. However, its production isn't exactly clean and green. It can be difficult to find tents that aren't made with synthetic—unless, of course, you're willing to get a canvas one. Army Surplus stores are a good place to look for these. Then again, lots of canvas tents are coated with polyurethane or a non-stick water-repellent coating. Some have eco-damaging vinyl (PVC) bottoms softened with potentially hormone-disrupting phthalates. Some are even treated with dodgy chemical insecticides and fungicides. If you're going to get the coated kind, polyethylene is a less toxic plastic.

Most nylon tents use both silicone and polyurethane, which Greenpeace considers the second-worst plastic out there

Sleeping Bags: Sleeping bags free of synthetic materials are even rarer, but they're not quite as toxic since they don't need to be waterproofed. They're often stuffed with polyester (which isn't so bad as far as petrol-based materials go) or down (which is natural but tends to

NO NEED FOR NEW

Before you shell out for new gear, think about buying used from an army surplus store or from Mountain Equipment Co-op's site **OutdoorGearSwap.com**. Bring worn or damaged tents, coats, bags—even Gore-Tex—back to the store where you bought them for repairs rather than tossing them. (Not that you'd throw them in the trash, right? Instead, donate any old gear to a local charity or the GearSwap.) And be honest with yourself. If you're the type who rolls out your Thermarest once a year, consider renting. There's no point in buying new products that just collect dust when dozens of people can rent a single tent over the course of a summer, putting it to much better use. Mountain Equipment Co-op and many camping stores offer rentals.

Now for a quickie lesson on biodegradable camp soaps. They may say they're "biodegradable," but that doesn't mean you should be sudsing away in the lake or river. These, and all soaps, shampoos and so on, can seriously harm aquatic life. Even the super-biodegradable kind (like **Campsuds** or **Druide**'s citronella line, available at most health and camping supply stores) are meant to be used about 60 metres from a body of water, where they can be filtered by the soil.

be a meat industry by-product, so vegans might want to skip it). Shells are generally made with nylon. Might not be a big deal to most, but if you have chemical sensitivities or are allergic to the dust mites that multiply in old sleeping bags, enjoying a good night's rest in the wilderness can be challenging. **Cottonfresh** makes a 100% cotton, dust mite–proof, allergen-free sleeping bag without any chemical treatments. But it's not super-warm. For a little luxury in warmer weather, there are even pure silk sleep sacks (for either option, punch in "sleeping bags" at www.allergybuyersclubshopping.com).

Waterproofing: No one wants to get rained out. Most waterproofing waxes, sprays and sealants are petroleum-based and filled with all sorts of stuff such as fluorochemicals. A popular alternative is **Nikwax** (available at camping stores), a water-and-beeswax-based repellent that can be washed into clothing and down or sprayed on tents, bags, shoes, gloves—you name it.

Water Purifying: Speaking of water, rather than dropping nasty chlorine or iodine tabs into a bottle of lake water and masking it with some sugary artificial powder, why not invest in a portable filter and truly enjoy that fresh water taste? **Katadyn** ceramic and activated carbon filters are touted by outdoor enthusiasts for removing all harmful bacteria, fungi, cysts and parasites and a long list of dangerous diseases without any chemicals.

Flashlights: Solar-powered, pump, shake or wind-up flashlights are much wiser options for the woods than the battery-operated kind. If you're rolling your eyes at the prospect of pumping and shaking to get a few minutes of flashlight time, lighten up—you can even make a little dance of it. Or try an **LED** flashlight. Your batteries are sure to last at least 20 times longer in one of these.

Food: All that fresh air and hiking can create a sasquatch-sized appetite. Try to minimize packaging by bringing bulk items such as couscous or rice in big PVC-free baggies (made by Ziploc or Glad). If you're looking for ideas on what to cook on the trail, pick up *The Leave-No-Crumbs Camping Cookbook* from your local bookstore or online (www.amazon.ca). Individually packaged camp foods create a lot of waste—which, by the way, should never be burned. I repeat: no burning plastics in the campfire, unless you want to suck back noxious and dangerous carcinogens, such as dioxin, that build up in the food chain! If you're going to buy ready-to-heat camp food, at least go for organic brands such as **Soft Path**, **Kettle Valley** or **Mary Jane's**. Mary Jane's comes in burnable packaging.

HOLIDAYS AND CELEBRATIONS

I must admit I love a big celebration (hence my three-day-long birthday party), and while I'm outing myself, I also secretly love Bing Crosby's rendition of "Silver Bells" and think a holiday dedicated to chocolate rabbits isn't so terrible (hey, who doesn't love bunnies?). What's so wrong with events that bring families and friends together for a big meal and maybe a bottle or two of wine? Well, if we were actually taking these moments to savour our relationships and the flavours of life, absolutely nothing. The problem comes when the holiday season warps into the high holidays of consumer culture. Aren't we putting the emphasis on the wrong syl-lable?

Gift-Giving: No matter how much you hate malls and the shop-till-you-drop philosophy, there are certain times of the year—birthdays, Christmas, showers, weddings, even Hanukkah—when people just expect presents. So why not let your gifts reflect your concern for the environment?

For one thing, you can cut back on fossil fuels by supporting local artisans and all their wonderful handmade crafts. Hunt down stores that sell hand-dyed scarves or recycled steel sculptures rather than mass-produced imports. Your regional crafts council or association will often have an online list of local guild shops and artist galleries (the Canadian Crafts Federation has a link to all the provincial sites at www.canadiancraftsfederation.ca). Or hit

(RE-)GIFT EXCHANGE

Having a gift swap with friends or co-workers? Make it "recycled": everyone wraps up an old unwanted gift, and participants can either draw from the unopened pile or steal someone else's. You might be surprised by how popular that tea cozy your aunt gave you for your birthday is.

a craft show, where you'll be able to buy work directly from the artist. Buying locally is even better if you can find craftspeople who work with recycled and eco-friendly materials. Keep your eye out for them and ask how they made their products.

Fair-trade shops are also great one-stop gift shops. While the items for sale are not made locally, they are made under good working conditions by artisan co-ops paid a fair price—a refreshing change from all the cheap imports made in sweatshops. Online catalogue shops such as **Peri Dar** out of Quebec (www.peridar.com) and national storefronts such as **Ten**

GREEN GIFT IDEAS

#1 Make your own gourmet food basket by hitting a health store and buying all sorts of yummy local organic jams, salsas and crackers and fair-trade organic cocoa.

#2 For the beauty buff, hit the personal care aisle of your local health store and grab an armful of great organic goodies such as lip gloss, bath salts and lotions.

#3 Everyone gives wine as a hostess gift. Why not take the opportunity to introduce friends and family to some of the more enjoyable fruits of organic agriculture? A growing number of liquor stores carry organic labels such as **Bonterra Chardonnay** (one of my faves). Introduce beer fans to a pretty bottle of **St. Peter's Organic English Ale** or a local organic brew. Serious gin mummies will love **Juniper Green Organic London Dry Gin**, made with organic coriander, savory and angelica root.

#4 Create homemade coupons. These could be anything, depending on your time and talents. You can suggest an hour of babysitting to a new mom or a three-course meal to an overworked friend, or offer to teach your pal how to snowboard, samba or strum a guitar. An hour massage is always nice when it comes from a main squeeze who's normally too tired to spend more than three minutes on your neck.

Tired of giving (or getting) unappreciated gifts that sit unused in dusty closets? Give something that actually means something—a goat. No, seriously. If you give a needy family in the developing world a goat through Oxfam or World Vision, they'll get about a litre of fresh milk a day, great fertilizing manure for vegetable gardens and about two or three offspring a year. For $60 you can give 10 fruit trees; $50 will stock a classroom. And $32? Two mosquito nets. You can feel good knowing your holiday presents actually mean something to someone somewhere, unlike that purple beret you got from Grandma last year (**www.worldvision.ca** and **www.oxfam.ca**).

Thousand Villages are crammed with gift ideas—ornate teapots, jewellery, carvings, pillows, throws, trinkets, chocolates, toys and treats—each with its own inspiring story. Plus, the goods tend to be made with eye towards sustainability and sometimes contain recycled or eco-friendly materials.

If there's a true environmentalist in your life, why not give him or her a tree? **Earthroots** has adopt-a-tree-in-Temagami packages, and **Canadian Physicians for Aid and Relief** has plant-a-tree-in-Africa options for any size donation. (You can also buy a cool plant-a-tree-in-Africa fleece or toque from www.cpar.ca, or Temagami posters at www.earth roots.org). You can even adopt a whole acre of wildlife habitat in someone's name through the **Nature Conservancy of Canada** (www.natureconservancy.ca). The **World Wildlife Fund** (WWF) has adopt-a-coral-reef and adopt-a-boreal-forest options (www.wwf.ca).

Kids will love the idea of saving the polar bears or whales through WWF's adoption kits— especially since they come with a plush teddy, a personalized adoption certificate, a sticker and a report on the work you'll be supporting. And what kind of uncle would you be if you handed your niece a toy moulded out of PVC that's been softened with harmful phthalates? Many toy manufacturers have phased one or both out, especially in toys for young children. **Brio**, **Lego** and **Chicco** are in the clear, and all **Plan Toys** are made of wood from rubber trees that have stopped producing latex. There are full worlds of Plan cities, Plan dollhouses and Plan toys geared towards preschoolers (www.plantoys.com). **HaPe** makes a line of sustainable bamboo games, like their balancing panda dice game (www.hapetoys.com). You can get fairly traded dolls and toys from Ten Thousand Villages. Got a nephew who loves building stuff?

Pick up the **Fuel Cell Car Science Experiment Kit**, with which you build a car that runs on water (www.mastermindtoys.com)! For more on green kids prezzies, see page 125.

When buying a gift for a gadget geek, look for the Energy Star symbol—it lets you know your electronics aren't sucking up gobs of energy when they're turned off (see page 166 for more on electronics). It's also a good idea to include rechargeable batteries (and a charger) when giving gadgets, gizmos and tech toys of any kind.

Gift Wrap: Wondering what to do about gift wrap? There's no need to reach for that fresh-cut-tree variety. Make your own from old road maps, cartoons, pictures, calendars, greeting cards, or even unwanted fabric. Or pick up some plain brown recycled kraft paper from your local art supply store and tie a leaf, fallen twig or wildflower onto it with twine. **Peri Dar** sells fair-trade wrinkly vegetable-dyed wrapping paper handmade by Nepali women (www.peridar.com). **UNICEF** also sells festive fair-trade gift wrap (www.shopunicef.ca).

WINTER HOLIDAY LIGHTS

Whether you celebrate Christmas with a rainbow of lights or Hanukkah with blue and white ones, December ain't December without a few strings of these. And no doubt all you folks who are trying to rival Chevy Chase's house in *National Lampoon's Christmas Vacation* know what a seasonal drain they can be on your energy bills. Sure, those little bulbs might only be 2.5 or 5 watts each, but they add up. Think of it this way: **California, which has almost the same population as Canada, uses about 1,000 megawatts on these mini lights alone, which, according to Grist.org, is enough to power 1 million homes.** No, I'm not asking you to spend the holiday season in the dark, but do you really need that many? If your house can be spotted by overhead planes, you know you've gone too far. Switch to efficient strings of LED lights, available at any hardware store. They use 95% less energy and last up to 20 times as long, according to B.C. Hydro. Plus, they don't get hot, so you won't burn down the Christmas tree. Some municipalities are even holding free festive lighting swaps, where you bring in your old, inefficient strings and get new LED ones. Now that's the spirit!

THE CHRISTMAS TREE DEBATE

You want a tree, but you're torn as to whether you should chop down a live one or go with long-lasting plastic. Many will tell you to save a perfectly healthy living tree from the chop. Trouble is, artificial trees are made of nasty PVC plastic. Sure, they last up to 10 years, but they clog our landfills for centuries to come and leach while they're at it. Real trees, on the other hand, are almost all harvested from tree farms. **The industry says trees are often grown on soils that can't support other crops and for every tree chopped another two to ten are planted.** They also note that farmed trees suck up greenhouse gases such as carbon dioxide and pump out oxygen—before they face the chop, of course, at seven or so years old. (But this is only really of any good if real forests aren't cleared for tree plantations, since pine plantations, for instance, don't hold as much carbon as a natural forest). For every tree bought at **IKEA**, by the way, the company will donate the cost of replanting a seedling to the Tree Canada Foundation for planting projects in parks, schools and riverside areas.

But here's the hitch—and it's a big one: the vast majority of Christmas trees are sprayed. All sorts of chemicals, including nasty insecticides and rodenticides, are used to keep them looking pretty. While Christmas tree groves often provide habitats for all sorts of wildlife, these chems can cause serious harm. And organic Christmas trees, Charlie Brown, are sadly hard to find.

If you go for the live tree, note that many municipalities have tree composting or mulching programs, so make sure to put yours out on the right days. Another option is to buy a potted version. These are great because they can be planted in your backyard when the holiday is over. Just note that they require lots of TLC at first. Talk to a greenhouse for tips or go to **www.christmastree.org/livecare.cfm**. The main thing is not to let your potted tree dry out, and don't keep it inside for more than a week.

India's festival of colour, **Holi**, is essentially a giant harvest party that banishes winter with bonfires, feasting and plenty of coloured-water- and powder-throwing in the streets. Canada generally doesn't have quite the street bash that northern India does, but powders and water-colours are still thrown at folks wearing white (and expecting stains) in places like temple parking lots. Trouble is, some of the Holi colours sold are actually industrial hues meant for processes like dying textiles and may contain very harmful chemicals and heavy metals.

Better to toss a dry mix of powdered turmeric and flour or pour some boiled beet-root juice in a water gun! Did I mention that you wear clothes you expect to stain? Because this stuff doesn't come out so easily.

Candy and Chocolates: The candy you buy in drugstores or supermarkets for Valentine's Day or Halloween might come in cute shapes, but it's also made with lots of cheap chemicals, preservatives and low-grade chocolate grown with highly toxic pesticides and picked by workers for appalling wages (see page 94). In the U.K. in the late '90s, Friends of the Earth found residues of lindane, a pesticide banned in many countries, in several supermarket chocolates. Larger health stores often carry organic fair-trade seasonally-inspired chocolates. If you can't find these goodies near you, local chocolatiers tend to create holiday treats in-house using all-natural ingredients.

Flowers: Oh, Poison, you were right: every rose does have its thorn. But we still love the prickly flowers, and we're compelled to show our feelings for our wives, girlfriends, mothers, party hosts and even ourselves with a big bouquet of them, or some sort of brightly coloured arrangement. Over 100 million blooms are grown and wrapped in cellophane for your buying pleasure every year. And each one is trucked and jetted thousands of polluting kilometres to reach your local flower shop.

Flower cultivation sucks back more pesticides than any other agricultural product

But the real ecological horror show happens in fields and greenhouses. Flower cultivation sucks back more pesticides than any other agricultural product, according to Sierra Club of Canada. To create flawless buds, hundreds of different pest-killing chems are used—many of them neurotoxins, others suspected endocrine disruptors, still others are probable carcinogens and considered either extremely toxic or just plain illegal in Canada.

277

All the groundwater used on needy plants has led to dropping water tables. And the quest for perfect, pest-free flowers often means that the super-toxic and ozone-depleting fumigant methyl bromide is applied to greenhouse soil (although an increasing number of countries have either banned or are trying to phase out the nasty substance).

Not only are flower farm chemicals contaminating groundwater through runoff or straight-up dumping (reports from Costa Rica document direct discharges into waterways, for instance), but workers aren't given much protection either. The distressing reality is they're often asked to go into greenhouses an hour or two after toxic spraying without any protective gear, and some have been forced to keep working while the spraying goes on. No wonder over 50% of Costa Rican flower labourers and nearly two-thirds of those surveyed in Ecuador complained of headaches, nausea, blurred vision, rashes and dizziness. And can we be surprised that pregnant workers have been found to have increased risks of birth defects, premature births and miscarriages, according to a study by the Colombian National Institute of Health? This is particularly troublesome knowing that 70% of Colombia's flower workers

WHERE DO OUR FRESH CUT FLOWERS COME FROM?

Here's a breakdown of just how many roses, carnations, lilies and the like we're importing and how far they have to travel to get to our nation's capital:

Colombia—$59,628,920 worth
(4,522 kilometres)

Ecuador—$26,458,603 worth
(5,054 kilometres)

United States—$9,187,140 worth
(3,941 kilometres, from northern California)

Netherlands—$5,666,511 worth
(5,645 kilometres)

Costa Rica—$2,705,919 worth
(4,013 kilometres)

(source: Industry Canada, 2005)

SIERRA ECO FLOWERS

Fair-trade buds have been widely available in Europe for a while now, thanks to programs like Germany's Flower Label Program (FLP). But for the longest time there was nothing tying together Canadian florists looking to sell stems with a clear conscience. Enter Sierra Eco. The label was developed by Montreal-based **Sierra Flower Trader**, the largest distributor of fresh cut flowers in eastern Canada. As with FLP flowers, the buds aren't organic, but far less pesticides are used, greener practices are in place and farm workers are treated according to International Labour Organization standards, often with good benefits. Sierra Eco's farms are certified and inspected by independent auditors. Housing, education, medical care and daycare are also funded. And the good news for us is that several florists across the country carry them. For a directory of these florists in Quebec, Ontario, Nova Scotia and New Brunswick, head to **www.sierraeco.com**. If you're a florist or know a florist who might be interested in selling fair-trade flowers, Sierra Eco's website also has a listing of wholesalers in Canada.

are women—women who are paid about 58 cents a day (covering less than half a family's basic needs), putting in long hours, especially before Valentine's Day and Mother's Day. Kind of ironic when you think about it: we honour the women in our lives with bouquets picked by women who are treated with little to no respect.

Sure, all this is happening, for the most part, in lands far away, but if we're demanding exotic bouquets of perfect flowers, we have to own up to our role in fuelling unsustainable practices. If you've wondered why flowers have grown so cheap in recent years, the answer is that we've switched from buying pricier petals from places such as northern California, B.C. and the Netherlands to flying in cheaper roses and carnations from Latin America—countries with lax worker and environmental regulations.

And all those chemicals are still sitting on that bouquet when you bring it home to your dining-room table. In Canada, blooms aren't tested for pesticide residues, but Environmental Working Group tests found that even flowers grown in the U.S. had up to 50 times more carcinogenic pesticide residues than food products. Are you going to lick your petunias? I hope not, but your kids or pets might, and we all bury our noses in them to get a deep whiff of the sweet aromas. And floral designers have been known to get rashes and

allergic reactions from arranging stems all day. To be safe, make sure to wash your hands well after handling your bouquet.

Floral Solutions: No doubt, certified organic flowers are hard to come by. But there are a couple of spots in this country where you can buy them. Toronto-based **EcoFlora** delivers Organic Bouquet flowers, as well as certified organic locally grown flowers (from May to October) and fair-trade flowers packed with wildcrafted greens. They even come wrapped in compostable cellophane wrapping (www.ecoflora.ca). **Whole Foods** in Toronto and Vancouver also sells some organic, fair-trade and local blooms—it's best to ask, since they also sell conventionally grown plants (though all such flowers are tested to make sure they don't exceed set levels of pesticide residues). **Cactus Flower House** in Edmonton offers pesticide-free petals and gets its blooms from a greenhouse just outside Edmonton, which dramatically cuts back on fossil fuel emissions. No matter where you live, tell your local florist you'd like to see a blossoming selection of pesticide-free blooms you'll feel good about buying.

MONEY
MATTERS

Dolly had it right:

working 9 to 5 is no way to make a living. But most of us don't have much choice in the matter (and slaving away from 1 to 9 on a graveyard shift can be such a drag it isn't even song-worthy). We spend at least half of our waking hours at work—and if you're out of a job, you probably spend almost as much time looking for one. After a long week, the energy you put in to the process feels about as renewable as a tank of gas. But how does the job itself fair? Is your workplace a waste glutton or a conservation keener? Maybe you're tired of your office's flagrant paper wastage and would rather apply your accounting skills to wind turbine inventory instead of disposable mops accounts. And if all of your hard-earned cash isn't instantly swallowed by bills, diapers and dog food, you've gotta figure out where to put it (a bank, for one, and mutual funds, if you're moderately ambitious). Might as well make it all as earth-friendly as possible.

FINANCES

The world of finance may be painted green, but that's not because of its heartfelt allegiance to the sustainability of double-crested cormorants. Still, while the banking and investment biz may have a bad rep for its nefarious connections to the dirtiest industries this side of Jupiter, that doesn't mean your money can't be different. From where you store your cash to how you invest it and what credit card you use to spend it, there are tons of ways to green your greenbacks. (Okay, Canada doesn't have greenbacks—they're more like purple-, pink- and bluebacks—but you get the point.)

Banks: We all groan about how banks gouge the hell out of us. But what doesn't get muttered around the water cooler quite so often is that they're also putting your hard-earned money to work financing dirty gold mines, oil digs and ecologically devastating dams around the world.

> **They're putting your hard-earned money to work financing dirty gold mines, oil digs and ecologically devastating dams around the world**

Some banks have taken baby steps towards earth-friendly practices. All five big Canadian banks (RBC, CIBC, BMO, TD Canada Trust and Scotiabank) signed on to the United Nations Environment Programme in 1992, but a decade later none of the banks had much to show for it. Royal Bank of Canada (RBC) says it often hires enviro consultants to investigate investment properties. Both RBC and CIBC have signed on to the Equator Principles (as have HSBC and Citibank)—voluntary guidelines that mean the bank can't invest in projects such as the Three Gorges Dam project in China—but at last check, no other Canadian bank had followed suit. TD Canada Trust is considered by environmentalists to be at the back of the eco-pack. Despite its funding of projects such as shoreline cleanups, TD has been accused of greenwashing and was slammed by ForestEthics and Rainforest Action Network in 2006 for "ignoring scientific consensus on global warming" and setting no greenhouse gas emission targets for its lending. All five major Canadian banks got the thumbs-down from the eco-orgs for loaning out cash to companies that rip up the boreal forest.

Citibank, an American bank with an online presence in Canada, is considered more progressive in terms of collaborating with enviro groups on setting best practices around endangered forest protection, illegal logging, carbon reduction, Native rights and renewable energy (www.citibank.com/canada/). The bank seems to be getting its act together after having been dogged by full-page ads in *The New York Times* and TV spots that targeted its poor record a few years back.

Citizens Bank of Canada is the only Canadian bank with a truly socially and ecologically responsible lending policy. It won't invest in any company with a poor eco-record or nuclear power ties. The full-service virtual bank also gives part of its profits to green charities (www.citizensbank.ca).

Credit Unions: Another great place to store your coin is a credit union. They offer all the same services as banks, plus every member has a share in the co-operative. There are thousands of them across Canada. In fact, according to the federal Department of Finance, Canada has the world's highest per capita membership in the credit union movement, with over 10 million members (about a third of us use them). In Quebec, a whopping 70% of the population belongs to one; in Saskatchewan, 60%. Some, like the **Alterna Credit Union**, have ethical policies and won't invest in corporations with ecologically destructive practices or poor labour relations or human rights standards. Not all credit unions have these policies, though, so it's best to ask before joining. To find a credit union branch near you, go to the Credit Union Central of Canada (www.cucentral.ca).

CREDIT CARDS AND CHEQUES

Okay, so you've almost got your finances in order. Now it's time to open that wallet and peek at your credit cards. Instead of handing all that interest straight to Visa, why not share a little with your charity of choice? Citizens Bank offers Oxfam and Amnesty International credit cards. The non-profit orgs get 10 cents with each purchase and 20 bucks right off the bat when you sign up for your card—a much better rate than many affinity cards. You can also get Citizens Bank Amnesty International Visa convenience cheques, which you can use wherever you can't use credit cards; the charge is added to your credit card bill.

The World Wildlife Fund (WWF) cancelled its credit card program in Canada, but you can get WWF cheques, Humane Society of Canada cheques and others at most financial institutions (visit **www.dhltd.com** and follow the links to affinity cheques). The downside is that the amount that actually makes it back to these charities is pretty low—roughly $1 per batch (and you know how long it takes to go through one of those batches, especially now that debit cards have taken over). Note that those pretty National Parks of Canada cheques are strictly for show; no cash is donated to the parks themselves.

Investing: Most of us start thinking about financial investments only come RRSP season, or maybe when we see pension fund payments coming off our paycheques. But whether you're planning for your retirement, dabbling in stocks or just looking to invest without sinking your cash into nasty oil, tobacco and mining, green funds are your main option. And it's an option that's growing in popularity and profitability. By 2004, Canadians were investing about $65 billion in socially responsible assets, according to the Canadian Social Investment Review—and that number jumps every year.

> By 2004, Canadians were investing about $65 billion in socially responsible assets— **and that number jumps every year**

The majority of the conscious investment funds out there are branded as ethical rather than just green. However, almost all say they factor environmental issues, along with other concerns such as human rights, into investment decisions. Plus, they all stay away from nuke-, military- and tobacco-related companies.

Socially responsible investors essentially want to reward good behaviour. Conscious funds generally invest in corporations whose management commits to making labour, ecological or human rights improvements (even if they're not saints). The funds leverage their buying power to push corporations to clean up their acts. And if they don't, they'll eventually be dumped. Overall, it's way beyond what mainstream funds offer; these sink their cash anywhere the money blows, with little regard for the planet and the people that have to live on it.

If you're shopping around for ethical funds, there are several to choose from in Canada. **Acuity** has a few socially responsible ones that screen for labour, enviro and human rights

BE A GREEN SHAREHOLDER

Already got investments that ain't exactly easy on the earth? Don't dump them. Go to annual general shareholder meetings and demand action through shareholder resolutions, which you're free to submit. If more than 50% of shareholders agree with your proposal, the company has to do what you say. Write letters to the company and lobby other shareholders to take action too. Amnesty International Canada has a whole campaign called Share Power dedicated to this concept. The group asks that you contact your mutual funds and pension funds to support shareholder proposals at a list of different corporations (see **amnesty.ca/campaigns/ sharepower** for details).

practices, nukes, booze, weapons and tobacco, on top of its line of **Clean Environment Funds**, which focus on screening for sustainability and green tech. The **Ethical Funds Company** puts out 14 funds filtered for eco-practices, tobacco, arms, racial inequality, nukes, labour and human rights. **Desjardins Funds** are managed through Quebec's credit union (and are also available at Desjardins Trusts) and have basically the same filters as the Ethical Funds Company. **Meritas Mutual Funds** have a comprehensive set of screens and are considered very good in terms of the environment (www.meritas.ca). Same goes for **Phillips, Hager & North Community Values Funds**. **Inhance Investment Management**'s funds have an interesting approach: their social researchers and portfolio managers actually meet to duke out which stocks should be included. **Manulife Canadian Balanced Ethics Fund** weeds out tobacco and gambling, but not much else. Despite old perceptions, many ethical funds do swimmingly well. Just ask your adviser for suggestions.

If you look closely at the list of investments on many of these funds, you'll probably notice some surprising choices, such as Shell. Yes, it's a fairly progressive oil company when you compare it to, say, Esso, but tell that to the people of Nigeria (where the company has been accused of dragging its feet on oil-spill clean-ups and of supporting the repressive military regime. Most infamously, its name was tied to the suppression of local protests against oil drilling in the early '90s that ended with the military's execution of nine protestors, including Ken Saro-Wiwa). Still, Shell's Canadian branch is judged independently on its support for action on climate change, among other things, and it's on the respected Jantzi Research social investment index of 60 ethically screened Canuck companies (see sidebar, below).

Companies on the Jantzi Research social investment index of 60 Canuck companies are screened for enviro, human rights and community factors, plus the index filters out companies affiliated with nukes, porn, alcohol, gaming, genetic engineering or weapons (www.jantzisocialindex.com). It's not meant to reflect the 60 best companies in Canada, nor, adds Jantzi's website, does it presume to represent the only 60 companies that meet social and environmental criteria.

Want to just play a few stocks, but not sure which to pick? Jantzi Research also puts out the Canadian Social Investment Database, which provides eco, social and governance performance ratings for 300 Canadian companies and income trusts (www.jantziresearch.com). It'll tell you if a company got an 8.5 out of 10 on Aboriginal relations, but only a 3 on environmental reporting, and provides plenty of details as to why. Pretty handy.

Among the few Canadian funds marketed as purely green are **Acuity's Clean Environment Equity Funds** and **Balanced Funds**. Both have holdings in small, mid-sized and sometimes large mining and oil and gas corporations, which seems kind of off, but they're considered the best of the sector. As Eugene Ellmen of the Social Investment Organization puts it, if you exclude oil, gas and forestry, you'll be knocking out 40% to 50% of the Canadian market, which would really drive up the risk of your portfolio.

The only investment that might satisfy green diehards is the **Clean Power Income Fund** (www.cleanpowerincomefund.com). It invests solely in wind, solar, biomass and other forms of renewable energy. It's also the first income fund to be certified under Environment Canada's Environmental Choice eco-labelling program (www.environmental choice.com), which is pretty cool. And the way renewable energy is taking off, this is definitely one to keep your eye on for the future.

COMMUNITY INVESTMENT

Got a big heart and a little cash to spare? Canadians (mostly Quebecers, actually) invest about $550 million in local community investment organizations every year. The money goes to loans to not-for-profits, co-ops and social housing. Your deposit and interest tend to be guaranteed, so you can't lose money. **VanCity** is one of the best-known examples, funding all sorts of inspiring social enterprises (**www. vancity.com**). In fact, it started the Citizen's Bank. **Montreal Community Loan Association** (**www.acemcreditcommunautaire.qc.ca**) and **Access Riverdale** in Toronto (**www. accessriverdale.com**) are other excellent examples. Nova Scotia has a provincially funded system called the **Community Economic Development Investment Fund** (**www.gov.ns.ca/ econ/cedif**). For more info, check out the Canadian Community Investment Network Co-op (**www.community investment.ca**)

Mainstream banks, by the way, don't really carry ethical funds (though some have been known to tell customers that all their funds are ethical when they're not). They say there's no demand for them. So if you want them to, might I suggest you start vocalizing your interest? Meanwhile, the Social Investment Organization's website not only links you up with such funds but lists tons of advisers across the country that know ethical funds well (www.socialinvestment.ca). These advisers can also help you if you're interested in putting some coin directly in ecologically screened stocks or bonds. Credit unions are another good place to find such funds.

If you work for a company or an organization with a pension plan, it probably has your pennies invested in the worst of polluting (but oh-so-lucrative) industries such as Big Oil and Tobacco. Do a little digging and see for yourself. If so, it's time to encourage fellow shareholders to push for a pension you can all be proud of, one that considers the environmental and ethical risks involved in corporate business practices and introduces screens (which can, for example, filter out tobacco or oil companies) so your retirement isn't built on Mother Nature's back.

CAREER

So you need a job, do ya? Who doesn't? Last I checked, my father was still right: lots of wonderful green things grow on trees, but not money. If only we could work for leaves instead of coins. Oh wait, you can—just work for the environment! Anyone willing to dedicate his or her entire professional life to an environmental cause of some sort deserves our support. Green headhunters should be chasing you down in your home and throwing enticing benefit packages at you. But until that day, there are plenty of resources at your fingertips to help you find the job you're looking for.

Environmental Job Hunting: You *could* contact each and every eco-bent company and organization you can think of to see if it happens to have a slot to fill—if you have all the time in the world. Or you can try more of a one-stop-shopping approach and check out online employment databases specifically for earth-lovin' people like you. EcoEmploy.com (which also goes by www.ejobs.org) is a good one. It lists government openings at the federal, provincial

> **Check out online employment databases specifically for earth-lovin' people like you**

GREEN BUSINESS COURSES

More and more universities offer courses in merging environmental concerns with business interests (yes, they are compatible!). York University in Toronto has a graduate diploma in business and the environment, and the universities of Victoria, Waterloo and Calgary offer similar programs and/or courses.

and municipal levels in Canada and south of the border, as well as postings at enviro agencies, non-governmental organizations (NGOs) and corporations looking for everything from foresters and oceanographers to media relations people and executive directors. It even offers resumé tips and advice on getting an American work visa. It's not very slick, but it is fairly user-friendly.

STARTING YOUR OWN GREEN BUSINESS OR ORGANIZATION

Perhaps you have visions of starting your own sustainable business, maybe an organic sock bunny store or a paper clip recycling centre. Check out Sustainable Business Online Resources to get info on accessing capital and lots of helpful links for small and mid-sized enterprises (**www.communityfutures.ca/ provincial/SustainableBusiness/**).

Want to start a save-the-purple-cockatoo campaign of your own? The Sustainability Network (**www.sustain.web.ca**) has all kinds of suggestions on finding funders, writing grants and so on. It also offers financial assistance to green NGOs for specific challenges and gives bursaries for training opportunities. And take a look at materials from the Greenability online training series on funding for the environmental community (**www.greenability.org**).

CanadianEnvironmental.com has a smaller database of jobs, divided by province. **People & Planet's GoodWork Canada** (www.planetfriendly.net/goodwork) is a more comprehensive listing of paid placements across the country, with a sprinkling from the U.S. and elsewhere.

If you're set on moving to the States, you should know about EnvironmentalCareer.com. Well-laid-out listings give you the down-low on working as an environmental planner or as a green teacher, in Vegas or Wyoming. You can search by categories (such as academic, accounting, activist or architect) or by city or state. You can post your resumé or, if you're an employer, post jobs. Set up a free search agent (a program that'll do the job hunting for you) and get offers by email! The site also has a publication dedicated to the topic—the *Green Careers Journal*.

Volunteering: If you're having trouble finding work, I have three tips for you: volunteer, volunteer, volunteer. Even if you're not looking to pad your resumé and just want to get off the couch and put your spare time to good use, there are countless organizations out there

GREAT GREEN BOOKS ON BUSINESS, JOBS AND VOLUNTEERING

How to Save the World in Your Spare Time
by Elizabeth May

Working with the Environment
by Tim Ryder

*The Eco Guide to Careers That Make a
Difference:*
Environmental Work for a Sustainable World
by the Environmental Careers Organization

Designing the Green Economy:
*The Postindustrial Alternative to Corporate
Globalization*
by Brian Milani

The Sustainable Company:
*How to Create Lasting Value Through Social and
Environmental Performance*
by Chris Laszlo

that could use a helping hand, whether you're willing to lick stamps or wash oil slicks off seabirds.

The Canadian Environment Network website (www.cen-rce.org) provides links to regional Environment Networks in each province, where you'll find complete directories of all the eco-groups in your province and links to their sites. Ontario's directory lists over 900 organizations. Browse through the lists to find a group that interests you, then give them a call. The networks are also good places to find action alerts, volunteer listings, conference postings and more.

For those open to a little globetrotting, PlanetVolunteer.net lists tons of exciting green opportunities, from electricians needed in southern France to stream monitors and publishing interns wanted in Toronto. More daring eco-warriors can find challenging postings such as an internship working with the Conservation Society of Sierra Leone, actually in Sierra Leone. University grads seeking experience abroad should look into the Canadian International Development Agency's International Youth Internship Program (www.acdi-cida.gc.ca/internships). You can search by host country, title or sector (for example, environment). An extensive list of environmental internships and volunteer postings in Canada and around the globe is also posted at Campusaccess.com.

Is getting down and dirty with Mother Earth your thing? WWOOFing has nothing to do with canine mating calls, but it does involve digging up gardens. It stands for World-Wide Opportunities on Organic Farms, an organization that provides volunteer opportunities to visit an organic farm anywhere in the world, get some fresh air and learn all about organic agriculture through enriching hands-on experience. You get free room and board in exchange. You can wwoof for a week, a month or a year—it's up to you. There are 400 places to wwoof in Canada alone, and wherever there's an organic farm in the world, you can probably be a wwoofer. Visit www.wwoof.ca if you want to sign up.

If you're serious about learning organic growing skills and have eight weeks to prove it, get in touch with the sustainable farming apprenticeship program run by B.C.-based Stewards of Irreplaceable Land (www.soilapprenticeships.org). It's kind of like starring in a green version of *The Apprentice*, with a hoe and pitchfork rather than a briefcase and suit.

OFFICE

When we're trying so hard to be conscientious in our own homes, it can be pretty frustrating to get to the office and see so much waste—lights blazing 24/7, endless photocopies destined for landfill, disposable cups piling up by the water cooler (most of which can't be recycled). Just because we're overworked doesn't mean the planet should be. Talk to your office manager (or whoever's in charge of this kind of thing) about bringing in more responsible options. Sure, most will gripe about the extra cost of buying recycled materials, but point out that they can offset the expense with energy-saving measures. You can make a nice spreadsheet or chart (or whatever it is you number crunchers do) to demonstrate that greening your office makes good fiscal sense.

For more resistant types, start by suggesting small steps that will save them money, such as turning off lights and computers at night and turning down the heat by a few degrees. Once they've warmed up to the benefits of going green, you can hit them up for new Energy Star computers. And, of course, lead by example—even if it's just from your little cubicle.

Lighting/Energy: A quarter of a building's energy bills go to lighting. Your company can save coin by switching to compact fluorescent bulbs, which use up to 80% less energy than regular incandescents. In terms of tubular fluorescents, switching to T8 types (which produce more light per watt and are a third more efficient than standard T12s) and adding electric ballasts (which regulate the current flow) will save 10% to 15% on energy bills. For detailed reports on which commercial fluorescent lighting to buy, see http://greenseal.org. Your office manager should also consider purchasing timers and occupancy sensors.

Also, ask your building manager or landlord to spend 90 bucks on an energy-saving programmable thermostat. You can set it so that the temperature drops to 15°C to 18°C at night in the winter and turns off the a/c altogether at night in the summer, then kicks back in to a comfortable but energy-saving temperature during business hours: 25°C in the summer and 21°C in the winter. And lowering the thermostat on the water heater from 130°F (55°C) to 120°F (50°C) can save 5% on water heating.

OFFICE RENOVATIONS

Looking to spruce up your old office building with some energy-saving renovations? Natural Resources Canada's Office of Energy Efficiency (OEE) hands out incentives for that kind of thing. For information and tools, visit **www.oee.rncan.gc.ca/commercial**. The site also lists regional incentives created by utility companies and the provinces.

Office Equipment: In the market for new computers? Printer dying on you? Make sure to look for the Energy Star label when you're shopping for new technology (including faxes, scanners, mailing machines, copiers and more). A home office using an Energy Star computer, printer and fax machine saves enough electricity every year to light your house for over four years. Now think about how much energy a whole office building can save. For instance, an Energy Star computer in sleep mode consumes about 80% less electricity than it does in full-power mode and can save up to $55 per monitor yearly and about 135 kilograms of carbon dioxide emissions. Multiply that by the number of people in your office, and it really adds up. Even an Energy Star water cooler will save about $30 a year. For more number crunching and info on rebates and incentives, check out www.oee.rncan.gc.ca/energystar.

Also, see if your office is interested in offsetting all the carbon emissions created to power your computers by making yours wind-powered! Yep, for $39 per desktop or $16 per laptop you can buy enough wind energy to power your work through Pembina Institute's Wind Powered Computers Campaign (www.pembina.org/wind).

COMPUTER MYTHS

Heard the one about how you save more power by leaving your computer on than by shutting it down and restarting it? Well, it's bull. Computers use about two seconds' worth of power to start up, according to the U.S. Office for Energy Efficiency and Renewable Energy. Turn off your electronic equipment when you leave the office.

FYI, pretty screensavers of the Amazon don't save energy. In fact, fancy graphics often more suck power than just letting the screen go dark in screensaver mode.

Machinery on the fritz? Don't toss it; contact the manufacturer. If you purchased wisely, say from **Xerox**, they'll not only provide you with the maintenance help you need to keep it running, they'll take it back when it dies and convert it into new equipment. Xerox kept 58 million kilograms of waste out of landfill in 2004 alone thanks to this program. The energy saved was enough to power 250,000 homes for a year. Apple, Dell and Hewlett-Packard also have take-back programs. Ask your manufacturer if it has one, and keep asking as you shop around for new gear (this applies to computers too). Also, don't forget about charities in your area that refurbish old computers and donate them to the needy (see page 166).

Disks and CDs: Got a stack of floppy disks from the early '90s lying around? Yes, you could reuse them hundreds of times, but that won't do you much good if your computer doesn't take them anymore. Send old diskettes to **GreenDisk Services** for recycling (www.greendisk.com). You can also send them old data-storing CDs if they're scratched or are just plain useless to you now. Next time, make sure to buy rewritable CDs so they can be used more than once.

Paper: Did you know that the average office worker goes through about 10,000 sheets of paper every year? Pretty appalling, really, considering it takes 19 full-grown trees to make a ton of virgin office paper, according to Environment Canada. Lots of businesses have recycling bins in place now (if yours doesn't, this is the first thing you should look into), but not many pay attention to what type of paper they're buying. Switching to 100% recycled printing and photocopy paper would save about 4,100 kilowatts of energy, 7,000 gallons of water, 60 pounds of air emissions and 3 cubic yards of landfill space, not to mention 17 trees for every ton of paper.

> The average office worker goes through about **10,000 sheets of paper every year**

Ideally, you'd be buying 100% post-consumer recycled (PCR), chlorine-free paper. (Bleaching paper is an incredibly toxic process that emits dangerous persistent dioxins that accumulate in our tissues. Elemental chlorine–free paper is better but not totally dioxin-free. Processed chlorine–free is best.) If that's too costly for your stingy office, Grand & Toy and Staples/Business Depot both sell office paper with about 30% PCR content for a decent price. They also carry hanging file folders and files, envelopes, portfolios, Post-it Notes and adding machine rolls with as much as 95% PCR, so don't limit your green paper supplies to what spits out of your printer.

TIPS FOR SAVING PAPER

#1 Photocopy and print on both sides of the page. Get the tech guy to change everyone's default settings.

#2 Email everything. Even pay stubs can be encrypted and sent to every worker's inbox.

#3 Don't print out a whole 60-page report willy-nilly. Take a quick look on-screen to decide which sections you really need.

#4 Use print preview religiously. I can't stress this one enough. It lets you see what you're about to print so you can assess whether you can make it fit on fewer pages or whether you need only the first three sheets.

#5 If you blow up your on-screen font to avoid eyestrain, make sure you shrink it down before you press the print button; otherwise, you'll turn a two-page document into a ten-page one.

#6 If an e-fax program is set up on your computer, use it. If not, ask your office manager to order **EFax** or **Comodo Trustfax** or, for high-volume corporate accounts, something like **Faxage**. Small businesses can even get free e-faxing. (And if your office insists on having a fax machine, make sure it uses regular paper, not chemically treated fax paper, which isn't always recyclable.)

#7 Hold on to paper that was printed on one side only and use the other side to take notes—or throw paper airplanes at people who don't recycle.

Writing Tools: We buy, toss and lose millions of pens and pencils a year in North America, and they all end up in landfill at the end of the day (although I swear little gnomes are stealing pens from my desk and using them as back scratchers). Why not scribble with a pencil certified by the Forest Stewardship Council (FSC), such as **Dixon Ticonderoga** pencils, or try ones made of recycled cardboard, reclaimed wood or old lunch trays instead of clear-cut trees? All of these options and more are available at **Frogfile** (www.frogfile.com) and **Green Earth Office Supply** (www.greenearthofficesupply.com) and some at Staples/Business Depot.

Look for **refillable** ballpoint pens or **recycled** plastic ones

Pen chewer? Ditch those petroleum-derived plastic ones and get corn-based pens instead. They're not edible, but they do biodegrade. If you can't find them, look for refillable ballpoint pens or recycled plastic ones. As for markers, the permanent ones are full of air-polluting VOCs (you can kind of tell by the

Gil Yaron went through a lot of paper back when he was a lawyer. Actually, he went through a lot of stuff—folders, pens, paper clips. When the Bowen Island–based B.C.er started hunting for eco-friendly versions of those products, he realized there was a glaring gap where a one-stop Canadian green office supply shop should be, That's where **Frogfile** jumps in (**www.frogfile.com**). The every-office-supply-you-need-under-one-roof shop was born in 2006. And a one-stop shop it is. Need supplies for your presentation? You'll find recycled flip chart pads, clipboards made from recycled circuit boards and recycled plastic transparencies. Frogfile carries eco-friendly supplies for your mailroom, desktop, filing cabinets, office kitchen and more. Each product is exhaustively researched with an eye towards the economic, social and environmental bottom line. Plus, a basket of Frogfile goods will cost you up to 13% less than a basket of mainstream office supplies. Guess Kermit was wrong: it is easy being green, you just need a little help from a file-friendly frog.

fumes). Better to get the water-based type. Same goes with correction fluid, by the way (get correction tape instead). With dry erase markers, look for alcohol-based, low-odour brands.

Coffee/Mugs: We all know coffee is the ultimate office supply—certainly productivity would plummet without it. But why would anyone want to brew up low-grade, pesticide-laden beans for which coffee pickers are paid starvation wages when several office coffee suppliers offer fair-trade java? Especially when the cheap stuff tastes like dishwater. Check out www.transfair.ca for a full list of your fair trade options. Oh yeah, and get everyone to bring in reusable mugs while you're at it. Those foam cups aren't recyclable in most municipalities, and they take forever to break down in landfill. If your workplace has a kitchen, talk to the office manager about supplying reusable mugs, dishes and cutlery.

ENVIRO FLEET

If your company has a fleet of cars—even if it's just three—it can save big time on gas bills by switching from gas-guzzling SUVs or sedans to more efficient models, including hybrids (see www.greenercars.com for recommendations). The fleet can even be converted to run on more efficient natural gas.

Cleaning: Tired of coming to work and choking on the chemical trail the cleaners left behind? Encourage your employers to consider eco-friendly alternatives. If you have a small business and don't need massive quantities, just wander into a health store and pick up some green cleaners. **Eco-Max** makes earth-friendly cleaning supplies for larger buildings that require bulk quantities (www.eco-max.ca). It also has a consumer line. Many cleaning companies will use whatever products you ask them to, as long as you supply them. Others market themselves as strictly green to begin with, but those willing to do large offices are harder to find. If you have an office kitchen, make sure it's equipped with environmentally friendly dishwashing soaps, such as **Ecover** (see page 183).

THE TOP 10 STEPS TO GREENING YOUR OFFICE

#1 Institute a paper-saving strategy using 100% recycled paper with high post-consumer content.

#2 Get energy-efficient lighting.

#3 Raise the temperature to 25°C in the summer and lower it to 21°C in the winter.

#4 Make sure all employees use their computers' energy-saving mode and turn off their computers at night. It takes two seconds.

#5 Lower the thermostat on the water heater to 120°F (do you really need it scalding hot?).

#6 Recycle your ink cartridges for printers and photocopiers.

#7 Make sure all employees have recycling bins at their desks and place one in the office kitchen. (And if your town collects food scraps from homes, ask if businesses can access the program. Some progressive offices even have composting bins at every work station, or at least in the kitchen.)

#8 Set up carpooling and bike-to-work programs with sign-up boards or list-servs. Also, make sure your office has bike racks.

#9 Use fair-trade coffee, reusable coffee filters (either cloth, steel or gold), reusable mugs and cutlery, and bulk sugar, milk and cream (not the individually packaged stuff).

#10 If you drive to work, talk to your employer about working from home one day a week to cut back on travelling emissions (this even has an official name: telework). Closing the office one day a week can save a fifth of its energy bills.

BIG
ISSUES

We can talk all you want

about the value of compact fluorescent bulbs and which kitty litter is more eco-friendly, but there's no denying that there are larger issues at play. I'm not talking about theological musings like whether god is a woman or a blanket of molecules or whether Angelina Jolie can single-handedly adopt all the world's needy children. I'm talking climate change, mass deforestation, wiping out wildlife—you know, end of the world stuff.

Not to propagate fear, but we should be freaked out—at least long enough to get off our butts to tell our elected representatives that we're not going to stand for Canada ranking 28th out of 30 industrialized nations for energy consumption, water use, greenhouse gas emissions, air pollutants, pesticide use and wildlife protection. Worse yet, the Organization for Economic Cooperation and Development (OECD) found that we've shown no improvement over the last 10 years! Rather than hang our heads in shame, it's time for a new form of "participaction"—one where we shake our fists, pick up the phone, write letters and take to the streets. Hell, if we're rigorous enough about it, we could tackle obesity rates at the same time.

Enough of the rant. Here's a breakdown of the major eco-hurdles we face and some tips on how to stay informed, get involved and nag politicians and polluting corporations. Don't forget to have a look at the Resource Guide at the back of the book so you'll know where to direct your ire.

CLIMATE CHANGE

The term "climate change" is now synonymous with "The planet is melting! The planet is melting!" But this is no imaginary concoction of some children's book chicken. Despite oil company–backed naysayers, the planet hasn't been this warm for at least 1,000 years, and carbon dioxide levels haven't been this high for about 20 million.

The planet hasn't been this warm for at least 1,000 years, and carbon dioxide levels haven't been this high for about 20 million

We can thank mass fossil fuel burning, industrial and agricultural pollution and deforestation for that (forests trap carbon, in case you were wondering about the forestry connection). Along with other greenhouse gases, all that CO_2 builds up in the earth's atmosphere, trapping the sun's heat (hence the "greenhouse" effect). The ramifications? Glaciers around the globe are melting faster than they have in 5,000 years, and polar bears are drowning after swimming 100 kilometres in search of vanishing ice floes. And although it's also called "global warming" (which sounds deceptively peachy to snow-bogged Canadians), climate change is perhaps more aptly associated with crazy storms, floods, freak cold snaps, droughts, sizzling temps and pretty much any extreme weather à la Hurricane Katrina and worse.

Action Needed: The Kyoto Accord, of course, is all about reining in our emissions and taking a step towards reversing the climate-change trend. And even though the accord doesn't go nearly far enough in setting targets for greenhouse gas reductions (we should be slashing greenhouse gas emissions to at least 80% below 1990 levels by 2050 if we're serious about this), it's certainly better than doing nothing, which is what the federal government has done for years.

The Chrétien-Martin Liberals did little to meet Kyoto targets, but at least they didn't embark on a campaign to eliminate all references to climate change and greenhouse gases from federal websites, as the Harper Tories did until it was politically unacceptable (case in point: the Tories took down the government's signature climate-change website, www.climatechange.gc.ca). Whoever's in charge needs to know Canadians want meaningful action on this pressing issue and won't put up with window dressing.

ENDANGERED SPECIES

Sure, many species came and went long before humans arrived on the scene (any *Jurassic Park* fan knows that), but since the 1500s, humans can take the blame for the vast majority of recorded extinctions. Destruction of habitat, pollution, climate change, and hunting have meant that we've put animals, birds, fish and plants species at risk of permanent obliteration around the globe—and 516 of those officially endangered are in Canada. Thirteen are already gone forever.

Action Needed: An internal audit released in August 2006 revealed that federal species protection is a mess in this country. The Species at Risk Act, passed in 2003, was designed to legally safeguard peregrine falcon, woodland caribou and others, but the Treasury Board reported that coordination of the act's implementation is in shambles, funds are being slashed and deadlines are being ignored. Much of the report was aimed at the old Liberal government, but (surprise, surprise) the Conservatives have done nothing to improve matters.

The spotted owl population plummeted by 67% between 1992 and 2002 thanks to rampant logging of its habitat

Environmental Defence has also given big fat F's to B.C., Alberta, the Northwest Territories and the Yukon for not having their own species-at-risk laws. Scary when you consider that B.C. is the most biologically diverse part of the country, home to over 70% of the nation's animal and bird species. Clearly, whatever tactics the outdoor-lovin' province is using to save at-risk creatures aren't working—the spotted owl population, for instance, plummeted by 67% between 1992 and 2002 thanks to rampant logging of its habitat. In 2006 five environmental groups even launched a lawsuit against then–Environment Minister Rona Ambrose for failing to protect the country's 17 remaining Northern spotted owls from loggers.

Nunavut, Saskatchewan, Ontario and Quebec all got D's for their abysmal attempts at protection. In some provinces, it's even legal to hunt threatened species. (Until 2006, Alberta, for example, allowed grizzly bear hunting, despite the fact that only 500 of the threatened animals are estimated to fall within its borders.) How 'bout we all call our elected representatives to tell them to take the extinction of Canadian animals seriously. Do they really want the eradication of yet another species on their hands?

ENERGY CRISIS

Our hyper-industrial society would be nowhere without power—not the hierarchical kind you find in boardrooms, but the type that fuels our cars, our hot water tanks and pretty much every plug-in apparatus you can imagine. Trouble is, our addiction to oil, coal and natural gas is a deadly double-edged sword. They not only choke out nasty air-clogging pollutants as we use them (particularly oil and coal), but digging for them comes with all kinds of disturbing ecological ramifications. Natural gas pipelines cut across northern Native lands and caribou mating grounds. Coal mines (even abandoned ones) release dozens of toxic chemicals tied to serious groundwater contamination. Hydro dams often flood wild habitats. And the uranium that fuels nuclear power plants isn't just polluting to mine, its dangerous radioactive waste is with us forever (plus uranium supplies are running out).

Then there's oil. Our dependence on the juice of million-year-old fossils is clearly unsustainable, and our hankering for it makes our other fuel addictions look child's play. Wars (both covert and overt) are waged in its name; fragile habitats are ravaged to excavate it and ship it. Lucky for us, Alberta has 1.7 trillion barrels' worth of it—in the

It takes more energy to squeeze oil from tar sand than it produces, and doing so emits two and half times more greenhouse gases than your typical oil production, making it the world's dirtiest oil

oil sands. Too bad it takes more energy to squeeze oil from sand than it produces, and that doing so emits two and half times more greenhouse gases than your typical oil production, making it the world's dirtiest oil, according to Sierra Club of Canada. Elevated cancer rates are being found in communities downwind (and downstream), acid rain is on the rise, and the predicted astronomical growth in tar sands production means that the west is sitting on what will soon be Canada's largest source of greenhouse gas emissions.

Action Needed: Wanna know why Stephen Harper has dragged his feet on our Kyoto commitments? Look no further than the tar sands. There's no way in hell we could meet the accord's targets if production in Alberta keeps climbing. Curbing production would, of course, also piss off our neighbours to the south, who now buy more oil from us than from any other country. Critics, such as University of Alberta's Parkland Institute and Sierra Club of Canada are calling for a five-year moratorium on all new tar sands development. Tell your MP you agree. While you're on the phone, call your MPP and tell him or her you want to see more than token investments in renewable energy and conservation efforts instead of building our future on fossils.

WATER SHORTAGE

Living in Canada, we tend to have a certain cockiness about our water supply. We know we're swimming in the stuff—I mean, hey, we have 20% of the world's fresh water. But what we don't realize is that we have only 7% of the globe's renewable water; the rest is glacial stuff left over from the ice ages, according to Environment Canada. And what good will our fresh lake water do us if it's thoroughly contaminated? The life-giving liquid becomes especially precious when you consider that a third of the world's population doesn't have enough. That's a position we weren't expected to be in until 2025, but a report released in the summer of 2006 by the International Water Management Institute in Sri Lanka says we're already there.

While Canada's thirst might not seem as dramatic as, say, Africa's, one in five Canadian municipalities have experienced shortages of late and have had to ask residents to curb use. The Prairies have been hit hard by drought, and the future is not bright for the region, which scientists, like University of Alberta's David Schindler, say is fast becoming a dust bowl (it doesn't help that oil sands extraction and livestock are both extremely water-intensive). Our water supply is also under serious threat from industrial pollution, invasive species and water exports to the U.S.

Action Needed: The Council of Canadians insists that we need a new national water strategy to make sure the resource is adequately protected. Canada must ban the export of water outright. We need national water conservation plans (after all, we manage to suck back more water per capita than any nation in the world other than the U.S.). We need national clean drinking water standards (so we don't see another Walkerton) and nation-wide policies about making water bottlers pay for the H_2O they take from our taps and springs and then charge us two bucks for. The feds have long had a laissez-faire attitude around protection of the Great Lakes and other shared water bodies, for which bulk water takings and pollution are joint responsibilities. Too many loopholes in existing regulations mean that we're slowly draining our water supply, drop by drop. The bottom line? Canada needs to recognize that access to safe water is a human right—we were the only country to vote against giving water this designation at the UN Commission on Human Rights in 2002.

A third of the world's population doesn't have enough of the life-sustaining liquid

DEFORESTATION

Up there with water wealth is our perception that Canada is covered with an endless canopy of trees. Hell, there are only 33 million of us living in the second-largest country in the world, and most of us hover as close to the southern border as you can get without having an American passport. What else is there, other than trees, to fill all that space? In truth, we do have vast forest coverage. Canada is home to the largest tract of ancient forest left in North America, the boreal. It makes up a quarter of the world's remaining old-growth forests, according to Greenpeace. Considering that nearly 80% of the planet's forests have been partly or fully destroyed, we need to make sure we hold on to what we've got (as Joni says, you don't know what you've got till it's gone). But do we care? Nah. We just raze it, then sell it to the States dirt cheap (heavily subsidized, of course), so they can sell it back to us as a table or toilet paper for 10 times the price. In fact, Greenpeace says an area the size of P.E.I. is cleared every year from Ontario, Quebec and Alberta. Canadian old-growth trees are making their way into building materials, tissue paper and catalogues. It's shameful, really. We're blowing our noses on and ordering bras off ancient trees that were home to countless numbers of animal species without a second thought.

An area the size of P.E.I. is cleared every year from Ontario, Quebec and Alberta

Action Needed: Environmentalists argue that Canada could very well create a market niche for itself by ensuring that every piece of lumber we sell is certified as sustainable by the Forest Stewardship Council (FSC). The program is backed by eco-activists like Greenpeace and ensures that biological diversity is preserved, environmental impacts are minimized and native land rights are respected. Ten percent of Canada's managed forests are already FSC-certified, we just need to go further. But even more importantly, we need to start freeing ourselves from our tree addiction and actively support tree-free alternatives like hemp and agricultural waste (which can be used to make products like strawboard cabinets, furniture and newsprint). Pushing for minimum recycled content regs for paper products would also be of help, that is if we want to have any forest around in 100 years.

CHEMICALS

We're surrounded. There are nearly 10 million synthetic chemicals out there and about 100,000 in commercial use, according to Environment Canada. They're in our homes, beauty products, clothing, food—and now they're in our bodies, rivers, soil and wildlife. Fine, you say, but they've all been tested for safety. Sorry, wrong. They might not instantly poison you, but about 23,000 chemicals that were in use in Canada before 1988 were grandfathered in under the Environmental Protection Act, meaning they were allowed to escape new safety testing standards because they were around before the act came in. "Age before brains" was clearly the motto there.

Health Canada recently reassessed the derelict bunch and found that about 4,000 chemicals of concern need to be properly investigated. For now, they are focusing on the 200 they think are the highest priority. That includes über-prevalent ones such as bisphenol A (which can be found in polycarbonate water bottles, ceramic dental fillings and tin can linings) and PFOAs (found in non-stick stuff).

We have a shocking cocktail of chemicals swimming in our blood and collecting in our fatty tissues

Let's just hope the feds don't fudge the investigation of potentially problematic chems, as the U.S. government has been accused of doing. (In May 2006, union leaders representing 9,000 government scientists, managers and employees publicly complained that the U.S. Environmental Protection Agency (EPA) was pressuring them to rush safety reviews and skip steps in the agency's review of 232 old pesticide ingredients already on the market.)

As it stands, we have a shocking cocktail of chemicals swimming in our blood and collecting in our fatty tissues. Environmental Defence tested a small pool of prominent Canadians and their families and found everything from flame retardants and DDT to nonstick chemicals and mercury. Health Canada researchers found that Canadian women's breast milk seems to have some of the highest levels of PBDEs (persistent flame-retardant chemicals found in furniture and electronics) in the world. In general, North Americans bear the dishonour of having 10 times the amount of chemicals in our systems as Europeans, who've been quicker at phasing out and banning persistent chemicals.

Action Needed: Health Canada finally announced that it would start systematically testing our blood for the presence of certain chemicals, including pesticides, lead and mercury (the study will look at 5,000 Canadians aged 6 to 79, starting in 2007). Hopefully, the results will lead to firmer and swifter action on persistent chems than we've seen in the past. The monitoring of lead and DDT levels in humans has proven that the faster we get rid of these

things in our world, the sooner we can eliminate them
from our bodies, so that maybe our grandchildren can
have a fighting chance.

FOOD

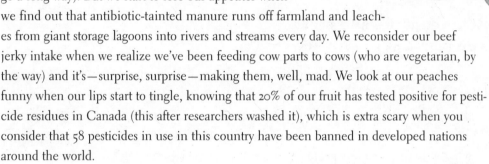

Toss food in basket. Lift fork to mouth. It's all so automatic there's nary a thought to what that food had to go
through to get to you. Most of us don't even do a little
"thank you, Lord, for this KFC" as they do in
American movies (although I believe a quick "thank
you, farmers, for the food we are about to eat" would
go a long way). But we start to lose our appetites when
we find out that antibiotic-tainted manure runs off farmland and leaches from giant storage lagoons into rivers and streams every day. We reconsider our beef
jerky intake when we realize we've been feeding cow parts to cows (who are vegetarian, by
the way) and it's—surprise, surprise—making them, well, mad. We look at our peaches
funny when our lips start to tingle, knowing that 20% of our fruit has tested positive for pesticide residues in Canada (this after researchers washed it), which is extra scary when you
consider that 58 pesticides in use in this country have been banned in developed nations
around the world.

Maybe it's no surprise that we're so out of touch with our food when you consider that
our meals come from thousands of kilometres away, a situation that's bound to get worse if
our cities keep sprawling out and converting prime agricultural lands into sub-
developments. And we can't count on the seas to feed us if we keep vacuuming our waters
bare so that the majority of our fish stocks are on the verge of collapse.

Action Needed: So what can you do about it? Well, besides buying local and organic with
minimal packaging, you need to start harassing your politicians about a thing or two. Like,
say, the fact that the feds sabotaged a UN ban on bottom trawling in international waters
(which make up 64% of the world's oceans), though even eco-foe U.S. president George W.
Bush called for an end to such trawling. And if Denmark and Sweden have banned the use
of antibiotics as a livestock growth promoter, why haven't we? The Canadian Medical
Association called for such a ban nine years ago. We also need serious greenbelt protection
across the country to preserve local farmland. And if we're going to subsidize farmers so

heavily, we should be doing the same for organic growers, since they not only feed our bellies but do our bodies—and the environment—more good than any pesticide-laden genetically modified patch of refined white wheat ever could.

WHAT YOU CAN DO

"Oh, but the world's problems are so big, what can I really do to make a difference?" you say. Don't worry, I have some handy tips to make it nice and easy. Reclaiming the reins of power from the oil companies, lumber mills and chemical corporations that seem to run this joint is not as hard as it seems if we all grab our elected representatives by the lapels and remind them that we the people hold the ultimate power in a democracy. You've just gotta take that first step. Start by picking a cause that's dearest to you and get informed.

Every letter you write and every petition you sign is an act of lobbying

Lobbying: Okay, so you're mad as hell. Now what? Time to take that frustration out on some politicians. Now, I'm not saying you want to be throwing spit balls at your local councillor, MP or MPP, but you do want make sure they remember that their job is to represent those who elected them. That includes you. You don't have to wear an alarmingly expensive suit and work for a shady corporation to do a little lobbying. Every letter you write and every petition you sign is an act of lobbying. Better still, get on the phone and tell your elected rep your thoughts on Canada's appalling pollution record or horrendous wildlife safeguards. No doubt they'll talk a good game, trying to convince you that plenty of impressive steps have already been taken to rectify the situation, but don't back down! You can argue your position best if you do your research beforehand. And google your politicians to dig up their environmental record or public position on the issue.

If you're really gung-ho, book an appointment to chat face to face. Bring along a mini delegation of two or three others who back your sound, earth-lovin' views. You'll get about 15 minutes to present your points, so be prepared with a written brief and printouts of any good research, charts or reports you can find. If you bend their ear enough, you can get them to hold community meetings, ask probing questions in the House, even submit private members' bills.

Using many of the same techniques—phone calls, letters, emails—you can also direct your lobbying efforts at the corporations doing the damage. For instance, Greenpeace, the David Suzuki Foundation, Friends of the Earth, the Pembina Institute, Sierra Club of

Canada and the Toronto Environmental Alliance encourage gas buyers to boycott climate change naysayer Esso. If you own shares in the company, use that foot in the door to launch a shareholder action (see page 285 for more info). You can even kick it up a notch by taking it to the streets. Help organize or participate in public protests outside the company's office. If you're actually a victim of a corporation's ecological recklessness (like, say, you live next door to a leaky plant), make like Erin Brockovich and file a class action lawsuit!

Joining Clubs: It can be hard to take effective action as just one person (not to mention lonely). So why not join an environmental organization? There are countless to choose from (see the Resource Guide for national, regional and local listings), and whether you want to save the unicorned snails, picket an oil company or help with a revitalization project in a sensitive wetland close to home, there's one out there for you. Making that first call can be a challenge if you've been spending most of your free time watching *Seinfeld* reruns or knitting, but once you go to a group meeting and get hooked on that feeling of accomplishment, of community, of hope you get from being involved in changing the world with a posse, you'll never look back.

Voter Power: Don't like what your councillor, MP or MPP is doing? Don't think they're standing up for the planet often enough or loud enough? Maybe they've sided one too many times in favour of developers over green space and polluters over communities. That little X you make in the ballot box is mighty powerful. Maybe it's time you changed your vote. And make sure all your family and friends are registered to vote and know why their vote matters.

If you know your local rep supports a new coal plant or voted in favour of paving through sensitive wetlands, tell people about it. Especially come election time. Print up flyers (on recycled paper, of course) with bullet points on the politician's dodgy record and slip it in your neighbours' mailboxes. If you join up with a group of like-minded citizens, you'll make a bigger splash.

Consumer Power: Buy, buy, buy—it's all we do. In fact, some rank shopping as their favourite pastime. And who am I to judge? I have a closet full of clothes and drawers full of necklaces and bangles that I'd no doubt want firefighters to save if flames ever licked

Why not use our consumer power for good? We can lend our dollars to products made with ethical policies and ecologically sound materials

my apartment. The point is, we all spend money on way too much stuff, even if you think you're a miser conservationist. And while we tend to focus on how a product will meet our needs (as in, "I need a bigger TV"; "I need a new cellphone"; "I need a teak coffee table"), we've got to own up to the fact that these purchases are fuelling chemical pollution, habitat destruction and landfill clogging. Why not use our consumer power for good? We can lend our dollars to products made with ethical policies and ecologically sound materials and yank money away from companies that are unresponsive to earthy considerations (Ethical Consumer in the U.K. has a long boycott list: www.ethicalconsumer.org). Lest we forget, money talks. And boy, do corporations speak its language.

For some local suggestions on stores, markets and organizations to support in your own home town, just flip to the Resource Guide at the back.

APPENDIX: PLASTICS

This petrochemical invention has enveloped nearly everything on the planet in a non-biodegradable sheath. But no matter how planet-conscious you are, sometimes you just can't get away from using plastic, so it's best to size up which type causes the least harm.

#1 Polyethylene terephthalate (PET): Pop bottle plastic, shampoo and water bottles. Probably the most commonly recycled plastic. Contains UV stabilizers and flame retardants, but has fewer harmful additives that will leach into landfills and your meal. Health Canada is, nonetheless, investigating it as one of 4,000 chemicals of potential concern that were brought onto the market without full safety assessments.

#2 High-density polyethylene (HDPE): Milk jugs, cleaning product bottles, shopping bags (which aren't necessarily recycled in municipalities that recycle #2 plastic—best to check). Most municipalities accept narrow-nose containers, but not all take wide-lipped ones such as margarine tubs. Not a bad plastic, compared to the others.

#3 Polyvinyl chloride (PVC): Greenpeace ranks this one as the biggest eco-villain of all. PVC, or vinyl, is made with vinyl chloride, a known human carcinogen. It's said to emit persistent dioxins in both its manufacture and incineration. Potentially hormone disrupting phthalates, lead and cadmium might be added to PVC products. Though it's used mostly by the construction biz (yes, your pipes just might be PVC if they're not lead), it's also the basis of vinyl records, old car seats, those shiny black outfits worn by the fetish crowd (sorry, gang!) and, scary but true, toys. The plastics people stand by its safety. If your plastic bottle has the number 3 or a V on the bottom, it's PVC. Rarely recycled.

#4 Low-density polyethylene (LDPE): Like its high-density sibling, #4 plastic isn't as toxic to manufacture as other plastics, but it's not commonly recycled.

#5 Polypropylene (PP): Not recyclable in many municipalities, which makes it unfavourable for single-use items, but it's not considered a bad player in terms of manufacturing.

#6 Polystyrene (PS): Perhaps a category best known by the trade name Styrofoam. Tied with polyurethane for second worst plastic since making the stuff involves carcinogenic benzene, plus it's not commonly recycled.

#7 Mixed bag: Basically any plastic other than #1–6. Under this broad umbrella sits polycarbonate (the hard plastic used for refillable baby and water bottles), which Greenpeace tosses in the second-worst category of plastics. That's a shocker because polycarbonate is often marketed to the green set as non-leaching, not to mention indestructible—perfect for outdoorsy types. But it's often made with a highly toxic chlorine gas derivative and carcinogenic solvents. "Yes, but does it leach?" you ask. The data is conflicting. While the industry says no (adding that even if it were to leach it wouldn't be enough to hurt you), some controversial studies suggest that, even at low doses, the hormone-disrupting chemical bisphenol A (found in the lining of food and beverage cans and polycarbonate bottles, including baby versions) can be harmful.

Bioplastic: Plastic made from plant sources such as cornstarch or soy instead of petroleum. Making it creates up to three times less carbon dioxide per ton of plastic than the petrol kind. Unlike regular plastic, you can often bury bioplastic in your backyard and it should biodegrade after several months (don't worry: it won't break down while you're using it, just under compost conditions). Health stores sometimes sell bioplastic cutlery, cups and plates—and keep your eye out for bioplastic computers and cars. Note: some concerns exist around the use of genetically modified corn (which makes up half the corn grown in the U.S.) to make these products. Corporate reps say they can't guarantee GMO-free crops were used, but insist say GMO molecules don't survive the fermentation process.

GLOSSARY

Ammonium nitrate: Made famous by its use in explosives (widely used in WWII), but mostly purchased as a fertilizer because it's a cheap source of nitrogen. Large spills can kill vegetation, and runoff from farms into waterways can create large algal blooms that choke rivers and bays and kill off fish.

Bioaccumulation: When chemicals build up in the tissues of a living thing, be it human, wildlife or plants. (Chemicals enter our bodies through the food we eat, the air we breathe and the water we drink.) Bioaccumulation explains why larger, older fish have higher levels of mercury, for instance, than smaller, younger ones.

Biomonitoring: A way of testing what happens to chemicals in the environment (for example, scientists test for persistent organic pollutants in polar bears and for dozens of chemicals in human blood, urine and saliva). Health Canada is about to embark on the biomonitoring of 5,000 Canadians.

Bisphenol A: Found in polycarbonate plastic bottles (the ones with the little #7 on the bottom), ceramic dental fillings and tin can linings, bisphenol A is an estrogen-mimicking hormone disruptor that several studies have tied to birth defects and breast and prostate cancer. It has been found to leach from products in small quantities. Manufacturers argue either that the levels are so low they're not a health risk or that their products (such as Nalgene and baby bottles) are special and don't leach like all the others.

Brominated fire retardants (PBDEs): These babies might make your mattress, couch and electronics less likely to erupt in flames, but they are part of a family of chemicals known as PBDEs, which are incredibly persistent and have the tendency to accumulate in human and animal tissue. Environment Canada has found skyrocketing levels of the stuff in arctic animals, lake trout, whales, water birds and human breast milk and considers the whole group toxic. Health Canada has asked manufacturers to phase out two types of PBDEs, namely penta and octa, but they're still found in commercial products.

Bt: A naturally occurring bacteria that's toxic to certain insects. Its gene has been cloned and spliced into plants, such as cotton, to make them insect-resistant.

C8: *See* PFOA.

311

Cadmium: A metallic element that is considered a probable human carcinogen.

Carcinogen: Anything that may trigger cancer.

Chemical sensitivities (a.k.a. multiple chemical sensitivities): A chronic syndrome caused by a person's intolerance to chemicals. There's even a medical term for it: idiopathic environmental intolerance. Even low doses of the offending chemicals can stimulate a negative reaction. Symptoms vary but can include headaches, a runny nose, aching joints, confusion, fatigue and sore throat. Symptoms generally improve or disappear when the chemicals are removed. A team of researchers recently found that people with multiple chemical sensitivities are missing certain enzymes that help metabolize chemicals.

Chloromethane (a.k.a. methyl chloride): A potent neurotoxin and possible human carcinogen found in air, water (including ground and drinking water) and soil samples. Sources include burning PVC and silicone rubber, as well as cigarettes, chlorinated pools and polystyrene insulation.

Chlorpropham: A pesticide used on many fruits and veggies to control weeds. It inhibits sprouting in potatoes. Long-term exposure to very high doses triggered tumours and stunted growth in lab animals, and in some instances caused death, but is generally considered to be of low toxicity.

Chlorpyrifos: A pesticide used on farms, lawns and pet collars and in home pest control. Chlorpyrifos is very toxic to animals, fish and birds and is a suspected endocrine disrupter, which is especially harmful for young children. Phased out for residential use in Canada and the U.S. Still allowed on crops.

Closed-cell: Used in reference to yoga mats, as in "100% closed-cell PVC mat." The term may imply that the product doesn't off-gas, but all it really means is that its plastic cells are sealed within their own little bubble, making it highly water-resistant.

DDT: Considered the first modern pesticide. DDT was first used during WWII to combat mosquitoes, then was commonly used on crops and sprayed in residential areas to combat tree infestations. It is extremely toxic to fish and birds, accumulates in the food chain and is classified as a probable human carcinogen. Most uses of it were phased out in the '70s, when its environmental impacts first came to light, and it was fully banned in Canada in 1989. It's still found in breast milk and in the bloodstreams of North American adults and, to a lesser extent, children. DDT is still used to fight insect-borne malaria and typhoid in some developing countries.

Diethanolamine (DEA): A suspected carcinogen common in shampoos, body wash and makeup. Cocamide DEA, MEA and TEA may be contaminated with DEA.

Dioxins (a.k.a. furans): Carcinogenic, endocrine-disrupting neurotoxins. There are lots of different types of dioxins, but they all contain chlorine, and they're all bad. The largest source of dioxins in Canada is the burning of municipal and medical waste. Burning plastics in your backyard releases dioxins too, as does chemically treated wood. They build up in animal tissues, which explains why the main way humans ingest dioxins is by eating meat, milk products and fish. Canada eliminated dioxin use as a pest control and says it requires the virtual elimination of dioxins in pulp and paper processing.

Diphenylamine: A fungicide used to prevent discoloration in apples. An impurity in it is considered a known carcinogen.

Ditallow dimethyl ammonium chloride: Found in anti-static products, fabric dyes, fertilizers and lubricating oil. Made from animal fat, it is toxic to fish and algae, and it isn't readily biodegradable.

Endocrine disruptors: *See* hormone disruptors.

Formaldehyde: Commonly found in pressed woods (particleboard and medium-density fibreboard), permanent press fabric (clothing and curtains) and insulation. There are two types: urea formaldehyde releases volatile formaldehyde gas, while the phenol type tends to off-gas less, according to the U.S. National Safety Council. Formaldehyde may cause cancer in humans, as well as wheezing, fatigue, rashes and eye, nose and throat irritations. Some people are especially sensitive to it. It's also a major component of smog.

Formic acid: *See* methyl formate.

Furans: *See* dioxins (these two are always lumped together, and Health Canada gives the same description for both).

Grandfathered: Refers to something that's exempt from new regulation.

High-density polyethylene (HDPE): *See* Appendix: Plastics.

Hormone disruptors (a.k.a. endocrine disruptors): Chemicals that mimic or block hormones, potentially throwing off normal body functions and triggering behavioural, reproductive and developmental problems.

Low-density polyethylene (LDPE): *See* Appendix: Plastics.

313

Malathion: An organophosphate pesticide in use in Canada since 1953. It's mostly sprayed on crops but is perhaps best known for its use to control adult mosquitoes in residential areas. Winnipeg has been misting the chemical around town for years. It's not really persistent in the environment, but it is deadly to all insects, including good ones such as honeybees, as well as fish and aquatic life. Health officials say it's not dangerous to humans, but environmentalists say it can cause kidney problems, intestinal problems and cancer in lab animals.

Mercury: The shiny stuff in old thermometers and the only metal that's liquid at room temperature. Mercury is used in dental fillings and batteries and as a preservative in some vaccines. Most of the mercury in landfill comes from car switches. Most human exposure to the potent neurotoxin comes from eating mercury-contaminated fish, according to the U.S. Environmental Protection Agency (EPA). Developing fetuses are most at risk and can develop severe disabilities from exposure—hence the 2004 EPA warning to women who want to become pregnant, pregnant or nursing moms and young children to curb their tuna intake (enviros say to ditch it altogether). The EPA estimates that 300,000 newborns each year have a higher chance of learning disabilities thanks to exposure to mercury in the womb. How do fish get so full of mercury to begin with? Emissions from coal plants and other factories send mercury up into the air, where it can travel great distances on wind currents and come down as rain or snow over bodies of water. It then collects in the bodies of aquatic animals and moves up the food chain. *See* bioaccumulation.

Methyl chloride: *See* chloromethane.

Methyl formate (a.k.a. formic acid): A suspected neurotoxin. Exposure can trigger eye, nose and skin irritations, shortness of breath, dizziness and headaches.

Methylene chloride: Emitted in polyurethane production and found in paint thinners and strippers, shoe polish, fabric protectors and pesticides—oh yes, and it's used in the production of decaf coffee and tea. EPA classifies it as a probable carcinogen. It doesn't dissolve well in water and can be found in drinking water.

Neurotoxin: A toxin that affects the central nervous system, harming neural tissue.

Nitrogen oxide: A gas present in car exhaust and a major component of smog.

Off-gas: Not a bodily function, but a reference to chemicals that are released into the air.

Organochlorines: A notorious group of chemicals that includes all kinds of bad boys such as DDT, PCB and dioxins. Some are carcinogens, and most accumulate in fatty tissues.

Organophosphates (OPs): An old-generation family of chemical pesticides that mess with an insect's nervous system. OPs are the most widely used pesticides in the world and are often quite toxic. They are also used for head lice, in sheep dips and as nerve gas in chemical warfare (in fact, the use of OPs as an insecticide was discovered in Germany during WWII in the production of nerve gas). OPs don't so much accumulate in the environment as they make wildlife and workers that come in contact with them sick. They're popular in the developing world, where they're cheaper than newer pesticides. But of a short list of pesticides that developing nations' governments are advised to restrict, all five, according to Pesticide Action Network, are OPs.

Parabens: All types of parabens (methyl, ethyl, etc.) have been found to be estrogenic—meaning they mimic female hormones. Parabens have been found in breast tumour samples but haven't been conclusively linked to cancer.

PBDEs: *See* brominated fire retardants.

PCB (polychlorinated biphenyl): An extremely persistent environmental contaminant. The industrial chemical was introduced in 1929 and used in the making of electronic equipment. Canada banned the substance in 1977 but it's still turning up in human tissues and farmed salmon.

Perfluorinated chemical (PFC): A slippery class of chemicals that can be found in Teflon, old Scotchgard products and Gore-Tex, to name a few. PFCs keep your eggs from sticking, repel stains and make rain bead off your jacket. For a shopper's guide to what products contain PFCs and detailed reports on the topic, check out www.ewg.org.

Permethrin: A suspected hormone disrupter and possible carcinogen. Permethrin is toxic to fish and tadpoles and can cause all sorts of physical reactions in humans, from nausea to asthma attacks.

Persistent: A chemical that does not readily biodegrade but instead accumulates in the environment. *See* bioaccumulation.

Petrochemical: Any chemical derived from petroleum, be it crude oil or natural gas. Petrochemicals are used to make plastic, fertilizers, paint, cleaning products, asphalt and synthetic fabrics such as polyester. All the ecological problems that arise from petroleum excavation, processing and shipping are also associated with its offshoots, plus the extra pollution created by refining and manufacturing each chemical.

PFOA (a.k.a. C8): An ingredient used to make non-stick surfaces on cookware, microwave popcorn bags, candy wrappers, fast-food french fry containers, cardboard pizza trays and burger wrappers. It does not break down in the wild (even DDT breaks down eventually) and has reportedly accumulated in 95% of Americans' tissues and in high levels in wildlife, including polar bears. (EPA documents showed that the company had known about PFOA's persistence in the broader population since 1976.) In early 2006, the EPA announced that it had reached an agreement with DuPont and seven other major manufacturers to cut their emissions and PFOA-containing products by 95% by 2010 and to eliminate PFOA altogether by 2015. Environment Canada has stopped the import of four new types of stain-resistant coatings that it worried might break down into PFOA, but hasn't taken action on PFOA itself to date.

PFOS: A chemical commonly found on older stain-repellent carpets, furniture and clothing. PFOS was the basis of Scotchgard's and Stainmaster's original formulation until it stopped production of the chemical in 2000 after the EPA threatened it with regulatory action. Studies found that PFOS was turning up everywhere in the environment, and that it killed some rat pups although it was their mothers that had been exposed in the womb, not the pups. Like PFOA, it was also used as a grease-repellent surface in fast-food wrappers, popcorn bags, candy bars and beverage containers. PFOS use has been phased out in Canada.

Phthalates: A chemical often added to PVC plastic as a softener, found in everything from kids' toys to sex toys, as well as all sorts of personal care products and perfumes. The industry insists they're safe, but one type of phthalate in particular, DEHP, has been found to cause birth defects in lab animals and is classified as a probable human carcinogen. Harvard researchers found that another, DEP, can cause DNA damage in the sperm of adult men. And Health Canada has asked that manufacturers of baby toys not make teethers and infant toys with one called DINP as it may cause kidney and liver damage over long-term use. Many toy companies have phased them out either entirely or at least in toys intended for younger children. Also found in water, household dust, breast milk and wildlife — phthalates clearly migrate from their source.

Polyethylene terephthalate (PET): *See* Appendix: Plastics.

Polypropylene (PP): *See* Appendix: Plastics.

Polystyrene (PS): *See* Appendix: Plastics.

Polyvinylidene chloride (PVDC): Used to make some cling wrap. Ten percent of PVDC wrap can be made up of potentially hormone-disrupting liver-damaging phthalates, which have been found to drift into food.

PTFE: Generally considered part of the PFC family (though a chemist might argue the point and say it's in the fluoroplastic family). The trade name for PTFE is Teflon. Gore-Tex products are basically PTFE with micropores. Gore-Tex swears its gear is so stable it'll never break down, but you wouldn't want to, say, accidentally throw your rain gear in a fire. A few groups of scientists have found that using PTFE-coated heat lamps to warm chicks and ducklings killed up to 52% of them within three to five days. Considered to be the compound in non-stick pans that may kill pet birds if a pan is heated to extremely high temperatures.

PVC (polyvinyl chloride, a.k.a. vinyl): Found in pipes, windows, toys, flip-flops, garden furniture, flooring, plastic bottles (check the bottom for recycling symbol #3), Venetian blinds, umbrellas, fake leather couches and even the puffy 3-D cartoon on your kid's T-shirt. Just the additives—phthalates, lead and cadmium—are super-controversial. In the late '90s, Greenpeace, after two years of investigation, concluded that vinyl is the absolute worst plastic for the environment. The building block of PVC, vinyl chloride, is not only a known carcinogen, but creates dangerous dioxins in the manufacturing process and when incinerated. The industry, of course, says vinyl is completely safe and that it has cleaned up its practices since its dirtier days and now emits very few dioxins and furans. Even so, many companies, such as Adidas, Reebok, Puma, Nike, Microsoft, Hewlett-Packard, Toyota and Honda, are committed to reducing or limiting the plastic. IKEA outlaws the substance altogether, and several municipalities have been making moves to do the same. (*See also* Appendix: Plastics.)

Sodium laurel sulphate (SLS): A sudsing surfactant found in shampoos, soaps and toothpaste and a known skin and eye irritant that may aggravate dandruff and mouth ulcers. Rumours of it being a carcinogen are considered urban myths. Health food products often contain SLS made from coconut oil.

Sodium laureth sulphate: Similar to sodium laurel sulphate, but somewhat gentler. Still maligned for the same reasons.

Surfactant: A type of chemical found in cleaning products, dish and laundry detergent, shampoos and washes. Surfactants make things lather, spread and penetrate well. Hundreds of surfactants are in existence, many petroleum-based. Most surfactants biodegrade in sewage treatment plants, but

317

nonlyphenol ethoxylates (NPEs) are of environmental concern since they don't really biodegrade, are toxic to algae and aquatic life and have been associated with hormone-disrupting effects.

Teflon: A brand name (owned by DuPont) for non-stick coating made with PFOA. The generic chemical name is PTFE.

Toluene: A common solvent used in paints, glues, disinfectants and rubber, as well as in tanning leather and used to make polyurethane foam. Inhaling toluene regularly over time can lead to brain and kidney damage. Even low doses can cause confusion as well as memory, hearing and vision loss. Pregnant women should minimize exposure. Toluene is a petroleum by-product.

Triclocarbon: A chemical disinfectant found in some antibacterial soaps, though it's less common than triclosan. Triclocarbon is persistent and has been surviving the sewage treatment process and turning up in lakes, rivers and streams.

Triclosan: The active ingredient in many antibacterial soaps, deodorants and toothpastes. Beyond accumulating in fatty tissues (it's been found in fish and in breast milk), it has made its way into lakes, rivers and streams (the U.S. Geological Survey found triclosan to be one of the top ten stream contaminants).

When it's exposed to sunlight in water, a mild dioxin forms. And when you throw chlorinated water into the mix, it could turn into a much nastier dioxin. *E. coli* that survived being treated with triclosan became resistant to 7 of 12 antibiotics.

Vinyl: *See* PVC.

Volatile Organic Compounds (VOCs): Found in paint, glue, gasoline, cleaning products, ink, permanent markets, correction fluid, pesticides and air fresheners. Don't be fooled by the word "organic" in the name—VOCs aren't good for us. They're carbon-containing gases and vapours that evaporate readily into the air, contributing to air pollution. VOCs can even off-gas from non-liquid sources, such as office furniture, that contain formaldehyde and cause serious indoor air pollution. Exposure can cause dizziness, headaches and nausea. Some VOCs are more toxic than others and are tied to cancer and kidney and liver dxamage. Some react with nitrogen oxide to form smog-inducing compounds.

RESOURCE GUIDE

COUNCILLOR LINKS

Calgary
www.calgary.ca

Halifax
www.halifax.ca/districts/index.html

Montreal
http://ville.montreal.qc.ca

Ottawa
www.ottawa.ca/city_hall/mayor_
council/councillors/index_en.html

Toronto
http://app.toronto.ca/im/council/
councillors.jsp

Winnipeg
www.winnipeg.ca/council

Vancouver
www.city.vancouver.bc.ca/ctyclerk/
councilmembers.htm

FEDERAL CONTACTS

Agriculture and Agri-Food Canada
Public Information Request
Services
Sir John Carling Building
930 Carling Avenue
Ottawa, Ontario K1A 0C7
Tel: (613) 759-1000
Fax: (613) 759-7977
www.agr.gc.ca

**Canadian Environmental
Assessment Agency**
22nd Floor, Place Bell
160 Elgin Street
Ottawa, Ontario K1A 0H3
Tel: (613) 957-0700
Fax: (613) 957-0935
www.ceaa-acee.gc.ca

Canadian Food Inspection Agency
59 Camelot Drive
Ottawa, Ontario K1A 0Y9
Tel: (613) 225-2342
Fax: (613) 228-4550
www.inspection.gc.ca

**Canadian Nuclear Safety
Commission—Headquarters**
280 Slater Street
P.O. Box 1046, Station B
Ottawa, Ontario K1P 5S9
Toll-free: (800) 668-5284
www.nuclearsafety.gc.ca

Environment Canada
Inquiry Centre
70 Crémazie Street
Gatineau, Quebec K1A 0H3
Tel: (819) 997-2800
Toll-free: (800) 668-6767
www.ec.gc.ca

Health Canada
Public Inquiries
Tel: (613) 957-2991
Toll-free: (866) 225-0709
www.hc-sc.gc.ca

National Energy Board
444 Seventh Avenue SW
Calgary, Alberta T2P 0X8
Tel: (403) 292-4800
Toll-free: (800) 899-1265
www.neb-one.gc.ca

Natural Resources Canada
Tel: (613) 995-0947
www.nrcan-rncan.gc.ca
Office of the Auditor General of
Canada
Commissioner of the Environment
and Sustainable Development
240 Sparks Street
Ottawa, Ontario K1A 0G6
Tel: (613) 995-3708
www.oag-bvg.gc.ca

Public Health Agency of Canada
130 Colonnade Road
A.L. 6501H
Ottawa, Ontario K1A 0K9
Tel: (613) 946-3538
www.phac-aspc.gc.ca

GREEN ENERGY SUPPLIERS

MARITIMES

Maritime Electric Green Power
Program
(commercial and residential)
Tel: (902) 629-3799
Toll-free: (800) 670-1012
www.maritimeelectric.com/green
power.html

QUEBEC

No green power programs

ONTARIO

Bullfrog Power
(commercial and residential)
Tel: (416) 360-3464
Toll-free: (877) 360-3464
www.bullfrogpower.com

Energy Ottawa Green Power
Program
(commercial)
Tel: (613) 225-0418
www.energyottawa.com (Click on
"Green Power")

Green Tags Ontario
(commercial and residential)
Tel: (519) 371-8739
Toll-free: (866) 546-8414
www.greentagsontario.com

Oakville Hydro Green Light Pact
Program
(small business and residential)
Tel: (905) 825-6370
Toll-free: (866) 521-0192
www.oakvillehydro.com/
greenpower_residential.asp

Ontario Power Generation
Evergreen Energy Green Power
(commercial)
Tel: (416) 592-2555
Toll-free: (877) 592-2555

www.opg.com/safety/sustainable/
evergreen.asp

Permanent Power Solutions
(commercial and residential)
Toll-free: (888) 304-3888
www.permanentpowersolutions.com

Selectpower Selectwind Program
(commercial and residential)
Tel: (519) 780-1209
Toll-free: (866) 780-7880
www.selectpower.ca/contribute/
selectwind/selectwind.aspx

Windshare Co-operative
(commercial and residential)
Tel: (416) 977-5093
www.windshare.ca

MANITOBA

No green power programs

SASKATCHEWAN

Saskpower's Green Power
Program
(commercial and residential)
Tel: (888) 757-6937
www.saskpower.com/greengen/
greengen.shtml

ALBERTA

ENMAX Greenmax Program
(commercial and residential)
Toll-free (in Alberta):
(403) 310-2010
Toll-free (across Canada):
(877) 571-7111
www.enmax.com/Energy

BRITISH COLUMBIA

B.C. Hydro Power Smart Green
Power Certificates
(commercial)
Tel: (604) 224-9376
Toll-free: (800) 224-9376

www.bchydro.com/business/gpcerts/
gpcerts3621.html

EPCOR EnVest Renewable Energy
(commercial)
Toll-free: (877) 441-7162
www.epcor.ca/Customers/
Commercial+and+Industrial/
EnVest/

Vision Quest Green Energy
(commercial)
Tel: (403) 267-2000
Toll-free: (877) 547-3365
www.visionquestwind.com

ACROSS CANADA

Canadian Hydro Developers
Renewable Energy Certificates
(commercial and residential)
Tel: (403) 269-9379
www.canhydro.com/www2005/
greensales.htm

Pembina Institute Wind Power
Certificates
(commercial and residential)
Tel: (403) 269-3344, ext. 117
www.pembina.org/wind/
wind_power.php

Vision Quest's Green Tags
Program
(commercial and residential)
Tel: (403) 267-2000
Toll-free: (877) 547-3365
www.visionquestwind.com

HEALTH FOOD STORES

Amaranth Whole Foods Market
7 Arbour Lake Drive NW
T3G 5G8
Tel: (403) 547-6333

Bowness Health Food
6435 Bowness Road NW
T3B 0E6
Tel: (403) 286-2224

Brentwood Health Foods
Brentwood Village Mall
322-3660 Brentwood Road
T2L 1K8
Tel: (403) 284-3133

Community Natural Foods
1304 10th Avenue SW
T3C 0J2
Tel: (403) 229-2383
   and
202 61st Avenue SW
T2H 0B4
Tel: (403) 541-0606
www.communitynaturalfoods.com

Deer Valley Health Foods
Deer Valley Shopping Centre
27-1221 Canyon Meadows Drive SE
T2J 6G2
Tel: (403) 271-5023

Golden Sun Health Foods
210 Southcentre Mall
T2J 3V1
Tel: (403) 278-0080

Planet Organic Market
10233 Elbow Drive SW
T2W 1E8
Tel: (403) 252-2404
www.planetorganic.ca

Sangster's Health Centres
Country Hills Town Centre
418-500 Country Hills Boulevard NE
T3K 5H2
Tel: (403) 226-5910
   and
Marlborough Mall
1215-3800 Memorial Drive NE
T2A 2K2
Tel: (403) 248-1077
www.sangsters.com

Sunnyside Market
10-338 10th Street NW
T2N 1V8
Tel: (403) 270-7477

Trinity Health Foods
Woodbine Square
206-2525 Woodview Drive SW
P2W 4N4
Tel: (403) 281-5582

FARMERS' MARKETS

Blackfoot Farmers' Market
5600 11th Street SE
Tel: (403) 243-0065
www.blackfootfarmersmarket.com
Fridays and Saturdays: 8:00 a.m. to
5:00 p.m.
Sundays: 10:00 a.m. to 4:00 p.m.

Calgary Farmers' Market
Hangar H6, 4421 Quesnay Wood
Drive SW
Tel: (403) 244-4548
www.calgaryfarmersmarket.ca
Fridays and Saturdays: 9:00 a.m. to
5:00 p.m.
Sundays: 9:00 a.m. to 4:00 p.m.

**Hillhurst Sunnyside Farmers'
Market**
Hillhurst Sunnyside Community
Centre
1320 5th Avenue NW

Tel: (403) 283-0554, ext. 223
Wednesdays: 3:30 p.m. to 8:00 p.m.

LOCAL FOOD BOXES

**Farm Fresh Organics Home
Delivery**
Tel: (403) 210-3700
www.freshorganics.ca

Small Potatoes Urban Delivery
Tel: (403) 615-3663
www.spud.ca

COMMUNITY-SUPPORTED
AGRICULTURE (CSA)

Blue Mountain Bio-Dynamic Farm
Carstairs
Tel: (403) 337-3321
http://members.shaw.ca/bluemtn
bio-dynamics

GREEN GENERAL STORES

**Clean Calgary Association
EcoStore**
809 4th Avenue SW
T2P 0K5
Tel: (403) 230-1443, ext. 222
www.cleancalgary.org/ecostore/

GREEN RENO STORES

Habitat for Humanity ReStore
2323 32nd Avenue NE, Suite 125
T2E 6Z3
Tel: (403) 291-6764
   and
5200 64th Avenue SE
T2C 4V3
Tel: (403) 205-4180
www.habitat.ca

**The Healthiest Homes and Building
Supplies**
833 1st Avenue NE
T2E 0C2
(see over)

Tel: (403) 290-1746
Toll-free: (877) 326-4211
www.thehealthiesthome.com

FAIR-TRADE STORES

Ten Thousand Villages
220 Crowchild Trail NW
T2N 2R2
Tel: (403) 270-0631
    and
8318 Fairmount Drive
T2H 0Y8
Tel: (403) 255-0553
www.tenthousandvillages.ca

CAR SHARING

Calgary Alternative Transportation
Co-operative
Tel: (403) 270-8002
www.catco-op.org

ENVIRONMENTAL ACTIVIST GROUPS

Alberta Ecotrust Foundation
1202 Centre Street SE
T2G 5A5
Tel: (403) 209-2245
www.albertaecotrust.com

Alberta Wilderness Association
455 12th Street NW
T2N 1Y9
Tel: (403) 283-2025
www.albertawilderness.ca

Canadian Parks and Wilderness
Society—Calgary/Banff Chapter
Kahanoff Centre, Suite 1120
1202 Centre Street SE
T2G 5A5
Tel: (403) 232-6686
www.cpawscalgary.org

Clean Calgary Association
809 4th Avenue SW
T2P 0K5
Tel: (403) 230-1443
www.cleancalgary.org

Nature Conservancy of Canada—
Alberta Chapter
1201 Centre Street SE, Suite 830
T2G 5A5
Tel: (403) 262-1252
Toll-free: (877) 262-1253
www.natureconservancy.ca

Residents for Accountability in
Power Industry Development
(RAPID)
414 Frobisher Boulevard SE
T2H 1G5
Tel: (403) 259-3025 or
(403) 248-0435

Sierra Club of Canada—
Chinook Group
#221, 223 12th Avenue SW
T2R 0G9
Tel: (403) 233-7332
www.sierraclubchinook.org

Sustainable Calgary
201-1225a Kensington Road NW
T2N 3P8
Tel: (403) 270-0777
www.sustainablecalgary.ca

Trout Unlimited Canada
P.O. Box 339, Station T
T2G 2H9
Tel: (403) 221-8360
Toll-free: (800) 909-6040
www.tucanada.org

HALIFAX

HEALTH FOOD STORES

The Healthy Bug
3514 Joseph Howe Drive
B3L 4H6
Tel: (902) 454-2225

Healthy Selection
1129 Bedford Highway
Bedford, NS
B4A 1B9
Tel: (902) 832-7511
www.healthyselection.ca

Planet Organic
6485 Quinpool Road
B3L 1B2
Tel: (902) 425-7400
www.planetorganic.ca

Sangster's Health Centres
Halifax Shopping Centre
7001 Mumford Road
B3L 4N9
Tel: (902) 454-2024
www.sangsters.com

Staff of Life Healthfood Bakery
6080 Quinpool Road
B3L 1A1
Tel: (902) 422-7799

Super Natural Health Products
5755 Young Street
B3K 1Z9
Tel: (902) 454-9999

Village Farm Market
5229 St. Margaret's Bay Road
B3Z 4R5
Tel: (902) 826-7077

CO-OPS

The Grainery Co-op
2385 Agricola Street
B3K 4C5
Tel: (902) 446-3301

FARMERS' MARKETS

Halifax Farmers' Market
1496 Lower Water Street
B3J 1R9
Tel: (902) 492-4043
www.halifaxfarmersmarket.com
Saturdays: 7:00 a.m. to 1:00 p.m.

LOCAL FOOD BOXES

Home Grown Organic Foods
Tel: (902) 492-1415
www.hgof.ns.ca/

COMMUNITY-SUPPORTED AGRICULTURE (CSA)

Mid Ridge Acres Farm
Springfield, NS
Tel: (902) 547-2424
www.midridgeacres.ca

GREEN GENERAL STORES

P'lovers
5657 Spring Garden Road
B3J 3R4
Tel: (902) 422-6060
Toll-free: (800) 565-2998
www.plovers.net

GREEN RENO STORES

Habitat for Humanity ReStore
121 Ilsley Avenue, Unit U
Dartmouth, NS
B3B 1S4
Tel: (902) 405-3755
www.habitathalifax.eastlink.ca

ENVIRONMENTAL ACTIVIST GROUPS

Canadian Parks and Wilderness
Society—Nova Scotia Chapter
4th Floor, 1526 Dresden Row, Unit 2
B3J 3K3
Tel: (902) 446-4155
www.cpaws.org

Ecology Action Centre
2705 Fern Lane
B3K 4L3
Tel: (902) 429-2202
www.ecologyaction.ca

NSPIRG (Nova Scotia Public
Interest Research Group)
6136 University Avenue, Room 314
B3K 4B8
Tel: (902) 494-6662
www.nspirg.org

Sierra Club of Canada—Atlantic
Canada Chapter
1657 Barrington Street
Roy Building, Suite 507
B3J 2A1
Tel: (902) 444-3113
www.sierraclub.ca/atlantic

World Wildlife Fund—Halifax
Chapter
5251 Duke Street
Duke Tower, Suite 1202
B3J 1P3
Tel: (902) 482-1105
www.wwf.ca

MONTREAL

HEALTH FOOD STORES

Au Bon Grenier
6610 Marseilles Street
H1N 1L9
Tel: (514) 223-8644

A Votre Santé
5126 Sherbrooke Street West
H4A 1T1
Tel: (514) 482-8233

Bonne Santé
1500 Atwater Ave
H3Z 1X5
Tel: (514) 937-4061

Club Organic
4341 Frontenac Street
H2H 2M4
Tel: (514) 523-0223

EcollegeY—The Real Green
Grocer
(will also deliver your order)
4627 Wilson Avenue
H4A 2V5
Tel: (514) 486-2247
www.ecollegey.com

Fleur Sauvage Natural Foods
5561 Monkland Avenue
H4A 1E1
Tel: (514) 482-5193

Nature Santé 2000
5006 Queen Mary Road
H3W 1X2
Tel: (514) 738-4638

P'tit Bonheur au Naturel
5412 Park Avenue
H2V 4G7
Tel: (514) 277-3434

Rachelle-Bery Produits Naturels
505 Rachel Street East
H2J 2H3
Tel: (514) 524-0725
www.rachellebery.com

Tau Natural Foods Stores
4238 rue Saint-Denis
H2J 2K8
Tel: (514) 843-4420
   and
7373 Langelier Boulevard
H1S 1V7
Tel: (514) 787-0077
www.taufoods.com

CO-OPS

Coop La Maison Verte
5785 Sherbrooke Street West
H4A 1X2
Tel: (514) 489-8000
www.cooplamaisonverte.com

FARMERS' MARKETS

Atwater Market
(has 4 organic vendors)
138 avenue Atwater
H4C 2H6
Tel: (514) 937-7754
www.marchespublics-mtl.com

Maisonneuve Market
(organic Saturdays)
4445 Ontario Street East
H1V 3V3
Tel: (514) 937-7754

LOCAL FOOD BOXES

Jardin des Anges
Tel: (450) 258-4889
Toll-free (in Quebec):
(888) 899-4889
www.jardindesanges.com

COMMUNITY-SUPPORTED AGRICULTURE (CSA)

(All deliver to drop-off points in Montreal)

D-Trois-Pierres
Pierrefonds & Saint-Paul
Tel: (514) 280-6743
www.d3pierres.com

Ferme Cadet-Roussel
Mont-Saint Grégoire
Tel: (514) 845-8341
www.fermecadetroussel.org

Ferme Chez Joly
L'Île-Bizard
Tel: (514) 626-4861

Ferme du Zéphyr
Senneville
Tel: (514) 488-2985
www.fermeduzephyr.com

Ferme Mange-Tout
Senneville
Tel: (514) 942-8473
www.fermemangetout.ca

Ferme Tourne-Sol
Les Cèdres
Tel: (450) 452-4271
www.fermetournesol.qc.ca

Les Jardins de la Montagne
Rougemont
Tel: (450) 469-5358
www.jardinsdelamontagne.com

Les Jardins de Tessa
Frelighsburg
Tel: (450) 298-1227
www.jardinsdetessa.com

Les Jardins Glenorra
Ormstown
Tel: (450) 829-2411
www.glenorra.com

Verger au Quatre Vents
Henryville
Tel: (450) 299-2183
www.verger-biologique.com

More CSAs can be found at
www.equiterre.org

GREEN BUTCHERS

(All deliver to drop-off points in Montreal)

Ferme Boréalis
Ulverton
Tel: (819) 826-2056
www.fermeborealis.com

Ferme des Prés
Sainte-Marie-de-Salomé
Tel: (450) 754-3307
www.fermedespres.com

Ferme Le Crépuscule
Yamachiche
Tel: (819) 296-1321
www.fermelecrepuscule.com

Fermes Morgan
(also delivers organic bakery
products)
Weir
Tel: (819) 687-2434
www.fermemorgan.com

GREEN GENERAL STORES

Coop La Maison Verte
5785 Sherbrooke Street West
H4A 1X2
Tel: (514) 489-8000
www.cooplamaisonverte.com

FAIR-TRADE STORES

Kif Kif
1228 rue Mont-Royal Est
H2J 1Y1
Tel: (514) 527-0404

Ten Thousand Villages
4128 rue St-Denis
H2W 2M5
Tel: (514) 848-0538
    and
5674 avenue Monkland
H4A 1E4
Tel: (514) 483-6569
www.tenthousandvillages.ca

CAR SHARING

CommunAuto
(various locations)
Tel: (514) 842-4545
www.communauto.com

ENVIRONMENTAL ACTIVIST GROUPS

Canadian Parks and Wilderness Society—Montreal Chapter
4871 avenue du Parc
H2V 4E7
Tel: (514) 278-7627
www.snapqc.org

Coalition Eau Secours
P.O. Box 55036
CSP Fairmount
H2T 3E2
Tel: (514) 270-7915
www.eausecours.org

Coalition pour les Alternatives aux Pesticides (CAP)
460 rue Ste-Catherine Ouest
Bureau 937
H3B 1A7
Tel: (514) 875-5995
www.cap-quebec.com

Coalition Quebec Vert Kyoto
(no offices)
Tel: (514) 979-8378
www.quebec-vert-kyoto.org

Équiterre
2177 Masson Street, Suite 317
H2H 1B1
Tel: (514) 522-2000
www.equiterre.org

Greenpeace—Montreal Office
454 Laurier East, 2nd Floor
H2J 1E7
Tel: (514) 933-0021
www.greenpeace.ca

Réseau Québecois des Groupes Ecologistes
4200 rue Adam
H1V 1S9
Tel: (514) 392-0096
www.rqge.qc.ca

Rivers Foundation
5834 rue Clark
H2T 2V7
Tel: (514) 272-2666
Toll-free: (866) 774-8437
www.rivers-foundation.org

Sierra Club of Canada—Quebec Chapter
3388 rue Adam
H1W 1Y1
Tel: (514) 651-5847
www.quebec.sierraclub.ca

Urban Ecology Centre
3516 avenue du Parc
H2X 2H7
Tel: (514) 282-8378
www.urbanecology.net

OTTAWA

HEALTH FOOD STORES

Bonnie's Natural Foods
1500 Bank Street
K1H 7Z9
Tel: (613) 523-1372

Herb and Spice
375 Bank Street
K2P 1Y2
Tel: (613) 232-4087

Kardish Specialty Foods
2515 Bank Street
K1V 0Y4
Tel: (613) 737-0305
    and
841 Bank Street
K1S 3V9
Tel: (613) 234-6795

Mother Hubbard's Natural & Bulk Foods
250 Greenbank Road
K2H 8X4
Tel: (613) 820-3178

Natural Food Pantry
Westgate Plaza
1309 Carling Avenue
K1Z 7L3
Tel: (613) 728-1255
    and
Billings Bridge Plaza
2277 Riverside Drive
K1H 7X6
Tel: (613) 737-9330
    and
126 York Street
K1N 5T5
Tel: (613) 241-6629
www.naturalfoodpantry.com

Nature's Buzz Organic Food
Market
23 Beechwood Avenue
K1M 1M2
Tel: (613) 842-0280

Peter's Health Foods
2525 Carling Avenue
K2B 7Z2
Tel: (613) 829-1122

Rainbow Natural Foods
Britannia Shopping Plaza
1487 Richmond Road
K2B 6R9
Tel: (613) 726-9200

Wheat Berry
206 Main Street
K1S 1C6
Tel: (613) 235-7580

CO-OPS

Ontario Natural Food Co-op
Toll-free: (800) 387-0354
www.onfc.ca

FARMERS' MARKETS

Ottawa Organic Farmers' Market
(located at Bank Street and Heron
Street, behind the Canadian Tire)
Tel: (613) 256-4150
Saturdays: 10:00 a.m. to 2:00 p.m.

LOCAL FOOD BOXES

Aubin Farm
Tel: (613) 658-5721
Email: aubinfarm@aol.com

Bryson Farms
Tel: (819) 647-3456
www.brysonfarms.com

COMMUNITY-SUPPORTED AGRICULTURE (CSA)

Bunching Onions CSA
Clarence
Tel: (613) 230-5993

Connaught Acres
Chesterville (with drop-off points
around Ottawa)
Tel: (613) 448-3540
www.connaughtacres.ca

Covenant Farm
Clarence Creek (will deliver)
Tel: (613) 488-3589
www.fermeducovenant.ca

Elm Tree Farm
Arden (will deliver)
Tel: (613) 335-3361
Email: elmtree@kos.net

Teamwork CSA
Almonte (with drop-off points
around Ottawa)
Tel: (613) 296-0599
Email: teamworkcsa@hotmail.com

Valentino's Organic Family
Gardens & CSA
Cumberland (will deliver)
Tel: (613) 834-9637

GREEN BUTCHERS

Saslove's Meat Market
1333 Wellington Street
K1N 7A2
Tel: (613) 722-0086
www.saslovesmeat.com

GREEN GENERAL STORES

Arbour Environmental Shoppe
800 Bank Street
K1S 3V8
Tel: (613) 567-3168
Toll-free: (800) 766-3324
www.arbourshop.com

FAIR-TRADE STORES

Ten Thousand Villages
371 Richmond Road, K2A 0E7
Tel: (613) 759-4701
www.tenthousandvillages.ca

GREEN RENO STORES

Habitat for Humanity ReStore
2370 Walkley Road, Unit 170
K1G 4H9
Tel: (613) 744-7769

The Healthiest Homes and Building
Supplies
135 Holland Avenue, K1Y 0Y2
Tel: (613) 715-9014
www.thehealthiesthome.com

CAR SHARING

VrtuCar
Tel: (613) 798-1900
www.vrtucar.com

ENVIRONMENTAL ACTIVIST GROUPS

Canadian Parks and Wilderness
Society—Ottawa Valley Chapter
601-250 City Centre Avenue
K1R 6K7
Tel: (613) 232-7297
www.cpaws-ov.org

Friends of the Earth
260 Saint Patrick Street, Suite 300
K1N 5K5
Tel: 1-888-385-4444
www.foecanada.org

Greenspace Alliance of Canada's
Capital
P.O. Box 55085
240 Sparks Street
K1P 1A1
Tel: (613) 733-7727
www.flora.org/greenspace/

Ottawa Riverkeeper
P.O. Box 67008
421 Richmond Road
K2A 4E4
Tel: (613) 864-7442
www.ottawariverkeeper.ca

The Peace and Environment
Resource Centre
  Mailing Address
P.O. Box 4075, Station E
K1S 5B1
  In Person
174 First Avenue (top floor)
Tel: (613) 230-4590
www.perc.ca

Pollution Probe
63 Sparks Street, Suite 101
K1P 5A6
Tel: (613) 237-8666
www.pollutionprobe.org

Sierra Club of Canada—Ottawa
Group
1 Nicholas Street, Suite 412
K1N 7B7
Tel: (613) 233-7889 or
(613) 567-4334
www.ontario.sierraclub.ca/ottawa

World Wildlife Fund—Ottawa
Chapter
85 Albert Street, Suite 900
K1P 6A4
Tel: (613) 232-8706
www.wwf.ca

TORONTO

HEALTH FOOD STORES

Appletree Natural Foods
845 Queen Street West
M6J 1G4
Tel: (416) 504-9677

Baldwin Naturals
16 Baldwin Street
M5T 1L2
Tel: (416) 979-1777
  and
1947 Queen Street East
M4L 1H7
Tel: (416) 698-8805

Essence of Life
50 Kensington Avenue
M5T 2K1
Tel: (416) 506-0345
www.essenceoflifeorganics.com

Evergreen Natural Foods
513 St. Clair Avenue West
M6C 1A1
Tel: (416) 536-2932
  and
161 Roncesvalles Avenue
M6R 2L3
Tel: (416) 534-2684

Foods for Life
2184E Bloor Street West
M6S 1N3
Tel: (416) 762-5590

Noah's Natural Foods
322 Bloor Street West
M5S 1W5
Tel: (416) 968-7930
  and
2395 Yonge Street
M4P 3E7
Tel: (416) 488-0904
  and

667 Yonge Street
M4Y 1Z9
Tel: (416) 969-0220

Peaches & Green
1561 Bayview Avenue
M4G 3B5
Tel: (416) 488-6321
www.peachesandgreen.com

Taste of Nature
380 Bloor Street West
M5S 1X2
Tel: (416) 925-8102

Whole Foods Market
87 Avenue Road
M5R 3R9
Tel: (416) 944-0500
www.wholefoodsmarket.com

CO-OPS

**The Big Carrot Natural Food
Market**
348 Danforth Avenue
M4K 1N8
Tel: (416) 466-2129
www.thebigcarrot.ca

Karma Co-op
739 Palmerston Avenue
M6G 2R3
Tel: (416) 534-1470
www.karmacoop.org

Ontario Natural Food Co-op
70 Fima Crescent
Etobicoke M8W 4V9
Tel: (416) 503-1144
Toll-free: (800) 387-0354
www.onfc.ca

FARMERS' MARKETS

Dufferin Grove Organic Farmers' Market
Dufferin Grove Park
Rink House (south of Bloor Street, east of Dufferin Street)
Tel: (416) 392-0913
Thursdays: 3:00 p.m. to 7:00 p.m.

Toronto Riverdale Organic Farmers' Market
Riverdale Park (outside gates to the farm)
http://friendsofriverdalefarm.com
Tuesdays: 3:00 p.m. to 7:00 p.m.

Village Market
Toronto Waldorf School
9100 Bathurst Street
Thornhill L4C 8C7
Tel: (905) 707-5771
www.villagemarket.ca
Saturdays: 9:00 a.m. to 1:00 p.m.

LOCAL FOOD BOXES

Eat Organics
Tel: (647) 393-3005
www.eatorganics.net

Front Door Organics
Tel: (416) 201-3000
www.frontdoororganics.com

Green Earth Organics
Tel: (416) 285-5300
www.greenearthorganics.com

Organics Delivered
Tel: (416) 556-7833
www.organicsdelivered.com

WOW Foods
Tel: (905) 595-0286
Toll-free: (877) 926-4426
www.wowfoods.com

COMMUNITY-SUPPORTED AGRICULTURE (CSA)

Devon Acres Farm
Brantford area
Tel: (519) 752-3980

Everdale Organic Farm
Hillsburgh
Tel: (519) 855-4859
www.everdale.org

ManoRun Organic Farm
Hamilton area
Tel: (905) 304-8048
Email: manorun@hwcn.org

Natures Way Organics
Walsingham (will deliver to Toronto)
Tel: (519) 586-3343
www.natureswayorganics.ca

Plan B Organic Farm
Hamilton area (with drop-off points in Toronto)
Tel: (905) 659-2572
www.planborganicfarms.ca

Simpler Thyme Organic Farm
Hamilton area (with drop-off points in Burlington and Hamilton)
Tel: (905) 659-1576
Email: simpler_thyme@hotmail.com

Thurston Organic Farm
Dunsford (with drop-off points in Toronto)
Tel: (705) 793-2327
www.thurstonorganicfarm.com

GREEN BUTCHERS

Beretta Organic Farms
(meat delivery service)
Tel: (416) 674-5609
www.berettaorganics.com

Butcher by Nature
520 Annette Street
M6P 1S3
Tel: (416) 241-8187

The Butchers
2636 Yonge Street
M4P 2J5
Tel: (416) 483-5777

Cumbrae's Naturally Raised Fine Meats
481 Church Street
M4Y 2C6
Tel: (416) 923-5600
and
1636 Bayview Avenue
M4G 3B7
Tel: (416) 485-5620
www.cumbraes.com

The Healthy Butcher
565 Queen Street West
M5V 2B6
Tel: (416) 674-2642
www.thehealthybutcher.com

Fresh from the Farm
350 Donlands Avenue
M4J 3B7
Tel: (416) 422-FARM
www.freshfromthefarm.ca

GREEN GENERAL STORES

Grassroots
372 Danforth Avenue
M4K 1N8
Tel: (416) 466-2841
and
408 Bloor Street West
M5S 1X5
Tel: (416) 944-1993
Toll-free: (888) 633-5833
www.grassrootsstore.com

Organic Lifestyle
Hazelton Lanes
260-87 Avenue Road
M5R 3R9
Tel: (416) 921-7317
www.organiclifestyle.ca

GREEN RENO STORES

Habitat for Humanity ReStore
1120 Caledonia Road
M6A 2W5
Tel: (416) 783-0686
    and
29 Bermondsey Road
M4B 1Z7
Tel: (416) 755-8023, ext. 33
Toll free: (800) 320-7183
www.habitat.ca

FAIR-TRADE STORES

Ten Thousand Villages
2599 Yonge Street
M4P 2J1
Tel: (416) 932-1673
    and
362 Danforth Avenue
M4K 1N8
Tel: (416) 462-9779
www.tenthousandvillages.ca

CAR SHARING

AutoShare
Tel: (416) 340-7888
www.autoshare.com

Zip Car
Tel: (416) 432-3114
Toll-free: (866) 494-7227
www.zipcar.com

ENVIRONMENTAL ACTIVIST GROUPS

Earthroots
401 Richmond Street West,
Suite 410
M5V 3A8
Tel: (416) 599-0152
www.earthroots.org

Environmental Defence
317 Adelaide Street West, Suite 705
M5V 1P9
Tel: (416) 323-9521
www.environmentaldefence.ca

FoodShare
200 Eastern Avenue
M5A 1J1
Tel: (416) 363-6441
www.foodshare.net

Greenpeace
250 Dundas Street West, Suite 605
M5T 2Z5
Tel: (416) 597-8408
www.greenpeace.ca

RiverSides Stewardship Alliance
511 Richmond Street West
M5V 1Y3
Tel: (416) 868-1983
www.riversides.org

Save the Oak Ridges Moraine
Coalition
401 Richmond Street West,
Suite 380
M5V 3A8
Tel: (647) 258-3281
www.stormcoalition.org

Sierra Club of Canada—Ontario
Chapter, Toronto Group
24 Mercer Street
M5V 1H3
Tel: (416) 960-9606
www.ontario.sierraclub.ca/toronto

Task Force to Bring Back the Don
55 John Street, 23rd Floor
M5V 3C6
Tel: (416) 392-0401
www.toronto.ca/don

Toronto Environmental Alliance
30 Duncan Street, Suite 201
M5V 2C3
Tel: (416) 596-0660
www.torontoenvironment.org

World Wildlife Fund Canada
245 Eglinton Avenue East,
Suite 410
M4P 3J1
Tel: (416) 489-8800
www.wwf.ca

VANCOUVER

HEALTH FOOD STORES

Capers Community Market
2285 West Fourth Avenue
V6K 1N9
Tel: (604) 739-6676
    and
1675 Robson Street
V6G 1C8
Tel: (604) 687-5288
    and
2496 Marine Drive
V7V 1L1
Tel: (604) 925-3316
www.capersmarket.com

Choices
1202 Richards Street
V6B 3G2
Tel: (604) 633-2392
  and
3493 Cambie Street
V5Z 2W7
Tel: (604) 875-0099
  and
2627 West 16th Avenue
V6K 3C2
Tel: (604) 736-0009
  and
1888 West 57th Avenue
V6P 1T7
Tel: (604) 263-4600
www.choicesmarket.com

Drive Organics
1045 Commercial Drive
V5L 3X1
Tel: (604) 678-9665

Famous Foods
1595 Kingsway
V5N 2R8
Tel: (604) 872-3019

The Grainry
1689 Johnston Street
V6H 3R9
Tel: (604) 681-6426

Green Leaf Organic Health Co.
9-1128 West Broadway
V6H 1G5
Tel: (604) 730-1162

Justin's Natural Food Store
4521 West 10th Avenue
V6R 2J2
Tel: (604) 221-0066

Mainly Organics
4348 Main Street
V5V 3P9
Tel: (604) 872-3446

Nature's Best Natural Foods
8279 Granville Street
V6P 4Z6
Tel: (604) 264-1252

Whole Foods Market
925 Main Street
V7T 2Z3
Tel: (604) 678-0500
www.wholefoodsmarket.com

CO-OPS

East End Food Co-op
1034 Commercial Drive
V5L 3W9
Tel: (604) 254-5044
www.east-end-food.coop

FARMERS' MARKETS

Organics @ Home Farmers'
Market
1479 Hunter Street
V7J 1H3
Tel: (604) 983-6657
www.organicsathome.com
Saturdays: 9:00 a.m. to 4:00 p.m.

UBC Farm & Market
6182 South Campus Road
Tel: (604) 822-5092
www.landfood.ubc.ca/ubcfarm
Saturdays: 9:00 a.m. to 1:00 p.m.

Your Local Farmers Market
Society
(various locations, some organic
foods)
Tel: (604) 879-3276
www.eatlocal.org

LOCAL FOOD BOXES

Green Earth Organics
Tel: (604) 708-2345
www.greenearthorganics.com

Ladybug Organics Home Delivery
Service
Tel: (604) 513-8971
www.ladybugorganics.com

Organics @ Home
Tel: (604) 983-6657
www.organicsathome.com

Small Potatoes Urban Delivery
Tel: (604) 215-7783
Toll-free: (877) 473-5001
www.spud.ca

COMMUNITY-SUPPORTED AGRICULTURE (CSA)

UBC Farm CSA Box Program
www.landfood.ubc.ca/ubcfarm/
csa.php

Yarrow EcoVillage Farm
Chilliwack
Tel: (604) 824-0800
www.yarrowecovillage.ca/farm/
csa.html

GREEN BUTCHERS

Organa Farms
(meat delivery service)
Tel: (604) 855-7104
Toll-free: (866) 611-3311
www.organafarms.com

GREEN GENERAL STORES

T.h.e. Store
The Village at Park Royal
H5-925 Main Street
V7T 2Z3
Tel: (604) 922-4665
www.t-h-e-store.com

GREEN RENO STORES

Habitat for Humanity ReStore
2475 Douglas Road
Burnaby V5C 5A9
Tel: (604) 293-1898
www.habitat.ca

FAIR-TRADE STORES

Ten Thousand Villages
Vancouver Commercial
1204 Commercial Drive
V5L 3X4
Tel: (604) 323-9233
   and
2909 West Broadway
V6K 2G6
Tel: (604) 730-6831
www.tenthousandvillages.ca

CAR SHARING

Co-operative Auto Network
Tel: (604) 685-1393
www.cooperativeauto.net

ENVIRONMENTAL ACTIVIST GROUPS

Better Environmentally Sound Foundation
822-510 West Hastings Street
V6B 1L8
Tel: (604) 669-2860
www.best.bc.ca

David Suzuki Foundation
2211 West 4th Avenue, Suite 219
V6K 4S2
Tel: (604) 732-4228
Toll-free: (800) 453-1533
www.davidsuzuki.org

FarmFolk/CityFolk Society
1937 West 2nd Avenue
V6J 1J2
Tel: (604) 730-0450
Toll-free (in B.C.): (888) 730-0452
www.ffcf.bc.ca

Forest Ethics
850 West Hastings Street,
Suite 604
V6C 1E1
Tel: (604) 331-6201
www.forestethics.org

Greenpeace—Vancouver Office
1726 Commercial Drive
V5N 4A3
Tel: (604) 253-7701
www.greenpeace.ca

Living Oceans Society
207 West Hastings Street,
Suite 204
V6B 1H7
Tel: (604) 696-5044
www.livingoceans.org

Sierra Club of Canada—B.C. Chapter
302-733 Johnson Street
Victoria V8W 3C7
Tel: (250) 386-5255
www.sierraclub.ca/bc

Smart Growth B.C.
314-402 West Pender Street
V6B 1T6
Tel: (604) 915-5234
www.smartgrowth.bc.ca

Society Promoting Environmental Conservation
2150 Maple Street
V6J 3T3
Tel: (604) 736-7732
www.spec.bc.ca

Western Canada Wilderness Committee
227 Abbott Street
V6B 2K7
Tel: (604) 683-8220
Toll-free: (800) 661-9453
www.wildernesscommittee.org

WINNIPEG

HEALTH FOOD STORES

Aviva Natural Health Solutions
(online shopping and retail centre)
52 Adelaide Street
R3A 0V7
Tel: (204) 947-6789
Toll-free: (866) 947-6789
www.aviva.ca

Borowski's Health Foods
437 St. Anne's Road
R2M 3C7
Tel: (204) 257-7667

Eat It.ca
(online shopping and organic depot)
603 Wall Street
Tel: (204) 772-2136
www.eatit.ca

Organza Foods
230 Osborne Street
R3L 1Z5
Tel: (204) 453-6266
www.organzamarket.com

Sangster's Health Centres
(4 locations)
www.sangsters.com

Sunrise Health Foods
(4 locations)
21-1225 St. Mary's Road
R2M 5E2
Tel: (204) 255-9213

Vita Health Natural Food Stores of
Manitoba
(7 locations)
www.vitahealthstores.ca

CO-OPS

Earthshare Agricultural
Co-operative
(delivers weekly shares to drop-off
points around Winnipeg)
1655 McCreary Road
Tel: (204) 947-9577
www.earthsharemanitoba.ca

Organic Planet Worker Co-op
877 Westminster Avenue
R3G 1B3
Tel: (204) 772-8771
www.organicplanet.coop

Save Your Fork . . . There is Pie
Organic Food Buying Cooperative
(delivers to your home)
244 Hindley Avenue
Tel: (204) 255-6494

FARMERS' MARKETS

Exchange District Farmers'
Market
Old Market Square
Tel: (204) 942-6716
www.exchangedistrict.org/Farmers
Market.aspx
Thursdays: 10:00 a.m. to 2:00 p.m.
Saturdays: 9:00 a.m. to 2:00 p.m.

Red River Exhibition Park
Farmers' Market
Red River Exhibition Park (Portage
Avenue at the Perimeter Highway)
Tel: (204) 888-6990
www.redriverex.com/farmers
market/index.aspx
Saturdays: 8:00 a.m. to 2:00 p.m.
(August through September)

St. Norbert Farmers Market
3514 Pembina Highway
R3V 1A1
Tel: (204) 275-8349
www.stnorbertfarmersmarket.ca
Saturdays: 8:00 a.m. to 3:00 p.m.

LOCAL FOOD BOXES

Fresh Option Organic Delivery
Tel: (204) 772-1479
www.freshoption.ca

GREEN GENERAL STORES

Humboldt's Legacy
887 Westminster Avenue
R3G 1B4
Tel: (204) 772-1404

GREEN RENO STORES

Habitat for Humanity ReStore
60 Archibald Street
R2J 0V7
Tel: (204) 233-5160
www.habitat.ca

FAIR-TRADE STORES

Ten Thousand Villages
Northdale Shopping Centre
10-963 Henderson Highway
R2K 2M3
Tel: (204) 661-5545

and
134 Plaza Drive
R3T 5K9
Tel: (204) 261-0566
www.tenthousandvillages.ca

ENVIRONMENTAL ACTIVIST GROUPS

Boreal Forest Network
3-303 Portage Avenue
R3B 2B4
Tel: (204) 947-3081
www.borealnet.org

Campaign for Pesticide Reduction
c/o 3-303 Portage Avenue
R3B 2B4
Tel: (204) 889-6021

Canadian Parks and Wilderness
Society—Manitoba Chapter
3-303 Portage Avenue
R3B 2B4
Tel: (204) 949-0782
www.cpawsmb.org

Climate Change Connection
3-303 Portage Avenue
R3B 2B4
Tel: (204) 943-4836
www.climatechangeconnection.org

Manitoba Naturalist Society
401-63 Albert Street
R3B 1G4
Tel: (204) 943-9029
www.manitobanature.ca

Manitoba Wildlands
1000-191 Lombard Avenue
R3X 0X1
Tel: (204) 944-9593
www.manitobawildlands.org

Nature Conservancy of Canada—
Manitoba Chapter
611 Corydon Avenue, Suite 200
R3L 0P3
Tel: (204) 942-6156
www.natureconservancy.ca

Western Canada Wilderness
Committee—Manitoba Chapter
3-303 Portage Avenue
R3B 2B4
Tel: (204) 942-9292
www.wildernesscommittee.mb.ca

KICK-ASS WEBSITES

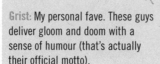

Grist: My personal fave. These guys deliver gloom and doom with a sense of humour (that's actually their official motto).
www.grist.org

The Green Guide: Full of practical reports on green problems and solutions for everyday things.
www.thegreenguide.com

E Magazine: A great eco magazine with both online and hard copy versions available by subscription. Some online content is free.
www.emagazine.ca

Environmental Health News: Check it every day to stay on top of extensive enviro news coverage from around the globe.
www.environmentalhealthnews.org

Treehugger: Get the scoop on all the latest and coolest green designs, gismos and goods.
www.treehugger.com

Care2 Make a Difference: Goes by Care2. It's got a news section and a petition section, but the Healthy Living section crammed with DIY tips on everything is the most handy.
www.care2.com

INDEX

ACKNOWLEDGEMENTS

There comes a time in every book when you get to pretend you're at the Academy Awards and start thanking everyone (I promise not to cry or name my accountant). Oh, let's see, where to begin? I've got to thank my NOW *Magazine* publishers, Alice and Michael, and NOW editor, Ellie, for sliding the idea for the "Ecoholic" column onto my lap and being incredibly supportive about turning the little-column-that-could into a book. Kendall, my editor at Vintage Canada, for thinking about transforming the column into a big ole' book in the first place (and to think, I nearly junked your first email, thinking it was spam!). My caring, earth-conscious readers who write in every week with thoughtful questions and kind words. Everyone that I've roped into helping me research material over the years (Andrea, Victoria, Sarah, Yee-Guan, Brad, Rick, Paul) and my tireless research assistants/*Ecoholic* book interns (Katie, Naomi, Loretta, Susan), you all rock my world and saved my butt. The Random House design and production department (Kelly, Beate, Carla) deserve a round of applause (as does the NOW design and production team for the work they do on the weekly column).

This book couldn't have been written without the love, support and sense of humour of my amazing family, friends and my personal cheerleader and eternal love, Brad. Not to mention, my muse, a.k.a. The Mews, who purred by my laptop through every draft of the book.

And finally, I have to thank the Earth for putting up with all of us. I know it's been rough lately, but hopefully the Ecoholics of the world will unite to turn all that around.

Corrections and Additions: If you have found an error in *Ecoholic* or if you are a producer who would like to be considered for upcoming editions of this indispensable guide, please contact the author at her website—www.ecoholic.ca.

For bonus material as well as a bibliography of sources and corrections please visit www.ecoholic.ca.

Adria Vasil has been writing the "Ecoholic" column for *NOW* magazine since the spring of 2004 and has been covering environmental issues for *NOW*'s news section for five years.

Vasil has a degree in politics and cultural anthropology from University of Toronto and a degree in magazine journalism from Ryerson. She's been an advocate for the earth since her teens, as well as an advocate for women's issues and human rights issues. She has appeared a number of times on television to promote environmentalism and discuss our role in climate change, including CBC *Newsworld*, MTV Canada, Much Music, TVO Vox and Book TV.

Please visit her website at www.ecoholic.ca.